T0399764

Biophilic Urbanism

Biophilic Urbanism provides readers with the tools to create more nature-based urban environments that are climate positive, sustainable, and healthy. The principles of biophilia are intended to support appreciation and direct engagement with nature, to responsibly utilize on-site natural resources, and to plan according to climatic conditions and local ecological processes. It seeks to create resilient and equitable human places capable of providing critical life-support functions and a strong sense of community, and to foster experiences that raise the human spirit creating a sense of awe. Twenty-five pattern attributes are defined and explored, each of which contributes to these goals.

Because of the dire necessity to respond to the COVID-19 pandemic, *Biophilic Urbanism* includes discussion of our need for connections, both to nature and one another, and the physical characteristics of cities and buildings relative to the contagious qualities of the air-borne virus.

Case studies, found throughout the world, are presented illustrating detailed biophilic planning and design strategies. The book will be of use to practitioners and students in the fields of natural and social sciences, behavioral science and psychology, environmental engineering, health and wellness professionals, architecture, landscape architecture, interior architecture, and planning.

Phillip James Tabb is Professor Emeritus of Architecture at Texas A&M University and founder and principal of Phill Tabb Studio. He received his Bachelor of Science degree in Architecture from the University of Cincinnati, Master of Architecture from the University of Colorado, and his PhD in the Energy and Environment Programme from the Architectural Association in London. Among his publications are *Solar Energy Planning* published by McGraw-Hill in 1984, co-authored *The Greening of Architecture: A Critical History and Survey of Contemporary Sustainable Architecture and Urban Design* published by Ashgate in 2013, co-edited *Architecture, Culture and Spirituality* also published by Routledge in 2015, *Serene Urbanism: A Biophilic Theory and Practice of Sustainable Placemaking*, published by Routledge in 2017, and *Elemental Architecture: The Temperaments of Sustainability*, published by Routledge in 2019. He is the master plan architect for the Serenbe Community – an award-winning biophilic community being realized near Atlanta, Georgia.

"In his new book, *Biophilic Urbanism*, Phillip Tabb provides a view of how cities can be places of companionship, emotional renewal, and flourishing through the thoughtful integration of nature and natural systems in the built environment. A central theme throughout the book is a recognition that people are not 'masters of the universe' but rather 'humble citizens of a planet that includes other living entities together in ecological systems.'

While many others have made similar claims, Professor Tabb addresses how to turn these thoughts into practice. He focuses on examples of small-scale urban environments and addresses how biophilic design – from backyard gardens to woodland pathways and shared green spaces – can contribute to social, emotional, and physical well-being of the inhabitants as well as the place we all call home – planet Earth."

—Judith Heewagen, PhD, Affiliate Faculty, University of Washington,
Department of Architecture

"Experiences of nature improve our health and wellbeing. Yet, on average Americans spend more than 90% of our lives indoors, then when we come outside, many times, we are in communities that offer little of the living world. In *Biophilic Urbanism*, architect and community planner Phillip Tabb, shows how to make vibrant experiences of nature in our urban fabric.

Tabb explores the theory and history of biophilia as a scientific endeavor and how it connects to design. He then lays out a biophilic pattern language, a set of design elements, to help make urban experiences of nature effective. Through case studies the lessons from a number of communities where experiencing nature is part of daily life. Tabb is the master planner of Serenbe, a new community outside of Atlanta that intentionally focuses on bringing nature into the lives of the inhabitants."

—William Browning, Managing Partner, Terrapin Bright Green

"This important book gathers up and clearly presents, in design relevant form, the essential understandings, research findings and arguments for the integration of nature into the design of the human environment, from the scale of the individual building to the street, block, neighborhood, community and bioregion. Professor Tabb illustrates how the basic principles and patterns of biophilic design are present in a diverse range of precedents, and in one detailed case study of the new community of Serenbe, located in the Chattahoochee Hills of Georgia, for which Tabb was the Master Planner and in which he now lives in a biophilic dwelling and garden that he designed for himself. The book is timely because biophilic design is increasingly recognized as an essential response to the cascading crises of climate destabilization, species extinction, and global ecosystem collapse. Of particular relevance to readers today is the author's consideration of how biophilic urbanism can exert a restorative and healing effect on everyday human life in the emerging age of global pandemics.

Biophilic Urbanism is a book that not only should be of interest to design and planning students and professionals, but also anyone who is committed to creating a more sustainable, beautiful and life-enhancing home for human dwelling that is in harmony with the natural world."

—*Gary J. Coates, ACSA Distinguished Professor, Kansas State University, (editor)* Resettling America: Energy, Ecology and Community, *and author of* Erik Asmussen, architect *and* The Architecture of Carl Nyrén

"There is no better time than now to reconsider how we design and build the environment in which we reside as a humanity and Dr. Tabb's *Biophilic Urbanism* is a practical guide to this transformational process. Due to the COVID pandemic the world is rethinking how to stay healthy in cities, hospitals, nursing homes, schools and other institutions. Dr. Tabb explains the science supporting our need to connect with nature for both human and environmental wellbeing, outlines the various scales of interventions, and lists key precedents with their positive outcomes. Design and engineering students, practitioners, owners and project team members will find the book clear and informative and the precedent tables a helpful metric to use for understanding the effectiveness of biophilic pattern attributes on projects. *Biophilic Urbanism* in debuting at a time when the world is reconsidering what constitutes progress and how best to move forward to promote human and environmental health. Now indeed is the time to open the doors and windows, let in the sunshine in and the fresh air flow through, infuse buildings with their landscapes, weave nature throughout our cities and shade them with trees, listen to the birds sing and embrace the local culture and ecology of place."

—*Elizabeth Freeman Calabrese, AIA, NCARB, LEED AP, WELL AP, WELL Faculty*

Biophilic Urbanism

Designing Resilient Communities for the Future

Phillip James Tabb

Routledge
Taylor & Francis Group

NEW YORK AND LONDON

First published 2021
by Routledge
52 Vanderbilt Avenue, New York, NY 10017

and by Routledge
2 Park Square, Milton Park, Abingdon, Oxon, OX14 4RN

Routledge is an imprint of the Taylor & Francis Group, an informa business

Library of Congress Cataloging-in-Publication Data
Names: Tabb, Phillip, author.
Title: Biophilic urbanism : designing resilient communities for the future /
Phillip James Tabb.
Identifiers: LCCN 2020033647 (print) | LCCN 2020033648 (ebook) |
ISBN 9780367473273 (hbk) | ISBN 9780367473266 (pbk) |
ISBN 9781003034896 (ebk)
Subjects: LCSH: Urban ecology (Sociology) | City planning–Environmental
aspects. | Sustainable development. | Nature--Effect of human beings on.
Classification: LCC HT241 .T333 2021 (print) | LCC HT241 (ebook) |
DDC 307.1/216–dc23
LC record available at https://lccn.loc.gov/2020033647
LC ebook record available at https://lccn.loc.gov/2020033648

ISBN: 9780367473273 (hbk)
ISBN: 9780367473266 (pbk)
ISBN: 9781003034896 (ebk)

Typeset in Univers
by KnowledgeWorks Global Ltd.

MIX
Paper from
responsible sources
FSC™ C013985

Printed in the United Kingdom
by Henry Ling Limited

This work is dedicated to my grandsons,
Emrys, Caius, and James Tabb

Contents

List of Figures   xiii
List of Tables   xviii
About the Author   xix
Foreword by Tim Beatley, PhD   xxi
Preface   xxvii
Acknowledgements   xli

Part 1
Principles   1

1   Introduction   3

Biophilia   3
The Crisis of Nature   13
   Nature versus Humanity   13
   Climate Change   14
   Diminished Contact with Nature   15
   Loss of Biodiversity   15
   Wildlife Destruction   16
   The Question of Zoos   16
   Increased Pollution   16
   Global Pandemic   18
   Primarily Living Indoors   20
The Crisis of Urbanism   21
   Unsustainability   21
   Population Growth and Migrations   22
   Growth by Addition   23
   Functional Land Use Zoning   24
   Placelessness   24
   Impact of the Automobile   25
   Pollution and Waste   26
Biophilic Urbanism and Biourbanism Defined   28

Scales of Application | 30
Buildings | 31
Streets | 32
Blocks | 32
Neighborhoods | 32
Communities | 33
Ecoregions | 33

2 Principles | **40**

Principles, Patterns, and Outcomes | 40
Biophilic Principles | 41
Derivation of the Patterns | 43
Biophilic Pattern Attributes | 46
Nature-Based Patterns | 46
Element-Based Patterns | 48
Form-Based Patterns | 50
Place-Based Patterns | 52
Numinous-Based Patterns | 54
Biophilic Positive Outcomes | 57
Outcome Descriptions | 57
Outcome Research Sources | 68
Climate-Positive Outcomes | 68
Sustainability Outcomes | 69
Placemaking Outcomes | 69
Health and Wellness Outcomes | 69
Numinous Outcomes | 69

Part 2
Precedents | **75**
Precedent Studies | 75

3 Castello di Gargonza | **77**

Castello di Gargonza | 77
Background and History | 77
Analysis of the Masterplan | 80
Primary Pattern Attributes | 82
Positive Outcomes | 83

4 Google Headquarters | **85**

Google Headquarters | 85
Background and History | 85
Analysis of the Masterplan | 89

Primary Pattern Attributes 90
Positive Outcomes 92

5 Helsinge Haveby (Garden Village) 95

Helsinge Haveby 95
Background and History 95
Analysis of the Masterplan 100
Primary Pattern Attributes 100
Positive Outcomes 102

6 Kronsberg District 105

Kronsberg District 105
Background and History 105
Analysis of the Masterplan 109
Primary Pattern Attributes 111
Positive Outcomes 112

7 Pontevedra City Center 114

Pontevedra City Center 114
Background and History 114
Analysis of the Masterplan 119
Primary Pattern Attributes 119
Positive Outcomes 121

8 Singapore Park Connector Neighborhood 124

Singapore Park Connector Neighborhood 124
Background and History 124
Analysis of the Masterplan 127
Primary Pattern Attributes 129
Positive Outcomes 130

Part 3
Case Study 133

9 Serenbe Community 135

Serenbe Community 135
The Settlement Form 137
The Hamlets 138
Constellating Urbanism 141
The Biophilic Principles 142
Serenbe Biophilic Pattern Attributes 144

1. The Plant Kingdom 145
2. The Animal Kingdom 147
3. Views and Vistas 150
4. Sensory Connections 152
5. Ecological and Biological Contexts 154
6. Fire and Energy 156
7. Earth and Grounding 158
8. Air and Natural Ventilation 160
9. Water and Waste 162
10. Ether and Celestial Moments 165
11. Orientation and Direction 167
12. Prospect and Refuge 169
13. Inside–Outside Relationships 171
14. Topography and Geography Patterns 173
15. Spatial Order and Connectiveness 175
16. Centering and Nucleation 178
17. Bounding and Containment 180
18. Natural Materiality 182
19. Form Language and Natural Analogs 184
20. Cultural, Social, Historic Connections . 186
21. The Arts and Mythopoeia 189
22. Living Color 191
23. Temporal and Transformative Processes . 193
24. Light in All Forms 195
25. Numinous and Noetic Moments 198

10 Conclusions **203**

Summary of Pattern Attributes and Positive Outcomes ... 203
Conclusions about Biophilic Urbanism 214

Suggested Reading 219
Index 222

List of Figures

0.1 Morphology of English village form (2800 BC–future):
(a) Stone/Bronze Age homestead, (b) Celtic hamlet,
(c) Romano-British hamlet, (d) Anglo-Saxon village, (e) Medieval
village, (f) industrial village, (g) modern village, and
h) biophilic village (*Source: Phillip Tabb*) xxxi
0.2 Titchfield Village, Hampshire, UK (*Source: Phillip Tabb*) xxxii
0.3 Castiglion Fiorentino, Italy (*Source: Phillip Tabb*) xxxiii
0.4 Walled-in garden (*Source: Phillip Tabb*) xxxv
0.5 Watercolor Cottage (*Source: Phillip Tabb*) xxxv
0.6 Serenbe, Chattahoochee Hills, Georgia: (a) drone image of
residence, (b) students at waterfall, (c) Serenbe farmers'
and artists' market (*Source: David Tabb and Phillip Tabb*) xxxvi
1.1 Paleolithic cave paintings, Altamira, Spain
(*Source: Alamy Stock*) 6
1.2 Makoko Floating School, Lagos, Nigeria
(*Source: Public Delivery*) 8
1.3 The Vertical Forest, Milan, Italy (*Source: Getty Images*) 9
1.4 The Eden Project, Cornwall, UK (*Source: Shutterstock*) 10
1.5 High Line Park, New York City (*Source: Shutterstock*) 10
1.6 Mexcaltitán, Mexico (*Source: Wikimedia Commons*) 11
1.7 Savannah, Georgia (*Source: Shutterstock*) 12
1.8 Impacts of the Coronavirus 2020: woman receiving groceries
(*Source: Shutterstock*) 19
1.9 Crisis of nature (*Source: Shutterstock*) 21
1.10 Crisis of urbanism (*Source: Wikimedia Commons*) 27
2.1 Biophilic Principles: (a) Yellowstone National Park, (b) Siena
Compo, (c) Dubai night scene (*Source: Shutterstock, Phillip
Tabb, Shutterstock*) 42
2.2 Climate-positive outcomes (*Source: Phillip Tabb*) 59
2.3 Sustainability outcomes (*Source: Phillip Tabb*) 60
2.4 Placemaking outcomes (*Source: Phillip Tabb*) 61
2.5 Health and wellness outcomes (*Source: Phillip Tabb*) 63
2.6 Numinous outcomes (*Source: Phillip Tabb*) 64

2.7	Social distancing (*Source: Shutterstock*)	65
3.1	Aerial view of Castello di Gargonza (*Source: Phillip Tabb*)	78
3.2	Gargonza center well (*Source: Phillip Tabb*)	79
3.3	Natural materials: (a) cottage entry stair, (b) cottage covered terrace (*Source: Phillip Tabb*)	80
3.4	Gargonza masterplan analysis: (a) base map, (b) biophilic patterns (*Source: Phillip Tabb*)	81
3.5	Gargonza lemon tree garden (*Source: Phillip Tabb*)	83
4.1	Aerial view of the Googleplex in Mountainview, California (*Source: Alamy Stock*)	87
4.2	The Googleplex: (a) inner commons, (b) outdoor seating (*Source: Alamy Stock*)	87
4.3	Charleston East biome: (a) biome under construction (*Source: Wikimedia Commons*), (b) biome canopy (*Source: Getty Images*)	89
4.4	Google masterplan analysis: (a) base map, (b) biophilic patterns (*Source: Phillip Tabb*)	90
4.5	Interior lobby of building 1900 (*Source: Shutterstock*)	93
5.1	Helsinge Haveby, Denmark (aerial image) (*Source: EFFEKT Architects*)	96
5.2	Helsinge Haveby food and social hub (*Source: EFFEKT Architects*)	97
5.3	Helsinge Haveby cluster center (*Source: EFFEKT Architects*)	99
5.4	Helsinge Haveby masterplan analysis: (a) base map, (b) biophilic patterns (*Source: Phillip Tabb*)	101
5.5	Helsinge Haveby moments (*Source: EFFEKT Architects*)	103
6.1	Kronsberg District aerial view (*Source: Alamy Stock*)	106
6.2	Kronsberg super-block interior park (*Source: Gary J. Coates*)	107
6.3	Kronsberg super-blocks: (a) interior lawns and apartment blocks, (b) pedestrian circulation and rainwater swale (*Source: Gary J. Coates*)	108
6.4	Kronsberg masterplan analysis: (a) Kronsberg base map, (b) Kronsberg biophilic patterns (*Source: Phillip Tabb*)	110
6.5	Kronsberg Hill and farm animals (*Source: Alamy Stock*)	112
7.1	Pontevedra, Spain, city center aerial view (*Source: Alamy Stock*)	115
7.2	Pontevedra central plaza (*Source: Alamy Stock*)	116
7.3	Pontevedra pedestrianization: (a) Plaza de la Lena (Firewood Square) (*Source: Alamy Stock*), (b) Pontevedra Metrominuto (*Source: City of Pontevedra, Spain*)	117
7.4	Plaza de Verdura, Pontevedra (*Source: Alamy Stock*)	118
7.5	Pontevedra city center analysis: (a) Pontevedra base map, (b) Pontevedra biophilic patterns (*Source: Phillip Tabb*)	120
7.6	Herreria Square, Pontevedra (*Source: Getty Images*)	122
8.1	Singapore aerial view (*Source: Alamy Stock*)	125

8.2 Singapore Bukit (Hill) Timah Public Nature Park
(*Source: Alamy Stock*) 128

8.3 Singapore Bukit (Hill) Batok (*Source: Wikimedia Commons*) 128

8.4 Singapore masterplan analysis: (a) Park Connector
Neighborhood base map, (b) Park Connector Neighborhood
biophilic patterns (*Source: Phillip Tabb*) 129

8.5 Singapore Gardens by the Bay (*Source: Alamy Stock*) 131

9.1 Serenbe masterplan, April 2019 (*Source: Phillip Tabb*) 137

9.2 Selborne hamlet aerial view (*Source: Serenbe Development*) 138

9.3 Grange hamlet and Serenbe Farms aerial view (*Source:
Serenbe Development*) 139

9.4 Mado aerial views: (a) west leg of Mado hamlet,
(b) the healing garden (*Source: Serenbe Development*) 140

9.5 Constellating Serenbe hamlets (*Source: Phillip Tabb*) 142

9.6 Serenbe base map (*Source: Phillip Tabb*) 145

9.7 Pattern attribute 1: the plant kingdom (*Source: Phillip Tabb*) 146

9.8 Nature in Serenbe: (a) Serenbe Farms, (b) father and son
looking at raspberries (*Source: Phillip Tabb*) 146

9.9 Pattern attribute 2: the animal kingdom (*Source: Phillip Tabb*) 148

9.10 The animal kingdom in Serenbe: (a) Serenbe Camp horseback
riding, (b) local red-tailed hawk (*Source: Phillip Tabb*) 148

9.11 Pattern attribute 3: views and vistas (*Source: Phillip Tabb*) 151

9.12 Views and vistas: (a) dusk sky vista over pasture, (b) view of
path between two buildings (*Source: Phillip Tabb*) 151

9.13 Pattern attribute 4: sensory connections (*Source: Phillip Tabb*) 153

9.14 Sensory experiences: (a) Serenbe waterfalls, (b) rose
(*Source: Phillip Tabb*) 153

9.15 Pattern attribute 5: ecological and biological contexts (*Source:
Phillip Tabb*) 155

9.16 Ecology: (a) swale next to the Montessori school, (b) swale
along Tabb Way (*Source: Phillip Tabb*) 155

9.17 Pattern attribute 6: fire and energy (*Source: Phillip Tabb*) 157

9.18 Fire and energy: (a) solstice bonfire, (b) net-zero dwelling
(*Source: Phillip Tabb*) 157

9.19 Pattern attribute 7: earth and grounding (*Source: Phillip Tabb*) 159

9.20 Earth and grounding: (a) Mado wetlands, (b) newly planted
basil (*Source: Phillip Tabb*) 159

9.21 Pattern attribute 8: air and natural ventilation (*Source:
Phillip Tabb*) 162

9.22 Air and natural ventilation: (a) mid-day moon, (b) wind
sculpture, (c) ceiling fan (*Source: Phillip Tabb*) 162

9.23 Pattern attribute 9: water and waste (*Source: Phillip Tabb*) 163

9.24 Water and waste: (a) vegetated wetlands, (b) Mado fountain
(*Source: Phillip Tabb*) 163

9.25 Pattern attribute 10: ether and celestial moments (*Source: Phillip Tabb*)   166

9.26 Ether and celestial moments: (a) evening sunset, (b) night sky (*Source: Phillip Tabb*)   166

9.27 Pattern attribute 11: orientation and direction (*Source: Phillip Tabb*)   168

9.28 Orientation and direction: (a) axial view through Anders Court to the yoga field, (b) view of the healing garden in Mado (*Source: Phillip Tabb*)   168

9.29 Pattern attribute 12: prospect and refuge (*Source: Phillip Tabb*)   170

9.30 Prospect and refuge: (a) hamlet omega form as prospect and refuge, (b) refuge within a barrel vault dwelling (*Source: Phillip Tabb*)   170

9.31 Pattern attribute 14: inside–outside relationships (*Source: Phillip Tabb*)   172

9.32 Inside–outside: (a) outside dwelling space, (b) inside dwelling space (*Source: Phillip Tabb*)   172

9.33 Pattern attribute 14: topography and geography (*Source: Phillip Tabb*)   174

9.34 Topography and geography: (a) hillside toward Mado hamlet, (b) hillside toward Grange hamlet (*Source: Phillip Tabb*)   174

9.35 Pattern attribute 15: spatial order and connectiveness (*Source: Phillip Tabb*)   176

9.36 Spatial order and connectiveness: (a) Thorburn transect diagram, (b) Thorburn transect along Selborne Lane, (c) Selborne Hamlet (*Source: Phillip Tabb*)   176

9.37 Pattern attribute 16: centering and nucleation (*Source: Phillip Tabb*)   179

9.38 Centering: (a) omega center walking path and bridge, (b) Serenbe labyrinth (*Source: Phillip Tabb and Serenbe Development*)   179

9.39 Pattern attribute 17: bounding and containment (*Source: Phillip Tabb*)   181

9.40 Bounding: (a) Grange hamlet omega bounding, (b) Selborne hamlet and fresco dining with architectural bounding (*Source: Serenbe Development and Phillip Tabb*)   181

9.41 Pattern attribute 18: natural materiality (*Source: Phillip Tabb*)   183

9.42 Natural materiality: (a) Swan Ridge bridge, (b) the Inn pond folly (*Source: Phillip Tabb*)   183

9.43 Pattern attribute 19: form language and natural analogues (*Source: Phillip Tabb*)   185

9.44 Form language and natural analogues: (a) Serenbe stables (rural), (b) Blue Eyed Daisy Bakeshop with outdoor social distancing (urban) (*Source: Phillip Tabb*)   185

9.45 Pattern attribute 20: cultural, historic, social connections
(*Source: Phillip Tabb*) 188

9.46 Cultural and social activities: (a) Serenbe Playhouse poster,
(b) farmers' and artists' market (*Source: Phillip Tabb*) 188

9.47 Pattern attribute 21: the arts and mythopoeia (*Source:
Phillip Tabb*) 190

9.48 The arts and mythopoeia: (a) artists in residence,
(b) wall mural (*Source: Phillip Tabb*) 190

9.49 Pattern attribute 22: living color (*Source: Phillip Tabb*) 192

9.50 Living color: (a) local fuchsia thistle, (b) Serenbe swim club
building, (c) butterfly (*Source: Phillip Tabb*) 192

9.51 Pattern attribute 23: temporal connections (*Source:
Phillip Tabb*) 194

9.52 Temporal connections: (a) crossroads in spring, (b) autumn
deciduous trees (*Source: Phillip Tabb*), (c) Mado hamlet under
construction (*Source: Serenbe Development*) 194

9.53 Pattern attribute 24: light in all its forms (*Source: Phillip Tabb*) 197

9.54 Light in all its forms: (a) tree shadows along footpath, (b)
moonlight in Crossroads (*Source: Phillip Tabb*) 197

9.55 Pattern attribute 25: numinous and noetic experiences
(*Source: Phillip Tabb*) 199

9.56 Numinous and noetic experiences: (a) exterior light from Mado
lantern, (b) message embedded in a concrete pad next to small
waterfalls (*Source: Phillip Tabb*) 199

9.57 Serenbe biophilic experiences: (a) Serenbe Farms,
(b) farm-to-table, (c) children at fountain, (d) Serenbe
Playhouse (*Source: Phillip Tabb*) 200

10.1 Social distancing: (a) Washington Square Park, San Francisco,
California (*Source: Shutterstock*), (b) fresco dining in Siena,
Italy (*Source: Phillip Tabb*) 217

10.2 The Great Rift Valley, East Africa (*Source: Getty Images*) 218

List of Tables

10.1 Castello di Gargonza – Key Biophilic Pattern Attributes and
Outcomes (*Source: Phillip Tabb*) 205

10.2 Google Headquarters – Key Biophilic Pattern Attributes and
Outcomes (*Source: Phillip Tabb*) 206

10.3 Helsinge Haveby – Key Biophilic Pattern Attributes and
Outcomes (*Source: Phillip Tabb*) 208

10.4 Kronsberg District – Key Biophilic Pattern Attributes and
Outcomes (*Source: Phillip Tabb*) 209

10.5 Pontevedra city center – Key Biophilic Pattern Attributes and
Outcomes (*Source: Phillip Tabb*) 210

10.6 Singapore Park Connector Network – Key Biophilic Pattern
Attributes and Outcomes (*Source: Phillip Tabb*) 211

10.7 Serenbe Community – Biophilic Pattern Attributes and
Outcomes (*Source: Phillip Tabb*) 212

About the Author

Phillip James Tabb is Professor Emeritus of Architecture at Texas A&M University and was the Liz and Nelson Mitchell Professor of Residential Design. He served as Head of the Department from 2001–2005 and was Director of the School of Architecture and Construction Management at Washington State University from 1998–2001. He completed a PhD dissertation on *The Solar Village Archetype: A Study of English Village Form Applicable to Energy Integrated Planning Principles for Satellite Settlements in Temperate Climates* in 1990. Among his publications are: *Solar Energy Planning* published by McGraw-Hill in 1984; *The Greening of Architecture: A Critical History and Survey of Contemporary Sustainable Architecture and Urban Design* published by Ashgate in 2013; co-edited *Architecture, Culture and Spirituality* also published by Routledge in 2015; *Serene Urbanism: A Biophilic Theory and Practice of Sustainable Placemaking*, published by Routledge in 2017; and *Elemental Architecture: The Temperaments of Sustainability*, published by Routledge in 2019.

In the late 1960s he worked for Walter Netsch at SOM in Chicago and was exposed to his Field Theory method of design. He worked with Keith Critchlow and taught sacred drawing in the Kairos School of Sacred Architecture (1986–1987), at Dar al Islam in Abiquiu, New Mexico (1988–1989), and at Naropa Institute, Boulder (1996). Since 2001, Tabb is the master plan architect for the Serenbe Community – an award-winning sustainable community being realized near Atlanta, Georgia. He was a planning consultant for the Peppler Neighborhood in Colorado, the Babcock Ranch Community in Florida, the Millican Reserve project in Texas, the Summit Series Community in Utah, the Howell Mountain Conservation Community in California, the Bellefield Agri-neighborhood in New York, and the Roots Farm in North Carolina. He has lectured internationally on the concepts of placemaking as a viable sustainable strategy and biophilic design.

He received six solar energy research and demonstrations awards from the AIA/RC, HUD, and DOE, and was a consultant to SERI. He was a board member of the Architecture, Culture, and Spirituality Forum and is a board member of the Serenbe Biophilic Institute. He was also a founding fellow of the Sustainable Urbanism Certificate Program at Texas A&M University. He received his Bachelor of Science degree in Architecture from the University of Cincinnati, Master of Architecture from the University of Colorado, and his PhD in the Energy and Environment Programme from the Architectural Association in London. Dr Tabb has taught studio design, sustainable architecture, and the theory of place-making, and he taught in the study abroad program in Castiglion Fiorentino, Italy. Currently he is principal of Phill Tabb Studio, as an urban designer and licensed architect. He has been a long-time member of the American Institute of Architects and holds a NCARB Certificate.

Foreword

I think that it is undeniable that we are in the midst of a collective global reconnection with the natural world; it is a kind of renewal of our vows to nature, if you will, one that rarely happens in a generation. And so, it is difficult to write this foreword without explicit mention of the global pandemic gripping us all. The news is largely grim but there are glimmers of hope and of a hopeful future lived more intensely and in closer contact with nature. Our approaches to urban planning and design will undoubtedly change forever and mostly for the good, more in line with the philosophy and practices advocated in the book to follow. There is little doubt that the subject of this book is even more important now than just a few months ago, and that the patterns and design ideas presented here are even more potent and relevant as we recover and reimagine our lives and communities moving forward post pandemic.

If there has been any sort of silver lining to the massive disruption, unemployment, human pain, and turmoil wrought by the Coronavirus it is the reconsideration of what is important in our lives, and in particular the demonstration for many of us of the power and importance of the natural world. In the US and elsewhere nature has been a balm and a salvation; a constant and stabilizing element amidst the backdrop of chaos and uncertainty. Watching and listening to birds has been my own personal salvation. Early on the Audubon rightly declared "it has never a better time to learn to birdwatch...," and downloads of bird-identification guides have soared.[1] Visits to parks, strolls around one's neighborhood, planting gardens in our front yards, backyards, in containers in balconies; we seek at once the benefits of biophilia by seeing, touching, hearing the wildness of nature, and respite from the daily news of infection and death. These are precisely the qualities of place Phillip James Tabb admires and elevates herein.

Phill Tabb's wonderful set of biophilic principles, patterns, and detailed precedents comes at an especially helpful time as we prioritize our lives around nature. As he shows here convincingly, it is possible to design new communities that are at once place-strengthening, climate-neutral, and biophilic. These are the kinds of places where we would want to quarantine. Communities like Serenbe, that Tabb analyzes in particular detail and has personally master planned, inspire and demonstrate that living and walking in conditions of immersive nature is possible and preferable now more than ever.

Our daily life-adjustments to lockdown are a constant reminder of the essential importance of nearby nature. One of our most popular national parks, and the closest to where I live, shut its gates early in the outbreak. Pre-pandemic we already knew that satisfying our daily (and hourly) doses of nature, the bulk of nature-diet if you will, would need to be provided by the spaces around where we live and work. That is one of the important insights from the stories collected in this book. We will continue to value and want to spend time in national parks and other more distant places of nature, and we can and must care about and work to protect these large expanses of nature, but it is the daily delights around us that will be the most meaningful and therapeutic. Keeping healthy and sane will increasingly depend on the ability, as in Tabb's descriptions of Serenbe and the other case studies show, of seeing, hearing, walking in the nature around us, daily or hourly, where we live.

A growing importance given to nature in the design of communities and neighborhoods has been a strong global trend even before the emergence of COVID-19. Biophilic Urbanism goes by many different names – natural capitalism, green infrastructure, nature-based solutions to urban problems – and is reflected in the growing importance of global networks of cities emphasizing the importance of nature (e.g. ICLEI's Cities With Nature and Cities With Forests, and our own Biophilic Cities Network). Tabb's book is a highly useful addition, providing both a systematic framework for understanding the natureful qualities of neighborhoods and cities, but also serving to inspire, motivate, and guide future design and planning work.

I like very much that Tabb has structured his principles and patterns by scale (buildings, streets, blocks, neighborhoods, communities, and regions). Implicit here is the possibility of nested outcomes: buildings contributing to larger biophilic neighborhoods, neighborhoods fitting together to form biophilic communities. It suggests ways that biophilic design at one scale can be transformative at larger scales. Serenbe is illustrative: while conserving 70 percent of the land on its 1200 acres, it has helped to create a regional conservation strategy with the promise of saving several hundred thousand acres.

Consistent with this Serenbe outcome, another nature-lesson of COVID-19 is that we need always to think well beyond the local and the nearby. An overarching insight from the pandemic is the need to profoundly change our relationships with the natural world. As the Coronavirus likely found its origin in wildlife markets and is a symptom of the larger patterns of habitat destruction (for humans as well as other species), there is the need to redouble our efforts at protecting these larger ecosystems and more far-away nature that we depend upon. Just as we must work to protect and integrate into our lives the nature around us, a biophilic community or city must also acknowledge and work on behalf of distant nature as well. As we embrace and apply wonderful biophilic design and panning patterns to our local buildings, neighborhoods, and urban spaces, we must at the same time work on behalf of larger planetary health. This can take the form of efforts to reform the resource flows and supply lines – for instance, shifting to local sources of wood – but it can also take the form of leadership and advocacy in support of global conservation. EO Wilson's bold idea of *Half Earth* – setting aside at least half the Earth for nature – is one such example and a conservation ethic and commitment that springs naturally from our innate love of nature.[2] We need then a version of Biophilic Urbanism that values local nature but situates it in a larger global ecosystem and understands the need to protect and restore more than just local natural world.

That we can bring about natureful living environments and also address other pressing social and environmental challenges seems apparent in much of the work to follow. There are of course many co-benefits of Biophilic Urbanism. While bringing more nature near to where we live, we can also reduce the energy consumption and carbon footprint of buildings and cities. Years ago, I had the chance to take a group of UVA students to Kronsberg. Most memorable was a walk to the largest of two wind turbines on site, at the time a mammoth 2.8 MW turbine at the edge of the development. Producing more energy (at least at that point) than needed by the entire neighborhood, it demonstrated the possibility of highly beautiful, livable, and natureful places that also exert a minimal ecological footprint on the world.

The benefits of spending time outside are even more evident in a pandemic. Chance of infection from COVID-19 is substantially greater in indoor work, home, and restaurant environments, to the point where social distancing simply doesn't work.[3] Eating outside will become the new normal in many cities and thus programs like San Francisco's, to facilitate the creation of a variety of different and informal nature-spaces, from parklets attached to restaurants and bars to new sidewalk gardens, even media spaces of roads through an innovative street parks program. Cities like Cincinnati and Tampa have already been shifting street space to make room for outdoor eating, perhaps the beginning of an al fresco dining revolution in the US. We will need to rely more on outside life in many ways and in many sectors (during the 1918 influenza epidemic many things, including even court proceedings, were held outside). Much of the life of communities like Serenbe already occurs outside. I am reminded of a delightful evening there watching an outdoor theater presentation of the musical *Grease*. We will need to design for more outside spaces and the communities profiled here, like Serenbe, will serve as important examples of what is needed.

Paradoxically, just as we need to design for more time outside we will also see major adjustments in the design of interior spaces, especially those of our homes. Here again the pandemic is instructive. There have been a host of creative ideas for bringing nature inside and for more intensively enjoying the spaces around our homes. The images of quarantined Italians serenading each other from their balconies serves to highlight the critical role these interstitial spaces play, and the need to continue to overcome the inside/outside barrier. More generally we will need to redouble our efforts to design and build more natureful homes, offices, schools, and libraries. The uplifting shapes and forms of nature and especially the ability to open windows, and to hear and see the nature around us, will be an essential source of health and meaning in this unsettling era. Tabb's patterns and precedents again provide timely guidance. Serenbe's approach to spatial design, its omega-shaped hamlets, maximize views of trees and nature, and abundant porches and terraces and outside rooms allow the kinds of nature-connected experiences so essential today.

Priorities have already been shifting in other ways as well, with an impressive variety of creative strategies evident in many cities across the US and the world. There has been a resurgence of interest in local food, for instance, and in the installation of food-producing gardens. One of the clearest outcomes of COVID-19 has been a concern about the security and dependence of long-distance supply lines, as shortages in eggs and flour and other foodstuffs has led to understandable angst. Images of unimaginably tall stacks of russet potatoes at Iowa farms going to rot, and dairy farmers dumping milk, we will likely carry with us, reminding us of the wastefulness and illogic of our anonymous agribusiness approach to growing and delivering food, and of the need to rethink and renew our local foodways. In some cities this is leading to new commitment about protecting peripheral urban farms from suburban sprawl, and in a number a new-found desire to reinvigorate and re-stitch (together) local and regional food systems. The Tabb patterns and precedents again connect well with these new realities. Food production is a central element of Biophilic Urbanism at Serenbe, Helsinge, and Kronsberg, for instance (at Kronsberg a demonstration organic farm and at Serenbe enough farm production to run a CSA). This is a pattern that will undoubtedly strengthen following concerns about the fragility of our food production and distribution system.

The creative responses to this desire for contact with outdoor nature have been numerous. Cities from London to Vancouver, from Bogotá to Mumbai, have taken steps to close streets to create more space for residents to walk, run, and bicycle. There has been a renewed importance given to urban trails and those spaces that allow for active movement and social distancing. As the Seattle Parks and Recreation Department admonishes in its signs, "Keep it Moving!" "This park is for walking, running, and passing through." Wonderful cities are marked by the pathways and trails that provide landscape connections and unusual vantage points. From Rio de Janeiro's Transcarioca Trail to Sydney's Coastal Walks to the San Francisco Bay area's parallel Bay and Ridge Trails (that together will eventually afford 1000 miles of natural trails in close proximity to where millions live), such corridors provide virus-safe opportunities to enjoy nature. An out-of-doors walking existence is an essential part of the DNA of places like Serenbe, as Tabb shows.

A renewed appreciation for the biophilic qualities of wood is combined with a realization of the low-energy and carbon-sequestering benefits of wood as a building material. New examples such as the Bullitt Center in Seattle and the Kendeda Building on the campus of Georgia Tech in Atlanta are helping to demonstrate how wood, sustainably and locally sourced, can deliver significant biophilic qualities to the interior spaces in which we work, learn, and live. In the case of Kendeda, the extensive wood used in this certified living building sequesters carbon and creates impressive interior biophilic spaces for learning and studying, and the wood is sourced from a local mill that salvages and recycles wood from local trees killed by weather or disease.[4]

The need to address the quality and safety of the living environments in which our elder residents live is yet another insight gained from the Coronavirus crisis. In California alone about one-third of the deaths from COVID-19 have been from residents in nursing homes. Why for us as a society it is acceptable to house (or warehouse many would say) one segment of the population in such dismal settings is unclear. Better would be a return to walkable, multi-generational communities like those described by Tabb here. Cottage forms of housing as in Castello di Gargonza, smaller housing clusters described in Helsinge Heveby, and the pedestrianized and auto-free zones of Pontevedra would all create more humane and livable (and safer) environments for elder residents. A better and more humane quality of life, but also a design and planning solution better suited to a pandemic world.

The difficulties of grappling with deep, structural inequalities comprise yet another insight provided by the Coronavirus. We have seen the many ways that pre-existing inequalities manifest and amplify inequalities during a pandemic. There are wide disparities in access to parks, trees, and other forms of nature. Tree canopy cover and exposure to extreme heat have been found to correlate well spatially with red-lining maps going back to the 1930s, and showing just how persistent these inequalities are.[5] It is no surprise that a pandemic exacerbates these inequalities even further—it is clear, for instance, that neighborhoods experiencing higher levels of air pollution (mostly lower-income neighborhoods of color) will experience higher infection and mortality rates.[6]

Part of the challenge will be to make sure that we design and build in ways that are deeply and profoundly inclusive. Wonderful biophilic projects like the High Line in New York, or Atlanta's newest and largest park, Westside Park (the restoration of Bellwood Quarry) raise worries of neighborhood displacement and eco-gentrification. As a result of precisely such fears, the mayor of Atlanta recently suspended issuance of new development permits in the surrounding older neighborhoods. There are currently few effective design and planning tools that adequately address this concern; Biophilic Urbanism moving forward must indeed put equity and social justice front and center.

In many ways it has the promise as a movement to be truly inclusive, taking into account and effecting a deeper and fuller ethical posture towards the world. While the economic benefits of biophilic design and planning may carry the day in city halls and statehouses (e.g. the higher worker productivity enjoyed through biophilic office design), or biophilic cities and urbanism hold dearly the premise that, as Stephen Kellert has argued, nature is a birthright, to be enjoyed and experienced by everyone, regardless of race or income (or age or gender). It is essential to a flourishing life, the kind of life every human is entitled to. Equally true, the ethics of Biophilic Urbanism include other non-human forms of life, acknowledging duties of inclusion, sharing, and care. One of our partner cities in the Biophilic Cities Network, Curridabat, Costa Rica, has established "every bee, bat, hummingbird and butterfly as a citizen…," and has given space and attention in the design of the city, especially in emphasizing through its "sweet city" initiative the planting of native plants and the creation of bio corridors.[7] Serenbe, too, certainly seems to reflect this kind of biocentrism, with room made for birds and wildlife, horses and farm animals, and dogs and other domestic pets – a kind of "zoopolis," in the words of UC-Berkeley planner Jennifer Wolch.[8]

Ultimately what Phill Tabb shows us so well in the wonderful book to follow is how nature can deepen our lives, strengthen a sense of meaning and purpose, foster greater connectedness to place and community, and generally improve the quality of the lives we lead. It is a pantheon to the power of community design. I recall one of the most memorable visits to Singapore in which I had the chance to walk along my favorite segment of the Park Connectors described so well in Chapter 8. After only an hour of walking along the Southern Ridges I had encountered numerous butterflies and birds, had walked through a diverse urban forest much of it at canopy level, and had even had an encounter with a monitor lizard. All experienced against the backdrop of a bustling port and dense vertical city. There was a wildness and beauty on that day and a sense of connection to things larger than myself: when it's done right that's what Biophilic Urbanism can bring about, the kinds of places Phill Tabb hopes we will all be able to enjoy.

Tim Beatley
University of Virginia

NOTES

1. "Birding is gaining flocks of new followers" found here: https://www.observertoday. com/news/page-one/2020/05/birding-is-gaining-flocks-of-new-followers/ (accessed May 10, 2020).
2. Edward O. Wilson. *Half-Earth: Our Planet's Fight for Life* (New York, NY: Liveright publishers, 2017).
3. For a good discussion of this see Erin Bromage's blog, "The Risks – Know Them – Avoid Them," found here: https://www.erinbromage.com/post/the-risks-know-them-avoid-them (accessed May 10, 2020).
4. Eutree Mill follows something it calls a "forest free approach" – see https://www. eutree.com/about/sustainable-wood-sourcing-forest-free-approach (accessed May 10, 2020).
5. See Jeremy Hoffman et al. "The Effects of Historical Housing Policies on Resident Exposure to Intra-Urban Heat: A Study of 108 US Urban Areas," *Climate 2020*, 8(1): 12 https://doi.org/10.3390/cli8010012 (accessed May 10, 2020).
6. See e.g. Aaron van Dorn, Rebecca Cooney, and Miriam Sabin, "COVID-19 exacerbating inequalities in the US," *The Lancet*, April 18, 2020, found here: https://www.thelancet. com/journals/lancet/article/PIIS0140-6736(20)30893-X/fulltext (accessed May 10, 2020)
7. Patrick Greenfield, "'Sweet City': the Costa Rica suburb that gave citizenship to bees, plants and trees," *The Guardian*, April 29, 2020 found here: https://www.theguardian. com/environment/2020/apr/29/sweet-city-the-costa-rica-suburb-that-gave-citizenship-to-bees-plants-and-trees-aoe (accessed May 10, 2020).
8. See https://ced.berkeley.edu/events-media/news/zoopolis-professor-and-former-dean-jennifer-wolch-imagines-the-future-of-cities-alongside-animals (accessed May 10, 2020).

Preface

I grew up along the Snake River on the Idaho side of the Teton Mountain Range. As a young boy I experienced an unspoiled natural environment in all forms, from the mysterious lava caves at Craters of the Moon to the Grand Teton National Park. Yellowstone National Park was nearby as well with its active volcano, incredible waterfalls and lakes, and its unique geothermal features – erupting geysers, hot springs, mud pots, and fumaroles. The variety of North American wildlife that inhabited this land was inspiring. Idaho has the largest percentage of land under national forests in the US, with approximately 20 million acres. I was constantly engaged with nature and, even though I was unaware at the time of the biophilic effect, I developed a healthy respect for nature's powerful forces, positive outcomes, and nourishing benefits.

Back in the late 1950s, my father gave me an interest and career aptitude test that indicated architecture would be a good career path for me. In high school my best subjects were fine art, math, geometry, and biology, certainly disciplines integral to biophilia. All this came to fruition some 50 years later. After six years of undergraduate architecture, I found myself in a profession that was defining itself by modernist principles of architecture with a backdrop of tumultuous political upheaval and social change. It was the 1973 OPEC oil embargo that ultimately shaped the direction of my career. I became a supporter of the utilization of solar energy and the logic behind the integration of other on-site renewable resources. Initially I became aware of the ways it could be applied to single buildings, and later I became interested in the ways in which solar energy could be implemented at the community scale. My first book, published by McGraw-Hill in 1984, focused on solar planning issues of variable scales of application, increases in density, and designs for solar access.

For 25 years I lived and worked in Boulder, Colorado, a city tucked up against the front range of the Rocky Mountains and surrounded by an expansive greenbelt. With help from the American Institute of Architects Research Corporation, my architectural practice was able to engage in solar energy research. Later we received five HUD and DOE solar demonstration awards. While I was able to confirm the practicality of this emerging technology, I was also intrigued with its spiritual implications, its ability to effect social change, its inherent connections to nature, and its capacity to empower. After the 1973 oil embargo and in graduate school, I became interested in climatology, sustainability, environmental psychology, and placemaking. While on-site energy sources could clearly be adapted to individual buildings, I became concerned with larger applications in order to find out how renewable energy could become viable at larger scales. In my doctoral studies in England, I researched the embodied energy conservation characteristics and on-site solar utilization potentials applicable to English village form. In order to better understand and interpret these measures and potentials, I began looking at the history and the evolution of villages in Great Britain. William Hoskin's seminal text *The Making of the English Landscape* presented a chronological development of English landscape and settlement forms.[1] I found seven defined periods that evolved in roughly five hundred-year increments, and added an eighth as a hopeful projection into the future. They were the Stone and Bronze Age farmsteads (2800–500 BC), Celtic hamlets (500–55 BC), Romano-British hamlets (55 BC–500 AD), Anglo-Saxon villages (446–1066 AD), medieval villages (1066–1600 AD), industrial villages (1600–1900 AD), modern villages (1900–present), and biophilic villages (2020–future).

The Stone and Bronze Age settlements tended to be nomadic as principal sustenance was provided by hunting and gathering. These settlements were typically found in thick woodlands where wild game was plentiful. When farming appeared, it necessitated a more settled form of habitation. The Bronze Age farmsteads usually contained extended families involved with crop-growing and animal husbandry. Typically, the homestead had one or more round communal huts with a central hearth.[2] Characteristics of this form included early placemaking, relative permanence, cultivation and the beginning of specialization.

The Celtic Hamlets consisted of dispersed farmsteads, hillforts, hamlets and small villages. They accommodated slightly greater numbers of people and were denser. The farming areas and field patterns were irregular and expanded, and they were bounded with massive rubble walling.[3] Some settlements developed what might be called "industrial zones" because craft and tool work occupied its own designated space. Typically, the hamlets housed storage pits, animal pens, and a watchtower and gate. Characteristics of this form included bounded cultivation, growing diversity, increased specialization, and fortification.

The Roman invasion of Britain in 55 BC resulted in further expansion and a substantial increase in population. The expanded road system was designed for military purposes for the movement of people, goods, and information. The Romano-British hamlet was essentially Celtic with an increase in industrial activity such as iron-making, pottery-making, and other crafts. The most dominant changes included transportation and the introduction of new technologies and interventions, including the plough, bridges, the planning grid, and new building types like the manor house or Roman villa, public baths, the theater, and the forum. Characteristics of this period included increased order, solar energy orientation, expansion, transportation advancements, and greater interconnectedness.

Anglo-Saxon settlements spread over twenty generations, representing a time when most of the hamlets and villages were founded and England became what William Hoskins called a "*landscape of villages*." They formed an interconnected constellation of thousands of settlements on the English landscape. According to Della Hooke, the dominant pattern was dispersed development and open farming in the more accessible and fertile lands.[4] The Anglo-Saxons practiced crop rotation and made use of the ox-driven plough. Where Christianity influenced the nucleation process of mainland Europe, in England it was the central market. Characteristics of this period included proliferation, site-fitted development, open-field strip farming, and agglomeration.

The medieval village resulted in further expansion, specialization, and the introduction of new building types and construction technologies. Tiled roofs and masonry construction allowed for greater density. Nucleation was a major formal pattern against the backdrop of dwindling resources, causing for the need for more control, organization, and land management. Typically, specialized functions of the village were provided by the market and shopping street, builder, baker, butcher, ironmonger, miller, weaver, and lacemaker. New technologies were also introduced such as the water mill, and stone and brick construction, also allowing for denser development. Characteristics of this period included proliferation, specialization of crafts and services, open-field cultivation and enclosure, and nucleation.

The industrial village tended to be larger, denser, industrialized, and connected to larger urban settlements. Wider roads, rail, and canal connections had the effect of bringing settlements closer together. According to William Marshall, the medieval open fields were due to the Parliamentary Enclosure Act, which converted them to enclosed fields and a continuous swathe of hedgerows.[5] Where the early industrial village was supported by agrarian life, having inherited the medieval form and architectural inventory, by the late industrial period the village was rebuilt and often relocated. It was difficult to avoid the pollution from factories, overpopulation, and lack of sanitation. Characteristics included densification, industrialization, and further connectedness.

The modern village experienced the greatest number of changes within the shortest amount of time. No longer self-governing, the modern village became part of an extremely complicated, interrelated administrative, social, and economic system. It was connected through telecommunications, television, radio, and now the World Wide Web, and physically through a complex system of rails, roads, and motorways. Remnants of the medieval and industrial villages were infused with cars and busses, car parks, electricity and telecommunication lines, and large single-ownership farms. Pedestrian village centers were now replaced with vehicle traffic and parked cars. The physical character was increased density with infill development, automobile-oriented, and suburban additions to the original form.

The biophilic village is transformed from the modern village utilizing the same spatial structure but eliminating the automobile from most of the village.

Parking occurs in several strategically located remote lots at the perimeter. The central space is now pedestrianized, encouraging the reintroduction of sustainable businesses such as pharmacies, green markets, grocery stores, shops, and cafes to extend into it. Reforestation occurs surrounding the settlement. Agriculture is more diversified providing local food for the village residents. To the northeast is a solar photovoltaic farm with a micro waste-to-energy plant adjacent to it. Characteristics of this form include pedestrianization, utilization of on-site renewable energy systems, perimeter greening, and diversified agriculture.

What can be observed in this sequence is the transformation of a predominantly natural forested environment with small nomadic farmsteads to completely developed and urbanized commuter villages or peri-urban settlements. The more primal characteristics of biophilia have evolved to more controlled and civilized ones. I couldn't help but sense in this sequence of human settlement-making from the Stone Age to the present that there was an inherited memory in the ways in which we lived together and with nature. Refer to Figure 0.1 that shows the morphology of English village form through these eight periods of time.

It was helpful to see the time lapse of village form-making and to understand its changing relationship to nature. From these studies, I found some interesting transformations that directly related to Biophilic Urbanism. First was the change from a primarily forested context to one where the woodlands have essentially perished to modern villages surrounded by farmland, and landscapes that are integrated within the settlement. Second, individual strip-farming within the settlement changed to large farms located outside of the villages. Third, the incremental increase of non-residential and specialized land uses, trades, and services occurred within the settlement, which mainly remains today. Fourth, an increase of density due to the evolution of construction technologies, such as clay tile roofs and masonry building, reduced fire risk, and infilling. Fifth, the influence of the automobile, which in many ways did not change the village form but often changed the center function. Due to its relatively small size, the village remains a pedestrian place punctuated with opportunities for social interactions and connections to nature.

During my studies and over a two-year period, I lived near the Village of Titchfield located along the south coast of England in Hampshire County. Titchfield appeared as a settlement in the Anglo-Saxon period, but most likely was established by the Romans due to its proximity to the coastline and its obvious cardinal street orientations such as East Street, South Street, and West Street. The urbanized portions of Titchfield occurred within a 1-kilometer-diameter circle and housed 2517 people in 891 dwellings according to the 1981 census. My research revealed that for this population, there were 67 non-residential land uses, businesses, and services, including two schools, four greengrocers, a grocery store, chemist, medical surgery, post office, bookstore, butcher, baker, hair salon, hardware store, two hotels, a parish church, gasoline station, and four pubs. A photograph taken in 1840 showed the commercial businesses and trades that existed in the central square. They still remain today, almost

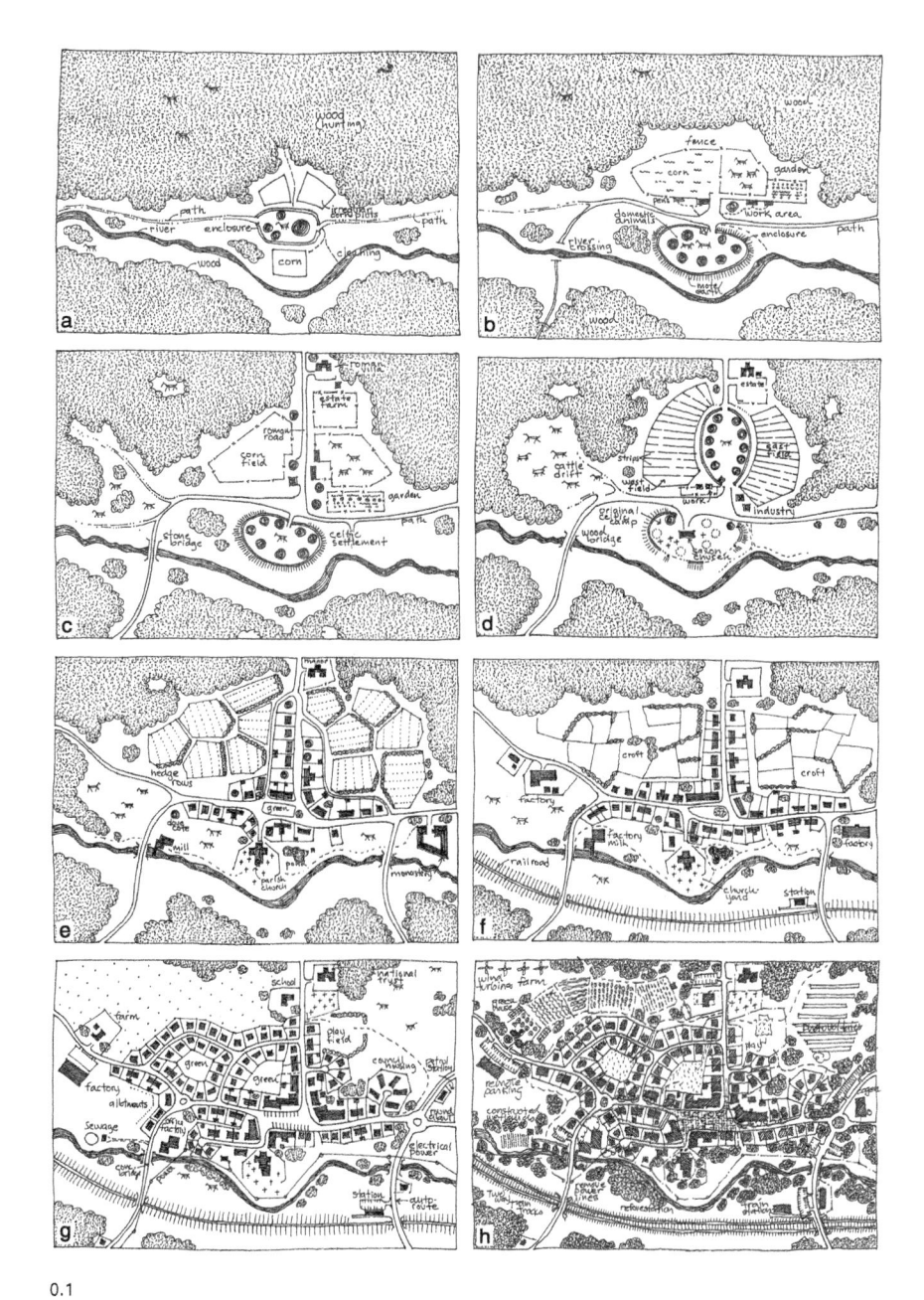

0.1
Morphology of English village form (2800 BC–future):[6] (a) Stone/Bronze Age homestead,
(b) Celtic hamlet, (c) Romano-British hamlet, (d) Anglo-Saxon village, (e) Medieval village,
(f) industrial village, (g) modern village, and h) biophilic village (*Source: Phillip Tabb*)

intact and in the same locations. They represented the sustainable functions and village-scale activities mentioned above. I felt that the New Urbanism proposals existing at that time did not include as rich a mix of critical or essential everyday non-residential goods and services.

The biophilic characteristics of Titchfield include its natural terraced siting on the land down to the river Meon, nucleation with a strong village center surrounded by mixed uses, an evolved pedestrian circulation network with numerous sidewalks and footpaths, and landscape fingers that penetrated deep into the village. Further biophilic attributes occur in proximity to the river Meon and surrounding countryside, the village square which accommodates civic and cultural activities and encourages social interaction, the center green ball fields, and the numerous residential walled-in gardens. The spatial structure and double-loaded street network are oriented along cardinal directions and allow for excellent solar access for passive sun tempering. Figure 0.2 is an aerial view of Titchfield Village indicating both built and natural areas.

After I finished my doctoral work, I visited Expo 2000 in Hannover, Germany and was able to experience the first phase of the Kronsberg District, which is one of the precedent studies in this work. The next year, I was able to integrate climate-oriented design, sustainability, and placemaking in the biophilic planning of Serenbe community located southwest of Atlanta, Georgia. Competitive land costs, completion of the South Fulton Parkway, its close proximity to Hartsfield-Jackson International Airport, and the unspoiled natural environment rendered

0.2
Titchfield Village,
Hampshire, UK
(*Source: Phillip Tabb*)

this a prime location for a special kind of residential development.[7] Utilizing an overlay district allowing for the transfer of density rights (TDR), Serenbe proposed a large amount of open space, mixed uses, concentrations of higher-density clusters, and urban agriculture. Serenbe became an amenity-driven development promoting a healthy lifestyle, with a constellation of hamlets and a primary amenity focus on the large amount of natural forested open spaces.

While at Texas A&M University, I had the good fortune to teach four different semesters in Tuscany, Italy, and took groups of students each time to Castello di Gargonza, another one of the precedents in this work. One of my favorite experiences was to photograph the Tuscan hill towns and landscapes from above in a Cessna with Paolo Barucchieri, the director of the Santa Chiara Study Center. Living in the Tuscan medieval town of Castiglion Fiorentino as a pedestrian was wonderful. It allowed me to live for three or four months without being in a car. In the autumns of 2015 and 2016, I conducted two faculty-led study away programs at Serenbe. During this time, I was able to teach and observe the construction of my own home, which was located across the street from the students' accommodation. My new home in the Crossroads neighborhood of Serenbe was designed and constructed in 2016 using biophilic principles and pattern attributes, and technologies for net-zero energy production. I retired from university teaching and decided to move permanently to Serenbe in the spring of 2017. I named my home "*Watercolor Cottage*" because I had a dream of semi-retiring and focusing on gardening, writing, consulting, drawing, and watercoloring in a white-colored off-grid house. Refer to Figure 0.3 for an aerial view of Castiglion Fiorentino, Italy with our school in the lower right hand corner.

0.3
Castiglion
Fiorentino, Italy
(*Source: Phillip Tabb*)

The Crossroads contains 24 dwellings agglomerated along a T-junction intersection. All houses are painted white, and they all have front porches and balconies facing the street, and most have white picket fences. I wanted my home to fit in, yet express values that supported modesty in overall size, but generosity of space. I love the sacred barrel-vault form that reflects the heavens, and incorporated it as my roof form. My exterior walls were white painted wood with occasional corrugated metal pop-outs. And, of course, I was interested in sustainability and biophilic design principles. I incorporated a geothermal heating and cooling system, and, like the other homes in Serenbe, built to high energy standards. My dwelling has a small footprint with minimal impact on the site, and has a total of 1,650 square feet (153 m²) of enclosed space. It is completely surrounded by coniferous and deciduous trees. With its 10.5 kWh photovoltaic system (35 panels) and Tesla battery wall, it can function at net-zero. The south-facing living spaces are passively solar heated in winter. The walled-in garden serves as a natural focus with its peach trees, flowers, edible plants and reflecting pool. I must say that I thoroughly love my home and feel that it reflects who I am and the values I hold true. To me, it expresses the idea of "walking the talk."

In the mornings I awake next to a small operable window located near the head of my bed. My bed is oriented along cardinal directions, so my head is to the north. In summer, the morning's light pours through it, and tells me I have a little more time to sleep. In winter it is still dark at that time, but my internal clock seems to know when it is time to wake. I enjoy the feel of the cool concrete floor beneath my feet. Having coffee in my living space allows me to enjoy the overlook to my walled-in garden. The nine five-foot-square windows provide tremendous amounts of natural light and views of the surrounding forest and morning sky. It is a moment of calm before the day progresses.

I don't have a conventional lawn. My home is sited in the woods surrounded by southern pine, sweet gum, white oak, and red maple trees. Working in the garden is restorative, and there is nothing like watching the gentle breezes and occasional hummingbirds wisp the tree branches and flowers in rhythmic harmony. The sounds of the modest waterfalls in the pond provide a soothing and hypnotic quality to the garden. It is a blessing to watch the peach trees, herbs (rosemary, parsley, thyme, basil, and mint), flowering plants (roses, hydrangea, purple majesty sage, whirling butterfly gaum, blue vervain, iris, verbena, and wildflowers), and various ground covers emerge in the spring. The garden is visited by bumblebees, butterflies, dragonflies, fireflies, hummingbirds, cardinals, frogs, chipmunks, an eastern box turtle, red-tailed hawks, and owls, and there is a resident eastern kingsnake. Figure 0.4 is a photograph of my walled-in garden in spring and Figure 0.5 is the southern view of Watercolor Cottage.

Another dimension to biophilia is in the incorporation of on-site resources. In my home, this means the use of passive solar heating, photovoltaic electricity production and storage, daylighting, natural ventilation, as well as the food produced in the garden. The ground floor of the house is made with a 6-inch-thick insulated, structural slab-on-grade for thermal storage of the passive

0.4
Walled-in garden
(*Source: Phillip
Tabb*)

heating system. Additionally, I have a Yotul wood-burning stove for backup heat in winter. With my online applications, I can monitor how much energy is being generated by the panels, how much energy is being stored in the Tesla batteries, and how much electricity is being directly used by the house. I can also see how each individual panel is functioning. System performance varies across the seasons, with higher performance from March through September. A neighbor of mine constructed a beautiful compost bin for me located a short distance from my kitchen.

I love preparing food in my kitchen with herbs and a few vegetables from my garden and others from Serenbe Farms. My kitchen is not huge and pristine,

0.5
Watercolor Cottage
(*Source: Phillip
Tabb*)

but rather highly functional with Italian espresso maker, Viking range, barn sink, juicers, wok, and cooking utensils within easy reach. The dining table is within the two-and-a-half-story living space and looks out over the garden. Two Turkish floor carpets become place markers for the dining and living areas of this space. A separate 10-foot by 10-foot (3 x 3 meter) screened-in space, which I call the "Martini Hut," surrounded by trees was added to the east of the house for socializing with neighbors and friends when weather permits.

The quality of light is so changeable, especially from early morning throughout the day and from season to season where the sun's position in the sky raises and lowers. In winter, the low-solar-altitude sunlight passes into the house penetrating deep into the northern rooms. In summer, the high-altitude sunlight is blocked by the roof overhang and operable shades. Sunlight reflecting off the surface of the garden pond shimmers in rhythmic waves. At certain times of the year warm mystical light casts shadows of the nine windows onto the interior walls. A 12-inch glass block emits the most amazing warm amber light that sits atop the large south-facing nine windows. There are many opportunities to experience living color. In my garden are beautiful flowers, butterflies, dragonflies, fruits and vegetables, autumn deciduous tree leaves, and changing skies. Inside my house all the walls are white as a backdrop to all my drawings and painting, so color is introduced on the ceilings. Each room has a different color, giving a slight hue to each of the spaces.

The images in Figure 0.6 show the character of my world in Serenbe at different scales. First is a drone image of my house showing its siting in the woods, the barrel vault roof with photovoltaic panels, and the walled-in garden. Second are a few of my students enjoying the calm of one of the Serenbe waterfalls in the woods. Third is a street view of the Serenbe Saturday morning farmers' and artists' market in Selborne hamlet. It was important to me to realize within the design of the house and community the five classical elements, and to demonstrate biophilic design strategies. I wanted a functional, peaceful place for my creative work, health and wellness, and spiritual development.

0.6
Serenbe, Chattahoochee Hills, Georgia: (a) drone image of residence, (b) students at waterfall, (c) Serenbe farmers' and artists' market (*Source: David Tabb and Phillip Tabb*)

My sub-neighborhood of Crossroads is located in the center of the community surrounded by woods, and it is one of the smallest neighborhoods in Serenbe. My house is on an estate lot at the edge of the cluster of 24 homes. The front of my house is set back from the public street, and the other sides face the woods. The white houses and Southern vernacular architectural language, a common rural road junction urban pattern found in Georgia, create a harmonious and beautiful setting. White picket fences line the streets adding to the human scale of the neighborhood. This small cluster has a flower shop, which I visit weekly, and a bicycle shop.

It is wonderful to have the choice of either peace and quiet or the warm and supportive friendship of my neighbors. Walking through the community is a delight, due to either the engulfing qualities of the natural woods or the friendly connections to community residents. I walk my dog twice a day, which gives me the opportunity to check my mailbox. The ganged mailboxes live in a small, detached structure next to an intimate playground at the edge of Crossroads. A small house wren nests each spring in one of the open mail slots. It is very common to meet a fellow resident there and chat for a while. When I travel away from Serenbe, my Crossroads neighbors look after my house, water my houseplants, and sometimes take care of my dog, Piccola.

My Crossroads neighbors and I have our own Facebook page where we ask questions of one another or share ideas, concerns, or simply recipes. A couple of times a month, I have a morning coffee with a couple of my neighbors, and we sometimes go to dinner together either in Serenbe or another restaurant nearby. When my students from Texas A&M University lived in one of the townhomes in the Crossroads during their semester away, the neighbors organized potlucks for them so they could meet everyone. This was a wonderful opportunity for the students to learn about a biophilic community and experience daily the pattern attributes of everyday living. We worked on projects related to the community and had first-hand contact with the sites, residents, and developers.

At the community scale, the biophilic effect is present nearly everywhere in one form or another. It occurs in the natural world and within the community, as both are so present and accessible. I generally live a reclusive life, yet it is healthy to have the choice of interacting with the community just outside my door. It is a pleasant walk to the general store in Grange hamlet where the staff are so friendly, or again, enjoy a chance meeting with fellow neighbors. I may join the weekly wine-tastings or stop in the Hills and Hamlets bookstore and nose around the new selection of books. Grange green is often filled with parents watching their kids play on the trampoline. It is amazing how this small patch of grass is always so populated. Many residents, including teenagers, are constantly driving by in their electric carts waving at everyone as they pass.

On Saturday mornings in the summer the Serenbe farmers' and artists' market attracts visitors and residents alike. It's within walking distance and is a wonderful way to see neighbors, and very often have lunch at one of the nearby restaurants. Within the community, there are five restaurants that use produce from Serenbe farms. The pedestrian network is everywhere in Serenbe, with more than 15 miles (24 km) of trails. It is faster for me to walk from my home to the Blue Eyed Daisy restaurant using the trails rather than using the sidewalks along the streets.

The quality of experience is so different within the woods where it is peaceful and mysterious in contrast to the streets, which foster community interaction. The streets are lined with trees and edible plants, and every house with a front porch is positioned close to the street. There are many cultural events that connect residents and visitors alike. The non-profit Serenbe Institute for the Arts, Culture, and the Environment supports the Serenbe Playhouse, the Artist-in-Residence program, the Terminus Modern Ballet Theatre, and the Serenbe Fellows program. The Art Farm, Art Over Dinner, and the Chattahoochee Hills Artists' Gallery provide other cultural venues. There are a number of environmental programs, not the least of which is the preservation and maintenance of the 70 percent of open space. Included in their activities is the mapping and repairing the fifteen-mile trail system throughout Serenbe.

This book is written, in part, to connect biophilia, in an integrated and inclusive way, to the architectural, urban design, and planning scales of the built environment. It is also intended to reinforce the positive benefits obtained through the direct experience of nature in all its forms. Woven throughout this work is the notion that nature-oriented design can be sustainable, healthy, and desirable. The manuscript was created from about mid-December 2019 through the end of July of 2020, a time completely dominated by the novel Coronavirus (COVID-19) pandemic. While the actual source of the virus is still unknown, some suggest that it evolved from bats and crossed species to humans in the wet markets of Wuhan, China.[8] By the beginning of October 2020, it was estimated that there were more than 35.5 million coronavirus cases worldwide with more than 1 million deaths, and in the United States it was estimated to be more than 7.5 million cases and 212,000 deaths.

The intersections among biophilia, urbanism, and Coronavirus are complex because of the highly contagious nature of the disease and the benefits of social interactions associated with biophilia and urbanism. This is further exacerbated by a globally mobile population of contemporary culture. One of the intended outcomes of biophilia is engagement with nature and with one another. This is creating new challenges for planning design on all scales. The Coronavirus is cause for the need for retreat, isolation, and disengagement, and in some instances large numbers of people needing quarantine and hospitalization.[9] Biophilia, in contrast, is about interaction and engagement with one's surroundings. Writing within this time period has revealed an overarching feeling of uncertainty – uncertainty about the future and nature of the forthcoming "new normal." It underscores the need to change from economic-driven cities to public health-driven cities.

It is interesting to see the thread of biophilic patterns throughout the history of the English village, as it demonstrates how the English settlement pattern evolved in ways that were sustainable and supported a natural form of living. With appropriate responses to contemporary culture, it could be seen as a model for new residential developments and suburban restructuring, and it certainly informed the design of Serenbe. Sustainable urbanism, landscape urbanism, landform urbanism, agricultural urbanism, serene urbanism, biomimicry, biourbanism, and resilient and regenerative architecture all share characteristic similar to biophilia. They oppose single-use development or functional zoning, low-density suburban sprawl, separation from nature, over-dependence upon the automobile, and the creation of carbon emissions. Conversely, they promote more meaningful connections to nature, such as increased density, the sustainable mix of uses, the creation of community, vital placemaking, and preservation.

This raises several questions. How can we provide easier access to nature across the urban-to-rural transect? How can we accommodate urban growth and break the pattern of forever retreating deeper into the interiority of living? And in what ways does the global pandemic change our perception of space and contemporary living in pursuit of public health-driven Biophilic Urbanism? The challenge is with our need to connect to nature and redirect the alienation caused by technology and the modern built environment. Biophilic principles need to apply at all scales of the built environment, which has largely been created with non-renewable fossil fuels and in homage to the automobile. The principles of modern architecture and planning, with their need for functional zoning, serial production, efficiency and obsession with first costs in development and construction, and industrial and corporate facilities, have also contributed to the dehumanization of our urbanized environments.

Scalar integration of biophilic principles, patterns, and design strategies is important. To date, most applications of biophilic design apply to single buildings and building elements. There are few, if any, entirely biophilic contemporary urban examples operating at all scales of development. The limited and even excluded dimensions of spiritual considerations are often missing from the biophilia narrative, yet when mentioned, they are rarely developed and seldom give rise to specific pattern attributes. While it is difficult to define and to obtain a workable consensus or even a compatible language of understanding, this dimension is integral to both positive health and high-level wellness outcomes.

Will our contemporary history continue to be characterized by the indoor generation, dominated by an automobile culture, obsessed by a community created through social media, limited by agriculture known through deliveries from Amazon Fresh, energy derived from fossil fuels, and fear of recurring waves of infectious diseases? Or will the lessons learned from the recent past inform new, progressive models of Biophilic Urbanism and ways in which to create resilience through incremental transformations of existing built environments? The following chapters seek to address these questions.

NOTES

1. William Hoskins, *The Making of the English Landscape* (Middlesex, UK: Penguin Books, 1970).
2. T. Rowley, *Villages in the Landscape* (London, UK: Dent & Sons Ltd., 1971).
3. P. Reynolds, Iron Age Agriculture Review (Wessex, UK: Council for British Archeology Group 12, 1985).
4. Della Hooke, *The Anglo-Saxon Landscape: The Kingdom of the Hwicce* (Manchester, UK: Manchester University Press, 1985) p 78.
5. William Marshall, *Rural Economy of Norfolk V2: Comprising the Management of Landed Estates and The Present Practice of Husbandry in That County (1795)*, (London, UK: Hathi Trust, 2010).
6. Phillip James Tabb, *The Solar Village Archetype: A Study of English Village Form Applicable to Energy-Integrated Planning Principles for Satellite Settlement in Temperate Climates* (London, UK: PhD Dissertation, 1990).
7. Phillip James Tabb, *Serene Urbanism: A Biophilic Theory and Practice of Sustainable Placemaking* (London, UK: Routledge, 2015).
8. Lydia Densworth, How the COVID-19 Pandemic Could End, *Scientific American* https://www.scientificamerican.com/article/how-the-covid-19-pandemic-could-end1/ (accessed May 28, 2020).
9. Prem Chandavarkar, *The Covid Pandemic: Seven Lessons to be Learned for a Future* https://medium.com/@premckar/the-covid-pandemic-seven-lessons-to-be-learned-for-a-future-81792f7f175 (accessed May 4, 2020).

Acknowledgements

Thanks go to Fran Ford, the senior publishing editor; to Kathryn Snell, my initial commissioning editor; to Sean Speers, my editorial assistant; and to Elizabeth Spicer, my production editor throughout the completion of the work at Routledge (part of the Taylor and Francis Group). And thanks goes to Elizabeth King of KGL. They provided great encouragement, enthusiasm, and valuable feedback throughout the process. Special thanks go to Dr Timothy Beatley who wrote the foreword to this book and supplied useful information, particularly with regards to the scales of application of biophilic principles and the connections to COVID-19. His keen interest and dedication to biophilic cities was an inspiration to me.

I would like to thank my fellow Serenbe community members, especially Steve and Marie Nygren, who endured by daily posts on Facebook regarding my progress on preparation of the manuscript. The Serenbe Biophilic Institute provided a forum for the exchange of ideas in relation to biophilic design, and is where I have been able to meet some incredible leaders in the field. I also thank Monica Olsen, Megan Schaeffer, Gail O'Neil, John Graham, Judith Heerwagen, Bill Browning, Gary Coates, Liz Calabrese, Robert Armon, SEI Engineering, Thanos Stasinopoulos, and finally Simos Yannas who was my doctoral advisor at the Architectural Association. Thanks to all those who encouraged me throughout the manuscript process. Thanks go to Phyllis Bleiweis who edited the manuscript, dotted my "i's" and crossed my "t's", and to Judy Walker who helped design the biophilic outcome diagrams and cover for the book. And thanks to Patricia Chang whose photograph of Washington Square Park appears on the cover. It is so important to have the support of your friends, neighbors, and colleagues.

Very special thanks go to my family, especially to my sons Michael and David, and to Shea, Kristin, Emrys, Caius, and James Tabb, my sister Janice, brother-in-law Richard Nourse, niece Jing Nicholson, and to all my friends. I suppose the book was in part written to all of us now living in the hope the world will evolve so that future generations may enjoy and benefit from fresh, invigorating, and more direct experiences of nature. And very special thoughts go to the memory of my parents, Frank and Tryphosa Tabb, whom I am sure would be proud of this book.

Chattahoochee Hills
Georgia, 2020

Part 1 PRINCIPLES

1 INTRODUCTION

BIOPHILIA

Biophilia is an emerging discipline within the confluence of the fields of natural and social sciences, philosophy, anthropology, public health, biology, evolutionary psychology, environmental and civil engineering, planning, urban design, landscape architecture, architecture, and interior design. Biophilia's epistemology derives from the two Greek terms *bio* meaning "life," and *philia* meaning "affection or friendly feeling toward."[1] Biophilia is defined as the love of life. It is the inborn affinity human beings have for other life forms.[2] Many proponents of biophilia have posited this relationship between humans and nature in several ways. Some describe it as the tendency to affiliate, interact or be closely associated with forms of life in nature. Others describe it as a psychological orientation to the alive and vital. And finally, this attraction is considered to be innate, subconscious, and evinced in daily life. Life is interpreted broadly, from life processes and connections to nature to living organisms or to all life forms. In part, this attraction is ascribed to abstract manifestations – the diversity of shapes, forms, patterns, and colors found in the living natural world. There are even broader explanations of biophilia that span from planetary systems to grains of sand. Expressed in these ways, biophilia supports the mystery, fascination, and interest we have to connect to nature in beneficial ways, which includes connecting to ourselves.

In Edward O. Wilson's Biophilic Hypothesis several concepts are worth examining. The idea of "*innate or inborn tendencies*" toward nature and life and life-like processes is considered to be genetically inherited memory gained throughout human biological evolution. Biophilia ranges between extremes from attraction to aversion, from awe to indifference, and from peacefulness to fear-driven anxiety.[3] For example, the idea of "*affiliation*" is rooted in unconscious or irrational emotional responses, having proximate manifestations, such as survival-specific behaviors like fight or flight. These manifestations are represented by responses to the dangers, such as the fear of snakes, spiders, or wolves, or having the attraction to colorful sunsets, and flora and fauna, or preferences for finding food or a safe habitat. It also includes issues of language acquisition, mate selection, and infidelity. Yet, biophilic design generally seeks to advance the positive characteristics of the affiliation and that our relationship is a beneficial one. However, more than that, Erich Fromm would argue that a biophilous orientation expresses in the whole person as an entire way of being.[4]

Is biophilia strictly a human experience or does it extend beyond us? Where did it originate? The savannas of tropical Africa were presumably the habitat-specific locations of our species.[5] The Savanna Hypothesis, put forward by Lamarck, Darwin and Wallace in the 1800s, explains that in early human development apes (chimpanzees and bonobos) migrated from lush forests to the savanna. This location was preferable because of its open spaces that were uniform, with grasses, fresh water features, wetlands, woodlands, evidence of nearby animals, flowering and fruiting plants, and scattered climbable trees as in the Rift Valley in East Africa during the Pleistocene period (1.8 million years ago).[6] Today, the Great Rift Valley has been a rich source of hominid fossils, allowing for the study of human evolution. The savanna facilitated a survival advantage, and as a consequence it is suggested that these ancestors transitioned from an arboreal lifestyle to one on the open grassland. This led to the favorable evolutionary trait of an upright posture (bipedalism) and walking, suggesting that natural selection resulted in human development with an adaptive mind, problem-solving ability, and love of life. The Savanna Hypothesis would further suggest that this first evolutionary step would also include not only an affiliation and adaptation to the environmental characteristic of this landscape, but also a sense of beauty about it. To Wilson, these land features included open grassland with abundant animal life; undulating topography with vantage points above and protective caves below; and streams that provided nourishment, attraction to other animals, and a defensive border for protection.[7]

According to Kaplan and Kaplan, landscapes today that resemble savannas or are parklike are preferred.[8] The Savanna Hypothesis posits that those individuals who comprehended and appreciated the value of their native landscape survived and multiplied in greater numbers than those who did not.[9] An opposing view asserted that the terrestrial savannas did not play a significant role in human development, and our ancestors preferred seasonal wooded ecosystems, such as those suggested in the Aquatic Ape Hypothesis and the researches of Richard Wrangham.[10] The Lovejoy Hypothesis suggested that the need to have free arms in order to carry food was the determinant that led to bipedalism.[11] Peter Rodman and Henry McHenry theorized that it was climate change that caused the shrinking forests, instigating the migration to grassier lands.[12] And finally, according to Beery and Jonssen, the Topophilia Hypothesis, an expansion of the Biophilic Hypothesis, extends the affiliation of nature with non-human nature and place attachment.[13] This seems relevant to biophilic urbanism, which is also placed-based.

Does this mean that biophilia is exclusively a human experience? It is easy to observe similar behaviors in wild and domesticated life-forms around us. It is uncanny how house cats can find the safest and warmest spots with great surveillance. Erich Fromm would argue that it is our "awareness" of the connection to nature that renders it a human, rather than an animal, experience. This self-awareness creates a separation, and perhaps intensifies the biophilic attraction towards regaining a unity with nature. Regardless of which hypothesis is ultimately correct, the relationship between human development and advantage-settings suggests a genetically based connection to biophilia and upholds the human affiliation with favorable natural environmental conditions. Negative natural phenomena exist, and instead of "affiliating" with them, we tend to "adapt" or "deal" with them. Peter Kahn asks whether these positive/negative extremes reconcile one another.[14] *Homo erectus* then begins the Biophilic Hypothesis and the human–nature relationship. Evolutionary development and survival were influenced by connections to advantageous landscape features, such as access to water, plant and animal life, natural defenses, and sufficient views to warn of potential approaching threats – all considered recent biophilic patterns today. If we fast-forward to today, what are the survival instincts and attractions for contemporary culture? How do world population, globalization, and urbanization affect the Biophilic Hypothesis?

Ancient societies, such as the Amazonian, the Aboriginal, and Native Americans saw themselves as part of, not separate, from nature. Everyday life and survival were woven together with a respect for natural systems, organisms, and natural food supplies. There also is evidence of biophobia or the fear of nature, where humans are vulnerable to predation, and the fear of snakes (ophidiophobia), spiders (arachnophobia), and poisonous plants (botanophobia). Even with the advent of animal husbandry (cattle, goats, sheep, and pigs) around 15,000 years ago, and widespread settled farming around 12,500 years ago, there existed a balanced and respectful relationship to nature.[16] Some speculate that humans saw themselves apart from nature – a homocentric paradigm, possibly caused by religious beliefs, the industrial revolution, or even the fossil fuel era – and the Earth and its natural bounty were seen as a commodity and something to be exploited. Human populations expanded, territories across the globe were occupied, and the natural resources were consumed. We eventually became dependent upon fossil fuels, and we transformed into an urbanized culture, ultimately moving inside buildings for the duration of most of our lives.

Ancient cultures lived closer to nature. There is further speculation that the reason humans now view themselves as separate from nature is through natural selection, to favor intellectual endeavors rather than physical ones. Major consequences of this evolutionary change are the enormous increase in population, the degradation of natural resources, the development of unsustainable consumption patterns, and the emergence of climate change. The interest in biophilia is beginning to reverse these trends, as exemplified in Elonda Clay's comment, "Gardens and landscapes immerse humans in the cycles of nature, life, death, and rebirth, growing seasons, the rising sun and waning moon, planting seeds, growth, and harvest."[17] Figure 1.1 shows Cave painting found in the Cave of Altamira, located in Cantabria, Spain and dating from the Upper Paleolithic period. It is interesting to see images of animals and of human hands in juxtaposition.

1.1
Paleolithic cave paintings, Altamira, Spain (*Source: Alamy Stock*)

The evolution of the idea of biophilia begins in modern times with the first introduction of the concept by Erich Fromm in 1964 in his book *The Heart of Man*. He posited that there is a tendency for humans to be attracted to all that is alive and vital.[17] Edward O. Wilson introduced the Biophilic Hypothesis in 1984, suggesting our innate tendency to connections with nature, living forms, and biological systems.[18] Stephen Kellert in 2008 expanded on the health and wellness effects of biophilia and presented 72 attributes to biophilic design.[19] He further introduced the concepts of a conservation-based ethic and environmental stewardship. Rachel and Stephen Kaplan in 1989 worked on restorative environments that promoted stress recovery through interactions with nature.[20] Biourbanism was introduced by Eleni Tracada and Antonio Caperna in 2010, showing nature's interactions were seen in the context of more contemporary and complex considerations of urban form.[21] In 2011, Tim Beatley's Biophilic Cities at the University of Virginia proposed the proliferation of biophilic designs at varying scales of urban form.[22] Terrapin Bright Green in 2014 developed examples of 14 biophilic patterns of design and later added a 15th, awe.[23]

Two global migration trends are increasing the separation of human activity from nature. They are the migrations from rural to urban areas and the migrations from outdoor to indoor environments. Around 2009, most of the developed world was urban. Developing regions, including Africa and Asia, which are still mostly rural today, are projected to have more people living in urban areas than in rural areas by 2030. Cities are the focal points of economic growth, innovation, paid employment, cultural functions, and other social outcomes. Rural areas provide agriculture, recreation, species habitation, and preservation of natural reserves. Yet this bifurcation presents many challenges and has a tremendous impact on the forms of habitation appropriate for these differing environments.

The questions of the degree to which urban living separates us from nature and the decline of vital connections to nature in urban environments are still under study. However, access to urban parks and public greenspaces, tree-lined streets, and rear gardens in suburban developments are common examples. Urban agriculture is increasing. Public zoological parks and botanical gardens also provide contact with nature. Three key indicators of the quality of an urban-nature exposure are the *frequency* (how often), the *duration* (how long), and the *intensity* (how much) of the interaction.[24] Incidental exposure to nature was higher in rural areas. According to the World Health Organization, detrimental effects on health due to urbanization include increases in depression, overcrowding, pollution, and difficulty with food supply systems, and a decrease in physical activity.[25]

According to the Environmental Protection Agency (EPA), the average American spends as much as 93 percent of their time indoors, with 87 percent of that time is spent in buildings and 6 percent in automobiles.[26] This creates a tremendous separation from direct experiences of nature, approximating to 22 of the 24 hours in each day. Another survey from Velux has found that one in four Americans spend almost their entire day indoors.[27] This is exacerbated by the fact that the EPA has found that levels of some pollutants are as much as 2 to 5 percent higher when found indoors.

According to Wayne Ott, in the conclusion of his research on human activity, "*we are basically an indoor species.*"[28] The relationship between health and human activity reveals important distinctions. Too much time indoors can create physical health problems caused by inactivity, and detachment from the natural world. This can have deleterious effects, such as respiratory problems due to breathing indoor polluted air, seasonal affective disorder (SAD), depression, insufficient daylight causing mood swings, and lower levels of energy and alertness. In addition, circadian disorders can affect sleep cycles. Excessive indoor living increases instances of eye, nose, and throat irritation as well as causing higher levels of fatigue. And living in damp and moldy homes increases risk of asthma by as much as 40 percent. We now are being considered an "indoor generation."

Contemporary applications of biophilic principles have generally been limited primarily to the individual building scale. They often occur on isolated sites and do not extend beyond their own property lines. Several infrastructure works have also followed biophilic design principles. According to Stephen Kellert, five conditions contribute to the effective practice of biophilic design. These are: (1) creating more exposure to nature, (2) repeating and sustaining the engagement with nature, (3) providing design innovations that connect to the overall setting or place, (4) providing opportunities for emotional attachments to nature, and (5) facilitating the social dimension to place and nature.[29] Places like Savannah, Georgia with its fabric of parks; the Planty Park in Kraków, Poland with its 2.5 miles (4 kilometers) greenway encircling the medieval inner city; Frank Lloyd Wright's Falling Water along the scenic Bear Run River in southwestern Pennsylvania; and even BIG's Waste-to-Energy Plant in Copenhagen possess biophilic features. Following are several fairly recent projects that demonstrate exemplary biophilic principles.

The Makoko Floating School was constructed in 2013. It is located within the vulnerable coastline of the Lagos Lagoon in a largely fishing community. It was designed by Kunle Adeyemi of NRE Architects, and sponsored by the United Nations Development Programme and the Boell Foundation. The school is composed of a locally sourced wooden and bamboo triangular "A-frame" attached

1.2
Makoko Floating
School, Lagos,
Nigeria (*Source:
Public Delivery*)

to a 33 x 33-foot (10 x 10-meter) base of recycled plastic barrels. It supports photovoltaic panels on the roof providing electricity, and rainwater harvesting stored in the outermost barrels. On the main level of the structure is an outdoor playground. This remarkable project was developed as a resource protecting the community from unpredictable storms and floods, and it is a good example of passive survivability. There are many biophilic patterns including access to nature, views and vistas, sensory connections, on-site energy and water, fresh sea air, living color, abundant natural light, strong inside–outside relationships, prospect and refuge, and natural materiality. Figure 1.2 shows the Makoko Floating School.

The Bosco Verticale, or Vertical Forest, is a pair of residential towers completed in Milan, Italy in 2014. Their heights are 364 feet (111 meters) and 249 feet (76 meters) respectively. Together they host 900 trees on terraces and balconies, in planters positioned around their facades. The towers were designed by Boeri Studio, in consultation with horticulturalists and botanists. The buildings were conceptualized as a home for trees that simultaneously houses humans and birds. The buildings are self-sufficient by using renewable energy from solar photovoltaic panels and filtered wastewater to sustain their plant life. These green technology systems reduce the overall waste and carbon footprint of the towers and provide carbon sequestering. Lead designer Stefano Boeri stated, "It's very important to completely change how these new cities are developing."[30] The Vertical Forest (see Figure 1.3) is a prototype design for an emerging format of architectural biodiversity and carbon sequestering. It creates a direct opportunity for interactions between humans and living species. As inspiring as the facades are, they do raise the question of whether schemes like these are fully biophilic or merely visual.

1.3
The Vertical Forest,
Milan, Italy (*Source:
Getty Images*)

The Eden Project is located in Cornwall, UK and was designed by Nicholas Grimshaw and completed in 2000. It features two large biodomes that cluster with smaller domes. The biodomes' structure comprises hexagonal and pentagonal plastic cells that can be inflated or deflated to adjust the insulation levels responding to fluctuating outside temperatures. The biodomes enclose multiple complexes, covering more than 3.9 acres (1.56 hectares) of land and housing over 100,000 plants. The tectonic form language is biomorphic and encloses the world's largest man-made rainforest. Biophilic features include access to nature, water, plants, the earth, sensory connections, refuge, living color, natural light, and numinous experiences. The Tropical Biome was the world's largest enclosed greenhouse, representing 5,000 species from many of the climate zones of the world. Refer to Figure 1.4, which shows the biodomes set into the Cornish landscape.

New York City's remarkable High Line Park (2009 and 2011) (Figure 1.5) was designed in three sections by landscape architecture firm James Corner Fields Operation with architects Diller Scofidio + Renfro. Theirs was a competition-winning proposal created as an aerial greenway elevated above the ground for one mile along Manhattan's West Side, transforming the 1.45-mile (2.33-kilometer) section of the former New York Central Railroad spur running through the Chelsea neighborhood. The original rail link was a massive public–private infrastructure project done in the 1930s called the "West Side Improvement" that elevated dangerous freight trains 30 feet (9.1 meters) off the street level, thereby avoiding conflict with pedestrians and cars on the ground below. Inspired by the Promenade Plantée in Paris, nine entrances give access to the elevated platform and to the pebbledash walkways that expand and contract along the park. The design has been described as part promenade, part town square, and part botanical garden, and its integration of the urban and natural become an

1.4
The Eden Project,
Cornwall, UK
(*Source:*
Shutterstock)

'*agri-tecture.*' It is certainly an excellent example of biophilic urbanism at the infrastructure scale.

Mexcaltitán de Uribe, Mexico is an excellent demonstration of the expression of biophilic urban patterns. It is a man-made island-city off the coast in the municipality of Santiago Ixcuintla in the Mexican state of Nayarit. Mexcaltitán was Aztlán (cradle of Mexico), the ancient home of the Aztecs. The patterns include an identifiable cultural and social center, which is in the form of a public square and green surrounded by larger non-residential buildings including a museum, hotel, restaurant and the church. The boundary is a natural crenellated edge between the built space and the estuary of the mangrove swamps. Streets in a double-cross pattern and a circumferential road make the spatial order. The curb of this road is more than a foot deep, allowing for water containment during the rainy season. Residents navigate at this time using gondolas,

1.5
High Line Park,
New York City
(*Source:*
Shutterstock)

hence Mexcaltitán's reference as the 'Little Venice.'[31] The center of the island is the high point, and the spire of the Church of Saints Peter and Paul towers upward high above the city. The island is oriented with its slightly longer aspect along the north–south axis, giving both symbolic and good solar access to the city. Nature is found in the very center of the city in its double-square plaza, in courtyards brimming with tropical plants, and certainly around the perimeter at the water's edge. The streets and sidewalks are used to dry the shrimp, oysters, and fish caught in the estuary, and therefore perform a double function. The overall shape of the urban fabric suggests a celestial diagram of the sun, which played a central role in Aztec beliefs. Refer to Figure 1.6, which is an aerial view of the island city.

James Oglethorpe established Savannah, Georgia in 1733, which has long been an excellent example of early American planning and is a good example of biophilic urbanism as well. Originally it was planned with four squares named after each ward, and by 1851 there were an additional 20 established squares. It is for these 24 nature-filled squares located evenly throughout the original town fabric that Savannah is most recognized. Two of the squares were demolished, leaving 22 active squares today. Typically, a ward is made of 9 blocks with the park in the center. The parks are surrounded by four civic and four residential blocks. Buildings located along the east-west sides of the squares typically house civic (*trust*) functions, while north-south blocks are residential (*tythings*). All of the squares measure approximately 200 feet (61 meters) from east to west, but they vary north to south from approximately 100 to 300 feet (30–91 meters). Figure 1.7 is an aerial view of Savannah, indicating the spread of park wards integrated into the urban fabric.

1.7
Savannah, Georgia
(*Source:
Shutterstock*)

In looking at these examples, biophilic urbanism addresses key contemporary issues, which can be seen in the relationships between urban form and nature. The positive outcomes include moving toward what Farhana Yamin calls "*climate neutrality*,"[31] creating sustainable development and what John Ehrenfeld calls "*true sustainability*,"[32] promoting community and overcoming what Edward Relph calls "*placelessness*,"[33] achieving health and what Halbert Dunn terms "*high-level wellness*,"[34] and providing opportunities for what Rudolf Otto calls "*numinous*" experiences.[35]

Climate neutrality and carbon neutrality are often interchanged. Both promote the reduction of emissions-producing activities, improving efficiency, incorporating renewable energy technologies, and phasing out of the use of fossil fuels. Several strategies contribute to a more climate-neutral future. They include living smaller, planting trees, rethinking power production, instituting land-use reforms to increase density and life-supporting mix of uses, increasing accessibility, pedestrianization (especially in city centers), reinventing the suburbs, and making peri-urban development more self-sufficient.

According to the 1987 Brundtland Commission Report, sustainable development was defined as "meeting the needs of the present without compromising the ability of future generations to meet their own needs."[36] True sustainability goes beyond "*fixing unsustainability*," deriving from the very cultural structure of modernity, including harmful energy sources and technologies, buildings and design practices, and continued consumer-oriented living styles. True sustainability flourishes instead of sustains and pertains to all living systems – a biophilic dimension.

Placelessness is characterized by monolithic concrete surfaces, spatial incongruity, a lack of human scale or of any redeeming meaning, the fall into disrepair, and the absence of living things.[37] Countering this, placemaking is often an intended outcome of urban development, and it is characterized by diversity, authenticity, safety, human scale, and living vitality. It fosters community, social interaction, identity, and stewardship. Nature is an important part of place. Certain physical patterns are also integral to creating a sense of place.

Health and wellness are desired benefits as defined by a dynamic process informed by physical, nutritional, mental, social, emotional, and spiritual indicators. Growing empirical evidence shows that interacting with nature delivers a range of measurable human benefits. Health and wellness effect everyone directly. Health is the overall mental and physical condition of a person in the absence of injury and disease. Wellness is an active process of choices that contributes to holistic lifestyles informed by physical, emotional, intellectual, psychological, social, and spiritual dimensions.

Numinous experiences occur through a variety of channels and intimate factors. Rudolf Otto categorized the numinous experience into three interrelated qualities: fascination (*fascinans*) and exuberance; the mysterious (*mysterium*) – that which is hidden from view or knowledge; and the awe-ful (*tremendum*) – that which is fear-inspiring. These are all experiential qualities that are enabled by interactions with nature.[38] There are two critical causes that separate us from experiences such as these: the *crisis of nature* and the *crisis of urbanism*, and it is to these crises that biophilic urbanism is arguably addressed. According to Judith Heerwagen, the positive outcomes evolve from a continuum from biophobia, through bio-indifference, and finally to biophilia.[39] The causes present a profound challenge for policymakers, public officials, design professionals, and developers, as they run deeply through contemporary culture and the modern lifestyles they have produced. These conditions have given rise to the disconnect, distractions, and amnesia affecting the source experiences of nature.

THE CRISIS OF NATURE

Nature versus Humanity

The relationship between the natural world and human beings is complicated. There is a pervasive aloof disregard of nature. This is due in part to an anthropocentric world view promoting the idea that human beings are special, top of the food chain, and set apart from nature, with nature seen as a commodity of natural resources for our use, consumption, and recreation. For some, life's objective is the pursuit of comfort and convenience. According to sociologists William Catton Jr. and Riley Dunlap, there are four basic assumptions in the Western worldview:[40]

1. Human beings are fundamentally different from all other creatures on Earth, over which they have dominion. This is in part because humans have not only a genetic inheritance, but also a cultural evolutionary one.

2. People are masters of their own destiny, and they can do whatever is necessary to achieve their goals.
3. The world is vast and provides unlimited opportunities for humans.
4. Humanity's history is about problem solving (today, technologically without limit) and unceasing progress.

With this worldview, it is no wonder that we find the health of the planet under serious attack. This is due in part to climate change, diminished contact with nature, loss of biodiversity, wildlife destruction, the question of zoos, increased pollution, the global pandemic, and primarily living indoors. John Ehrenfeld would argue that true sustainability occurs through the flourishing qualities of dignified and authentic lives.[41] This world view and the conditions they create are contributing to this crisis of nature.

Climate Change

Climate change and environmental degradation are also the consequences of our contemporary condition, a situation the public has recently recognized. Cities and urban areas are the major cause of climate change and they also hold the greatest opportunity to mitigate it. According to Lamia Kamal-Chaoul and Alexis Roberts, they consume a great majority – between 60 to 80 percent – of energy production worldwide and account for a roughly equal share of global CO_2 emissions.[42] Carbon fixation or absorption capacity is directly related to changing land-use patterns, particularly from natural land to developed land.[43] Politicians are only now acknowledging that climate change is actually real; however, they do not agree on its source. The global scientific community explains that human activity is the cause, created by trapped solar radiation due to rising anthropogenic greenhouse gases and the burning of fossil fuels within the building, power, and transportation sectors of our culture. The year 2016 ranks as Earth's warmest since 1880, according to two separate analyses, by National Aeronautics and Space Administration (NASA) and National Oceanic and Atmospheric Administration (NOAA) scientists. Indicators of this phenomenon include shrinking ice sheets, warmer ocean temperatures, the rise of global air temperatures and global sea levels, ocean acidification, glacial retreat, declining Arctic sea ice, decreased snow cover, and increasingly frequent extreme weather events.[44]

Natural disasters, such as the Indian Ocean tsunami (2004), hurricane Katrina (2005), the Kashmir earthquake (2005), cyclone Nargis (2008), the Haiti earthquake (2010), the Tohoku earthquake and tsunami (2011), superstorm Sandy (2012), the Mount Everest avalanche (2014), Hurricanes Harvey, Irma, and Maria (2017), the lower Puna volcanic eruption (2018), the Australian wildfires (2019), and the West Coast wildfires and global COVID-19 pandemic (2020), all contributed to a greater awareness of the recurring dangers of our relationship with the natural environment. According to Christina Hill, "Hurricanes Sandy and Katrina were not so much natural disasters but were human disasters because of historically poor land-use decisions."[45] Some predictions concerning climate change suggest that the incremental shifts may eventually become more abrupt and even irreversible, leading to massive disruption.

Global cooling in winter accompanies global warming and an increasing number of storms and weather anomalies. Climate scientists are reporting that these changes are affecting urban areas in significant ways. Included are six different factors: sea-level rise; an increase of hurricanes in coastal regions; extreme precipitation with flooding; extreme drought; changes in average temperatures; and the urban island effect. Antarctica reached a record high temperature on February 6, 2020 with 65 degrees Fahrenheit (18.3 degrees Celsius). NOAA announced that, averaged globally, January of 2020 was the warmest since record-keeping began in 1880.[46]

Diminished Contact with Nature

There are two major causes of decreasing of contacts with nature. The first is the diminishment of natural land, and the other is the increasing limited access to the remaining land. Arable land has declined due to erosion, wildfires, pollution, and urban development, especially because of suburban sprawl. It is estimated that by 2030 urban areas will triple in size, expanding into cropland and undermining the productivity of agricultural systems that are already stressed by rising populations and climate change. And roughly 60 percent of the world's cropland lies on the outskirts of metropolitan areas. The rural-to-urban transect further exacerbates the problem as increased density and reduced greenspace moving toward city centers.

Loss of Biodiversity

Loss of biodiversity is defined as the decrease of diversity in the biological community of plant and animal species within an ecosystem or geographical area. The primary cause of the loss of biodiversity is human interventions in the world's ecosystems. According to Peter Newman and Isabella Jennings, the loss in biodiversity is affecting ecosystem productivity, and is increasing at an alarming rate.[47] They further state that preservation of biodiversity is necessary for sustainable development, and it is certainly at the core of biophilic urbanism. According to the University of Copenhagen, the world is losing species at a rate that is 100 to 1,000 times faster than the natural extinction rate.[48] A United Nations report estimates that as many as 1 million plant and animal species are currently threatened with extinction.[49] According to John Rafferty, there are considered to be five primary causes of biodiversity loss:[50]

- Habitat loss – *Destruction of an ecosystem's plant life, soils, hydrology and nutrient sources.*
- Invasive species – *Disruptive non-native species.*
- Over-exploitation – *Over-harvesting aquatic and terrestrial animals.*
- Pollution – *Addition of pollutants at a faster rate than the ecosystem can manage.*
- Climate change – *Rising temperatures and increasing weather anomalies.*

Wildlife Destruction

Loss of habitat is the primary threat to the survival of wildlife and occurs when an ecosystem has been drastically altered by human activity. Habitat that is no longer capable of supporting native species is considered habitat destruction. The primary causes of population decline in species include climate change; extinction events; and habitat loss due to mass deforestation in order to cultivate of land for agriculture, land conversion for development, and fragmentation of habitat resulting in the separating of animal inhabitants from crucial resources. Animal species with poor colonizing capabilities are most at risk. The health of world's ecosystems, on which we all depend, is deteriorating more rapidly than ever. According to the Intergovernmental Science-Policy Platform on Biodiversity and Ecosystem Services, around 1 million animal and plant species are now threatened with extinction.[51] The three current primary causes of extinctions are similar to the causes of biodiversity loss:[52]

- Over-hunting – *Fur, ivory, fins, organs, food sources, and sport.*
- Habitat destruction – *Deforestation and coral reef destruction.*
- Pollution – *Contaminants and unnatural chemicals in the air, soils, and seas.*

The Question of Zoos

Modern zoos strive to educate visitors about zoo animals and those who live in the wild, to promote needs and conservation messaging, while fostering appreciation for wildlife in general. Approximately 700 million people visit zoos worldwide annually.[53] On the face of it, experiencing urban-situated zoological gardens should support biophilia and the human–nature interactions; however, David Hancocks argues that today's zoos are not really advancing conservation efforts but are simply entertainment venues with superficial "Tarzanesque" aesthetics.[54] The problem is that zoos' environments are too small and are seemingly lacking in consideration of the animals' emotional needs, and that zoos are creating conditions where animals have less control over their own environments. Hancocks goes on to suggest that it is rare to find zoos demonstrating consideration for fair trade and sustainability or other basic conservation ethics, or awareness of environmental pollution, the evils of factory farming, carbon footprints, etc., and that smaller species can better promote biodiversity awareness and provide more illustrative stories. According to Ado Sa Samraj:

> "If you're going to bring animals into your sphere and take them out of theirs, you have to make some sort of arrangement with them in which they have the potential, through their contemplative life, to be just as happy as you want them to be."[55]

Increased Pollution

In the 1960s a growing awareness of the deleterious effects that contemporary life had on the environment became more evident. Rachel Carson's *Silent*

Spring was a startling wake-up call.[56] This work was credited with helping launch the environmental movement. Carson, a marine biologist, documented damage caused to the environment by the aerial spraying of pesticides to kill mosquitos. She focused on the example of birds whose populations had dwindled as a result of the damage caused to their eggshells by exposure to DDT. Unlike most pesticides, whose effectiveness is limited to destroying one or two species of insects, DDT, developed in 1939, was capable of killing hundreds of different kinds at once. Widespread use, she argued, harmed many other animals including humans. The title of the book was a call to bring back the singing of birds in springtime. The book marked the beginning of a growing awareness of the indiscriminate use of pesticides and other harmful chemicals in the environment. Health issues are becoming increasingly important. In the United States, for example, life expectancy is on a slight decline due to lack of exercise, poor diet, drug overdoses, suicides, alcohol-related illness, and obesity. There is a disparity in rural versus urban health. In rural areas there are fewer physicians per capita as well as fewer specialists in other medical fields. However, rural medical care offers a more personalized approach to healthcare, and there is easier access to nature. While there is a higher need for healthcare in urban areas, there is more access to treatment options.

The common definition of pollution is the introduction of both natural and human-made contaminants into the environment that causes disease, harm, instability, and destruction. Pollutants usually affect elemental substances – fire earth, water, and air – and can manifest in the very places we live – our homes, schools, places of work, and communities. Mining, drilling, and the burning of fossil fuels are harmful to human health and the environment. The burning of fossil fuels for transportation and electricity emits harmful pollutants. Nuclear power plants generate waste heat energy (a form of energy pollution) and radioactive wastes.

The materials used to construct buildings, roads, and infrastructure can be highly toxic. For example, prior to the 1970s friable asbestos-containing materials were used as insulation. When disturbed, asbestos crumbled into a dust of microscopic fibers which remained in the air for long periods of time. If inhaled they posed a serious health threat, as asbestos fibers can become permanently lodged in body tissues and eventually lead to cancer. Many other construction materials have been found to be harmful. Infrastructure also contributes to pollution, especially in our waterways through waste heat and chemical pollutants caused by electric power production, dams, and water channels.

A primary source of air pollution is the combustion of gasoline and other hydrocarbon fuels in automobiles, trucks, and jet planes, producing several primary pollutants: nitrogen oxides, gaseous hydrocarbons, carbon dioxide, and carbon monoxide, as well as large quantities of particulates, chiefly lead. Smog hanging over cities is the most familiar and obvious form of air pollution. Indoor air quality and urban air pollution are listed as two of the world's worst pollution problems. Key contaminants are sulfur oxides (SO_x), nitrogen oxides (NO_x), carbon monoxide (CO), volatile organic compounds (VOCs), carbon dioxide (CO_2), and fine particles. Where the external cause of air pollution is the burning of fossil fuels, the internal causes are chemical toxins from common household products resulting in indoor air pollution and sick building syndrome. This includes outgassing from building materials, combustion gasses from heating and kitchen appliances, smoking, and radon gas from the surrounding ground. It was in 1960 that the first Clean Air Act passed in the US Congress.

Global Pandemic

2020's global pandemic of the novel Coronavirus COVID-19 revealed our vulnerability to this highly contagious airborne virus. Within the context of a vastly mobile world population, it is speculated that the virus spread from its origin in the wet markets of Wuhan, China throughout the world. The zoonotic impact of this virus affected millions of people with countless deaths (880,000 deaths worldwide as of early September 2020) exposed weaknesses in the supply chain of essential goods and services, and placed extreme stress upon the surge capacity of healthcare facilities and surrounding communities. Mitigation measures included safe distancing between individuals, avoiding groups of people, staying at home, and the wearing of face masks in order to subdue the spreading of the disease. Older people aged 65 and above, those who have underlying medical conditions (especially weakened immune systems and respiratory illnesses), and those living with large numbers of people in confined places were at higher risk from COVID-19. People living within nursing homes, congregate housing, and long-term health facilities and/or receiving assisted living; those attending aggregate work environments; incarcerated prisoners; and employees in meat packing industries were highly susceptible to testing positive to the disease and spreading it to surrounding communities. By late June, it was reported that younger populations were also susceptible to the disease. Critical to the recovery from the pandemic was the difficult interplay between maintaining safe distancing and staying at home mitigation measures and the opening up of manufacturing and business premises and social and entertainment venues in order to kick-start the failing economy.

In the United States, where the disease was most prevalent, several causes were apparent: the slow initial response to the spread of the disease and to closing down travel, especially from Europe; the inability to institute effective nationwide mitigation practices; the stress placed upon the healthcare system and associated infrastructures (healthcare givers, police, fire protection, paramedics, and support staff); a breakdown in the supply chain of critical medical equipment; the inability of states to initiate a rapid, simultaneous, and unified mitigation strategy instead of the piecemeal approach over an extended period of time; the opening up the economy and relaxing mitigation measures before containment practices were put into place; the slow start to large-scale testing and little contact tracing; and the often ambiguous, contradictory, and misleading information that obfuscated the truth about what to do in response to the virus. Lessons learned include the effectiveness of regional and local responses to managing and controlling the spread of the disease over national responses.

Density has long been considered a positive sustainable planning strategy preserving land, providing large social and cultural venues, and creating infrastructural efficiencies. According to Camilla Cavendish, density has been the enemy during most plagues.[57] As a result, there may be a trend toward populations migrating out of dense megacities to suburbs and beyond enabled by sheltering at home, more space for social distancing, and teleworking. She goes on to call into question the value of city life and suggests that tradeoffs have changed from the cultural and economic benefits of urban environments to public health safety found in outlying communities. An opposing view is put forward in a study by Hamidi, Sabouri, and Ewing, where they suggest that higher Coronavirus infection, transmission, and mortality rates seem to be linked to a metropolitan area's size, not its density, and that cities that are very large and stretching across multiple counties are at higher risk.[58] Vulnerable populations – those aged over 65 living in congregate housing, nursing homes, and assisted and independent living facilities; and also inmates in prisons – normally live in concentrations outside of dense urban cores. Density per se contributes to infection rates only when combined with other factors, including failing in social distancing, sheltering-in-place, sanitation protocols, testing, contact tracing, the wearing of face masks, and travel behavior. This combinatory effect was evidenced by the higher infection rates in the dense cities of New York City and Milan versus the much lower rates in Hong Kong and Seoul, especially in the early stages of the pandemic. Figure 1.8 depicts an elderly woman receiving groceries from a courier with safe distancing, masks, and gloves.

1.8
Impacts of the Coronavirus 2020: woman receiving groceries (*Source: Shutterstock*)

According to Allison Aubrey, Laurel Wamsley, and Carmel Wroth, those activities that are considered low risk or reduced viral load include exercising out-doors, camping, going to a vacation house, a small gathering in your back yard, outdoor activities with less than ten people, and socially distancing at a beach or pool.[59] All of these are biophilic in nature. There is a need to re-evaluate the spa-tial characteristic of society, from churches and football stadiums to restaurants and elevators, where large or concentrated numbers of people gather. There is the need for a focus on congregate care facilities; scaled screening, testing, and re-testing of the triage high-risk patients; aggressive quarantine measures; and support of healthcare workers. There is the need for single voices from healthcare professionals and government leaders on clear information, scientific facts, and honest communications. And finally, there is the need to put into place future preparative measures before there are additional peaks or another pandemic occurs. Questions arise: is this disease is a singular event or one that may persist every year like the common flu?

Primarily Living Indoors

On average Americans spend as much as 93 percent of their time indoors.[59] Modern amenities, emergent technologies, more humane workspaces, and larger domestic dwellings have undoubtedly made contemporary life easier. However, there are health risks associated with too much indoor living. They include the reduction of physical activity, exposure to indoor air pollution and damp, and the reduction of exposure to daylight and fresh air. Within the home, children's' bedrooms are the most polluted within a house. Signs that you are spending too much time indoors could manifest as moodiness (and sometimes depression), increased anxiety and restlessness, sleep troubles, bone and mus-cle weakness, change in appetite, a weakening immune system due to ack of vitamin D, and fatigue.[60]

Neil Postman suggests that we are "*Amusing Ourselves to Death*" through our interactions and even obsessions with mass media.[61] Today the situation is compounded because of the ubiquitous nature of the Internet, social media, personal computers, tablets, the proliferation of mobile devices, and access to a plethora of programs, games, movies, and music. In an instant we have access to an immense number of entertainment and communications venues. This in large part contributes to the high percentage of time spent indoors. Where the Internet renders the world a smaller place, it also distances us from the direct experience of that same place. It is a misconception that we primarily get colds and flus more often in cold outdoor winters; in fact, we are more likely to catch these viruses inside because we are exposed to higher concentrations of airborne pollutants including cold and flu viruses. In contrast, the Coronavirus pandemic of 2020 has shown that staying in place and isolating indoors can also be a positive measure that slows down the spread of the disease.

Figure 1.9 depicts the crisis of nature showing an incredible scar deep in the landscape caused by copper mining.

1.9
Crisis of nature
(*Source:*
Shutterstock)

THE CRISIS OF URBANISM

Unsustainability

While most of our apparent concerns and efforts to improve the built environment were directed toward sustainability, they in fact focused upon correcting what John Ehrenfeld called "*unsustainability*" – that is, the unsustainable technologies, buildings, and design practices – and in fact continued consumer-oriented living styles. According to Ehrenfeld, "Unsustainability springs from the cultural structure of modernity itself; the way we hold reality and ourselves as human beings, and the hegemony of technology as the solution to every problem facing individuals and the society at large."[62] An unsustainable culture displays certain characteristics according to Ehrenfeld, including the following: reductionist determinacy, anthropocentrism, techno-optimism, and denial. Conversely, a sustainable culture supports wholeness, interconnectedness, bio-centrism, techno-skepticism and avowal (public affirmation). The 60-story Porsche Design Tower in Miami, Florida is a case in point, as the "sustainable building design" supports an "unsustainable program." Multi-million-dollar condominiums come complete with a special elevator for residents' cars, taking them to their two- or four-car garages adjacent to individual living rooms. A majority of the 132 units have been purchased by foreign investors and are used as second and third homes.

Unsustainability is a contemporary phenomenon that most dramatically occurs in large metropolitan areas. Defined by Ehrenfeld, the term refers to mainstream values and consumption patterns that continue to dominate production, use, and disposal of goods, and are the proximate cause of the damage to the environment.[63] Unsustainability's cultural characteristics support an over-rational optimism in science and technology, and a myopic determinacy. Further, it follows fragmented measures rather than interconnected ones, anthropocentric measures rather than eco-centric ones, and mechanistic measures rather than natural systemic approaches.

The consequences of unsustainable cultural structures and activities include climate change, renewable resource deletion, and environmental degradation. Scientists agree unequivocally that the climate is changing. Political debate continues to question the root cause and whether or not it is the result of a natural cycle or a function of human activity. If it is human activity, then this is a clear mandate to rethink and correct the unsustainable structures responsible for its cause. If caused by natural cycles and processes of nature, then does it absolve continuing unsustainable consumption and practices, or do we continue to seek increasingly more effective sustainability measures for our cities?

Population Growth and Migrations

Is our survival dependent upon maximizing population growth or should we be more strategic looking at other more controlled and balanced models? The world's population was less than 1 billion people until the 1800s; by 1930 it had doubled, and 30 years later it reached 3 billion. By the millennium it had reached 6 billion, and by 2015 it measured more than 7 billion.[64] In that same year over a billion people migrated both within their own countries and abroad. While the growth rate peaked in the 1960s at around 2 percent and presently is in slow decline, population as a whole continues to increase overall. The world population is projected to increase by more than a billion people within the next 10 years, reaching 8.5 billion in 2030, and to increase further to 9.7 billion by 2050 and 11.2 billion by 2100 (UN 2015). This will have an enormous impact on natural resources, increased consumption, and the built environment necessary to support these population increases.

The "Blue Marble" was a NASA photograph taken on December 7, 1972 by the crew of the Apollo 17 spacecraft, and was a vivid expression of the wholeness as well as the finite nature of our world. It gave us a perspective previously only imagined. Realization of these events has led to the understanding of planetary carrying capacity – a concept that posits that there is a finite quantity of resources, including potable water, fresh air, food, and energy, that are necessary to manage and sustain human habitation now and in the future.

"The Limits to Growth" published in 1972 was a pioneering report modeling the interactions between the natural and human-made systems, and their consequences. It was another poignant warning that the growing world population was reaching the limits of the world's carrying capacity of finite planetary resource supplies.[65] The pattern of exponential growth was analyzed using five variables: world population, industrialization, pollution, food production, and resource depletion. While generally dismissed by critics as a doomsday prophecy, it did reaffirm the dynamic interactions among important finite environmental factors and brought awareness of the probable consequences of societal growth.

According to Max Roser, Esteban Ortiz-Ospina and Hannah Ritchie, global life expectancy increased from 65 years in 1994 to 72.6 in 2019.[66] There is a planetary shift in population distribution from rural to urban areas. The developed world became mostly urban around 2009, and developing regions, including Africa and Asia, which are still mostly rural today, are projected to have more people living in urban areas than in rural areas by 2030. Cities are focal points of economic growth, innovation, cultural functions, and paid employment. Rural areas provide agriculture, recreation, species habitation, and preservation of natural reserves. Yet this bifurcation is the cause of many challenges and has a tremendous impact on the forms of habitation appropriate for these differing environments. Modernity's legacy manifests innumerable benefits as well as devastating assaults. We are a global culture, connected, mobile, and interdependent with improved living standards, health, life expectancy, production efficiency, and agricultural practices, and tremendous advancements in technology. Yet, the unintended consequences of many of these achievements threaten our contemporary ways of life, as evidenced by the increasing effects of climate change, species extinction, and the global pandemic.

As mentioned, in 2009 it became the case that more human beings live in urban areas than rural ones. It is estimated that in 2018, 55 percent of the world population lived in urban areas, a figure projected to increase to 68 percent by 2050.[67] Most future population increases are speculated to occur in Asia and Africa. By 2030, almost six in ten people will live in metropolitan areas. Every year millions of people leave their homes in rural areas and migrate towards urban centers, both within their own countries and across political borders. Some of these people move simply to seek new opportunities, greater employment prospects, and access to services, and to improve their lives. Others are forced to flee due to religious or political conflict or sudden or slow-onset disasters such as drought, flooding, or rising sea levels, often exacerbated by climate change and environmental stress. This migration to urban areas includes dynamic movement between inner cities, mature and emerging suburbs, exurbs, and rural areas. In the United States for example, in 2018, 46 million people lived in rural counties, 98 million in urban core counties, and 175 million in suburban counties.[68] This provides an interesting focus for biourbanism.

Growth by Addition

An important dimension of growth is the actual method and physical form of the growth. According to architect Leon Krier, urban growth by addition expanded beyond human scale. This pattern usually begins at a center and expands outward in concentric circles, by either urban extension, unplanned sprawl, or infill or conversion of nonurban to urban uses within the urban area. Isolated growth or peri-urbanism is characterized by development existing outside of the primary urban area. In the industrialized world, this process has been enabled by the automobile, which provides access to employment, education, health care, shopping, and cultural activities. Krier, however, preferred growth where community size reached rational human limits, and then grew by a process of multiplication.[69] This pattern suggests an optimum size based on nucleation and pedestrian access to goods and services. When this size is reached, it shifts to another location where the nucleation process occurs again. Growth by gross addition might be better achieved through intelligent multiplication of populations in sync with carrying capacities of local ecological regions. This, too, is referred to as *"systemic constellating urbanism."*[70]

Functional Land Use Zoning

Functional or single-use zoning is a land use planning process that assigns particular uses or activities to separate parcels of land. Originally known as "Euclidean zoning," this practice limits the activities and functions that are allowable within a specific area to singular or similar uses, and also prohibits certain uses within a specified parcel or district. It regulates what is permitted or prohibited on particular land parcels. This zoning practice was primarily implemented within suburban areas and was largely enabled by the widespread use of the automobile. This allowed access to distance-separating land parcels assigned to differing uses, such as residential districts, shopping centers, fast-food establishments, recreation areas, schools, office parks, and even the suburban church. Leon Krier saw this as a controlling divisive planning practice that isolated, fragmented, separated, and territorially regrouped critical cultural functions. These kinds of environments are inherently indistinct, segregationist, and lacking in both natural and built heterogeneity. To Krier, functional zoning was seen as an effective means of destroying the infinitely complex social and physical structure of community.[71] In contrast to this functional zoning, *integrated zoning* supports biophilic urbanism with the inclusion of nature, social spaces, and accessibility within walking distances.

Placelessness

Placelessness pervades the contemporary built environment with its soulless qualities that anesthetize the senses. It is characterized by the dominance of the automobile, monolithic concrete surfaces, spatial incongruity, lack of human scale or of any redeeming meaning, the fall into disrepair, and absence of living things. According to geographer Edward Relph, it is a less authentic attitude that is the "casual eradication of distinctive places and the making of standardized landscapes that results from insensitivity to the significance of place."[72] Placelessness manifests in different ways within the varying territories: urban, suburban, exurban, and the interstitial network environments connecting them all. Placelessness is one of the negative by-products of urbanism. It can occur everywhere, but most often is found in urban areas, particularly those in decline or experiencing neglect. Placelessness is pervasive there as previously functioning parts fall into disrepair and decrepitude caused by changing population and urban migration patterns, and zoning and political district restructuring. Example causes include highway insertions through discrete neighborhoods, political disenfranchisement, unemployment, and high rates of crime. The condition is often brought about by external events, and the aftereffects in economic changes and social conditions result in decay, blight, and dereliction. According to phenomenologist Christian Norberg-Schulz, it becomes a "flatscape," lacking in authenticity and intentional depth, with mediocre experiences.[73] The characteristics of placelessness include inauthenticity, monotony, uniformity, scalelessness, soullessness, and a lack of diversity and the presence of nature.

Placelessness is a geographic territory devoid of four important ingredients necessary for healthy human habitation – diversity, authenticity, meaning, and nature. According to Edward Relph, placelessness is not only confined to urban areas, but also to new industrial and commercial developments, instant new towns, and suburbs where mass culture is informed by mass consumerism and mass media. They display standardization and impersonal uniformity. Further, they are superficial expressions where "they not only look alike but feel alike and offer the same bland possibilities for experience."[74]

The topographical, ecological, geographical, historical, and cosmological conditions of architecture and urban environments are very much part of the present atmosphere that gives a place its meaning. When these reference points are missing, place seems to mutate into a vapid and profane spatiality of nothingness. And this is where the lifeless nature of placelessness sets in, devoid of any redeeming qualities. In his book *The Geography of Nowhere*, James Howard Kunstler suggests that suburbia is an abstract notion of place lacking particularity.[75] He goes on to say that the modern environment has few redeeming characteristics, and continues to be dominated by a car-centered culture. At center stage is our sedentary autocentric lifestyle and the settlement pattern it requires.

Placelessness also includes homelessness, with the displacement, temporary shelters, transiency, and lack of basic services. Although difficult to determine, it is estimated that there are 150 million homeless worldwide (around 2 percent of the world's population). In the United States alone, it is estimated that there are 500,000 homeless, equivalent to the population of Miami. According to Joseph Chamie, the causes include the shortage of affordable housing, privatization of civic services, investment speculation in housing, and unplanned and rapid urbanization, as well as poverty, unemployment, family breakdown, and more recently the COVID-19 pandemic.[76] People openly live on city streets, creating modern urban landscapes.

Impact of the Automobile

With the advent of the automobile and its wide acceptability, urban form has changed to accommodate its increasing numbers and improved individual accessibility. Automobiles began mass-production in the 1920s and quickly became a common household necessity in an expanding and more mobile society. One car per family evolved to one car per adult driver. Highways and interstates paved the way for a truck and automobile culture. They became and still are a necessity for everyday life in many places throughout the world. It was predicted that by 2016 there were estimated to be a 1.32 billion cars on the road worldwide, with China leading in numbers.[77] The automobile has brought many advantages, including increase convenience and accessibility, freedom of movement both when and where, and even a kind of social identity. The negative impacts include air pollution and smog; global warming; increased congestion and commute distances; vehicle purchase, maintenance, and insurance costs; and worst of all, traffic fatalities. According to the Energy Information Administration, carbon dioxide emissions from vehicles are the largest energy polluting sector, surpassing the power production sector.[78] There are approximately 1.35 million traffic fatalities each year, with more than half of the deaths among vulnerable users.[79]

Pollution and Waste

As mentioned, human-generated pollution remains a major environmental problem. In the 1960s a growing awareness of the deleterious effects that contemporary life had on the environment became more present. With continued growth in world population, pollution and waste today, pose increasing risks to biodiversity, health, and visual qualities of the natural and built environments. The common definition for pollution is the introduction of contaminants into the environment, both natural and human-made, that causes disease, harm, instability and destruction. Pollutants usually affect the elemental substances that include the earth, water, and air – and can manifest in the very places we live – our homes, schools, and places of work. As mentioned previously, the materials used to construct buildings can be highly toxic.

Water pollution derives from two general sources: direct and indirect contamination. Direct sources include effluent outfalls from factories, refineries, waste treatment, and power plants that emit fluids of varying quality directly into urban water supplies. Indirect sources include contaminants that enter the water supply from soils/groundwater systems and from the atmosphere via rainwater. Soils and groundwaters contain the residue of agricultural practices, including fertilizers, pesticides, and improperly disposed-of industrial wastes. The effects of water pollution are varied and include poisonous drinking water and poisonous food animals. These organisms have bio-accumulated toxins from the environment over their lifespans, as revealed by Rachel Carson in *Silent Spring*. There are also unbalanced river and lake ecosystems that can no longer support full biological diversity; deforestation from acid rain; and many other effects. Water tables are slowly shrinking as consumption surpasses renewable sources. In 1965 the US Congress passed the Water Quality Act, the Noise Control Act, and the Solid Waste Disposal Act, setting standards for all states. In 1968, Congress passed the Wild and Scenic Rivers Act and National Trails System Act.

Soil contamination is caused by the presence of xenobiotic (foreign, and usually harmful, to living organisms') chemicals or other alterations in the natural soil environment. Contamination or earth pollution typically arises from failure due to the corrosion of underground storage tanks or of the piping associated with them, historical disposal of coal ash, application of pesticides, percolation of contaminated surface water to subsurface strata, oil and fuel dumping, leaching of wastes from landfills, or direct discharge of industrial wastes into the soil. Large-scale agriculture and industrial incursions began to reduce the soil's restorative function, and the clearing of tropical rainforests, due primarily to cattle ranching, contributed to loss of species' habitat and global warming caused by disruption of the natural hydrologic cycle. In the late 1960s, then President Richard Nixon established the US Environmental Protection Agency to lead in the war on pollution following a decade of awareness and reflection on the environmental effects of modernity.

According to Josh Reno, North Americans don't think twice about what happens to the garbage they throw away, and the American dream of two cars, a single-family house, and a nice community is made possible by creating tons of waste.[80] According to Stephen Cohen, Americans in 2015 produced 4.48 pounds of waste a day per person.[81] The Great Pacific Garbage Patch of floating plastic is larger than Texas. While most garbage ends up in landfills, the growing trend now is to either recycle or burn to create electricity.

The combination of the crises of nature and urbanism paints a dire picture, yet the necessity to change will be the mother of invention. And this is where biophilia and biophilic urbanism can help mend the breach in natural and cultural restorative processes. There is a need to go beyond mere affiliation with nature. Lifestyles need to evolve to produce the positive outcomes of climate neutrality, true sustainability, equitable placemaking, high-level health and wellness, and spiritual awakening. This all must be accomplished within the context of an expanding population and changing migration patterns.

Figure 1.10 shows a street scene with homeless tents in Anchorage, Alaska, which is endemic of the crisis of urbanism.

1.10
Crisis of urbanism
(*Source: Wikimedia Commons*)

BIOPHILIC URBANISM AND BIOURBANISM DEFINED

Biophilia is our affiliation and attraction to nature, and urbanism is the larger context of the built environment where most of us live. Biourbanism or biophilic urbanism posits social, sustainable, and economic regeneration of the urban built environment through the development of healthy communities. According to professors Antonio Caperna, Alessandro Giuliani, Nikos A. Salingaros, Stefano Serafini, and Alessia Cerqua, "*Biourbanism focuses on the urban organism, considering it as a hypercomplex system, according to its internal and external dynamics and their mutual interactions.*"[82] Where biourbanism focuses on the dynamic natural and ecological processes of a place, biophilic urbanism on the other hand focuses on the ways in which the beneficial qualities of nature inform planning and design processes through specific design guidelines, thus contributing to positive outcomes for humanity.

Biourbanism is an open-sourced planning approach designed to foster regenerative relationships between the urban environment and the biological systems upon which it depends. Policies include climate resilience, low carbon generation and use, and divestment of fossil fuels. Biourbanism follows the premise of deep ecology that promotes the inherent worth of living organisms regardless of their perceived utility.[83] Deep ecology is "deep" because it looks extensively into the actual reality of humanity's relationship with the natural world, developing more philosophical and ethical conclusions than that of the prevailing view of ecology as a branch of biology. The theoretical foundations of deep ecology, advocated by Arne Naess in 1973, saw an ecological community of inclusive memberships where "everything was connected to everything."[84] This systemic view of part and whole was critical in understanding the scalar complexity of structural ordering and sustainability as the need for systems that could transcend scales in self-similar and efficient ways. In line with deep ecology and as opposed to a city as a linear machine, biourbanism focuses on the city as a complex living organism.

Biourbanism focuses on technology as well as social wellbeing. It promotes regenerative, renewable energy systems, self-organizing urban forms, and high-efficiency and low-emission technologies. The social grounds of biourbanism express by deepening the interactions between urban cultural and human health affecting equity factors within the ecological context in which they exist. It views the physical environment as being dynamic, complex, non-linear, and having systemic efficiencies. The principles of biourbanism follow:[85]

- Biophilic design – The integration of ecological, biological, and natural systems with the built environment.
- Scalar inclusiveness – The entire context is included, from the micro- to the macro-scale, from building to site to street to block to neighborhood to community to region and to macro-climatic context, into a systemic whole.
- Geometric coherency – The spatial structure must facilitate an optimal nature–human–built environment relationship.

- Self-organization – Urban environments are complex, adaptable, and resilient.
- Energy sectors – The creation of restorative systems for the production, transportation, and building sectors.

Biourbanism and biophilic urbanism derive from similar analyses of the contemporary urban condition, and therefore share similar principles. Biophilic urbanism is the application of a range of design pattern attributes or guidelines to varying urban scales, from building elements and interiors to neighborhoods and communities. Biophilic urbanism operates from three primary interactions: (1) the impacts of nature upon human beings and the built environment, (2) the impacts of human beings and the built environment upon nature, and (3) the impacts of the built environment on both nature and human beings. Biourbanism seeks to encourage positive benefits and outcomes from this triad of interactions, for example from climate neutrality to a healthier human biology, from human stewardship of the natural world to habitat exchange and nature's restoration, and finally from biophilic urbanism to true sustainable patterns of behavior and the inclusion of nature at all scales of development.

Biophilic architecture addresses the ways in which a building can help facilitate greater human–nature interactions. Biophilic urbanism addresses three other dimensions – the social dimension, broader environmental dimensions, and the transportation and traffic dimension. The social dimension focuses on the introduction of the mix of uses – the clustering and nucleation of mix of uses; density; creation of public gathering spaces; opportunities for interaction; public safety; and the provision of common activities such as recreation, education, and other cultural pursuits. The broader environmental dimension looks at open space, parks, recreation, natural disaster planning, and ecological corridors. The transportation dimension addresses ways to diminish the negative effects of automobiles and parking lots; the reduction of greenhouse gas emissions; the use of alternative fuels; the introduction of alternative modes of movement; carpooling; and pedestrianization. According to Peter Newman,

> "the importance of scale and density in creating these opportunities is now well understood. But there has been a parallel emergence of the evidence of the need for people to be more closely linked to nature, and to create cities that are more sensitive to natural systems. Thus an increasing number of cities are now actively engaged in the process of incorporating nature into their design and function to an increasing extent."[86]

The broad issues at each of the urban scales are in need of biophilic considerations that include energy production, transportation modes and circulation networks, infrastructure, water and waste, density and mix of uses, and building designs appropriate to typology and context. Nature affects and is affected by each of these urban issues. To accomplish all of the intended biophilic outcomes, it is important to re-examine development and construction practices with greater attention to climatic and ecological contexts, sustainable planning and design practices, limiting automobiles and promoting healthier modes of transportation, and human–nature placemaking.

SCALES OF APPLICATION

Nature's interactions with the physical environment occur at every scale, from atoms to galaxies. For biophilic urbanism these scales generally vary from a building interior to the ecological regions within which a community may occur. According to Eleni Tracada and Antonio Caperna, "In the natural environment, structural qualities exist on a variety of levels of scale, from the macroscopic to the microscopic (intermediate scales). Moreover, physical forms possess natural scaling hierarchies as a result of internal and external forces."[87] The biophilic principles and design patterns can be applied to any development scale, from building interiors to bioregions.

In the rural-to-urban transect, biophilic design approaches will likely vary as the more natural areas at the boundary transition to the denser urban center. A seamless gradient provides continuity. Typically, this gradient has greater land area dedicated to nature at the extremities, with cultural and commercial activities needing less area and concentrated at the center. The primary scales under consideration in this work include individual buildings, streets, blocks, neighborhoods, communities, and ecoregions.

- Buildings – provide a host of biophilic properties and design strategies enabled by a building's envelope, orientation, degree of transparency, spatial structure, use of color, landscaping, integration of renewable energy technologies, and kitchen gardens; encourage inside–outside flows, views to nature, solar access, utilization of natural light and ventilation, porosity, natural materiality, durability, and resilience. Dwellings can be designed for sheltering-in-place, spatial distancing, and quarantining.
- Streets – provide pattern attribute opportunities for increased accessibility and pedestrian movement, parking and traffic calming, climate-responsive and edible landscaping, and protective tree cover; include daylit swales, sidewalks, and porches for social interaction; reduce night-sky light pollution; and provide for safety and unobtrusive surveillance. Biophilic design also suggests car-free connections between places. Certain street orientations can contribute to good solar access.
- Blocks – provide an urban unit and human scale increment with place identity, clustered housing, small gardens, social gathering spaces, green courtyards, native species landscaping, street or natural boundaries, hidden car garages, alleys, potentials for shared geothermal heating and cooling and/or district heating and cooling, and unobtrusive trash collection and recycling. Blocks can be used for neighborhood-scale agriculture and play areas.

- Neighborhoods – provide pattern multiple land plots, infrastructure, housing and housing clusters, parks, play areas, primary schools; attribute opportunities for local gardens and greens, community outdoor rooms, and gathering places, clustered mixed use, creating views and pedestrian access to nature; use native vegetation in leu of traditional water-intensive lawns, providing porous boundaries and a clear sense of place. Car-free zones and pedestrian networks are also suggested.
- Communities – provide pattern attribute opportunities for nucleation and appropriate density, inclusion of mix of uses, increased accessibility, infrastructure planning, urban agriculture, recycling, vegetated wetland water-waste systems, environmentally oriented schools, extensive trail systems, reduced night-sky light pollution, and community-scale passive survival systems and solar farms. Community scale can support car-free or limited automobile access zones.
- Ecoregions – provide pattern attribute opportunities to integrate development with natural ecological flows and riparian areas, sensitivity to natural topography, ample for connections to nature, providing for habitat protection, connections to water, responses to surface water and flood plains, and the possibility for community renewable energy production. An ecoregion has connection to and is part of a larger bioregion and often contains peri-urban areas. Lockdowns should be considered for epicenter outbreaks of COVID-19.

Buildings

Buildings are defined as enclosed structures providing shelter, security, privacy, comfort, and accommodation for human activities and needs. Buildings are generally defined by construction size, type, and use or function. They are confined to a single plot of land and therefore have less impact upon the surrounding parcels of land. The single plot must conform to zoning restrictions that establish property line setbacks, building footprint and height limits, parking requirements, and open space ratios. Biophilic architecture can incorporate all the biophilic patterns, providing a rich environment for the building's occupants. This includes physical elements – interiors, primary architectural forms, and materials. Strategies common to biophilic buildings include emphasis on inside–outside relationships, views and sensory connection to nature, designs for prospect and refuge, spatial hierarchies, encouragement of natural light and ventilation, and incorporation of natural materials. More robust examples utilize on-site energy technologies, rainwater harvesting, natural analogies, provision of edible landscaping, the use of non-toxic building materials, and the inclusion of living color. Biophilic design needs to be sensitive to the building typology as differing building types have unique requirements and afford varying opportunities. At the residential scale, biophilic pattern attributes can be fully realized by rethinking sites and yards to on-site resource utilization and material choices. Buildings should make provisions for sheltering-in-place when necessary, and for effective interfaces with the people, goods, and services. During the global pandemic, sheltering-in-place provides new design challenges.

Streets

Roads' primary function is in aid of transportation, providing movement of people, goods and services. While streets are lands dedicated to public conveyance and circulation, they also serve for collection and treatment of stormwater, pedestrian movement, social interaction, and intimate interactions with trees, plants, and edible landscapes. A critical function of a street is to provide unobstructed access for emergency and fire-fighting vehicles. Streets form an outdoor network for architecture, with variable spatial characteristics and functions. Street surfaces should be permeable and relatively narrow and possess periodic traffic calming designs. The street can be designed as a variable space relating to the extremes of lower-density rural environments and higher-density urban centers. The former supports engagements with nature; the latter to more social and cultural interactions. Streets are becoming more and more pedestrianized as car-free environments are gaining currency, especially in larger cities. In relation the Coronavirus, there should be easy access to essential goods and services, provision of sidewalks and clear pedestrian travel paths, and provisions for physical distancing.

Blocks

A block is a replicating urban unit of space with individual land plots and buildings surrounded by streets. They are a repeatable urban element often organized by a larger grid or spatial ordering system. But more importantly, blocks are places. The block is an important scale for the social and natural interactions in everyday life that contribute to a sense of place. This scale offers an excellent opportunity to introduce nature, edible landscapes, protected courtyards, and to encourage social interactions. Often blocks are surrounded by a canopy of trees providing shading in summer and views year long. It is important to provide ample sidewalks for safety mobility, social distancing, and connectedness. Automobile parking is an important issue at the block scale, to minimize its negative impact while maintaining accessibility.

Neighborhoods

A neighborhood is defined as a geographically localized social unit and spatially specific setting capable of supporting face-to-face interactions. The neighborhood scale allows for the introduction of larger greenspaces, community gardens or allotments, a smaller-scale mix of uses, and a sense of place. This scale also includes infrastructure services to each building (water, sewer, waste disposal, electricity, natural gas, and telecommunications). It provides access to a network of paths and trails, playgrounds, treehouses, neighborhood parks, and water features such as streams and ponds. Neighborhoods tend to be coherent, have a clear sense of identity, and are relatively small with all buildings within walking distance. Neighborhood walking behavior is measured by walking distance, direction, time, and experience. Neighborhood destinations are within a walking distance of 1 mile (1.6 km). The size is further determined by the age and physical condition of residents. In the United States, another measure of a neighborhood's size is a 5-minute walking distance, or 1,312 feet (400 meters), after which the use of an automobile is preferred.[88] During Coronavirus surges, parks and public outdoor spaces should delineate safe distancing markers.

Communities

A community is defined as a social unit sharing a common place. It is important that the community is not a single use of functionally zoned development. The community level offers opportunities for access to larger numbers of commercial, institutional, and recreational facilities and services. This scale offers the introduction to community-wide energy, waste-water, and agricultural systems. Typical non-residential functions, that will help reduce between-place transportation, include a grocery store, healthcare facilities, primary and secondary schools, daycare, a library, a hardware store, a pharmacy, a hairdresser, a religious or community gathering space, outdoor recreation and playgrounds, a café or restaurant, agriculture, and gasoline (and electric charging) stations. At the community scale, water-waste systems, such as constructed wetlands, can be incorporated in new developments. Efforts should be made to provide light for night safety while reducing night light pollution. Infrastructure is in need of a rethink, and according to Tim Beatley, "roads, bridges, tunnels, ports, to name a few, could all be profoundly received and reimagined through a biophilic lens."[89]

The size of a community is under debate and may be determined by many factors. Size can affect the degree to which members either maintain meaningful relationships or live anonymous lives. If a community is automobile-free, then its size will likely be smaller, yet it can be more densely populated. The area covered by walking distance is generally defined as a mile (1.6 kilometers) in diameter, or about 3.3–4 feet (1–1.2 meters) per second.[89] The Dunbar number suggests that 150 is the ideal number for a group, so a community could be composed of a constellation of neighborhoods of 150 residents each.[90] A community size can also be determined by its urban or natural context. The concept of constellating urbanism is designed to respond to the needs of larger populations and the size constraints of walkable communities. Increase of density has long been seen as a good sustainability strategy, but with the Coronavirus pandemic communities may be reconsidering population density and agglomeration of vulnerable populations.

Ecoregions

An ecoregion is defined as an area of land with recurring patterns and common and distinctive characteristics including climate, landscapes, geography, hydrological processes, ecological features, and governance. A bioregion has the type, quality, and quantity of environmental resources, including biotic and abiotic phenomena. They rarely have abrupt edges, but typically have ecotones (transitions between two zones) and mosaic habitats that bind them. It is part of a larger bioregion and ecozone. The regional scale provides the opportunity for sensitivity to ecological processes, reforestation, agriculture, walking trails, recreation, and efficient between-place transportation modes and connections. Principal biophilic strategies at the ecoregion scale include preservation that seeks to prolong and maintain the present condition of an ecological region in an area that is untouched by humans. Conservation is the protection, sustainable use, and management of natural resources – wildlife, water, air, and earth. Typically, ecoregions are defined by major natural features such as shorelines, rivers and river basins, and other water features. Topological or landform variations and boundaries are largely informed by climatic factors, such as the daily and seasonal fluxes of energy and moisture.[91] Cooling corridors, river valleys, and green infrastructure have been found to provide regional benefits.[92] Ecoregions can contain a number of peri-urban settlements forming a rural–urban transition.

Fractals have been cited as being biophilic in nature due to the character of their pattern similarities crossing progressively smaller and larger scales and sizes of expression. While in nature the patterns are highly similar, they do possess slight variations, as in the case of snowflakes or the branching patterns of trees. Fractals are found in nature with four inherent characteristics – infinite intricacy, zoom symmetry, complexity evolving from simplicity, and a fractional dimension that exists between two and three dimensions.[93] The process of self-similarity is useful when conceptualizing biophilic pattern approaches to varying scales of physical design, from interior details of a building to entire cities. Fractals often are found in ornamentation, repetition of conceptual elements, spiraling proportional geometry, screen geometry, crenellations, hierarchy of street layouts, lotting schemes, and the multiplication of neighborhood configurations. Another useful quality of the fractal process is the seamless transition and nested patterns among scale development – interiors, buildings, neighborhoods, communities, and regions. Many of the biophilic pattern attributes function in this way, but not all possess self-similar characteristics through each of these scales from interiors to regions. For example, sensory connections, ecological and biological connections, water and waste, and inside–outside patterns may coexist, but may not be seamless and self-similar.

Scalar conflicts can occur when a biophilic pattern at one scale is opposed to a pattern at another. For example, the strategy for preserving land with higher density can conflict with the need for solar access, which is easier to accomplish in lower densities. At higher densities external views from dwellings can be problematic due to the need for privacy. Pedestrianization can also conflict with the need for emergency vehicle access to every building, especially for fire protection. In new residential developments, the mix of uses does not include critical life-support functions such as medical facilities, fire protection, paramedics, pharmacies, grocery stores, daycare, schools, religious spaces, and police. For example, some new urban communities primarily cater to commercial uses for visitors and tourists. In developing biophilic urban concepts, several paradoxes exist.

From the Savanna periods of human development to today, we have relied on evolving technologies to obtain critical natural resources for survival. This has enabled human expansion. As a consequence, we have overpopulated the entire planet. This increase in population and density concentrations has gradually separated us from the very nature that enabled this expansion. This in turn has landed us in the conflicts between nature and the urban environment that we currently experience, setting up several paradoxes. It is estimated that nearly 10 billion people will exist in 2050, with 75 percent occupying coastal regions. People are migrating to these vulnerable locations and experiencing the effects of climate change with rising sea levels. Another paradox exists in that, in our desire to preserve more natural land by densification into megalopolises, we have further alienated ourselves from nature. This is proving to be unhealthy. How can biophilic urbanism reverse this trend and create a better balance? Will planting trees on high-rise facades be enough? Or will we need more comprehensive approaches that dig deeper into contemporary culture, transforming the current urban condition?

Biophilic Urbanism is explored with six precedents found worldwide. These comprise, in increasing scale: Castello di Gargonza and its revitalization in Tuscany, Italy; the Google Headquarters at Charleston East in Mountainview, California; Helsinge Haveby planned for Helsinge, Denmark; Kronsberg District located in Hannover, Germany; Pontevedra City Center in Pontevedra, Spain; and the Singapore Park Connector Neighborhood. The precedents provide a wide range of biophilic planning and design strategies. This work concludes with a deep dive into the case study found with Serenbe Community, a mixed-use residential development found southwest of Atlanta, Georgia. In this case study the wide range of biophilic principles and design patterns are presented and examined in detail.

NOTES

1. Biophilia https://www.dictionary.com/browse/biophilia (accessed January 4, 2020).
2. Edward O. Wilson, *Biophilia* (Cambridge, MA: Harvard University Press, 1984).
3. Ibid.
4. Erich Fromm, *The Heart of Man: It Genius for Good and Evil* (Herndon, VA: Lantern Books, 2010).
5. Gordon H. Orians and Judith H. Heerwagen, "Evolved Responses to Landscapes," in Jerome H. Barlow, Leda Cosmides, and John Tooby (eds.) *The Adapted Mind: Evolutionary Psychology and the Generation of Culture*, (New York, NY: Oxford University Press, 1992). pp 557–561.
6. J.B. Lamark, C.R. Darwin, and A.R. Wallace, *Savanna Hypothesis* https://en.wikipedia.org/wiki/Savannah_hypothesis (accessed January 30, 2020).
7. Edward O. Wilson, *Biophilia: The Human Bond with Other Species* (Cambridge, MA: Harvard University Press, 1984). p 109.
8. R. Kaplan and S. Kaplan, *The Experience of Nature: A Psychological Perspective* (Cambridge, MA: Cambridge University Press, 1989). p 48.
9. http://people.sunyit.edu/~lepres/thesis/principles/213_pdfsam_POD.pdf.

10. J. Dirk Niles, Science to Live By: Beauty and the Savanna Hypothesis https://www.crozetgazette.com/2015/07/03/science-to-live-by-beauty-and-the-savanna-hypothesis/ (accessed January 30, 2020).

11. C. Owen Lovejoy, *The Origin of Man* (New Series, Vol. 211, No. 4480, Jan. 23, 1981). pp. 341–350.

12. Thomas Beery and Ingemar K. Jonssen, *Topophilia and Human Affiliation with Nature* http://hkr.diva-portal.org/smash/record.jsf?pid=diva2%3A857474&dswid=147 (accessed April 5, 2020).

13. Peter S. Rodman and Henry M. McHenry, *Biogenetics and the origin of hominid bipedalism* https://onlinelibrary.wiley.com/doi/abs/10.1002/ajpa.1330520113 (accessed February 3, 2020).

14. Peter H. Kahn, Jr., *Developmental Psychology and the Biophilic Hypothesis: Children's Affiliation with Nature*. https://faculty.washington.edu/pkahn/articles/Developmental_Psychology_Biophilia_Hypothesis.pdf (accessed February 10, 2020).

15. Graeme Barker, *The Agricultural Revolution in Prehistory: Why did Foragers become Farmers?* (Oxford, UK: Oxford University Press, 2009).

16. Elonda Clay, "Backyard Gardens as Sacred Spaces: An Ecowomanist Spiritual Ecology," *Religion and Nature: The Elements* (New York, NY: Bloomsbury Publishing, 2018). p 11.

17. Erich Fromm, *The Heart of Man* (New York, NY: Harper and Row, 1964).

18. Edward O. Wilson, *Biophilia: The Human Bond with Other Species* (Cambridge, MA: Harvard University Press, 1984).

19. Stephen R. Kellert, Judith H. Heerwagen, and Martin Mador, *Biophilic Design: The Theory, Science, and Practice of Bringing Building to Life* (New York, NY: John Wiley & Sons, Inc., 2008).

20. R. Kaplan and S. Kaplan, *The Experience of Nature: A Psychological Perspective* (Cambridge, MA: Cambridge University Press, 1989).

21. Eleni Tracada and Antonio Caperna, *Biourbanism for a Healthy City: Biophilia and sustainable urban theories and practices* (http://citeseerx.ist.psu.edu/viewdoc/download?doi=10.1.1.888.2688&rep=rep1&type=pdf), (accessed January 2, 2020).

22. Tim Beatley, *Biophilic Cities* (Washington, DC: Island Press, 2011).

23. Terrapin Bright Green, *14 Patterns of Biophilic Design: Improving Health and Wellbeing in the Environment* (Online: https://www.terrapinbrightgreen.com/reports/14-patterns/, 2014).

24. Christopher Dye, *Health and Urban Living, Vol. 319* (AAAS: Science, February 8, 2008) 766–769.

25. World Health Organization, *Bulletin of the World Health Organization, Urbanization and health,* http://www.who.int/bulletin/volumes/88/4/10-010410/en/ (accessed March 28, 2020).

26. Environmental Protection Agency, https://irp-cdn.multiscreensite.com/c4e267ab/files/uploaded/kt34RqduTlGgjxf3soeQ_EPA_Report%20to%20Congress%20on%20Indoor%20Air%20Quality_Volume%20II_Assessment%20and%20Control%20of%20Indoor%20Air%20Pollution_1989.pdf (accessed March 28, 2020) p i.

27. Velux, *The "Indoor Generation" and the health risks of spending more time inside* https://www.usatoday.com/story/sponsor-story/velux/2018/05/15/indoor-generation-and-health-risks-spending-more-time-inside/610289002/ (accessed March 28, 2020).

28. W.R. Ott, *Human activity patterns: a review of the literature for estimating time spent indoors, outdoors, and in transit. In: Proceedings of the Research Planning Conference on Human Activity Patterns* (Las Vegas, NV: EPA National Exposure Research Laboratory, EPA/600/4-89/004, 1989) 3-1 to 3-38.

29. Stephen R. Kellert, Judith H. Heerwagen, and Martin Mador, *Biophilic Design: The Theory, Science, and Practice of Bringing Building to Life* (New York, NY: John Wiley & Sons, Inc., 2008).

30. Stefano Boeri, *Vertical Forest* https://www.stefanoboeriarchitetti.net/en/project/vertical-forest/ (accessed June 1, 2020).
31. Farhana Yamin, What is 'carbon neutrality' – and how can we achieve it by 2050? https://theelders.org/news/what-carbon-neutrality-and-how-can-we-achieve-it-2050 (accessed February 16, 2020).
32. John R. Ehrenfeld, *Sustainability by Design*, (New Haven, CT: Yale University Press, 2008).
33. Edward Relph, *Place and Placelessness (Research in planning & design)*, (London, UK: Pion Ltd., 1984).
34. Halbert L. Dunn, *High Level Wellness* (Arlington, VA: Beatty, 1971).
35. Rudolf Otto, *The Idea of the Holy* (Oxford, UK: Oxford University Press, 1950).
36. World Commission on Environment and Development (WCED), *Our Common Future* (Oxford, UK: Oxford University Press,1987). p 43.
37. Edward Relph, *Place and Placelessness (Research in planning & design)* (London, UK: Pion Ltd., 1984).
38. Rudolf Otto, *The Idea of the Holy* (Oxford, UK: Oxford University Press, 1950).
39. Judith Heerwagen, Biophilic Design https://sftool.gov/learn/about/580/biophilic-design (accessed March 12, 2020).
40. J. William Cotton and Riley Dunlap, https://www.researchgate.net/figure/A-comparison-of-major-assumptions-in-the-dominant-western-worldview-sociologys-human_tbl1_267802272 (accessed June 1, 2020).
41. John R. Ehrenfeld, *Sustainability by Design* (New Haven, CT: Yale University Press, 2008). pp 58–59.
42. Lamia Kama-Chaoul and Alexis Robert (eds.), *Competitive Cities and Climate Change* https://www.oecd.org/cfe/regional-policy/44232251.pdf (accessed February 11, 2020).
43. Qian Xu, Yuxiang Dong, and Ren Yang, *Influence of different geographical factors on carbon sink functions in the Pearl river Delta* https://www.ncbi.nlm.nih.gov/pmc/articles/PMC5427894/ (accessed March 19, 2020).
44. NOAA, *Global Climate Indicators* https://www.climate.gov/news-features/understanding-climate/global-climate-indicators (accessed June 1, 2020).
45. Christina Hill, "Form Follows Flows: Systems, Design, and the Aesthetic experience of Ecological Change," *Nature and Cities: The Ecological Imperative in Urban Design and Planning* (Cambridge, MA: The Lincoln Institute of Land Policy, 2016). p 389.
46. National Oceanic and Atmospheric Administration, *Climate change impacts* https://www.noaa.gov/education/resource-collections/climate-education-resources/climate-change-impacts (accessed February 5, 2020).
47. Peter Newman and Isabella Jennings, Cities as Sustainable Ecosystems: Principles and Practices https://gnhre.org/2014/01/11/cities-as-sustainable-ecosystems-principles-and-practices-p-newman-and-i-jennings/ (accessed February 16, 2020).
48. University of Copenhagen, https://www.sciencedaily.com/releases/2012/01/120120010357.htm (accessed February 4, 2020).
49. *UN Report: 1 Million Animal and Plant Species at Risk of Extinction* https://www.forbes.com/sites/grrlscientist/2019/05/09/un-report-1-million-animal-and-plant-species-at-risk-of-extinction/#470c69ec5fa3 (accessed June 1, 2020).
50. John P. Rafferty, *Biodiversity Loss* https://www.britannica.com/science/biodiversity-loss (accessed January 21, 2020).
51. United Nations https://blog.nationalgeographic.org/2019/09/23/global-biodiversity-is-in-crisis-but-there-is-hope-for-recovery/ (accessed January 20, 2020).
52. National Geographic https://blog.nationalgeographic.org/2019/09/23/global-biodiversity-is-in-crisis-but-there-is-hope-for-recovery/.
53. Andrea M. Godinez and Edwardo J. Fernandez, *What Is the Zoo Experience? How Zoos Impact a Visitor's Behavior, Perceptions, and Conservation Efforts* https://www.frontiersin.org/articles/10.3389/fpsyg.2019.01746/full (accessed January 25, 2020).

54. David Hancocks, *The Future of Zoos* https://www.zoolex.org/media/uploads/2018/07/30/hancocks_2012_future_of_zoos.pdf (accessed January 25, 2020).

55. Adi Da Samraj, "Fear-No-More-Zoo," https://mailchi.mp/7e373b8e5b07/fear-no-more-zoo-europe-is-a-refuge-for-rare-and-endangered-species?e=aae253ddb0 (accessed June 15, 2020).

56. Rachel Carson, *Silent Spring*, anniversary edition (New York, NY: Haughton Miffin Company, 2002).

57. Camilla Cavendish, *The Pandemic is Killing the Attraction to megacities* https://www.placemakingresource.com/article/1683415/pandemic-is-killing-attraction-megacities (accessed May 24, 2020).

58. Shima Hamnidi, Sadegh Sabouri and Reid Ewing, "*Does Density Aggravate the COVID-19 Pandemic?*," https://www.tandfonline.com/doi/full/10.1080/01944363.2020.1777891 (accessed June 27, 2020).

59. Allison Aubrey, Laurel Wamsley, and Carmel Wroth, *From Camping to Dining Out: Here's How Experts Rate the Risks of 14 Summer Activities* https://www.npr.org/sections/health-shots/2020/05/23/861325631/from-camping-to-dining-out-heres-how-experts-rate-the-risks-of-14-summer-activit (accessed May 27, 2020).

60. Environmental Protection Agency https://snowbrains.com/brain-post-much-time-average-american-spend-outdoors/ (accessed March 30, 2020).

61. The Benefits of Vitamin D, https://www.healthline.com/health/food-nutrition/benefits-vitamin-d (accessed March 29, 2020).

62. Neil Postman, *Technopoly: The Surrender of Culture to Technology* (New York, NY: Vintage Books, 1993).

63. John R. Ehrenfeld, *Sustainability by Design* (New Haven, CT: Yale University Press, 2008).

64. United Nations Commission on Population and Development, http://stories.weather.com/disruptionindex, (accessed July 17, 2015).

65. Donella Meadows, Dennis Meadows, and Jorgen Randers, *The Limits to Growth* (Chelsea, VT: Chelsea Green Publishing, 1972).

66. Max Roser, Esteban Ortiz-Ospina, and Hannah Ritchie, *Life Expectancy*, https://ourworldindata.org/life-expectancy (accessed March 28, 2020).

67. Kim Parker, Juliana Menasce Horowitz, Anna Brown, Richard Fry, D'Vera Cohn, and Ruth Igielnik, *Demographic and economic trends in urban, suburban and rural communities* https://www.pewsocialtrends.org/2018/05/22/demographic-and-economic-trends-in-urban-suburban-and-rural-communities/ (accessed February 4, 2020).

68. Ibid.

69. Leon Krier, *Houses, Palaces, Cities* (London, UK: Architectural Design Editions, Ltd., 1984). pp 32–22.

70. Phillip James Tabb, *Serene Urbanism: A Biophilic Theory and Practice of Sustainable Placemaking* (London, UK: Routledge, 2017). p 146.

71. Leon Krier, *Leon Krier: Houses, Palaces, Cities* (London, UK: Architectural Design, 1984). p 34.

72. Edward Relph, *Place and Placelessness* (London, UK: Pion Ltd., 1984).

73. Christian Norberg-Schultz, *Genius Loci: Towards a Phenomenology of Architecture* (New York, NY: Rizzoli International, 1980).

74. Edward Relph, *Place and Placelessness* (London, UK: Pion Ltd., 1984).

75. James Howard Kunstler, *The Geography of Nowhere: The Rise and Decline of America's Man-made Landscape*, (New York, NY: Free Press, 1994).

76. Joseph Chamie, *As Cities Grow, So do the Numbers of Homeless* https://yaleglobal.yale.edu/content/cities-grow-so-do-numbers-homeless (accessed February 8, 2020).

77. Andrew Chesterton, *How Many Cars are There in the World?* https://www.carsguide.com.au/car-advice/how-many-cars-are-there-in-the-world-70629 (accessed February 28, 2020).

78. US Energy Information Administration, US Carbon dioxide Emissions by fuel (2005–16), https://www.eia.gov/todayinenergy/detail.php?id=30712 (accessed February 28, 2020).

79. World Health Organization, *Road Traffic Injuries*, 7 February 2020 https://www.who.int/news-room/fact-sheets/detail/road-traffic-injuries (accessed February 28, 2020).

80. Josh Reno, *Your modern lifestyle is made possible by creating tons of waste* https://www.sciencedaily.com/releases/2016/03/160303094324.htm (accessed February 6, 2020).

81. Steven Cohen, *Consumption, Waste and our Changing Lifestyle* https://blogs.ei.columbia.edu/2019/08/26/consumption-waste-changing-lifestyle/ (accessed February 7, 2020).

82. Antonio Caperna, Alessandro Giuliani, Nikos A. Salingaros, Stefano Serafini, Alessia Cerqua.

83. Eleni Tracada and Antonio Caperna, *Biourbanism for a Healthy City: Biophilia and sustainable urban theories and practices* (http://citeseerx.ist.psu.edu/viewdoc/download?doi=10.1.1.888.2688&rep=rep1&type=pdf), (accessed January 2, 2020).

84. Bill Devall and George Sessions, *Deep Ecology: Living as if Nature Mattered* (Layton, UT: Gibbs, Smith, Publisher, 1985) https://www.bustle.com/p/7-signs-youre-spending-too-much-time-inside-its-affecting-your-health-8209455 (accessed January 15, 2020).

85. Eleni Tracada, *A New Paradigm for Deep Sustainability: Biourbanism* https://www.researchgate.net/publication/257924206_A_New_Paradigm_for_Deep_Sustainability_Biourbanism (accessed February 5, 2020).

86. Peter Newman et al., Can Biophilic Urbanism Deliver Strong Economic and Social Benefits in Cities? https://sbenrc.com.au/app/uploads/2013/11/sbenrc_1.5biophilicurbanism-industryreport.pdf (accessed June 4, 2020).

87. Eleni Tracada and Antonio Caperna, *Biourbanism for a Healthy City: Biophilia and sustainable urban theories and practices* (http://citeseerx.ist.psu.edu/viewdoc/download?doi=10.1.1.888.2688&rep=rep1&type=pdf), (accessed January 2, 2020).

88. EV Studio, *The Five Minute Walk: Calibrated to the Pedestrian* https://evstudio.com/the-five-minute-walk-calibrated-to-the-pedestrian/ (accessed May 5, 2020).

89. Tim Beatley, *Biophilic Cities* (Washington, DC: Island Press, 2011). p 98.

90. Dunbar Number https://www.bbc.com/future/article/20191001-dunbars-number-why-we-can-only-maintain-150-relationships (accessed January 14, 2020).

91. Umberto Berardi, *Cooling Corridors: The Role of Green Infrastructure in Building Resilience to Extreme* Heat https://www.greenbelt.ca/cooling_corridors (accessed May 15, 2020).

92. Robert Bailey, Ecoregion Mapping and Boundaries. https://www.fs.fed.us/rm/ecoregions/docs/papers-presentations/ecoregion-mapping-boundaries.pdf (accessed January 15, 2020).

93. Michael Rose, *Explainer: what are fractals?* http://theconversation.com/explainer-what-are-fractals-10865 (accessed March 4, 2020).

2 PRINCIPLES

PRINCIPLES, PATTERNS, AND OUTCOMES

Biophilic urbanism is informed by specific principles, which guide patterns of planning and design. The principles emerge from the posits of the biophilic effect as applied to the urban context and can produce positive outcomes. The patterns are qualities and characteristics found within specific attributes embodying biophilic intentions. And the outcomes are positive consequences of experiencing the attributes within biophilic environments. The outcomes also determine our planet's future health. This *principal–pattern–outcome* relationship is seen as a dynamic and restorative process from buildings to ecoregions over time.

Fundamental to biophilia are other sets of relationships that occur among nature and its processes, human experiences, and lifestyles practices, and the quality of the ever-changing built environment. Correspondingly, nature as the source of the principles is reflected in the built environment through implementation of the pattern attributes. This results in engaging experiences with the support of healthy lifestyles as positive outcomes. In a triadic relationship, each process – nature, humans, and the built environment – interacts with the other two in positive and negative ways. For example, nature is both inspiring and destructive, humans are both giving and taking, and the built environment is both nurturing and polluting.

The principles represent the forces behind biophilic design; they are original, authentic, and archetypal, and are sourced from nature. They represent the primary posit of the Biophilic Hypothesis that we are inherently drawn to and use connections to affiliate with nature and other forms of life. The principles illuminate the critical interface between the nature and the human experience. The pattern attributes are model design guides and ectypes in that they are representations and physical expressions of the principles. It is important that the pattern attributes are applicable at varying scales, differing locations along the rural-to-urban transect, and in the varying contexts of the built environment. The outcomes are unique to each person, neighborhood, or community as realized typal examples of the pattern attributes.[1]

- Principles – *biophilic effect, the triadic relationship, and archetypal energies applied to the rural-to-urban scales in varying contexts.*

- Pattern Attributes – *qualitative design characteristics and ectypal transferable exemplifications, most of which have quantitative evidenced-based outcomes.*
- Outcomes – *positive consequences, experiences through typal, concrete examples with measurable outcomes.*

BIOPHILIC PRINCIPLES

The biophilic principles have evolved from a re-evaluation of the Western world view and its interplay with nature, human beings, and the built environment. Our role is to respect nature and build accordingly. It is to rethink the axiom that nature is simply a usable commodity and see it as something more inclusive and sustainable. We need to help restore and provide stewardship for the natural world around us. We need to build more responsively to both its powerful forces and intimate bounties. While the Biophilic Hypothesis places importance on our innate affiliation with nature and its processes, at its core are the principles that reinvigorate and elucidate a paradigm shift forging a new and more balanced world view. The biophilic principles are directly linked to the primary desired outcomes of biophilic design.

The first outcome is to respect, restore, and respond to the larger natural context within which we live. This includes the ecological regions and climatic contexts. The second outcome is to respond repeatedly and sustainably to interactions with nature and the renewable technologies they support. The third outcome is to support placemaking and the positive urban forms and social interactions that can result from it. The fourth outcome is to promote health and wellness through positive experiences with both the natural and built environments. And the fifth outcome is to create the opportunities for spiritual connections to nature and the experiences of sacred places, true sustainability and high-level wellness.

The three primary biophilic principles derive from the nature–human–built environment interactions. Refer to Figure 2.1. As in any triad, one part interacts with the other two, creating six relationships. The positive outcomes of nature effect humans in beneficial ways, and it is from nature that the built environment is materialized. Human interactions are influenced by both experiences of nature and the built environment. And, the built environment impacts both nature and humans in positive and negative ways. Intended outcomes of the triad follows:

- To be open and gain greater access to nature's connections to us.
- To repeat and sustain healthy lifestyles and relationships that positively impact nature.
- To build responsively, respecting and contributing to the natural world.

Biophilic planning and design principles are intended to support appreciation and direct engagement with nature, to interact and responsibly utilize on-site natural resources, to plan according to climatic conditions and local ecological processes, to create vital and equitable human places capable of providing critical life-support functions, to foster a sense of community, and to support experiences that raise the human spirit. Echoing the 2015 United Nations Sustainable Development Goals, biophilic urbanism principles seek to encourage respect for the natural world, provide locally grown organic food, support health and well-being, provide abundant and clean water and sanitation, provide affordable and renewable energy, provide easy access to employment and support economic growth, create innovations in infrastructure and clean industry, provide quality education, and ensure the formation of sustainable communities. In order to achieve these sustainability goals, clear guidelines, design strategies, model demonstrations, and new and exciting conceptions are required.

The biophilic principles are intended to guide planning and design processes offering the greatest opportunity to seamlessly realize the biophilic effect at varying scales. The attribute categories provide a nesting of patterns essential to biophilic design. They form a broader context and provide similar adjacencies to the patterns. Biophilia pattern attributes are planning and design guides intended to cross all areas of the rural-to-urban transect. This includes the span from a room to an entire community or region. The principles encode environmental values and respect for nature and inform the more actionable pattern attributes. The principles are the narrative, while the attributes are the language.

To better understand the principles, they are divided into five principle-pattern categories: nature-based patterns, element-based patterns, form-based patterns, place-based patterns, and numinous-based patterns. Each category contains five patterns, totaling 25 pattern attributes. Nature-based patterns encompass nature, natural systems, life forms, and our connections to them. Element-based patterns focus on the classical elements of fire, earth, air, water, and ether as natural constituents of the natural world. Form-based patterns represent biophilic ordering systems inherent in the built environment, especially in buildings. Place-based patterns represent a confluence of nature, culture, and ecology within a specific geological and climatic context. According to William James, Numinous-based patterns are experiences that have noetic and cognitive content. They produce an overwhelming sense of clarity, they are transient – usually

2.1
Biophilic Principles:
(a) Yellowstone National Park,
(b) Siena Compo,
(c) Dubai night scene (*Source: Shutterstock, Phillip Tabb, Shutterstock*)

lasting less than a half hour, and rarely more than a few hours – and they produce positive emotional affects.[2] It is important to contextually apply the principles through the rural-to-urban transect and at the varying scales of an ecological region. For the purpose of this work, the following categories serve to organize the various pattern attributes in complementary ways.

- Nature-based pattern attributes – *include designs that encourage greater direct and indirect interactions with and emersions in nature, including vegetation, animals, and minerals, views and other sensual connections to the natural world.*
- Element-based pattern attributes – *include designs that integrate the classical elements and their qualities of fire and energy, earth and groundedness, water and waste, and air and ether, responding to the dynamic processes of a place.*
- Form-based pattern attributes – *include planning measures and designs that inform direction and orientation, local topography, spatial order, surveillance, thresholds, and increase of inside–outside relationships.*
- Place-based pattern attributes – *include contextual considerations of nucleation, place identity, utilization of indigenous materials, and designs that respond to the ecological systems of the region and foster community.*
- Numinous-based attributes – *include designs that reflect growth and changes through time, express the transformative qualities created by the various forms of the arts, inclusion of living color, various forms of light, and are fascinating, mysterious, inspiring, and numinous conduit moments of awe.*

DERIVATION OF THE PATTERNS

The biophilic pattern attributes in this work have been carefully generated from analysis of previously published works and personal experiences. Ekistics was an interdisciplinary model published in 1968 by Constantinos Doxiadis. Christopher Alexander's *A Pattern Language* published in 1977 presented 253 patterns, with at least 54 relating directly to biophilic attributes. Michael Brill in 1985–1986 uncovered a set of 14 design guidelines, which when the patterns were combined appeared to contribute to charged places. Stephen Kellert in 2008 developed a restorative design approach and paradigm in which there were 72 comprehensive "*attributes of biophilic design*." In 2018, Kellert with Calabrese consolidated them into 25 pattern attributes. Across the urban context, Tim Beatley introduced biophilic elements for six different and overlapping urban scales (2011). In 2014, Terrapin Bright Green published *14 Biophilic Patterns of Design* intended to articulate the relationships between nature, human biology, and the built environment. And finally, Phillip Tabb in *Serene Urbanism*, published in 2017, developed 20 placemaking patterns.

Ekistics is the science of human settlement developed in the late 1950s, and was applied to regional, city, community, and dwelling scales.[3] It aids urban planning, and design works achieve harmony among inhabitants of a place and their physical and sociocultural environments. While the elements of Ekistics were broad in nature, they did possess an inferred connection to biophilia, which emerged as a discipline decades later. There were six Ekistics levels: *nature*, *anthropos*, *society*, *shells*, *networks*, and *settlements*. The first set of three certainly relate to biophilia, and the last set of three relate to urbanism.

A pattern language was developed in Volume II of the series of books written by Christopher Alexander et al.[4] Patterns were observed from the past and were intended as timeless planning and design instruments applied to current issues at varying scales of the environment. It was the grouping of the patterns that created a field of relationships and what they called a "language." Many of the 253 patterns related directly to biophilia, notably: agricultural fields, neighborhood boundary, access to water, green streets, animals, food stands, outdoor room, roof garden, indoor sunlight, fruit trees, pools of light, and windows overlooking life, to name a few.

With the aid of a two-year grant from the National Endowment of the Arts, architect Michael Brill and his students at the State University of New York in Buffalo developed a set of design guidelines for what they called "*charged spaces*."[5] They found that certain patterns appeared to be present in special or sacred places. They discovered 14 such patterns that ranged from "*acknowledging a center* and *nature within*" to "*differentiated boundaries* and *consecration of the place*." They posited that these places were immensely charged, triggered powerful feelings, and produced a wave of sensory unity. The places seemed to create an ancient stirring within them, or what the authors called the experience of an "original feeling."[6] They concluded that places such as these can be found in nature and within places we have made.

These special places contain a svelte veil that exists between our secular world and the sacred, where possible energetic connections can more easily be experienced. The sequence of patterns included centering, differentiated direction, succession of spaces, connections to the celestial order, verticality, control of the underground, bounding, a distinct passage, discerning views, rare materiality, nature contained within, and consecration. The relationship of these patterns to biophilia is significant, especially in placemaking.

Stephen Kellert et al. published biophilic design attributes that were composed in six categories with 72 patterns informing a biophilic experience.[7] Of the 72 pattern attributes, most are directly applicable to biophilic urbanism. In this work, many of his attributes have been consolidated into one pattern, such as all forms of light have combined Kellert's patterns for luminosity, natural light, filtered and diffused light, reflected light, warm light, light pools, light and shadows, and light as shape. These pattern attributes were one of the first attempts to present the biophilic effect in actionable design guidelines. Later these patterns were simplified and consolidated into a more manageable set of 25 patterns.

The work of Tim Beatley shifted the biophilic conversation from isolated buildings to a focus on design principles at the urban design scale, especially in cities. He articulates six expanding scales of the built environment starting with buildings, blocks, and streets, and going to larger contexts in neighborhoods, communities, and finally to regions.[8] The regional context set the spatial structure and ecological processes for all the other scales. According to Beatley, the best biophilic cities are those in which the cascading scales overlap and reinforce biophilic behaviors and lifestyles. This nesting of scales is an important dimension in biophilic urbanism.

Terrapin Bright Green's online-published paper "14 Patterns of Biophilic Design" offers a framework for exploring biophilia, identifying biophilic design patterns, and relating the science behind the intended outcomes.[9] More recently, they have added a 15th pattern – awe (2020). The patterns were seen as tools for understanding design opportunities primarily at the single building scale. This paper was one of the first publications that clearly defined biophilia in design terms, delineated design patterns, and articulated the outcomes, especially for health and wellness. The references to the scientific research regarding health and wellness benefits are extremely useful in understanding biophilia's functions and outcomes.

In *Serene Urbanism* by Phillip Tabb, he cited 20 ectypal place-creation patterns intended to guide the design of buildings and planning of communities (2015).[10] They were "ectypal" in the sense that they were concrete expressions of higher archetypal principles. The five principles in which the patterns were organized comprised: the unity principle, the generative principle, the formative principle, the corporeal principle, and the regenerative principle. The place patterns were designed to provide universal guidelines for creating place at any scale. At the core of this work was the need to reinvigorate a healthy relationship between the serene qualities of nature and the beneficial qualities of culture and the urban context.

In biophilic urbanism, the principles, pattern attributes, and intended positive outcomes are synthesized in the urban context in an attempt to provide a usable design tool applicable at any scale of development. Generally, the pattern attributes function at each of the development scales, although some may be more appropriate or more easily applied to a specific scale. For the purpose of this work, they are used to create seamless interactions at the building, street, block, neighborhood, community, and regional scales. And while there are differing issues occurring at each urban scale, there is a self-similarity within the natural world that binds them.

The pattern attributes are seen as strategies and guidelines, representing a standardized vocabulary and language in biophilic planning and design. They are typal in their representation of previously identified applications and benefits. They are ectypal in that they are carriers of embodied biophilic principles. At the archetypal level, biophilia expresses as pure principle and intention. It has a philosophical and theoretical basis, explained by the Biophilic Hypothesis. At the ectypal level, biophilia expresses through the pattern exemplifications as models with transferable and inherent design attributes. And finally, at the typal level, biophilia represents actual functioning designs and planning demonstrations that are particular to a region, program, site, and design.

The disclaimer here is that there is no fixed or absolute set or number of biophilic pattern attributes. Our relationship, affiliation, and affinity to nature is a changing and evolving process. It is affected by our growing understanding of the world around us and the quality of our direct experiences of it. Time is certain to expand and influence this process. In relation to biophilic urbanism, there are, perhaps, differing contexts, scales of application, and functional requirements that may propose a modified set of pattern attributes. Much like Christopher Alexander's 253 patterns, they represent an alphabet intended to create a language – in the case of this work, a language intended to contribute to positive climate change, greater levels of sustainability, more vital community-oriented placemaking, improved health and wellness, and opportunities for numinous experiences. While there is intended to be a universal quality to the principles, pattern attributes, and outcomes, it must be noted that locations worldwide will interpret them in context-specific ways.

BIOPHILIC PATTERN ATTRIBUTES

As mentioned, the biophilic pattern attributes in this work have been synthesized from an analysis of the previously published patterns and design guides. They, too, have been informed by actual experiences of natural and built places. The patterns are organized into the five groupings: nature-based patterns, element-based patterns, form-based patterns, place-based patterns, and numinous-based patterns; and five outcome categories. A pattern attribute is defined as a specific design guideline composed of the inherent qualities, characteristics, and coding of the principles. They are actionable models applicable to planning and architectural scales.

Nature-Based Patterns

1. *The plant kingdom* – Plants in all their manifestations are living organisms, vital expressions of life including trees, herbs, bushes, grasses, vines, ferns, mosses, and algae. The plant kingdom provides the taming quality of the wild, disordered and chaotic brought into safe and natural surroundings. This can include agriculture, orchards, vineyards, landscaping, water features, geological formations, or open spaces. Trees and plants provide the role of carbon sinks. The Global Seed Vault located in Svalbard, Norway is an excellent example of biophilic architecture with its 930,000 seed varieties. With seed scarification, sowing, tending, harvesting, preparing, cooking, and consuming our food, nutrition is central to health and wellness. Plants are essential to human survival for food, fiber, and fodder, as well as fascination and beauty. Agricultural urbanism is an emerging movement, although not a new one, that posits integrating a broad range of sustainable food and agricultural systems into city planning.[11] This approach increases access to

healthy food, and the knowledge of how and what is actually ending up on our kitchen tables. In biophilic urbanism, this suggests shifting large, distant monoculture farming production toward local organic farming practices. Farm-to-table is an emerging example representing this attribute. According to Prem Chandavarkar, one of the lessons learned from the pandemic is our problematic relationship with nature and food supplies.[12]

2. *The animal kingdom* – We are part of the animal kingdom, and our relationship to the other species is fundamental; they supply food, protection, companionship, and fascination. Wild, free-roaming, and domesticated animals are important and provide emotional stimulation and immense pleasure. According to the Centers for Disease Control and Prevention (CDC), domestic pets provide many health benefits. They can increase opportunities to exercise, to be outside, and to socialize.[13] Regular walking or playing with pets can decrease blood pressure, cholesterol levels, and triglyceride levels. Interacting with animals has shown to decrease levels of cortisol, a stress-related hormone. They can help manage or reduce loneliness and depression by providing companionship. Wild animals contribute to and play important regulatory roles in intact ecosystems, including regulating herbivore and mesopredator (racoon, snake, and skunk) populations that in turn affect floral, soil, and hydrological systems.

3. *Views and vistas* – We are a visual species, so views and vistas are extremely important to us, for several reasons. Intimate and framed views of nature are soothing and contribute to wellbeing. Large-scale vistas – such as views of the night sky and ocean's horizon line, or places like the Grand Canyon – are inspiring and remind us of how vast the natural world really is. Views to the woods where children play, and to the streets where there is social activity, are both desirable. Surveillance views are important for public safety. "Eyes on the streets," in the seminal work of Jane Jacobs, *The Life and Death of Great American Cities*, suggests the importance of natural managers of street-life.[14] Biophilic urbanism suggests a greater integration of nature along waterways and streets, on roofs, and between and within buildings.

4. *Sensory connections* – Exposure to nature produces positive effects as experienced by all our senses – visual, auditory, olfactory, haptic, and gustatory all contribute. There are other perceptions that could be considered senses, including those of balance and temperature, and proprioception or the sense of movement in space. Humans are dominantly visual, but the other senses are important in biophilic design. Natural sounds restore moods, and natural olfactory sensations are important for memory, language, and social attraction and reproduction. Tasting food can be transforming. Haptic or touch sensations are enjoyed in horticultural activities, a walk in the rain or snow, and playing with domesticated animals. Moving through varying spaces, either spatially intimate or generous, affects us. According to John Steele,

the combination of senses creates enhanced perception and more focused attention and memory.[15]

5. *Ecological and biological contexts* – The ecology of a region is determined by its latitude, its elevation, its relation to hydrological cycles, its climate, its dominant bio-geographical features, and its proximity to urban areas. To sustain the resulting ecosystems, development schemes need to design with topography, watersheds, rivers, estuaries, animal habitats, vegetated wetlands, and access to nature. Biophilic urbanism suggests visibility of and direct access to ecological processes. Infrastructure and natural analogs and biomorphic designs are often expressions of this pattern. The biological patterns are the ordering qualities of the natural world, processes of growth and proliferation, and organic forms used to inform certain planning and design situations. They are not a mimic or motif, but rather they have natural logic and authentic expression. They can appropriately simulate the natural world in natural sites and urban contexts. Examples include landform architecture and biological planning for diversity and advanced mitigation. In biophilic urbanism this suggests planning with the natural features of a site and inclusion of as much greenspace and tree cover as possible. In the instance of biologic contaminants, implement a pandemic preparedness plan across the urban-to-rural transect.

Element-Based Patterns

6. *Fire and energy* – For early humans, fire gave warmth, light, and protection as well as a means to cook, heat, and hunt. The primary benefits of fire in the built environment are the provision of energy for heating and cooling buildings, cooking, fuels for transportation, and renewable energy for power production.[16] The fireplace holds a more significant place in contemporary domestic architecture than merely as a source of heat; it also provides comfort, light, and mesmeric movement. It serves as an altar of sorts; a place for a family portrait or a mirror reflecting family keepsakes. It is important to understand that the production of carbon of fire contributes to soil restoration as well as to climate change. Reduction of both in-place and between-place automobile travel can reduce contaminants. At the biophilic urbanism scale, this attribute has implications for community energy production and distribution, and transportation systems, modes, and internal networks. Site planning for solar access is also important. "*Passive survivability*" and "*shelter-in-place*" combine in an increasingly desirable survival strategy.

7. *Earth and grounding* – As an element, earth is complex, manifesting as material and form, structure, weight, density, solidity, and materiality. It signifies tangibility, safety, protection, and stability, providing substantive protection. It is associated with geology, soils, and nutrients of the earth. Benefits of earth include the provision of shelter; the provision of nutrients and food grown in the earth; and protection from severe climate and weather conditions,

and from insects and predators. It also supplies strength of materials in construction, and allows us to build larger, higher, and in more complex ways. Earth supports the emergence and proliferation of technology in all its forms and uses, from wine bottle openers to spacecraft, and, finally, it imparts the sensual nature of materiality. Earth enhancing carbon removal and storage is another benefit of the attribute earth. Biological grounding or physical contact with the Earth's surface (gardening, bare feet, or walking on a beach) is beneficial to health. Within the urban context, vegetation can be formed by green indoor plants, green roofs, green walls, green verges, green islands, green corridors, and urban farming.

8. *Air and natural ventilation* – Anaximenes of Miletus (mid sixth century BC) was the first pre-Socratic philosopher to attach significance to air, naming it as the element holding the fabric of nature together. Oxygen is our most basic need; without it we very quickly experience brain damage and death. The average person can only survive for a couple of minutes before hypoxemia occurs. Indoor air quality has recently become increasingly important, affecting both comfort and the health of building occupants. It is important for a building to function by repelling outside polluted air from building interiors, expelling unwanted interior air to the outside, and permitting only healthy fresh air into and through the building. Air also mitigates temperature differences affecting comfort. Some of the health benefits of fresh air include boosting the immune system, providing fresh oxygen, and increasing energy. It is good for digestion, it cleans out the lungs, and it sharpens the mind. Important benefits of air are in its role in cross-ventilation and in global hydrological cycles. While there has been a great deal of research supporting the beneficial qualities of fresh air, the Coronavirus has brought new concerns, and the need for effective social distancing in response to the spreading of the airborne virus by speaking, coughing, and sneezing.

9. *Water and waste* – Water is necessary for life. According to Abby Phon, the health benefits of water for the human body include increasing energy, flushing out toxins, promoting weight loss, improving skin complexion, maintaining regularity, boosting the immune system, and preventing cramps and sprains.[17] Water can help maximize physical performance. Ecosystems are linked and maintained by water, which provides permanent habitat for many species. Water is essential for plant growth and landscaping, and is the main component of plant cells, transporting nutrients throughout the plant, and being used in photosynthesis. The experience of the element water is an emotional one, whether it is calm, soothing, warm, flowing, rushing, or rhythmic. In architecture and planning even small features – such as a drinking fountain, pool, wetlands, stream, or views of water features – are adequate to elicit positive responses. At the urban scale, rainwater can be managed through harvesting, swales, infiltration gardens, porous surfaces, climate-responsive landscaping, and retention ponds.

10. *Ether and celestial moments* – Our connections to the larger celestial context are a response to the open sky and the changing movements of the Sun, Moon, planets, and other celestial objects marking the changing seasons and times of the day.[18] Associated with these connections are potential numinous experiences with sunrises and sunsets, shooting stars, solar and lunar eclipses, and the Northern Lights. The celestial heavens arrive slowly, change gradually, and slip away imperceptibly, reflecting our place and time in the broader universe.[19] The endless stars, constellations, and wandering planets form patterns that embody myths, fantasies, and legends. Even today, they inspire mythopoeia and fictional myth-making. Phototropism derives from the botanical world and its chemical and biological processes; it is the tendency to respond to and follow the movement of the Sun by rearranging plant chloroplasts to enhance the process of photosynthesis. In biophilic urbanism, this suggests planning for solar access and the reduction of night light pollution. Viewing the heavens can provide inspiration, serve for self-reflection, and renew the understanding of our place in the scale of all things.

Form-Based Patterns

11. *Orientation and direction* – Meaningful orientation or finding direction gives purpose and connections to the terrestrial world of a given place through orientation to the natural features of the place, such as the cardinal directions, the natural contours or geology of a site, views and vistas of special features both near and far, solar movements like solstices and equinoxes, or to symbolic orientations. To orient is to situate oneself or a design in relation to something interesting or important. This pattern literally situates one in terrestrial and celestial space with distinctive place-defining markers. In biophilic urbanism, this suggests a more direct connection between residential enclaves, workplaces, and spiritual environments. It also includes the visibility of urban spaces in terms of wayfinding, visual merchandising, and surveillance. At the biophilic urbanism scale, this attribute has implications for site planning for solar access, ecological flows, topographical context, important views, and special site features.

12. *Prospect and refuge* – The Prospect–refuge theory was developed by Jay Appleton saying our innate desire for nature has prospect or critical viewing, while at the same time enjoying safety (refuge).[20] To Konrad Lorenz, prospect–refuge means one can "*see*, while not being *seen*."[21] Prospect creates discernable views of distant objects, of changes in weather, and of intruders and other potential sources of danger. Refuge provides a secure, safe, and protected setting at both the urban design and architectural scales. Modern security occurs not only with planning interventions and architectural designs, but also with the use of technology. In restaurants, cozy nooks and intimate settings are desirable. Refuge can also occur at the community level, where residents can observe suspicious activity. In biophilic urbanism

this includes the provision of dynamic public places with naturally occurring social surveillance; the creation of safe refuge within community commercial and cultural destinations with natural street and place surveillance. The global Coronavirus pandemic will certainly initiate new guidelines on ways in which we address this particular pattern, especially refuge. Appropriate measures for refuge include home sheltering, possibly the need for isolation, and designs for sanctuary spaces and passive survivability, and for workplaces, restaurants, and congregate settings is the need for safe distancing.

13. *Inside–outside relationships* – This pattern includes both direct and indirect relationships between the inside and outside, with emphasis on transparency, porosity, and fluid movement between the two. Visual connections to the outdoors are important, but direct source experiences of unstructured self-sustaining features of nature can involve more senses and produce vital outcomes.[22] This relationship can be encouraged with the provision of outdoor balconies, decks, patios, rooms, terraces, gardens, parks, and/or plazas. Further, walls of glass, movable walls, operable windows, and French doors can encourage a more seamless visual and physical connection between indoors and outdoors. Interstitial space occurs between the two. This is an incredibly important attribute because we spend so much time indoors. At the biophilic urbanism scale, this attribute has implications along the rural-to-urban transect, offering differing kinds of larger-scale inside–outside relationships. In times of a virus pandemic, the inside–outside relationship requires careful managing of this threshold. In restaurants, for example, there may be blurred thresholds of indoor and outdoor seating.

14. *Topography and geological patterns* – Most residential projects are developed on areas that are not very steep, making construction easier and accessible, control of surface water, patterns of erosion, and safety relatively easy to accomplish. With biophilic urbanism there are certain advantages to some variations in topography as long as they satisfy safety considerations. The orography of varying topography creates certain microclimates that vary our perceptions as we move through space. At the biophilic urbanism scale, changing topography and geographic features can create place location and form for landform communities, and contribute to place identity.[23] Carbon sequestering is affected by topological and geological factors as the carbon fixation capacity differs with varying soil depths and compositions. There is a preference for places with variations in elevation and distant views of the horizon. This preference could be linked back to the Savanna hypothesis with sculpted landscape highs and lows.

15. *Spatial order and connectiveness* – This pattern recognizes the unique differences among the various ordering systems, from monotony to simplicity to ambiguity to complexity to chaos. Each spatial order reflects systems found in nature and is employed for specific biophilic functions within the built environment. Simplicity orders tend to be economical and efficient, while

complex orders express diversity and varying ranges of detail. Ambiguous orders create mystery and can form transitions between extremes. In biophilic urbanism, ordering systems are sympathetic to overall climatic, ecological, and topological contexts. Connectivity is an important dimension of spatial structure, and contends with land use patterns, transportation modes, and safe pedestrian environments. This includes variations in space size and type, geometric networks, spatial sequencing, fractal-like nestings, density, mix of uses, and the degree of pedestrianization. Biophilic urbanism grows through a process of multiplication when the optimal size has been reached. Different space types generate different qualities, from spatial intimacy to spatial generosity, and from community to privacy.[24] In biophilic urbanism there is a paradigm shift from automobile-oriented spatial structures to pedestrian ones. According to Orians and Heerwgen, there is a natural preference for landscapes in which the spatial orders contain "moderate degrees of complexity, a sense of coherence, and semi-open spatial configurations."[25] Further, environments that have changes in elevation, distant views, focal points, the presence of water, and large trees are preferable to those that do not. The global Coronavirus pandemic is cause for re-evaluating spatial design and connectivity considerations in times of surges of the disease, and the need for spatial distancing, sheltering-in-place, and in extreme conditions, lockdown.

Place-Based Patterns

16. *Centering and nucleation* – Centering is a point of attraction and a seed encoding growth of the place. It can be a special space, square, green, temple, market, street, building, landmark, natural feature, or fountain. It can be a physical focal point and usually has an intense activity and meaning contributing to place demarcation. The center often possesses special energetic qualities as described by genius loci or spirit of place. According to Mircea Eliade, orientation to a fixed point within the chaos of homogeneity can create a revelation of the "found world."[26] In biophilic urbanism it possesses cultural and commercial activities with supporting amenities or a physical icon, such as the Eiffel Tower in Paris or Eero Saarinen's parabolic arch in St. Louis. The concept of pedestrianization is gaining currency as it not only creates safe places, but also provides a context for more robust forms of biophilia to emerge. Nucleation is the process by which urban design elements are attracted to a central and diverse focus and incubator of activity. In some instances, poly-nucleation is a settlement pattern with multiple centers. During pandemics, providing places with expanded and personalized functions for prolonged stays at home is important for stress reduction and mental health.

17. *Bounding and containment* – Bounding is the comprehensible edge with an integrating relationship to the center. It functions by creating containment within, protection from without, and porosity and control of natural

systems flowing through. It can be either natural or man-made. Bounding can also contribute to place demarcation and identity formation, and in this sense it adds to the comprehension and coherence of a place. According to Michael Brill, boundaries must reveal the different meanings found around the perimeter, such as the cardinal directions, and/or entry points.[27] Within biophilic urbanism, it suggests safe-place creation by reducing automobiles, traffic calming, and increasing pedestrian connections and activity places. Bounding should not be confused with "*gated communities*" as gated communities do not support community building, but encourage isolation and self-similarity. As with relationships, boundaries serve to clarify and provide protection of the place, while maintaining respect. Bounding and containment suggest other important pattern considerations in response to the novel Coronavirus pandemic. This is true for homes, but more importantly, places with large population densities, like nursing homes, schools, congregate housing, sporting events, hospitals, meat-processing plants, ships, military camps, and prisons. Containment is critical in reducing the spread of the disease.

18. *Natural materiality* – Natural materials usually come directly from the environment, as opposed to artificial materials that are man-made or created through industrialized processes. The building sector contributes up to 30 percent of global annual greenhouse gas emissions, making carbon sequestering and storage in buildings important. People respond to natural materials because they have an affinity to living organisms. Natural materials reflect the local ecology, creating a distinct sense of place.[28] At the urban design scale, natural materials for courtyard, plaza, street, sidewalk, parking, pathway surfaces, landscaping, and exterior envelope materials can contribute to carbon sequestering. Natural materiality expresses non-objective, nonlinear, and random patterns, and experiencing these materials creates a semiotic narrative back to a living source. Façade and roof greening are other material approaches currently being used. Natural building materials use far fewer toxins during their production process and facilitate carbon sequestering. On the whole, producing natural materials requires less embodied energy. Integrating natural materials inside buildings is another way of bringing nature inside. Natural materials can be used in creative and contemporary expressions as well.

19. *Form Language and natural analogs* – A biophilic form language is a reference to natural forms, structures, processes, and patterns. They often emulate natural forms, shapes, surfaces, materials, and colors. As a language, it suggests use of these elements in creating an overall expression and image of the place, which will often vary depending upon its geographical location, and its position along the rural-to-urban transect. A form language will also embody many of the other pattern attributes analogous to a kind of biophilic grammar. These vary across direct and indirect evocation (not copies), and from lattice structures of the plant kingdom to forms of the animal

world. Often today they take the form of tree-filled building facades, green walls and roofs, and agricultural urbanism. To Christopher Alexander, the language creates a coherent picture of an entire region with infinite forms and pattern details.[29] It is important to not simply copy nature (biomimicry), but rather to develop a deeper understanding of its processes and utilities (bio-influence). At the biophilic urbanism scale, this attribute has implications for the patterns of growth over time, and the image of the place as determined by the nature–urban integration. Numerical arrangements echo geometric, rhythmic, repeating, and three-dimensional patterns, which in turn are commonly found in nature as fractals. Natural analogs borrow from natural forms and processes. According to Michael Pawlyn, they contain sustainable principles and are inspiring. They can be superefficient structures, high-strength biodegradable composites, self-cleaning surfaces, and low-energy and waste-degrading systems.[30]

20. *Cultural, social, historic connections* – Cultural connections nurture and integrate historic, geographic, ecological, and collective values, and spiritual sensitivities to nature and place. They represent a shared identity and a sense of belonging. Often the visual, performing, and culinary arts, and both active and passive recreation, help further this connection. Community building is a qualitative social process directed toward facilitating interactions, enhancements, and engagements towards its success and wellbeing.[31] In biophilic urbanism, this suggests nature-based, sustainable, and wellness activities, programs, and amenities that all contribute to greater social interactions, opportunities, and shared experiences. At the biophilic urbanism scale, this attribute facilitates the creation of public spaces with easy access and multiple activities. Cultural and social activities, which the life-enhancing effects of social interactions support, extend to giver as well as to receiver. Aging in place creates seamless social connections through time, as social interactions are seen as a biomarker of health. During epidemics of air-borne viruses, concerted attention must be observed with physical distancing and sanitation protocols, especially for people living within nursing homes, assisted living and congregate housing, long-term health facilities, and aggregate work environments, and for incarcerated prisoners. Social gathering numbers should be completely eliminated in the case of severe episodes or limited to no more than ten people under normal circumstances of the epidemic.

Numinous-Based Patterns

21. *The Arts and mythopoeia* – Important cultural and aesthetic experiences are enabled through various forms of art, including the visual, literary, performing, and culinary arts. Three functions of the arts include the physical, social, and personal connections, and each of these can contribute to urban placemaking. Community arts activities contribute to health and subjective wellbeing, and meaningful social interaction; they promote tourism, civic

pride, and positive economic impacts. The performing arts can unify a community and provide an important venue for social interaction. Culinary arts support community, improved nutrition, and health and wellness. And the visual arts can be part of the physical expression of the place. Mythopoeia suggests sharing and ongoing creation of local myths and resident stories. Taken together, the arts can be transformative through cultural numinous experiences. There is evidence that engagement with artistic activities – either as an observer of the creative efforts of others or as an initiator of one's own creative efforts – can enhance one's mood, emotions, and other psychological states, as well as having a salient impact on important physiological parameters. Mythopoeia generally includes narratives of mythological themes and archetypes in fiction; in the context of biophilia it serves to reflect the stories created by residents within their communities and natural environments.

22. *Living color* – In Feng Shui the notion of *living color* invokes a transcendent dimension with regenerative powers. Color expresses a visible and vital element of life. Color, that is natural and is activated by varying qualities of light, can produce numinous experiences. Color is experienced as properties of surfaces, which change color over the course of a day. Morning light tends to be yellow with mid-level electromagnetic wavelengths; it becomes bluer in the middle of the day with shorter wavelengths; and shifts to red with even longer wavelengths in the late afternoon.[32] The rich color of an iris or rose petal, the intricate and vibrant colors of a butterfly's wings, and the fiery colors of a midsummer sunset are all living colors. In architecture, stained glass that is activated by the changing qualities of light can produce similar effects, such as the west transept rose window of Chartres Cathedral. The multicolored exteriors of fishermen's houses found in Burano, Italy suggest vitality and joy. Colors can also have symbolic associations and elicit certain emotional responses, such as the color of red representing passion and fire, blue the calmness of water, and green seen abundantly in nature and the edible plant world.[33]

23. *Temporal and transformative processes* – The environment, both natural and urban, is in constant change. Change is reflected in processes of growth and evolution over time. Natural environments transform in an ecological succession from pioneering to climax communities; urban environments through ever-evolving development practices and technologies. Changes that occur over time include daily fluctuations from day to night, seasonal changes from summer to winter, and the patina of time as reflected by trees growing taller, and annual plants being born and dying. The built environment changes, similarly, with population growth, expansion, renewal, and aging through degradation over time. Emergent technologies, construction materials, and densification and migration patterns are also subject to change. Materials must be durable, waterproof, changeable, and requiring low maintenance. Adaptability and resilience are important. A place becomes more

familiar over time and is embodied and storied, creating its own history and culture. Human interactions with certain materials, such as steps and handrails, reflect their use and human function. According to Christopher Day, the soul of a place incarnates progressively from conception to construction, and finally through occupation and use over time.[34]

24. *Light in all forms* – Light is an integral pattern to biophilia and manifests in so many ways. Daylight affects both our eye functions and our inherent circadian rhythms. In its many forms, light is related to luminosity, the ethereal, inspiration, and the numinous. Light is natural, dynamic, and can be direct, filtered, diffused, or reflected. Twilight occurring at dawn and dusk expresses as three types – civil, nautical, and astronomical twilight depending upon its position relative to the horizon. Fluid luminosity refers to the changing qualities of light, whether due to fluctuating conditions, source, color, or architectural design. It has a co-existing dance with shadow to give expression to form. Light can also derive from moon and starlight, campfires, fireplaces, and candles. According to Louis I. Kahn, silence is immeasurable while light is the giver of presence.[35] In biophilic urbanism, this suggests lotting schemes and building forms that promote potential access to natural light for every living space with dynamic systems of modulation. Not all light is desirable. Glare creates a loss of visual performance, and both sunlight and artificial light produces skyglow, light trespassing, and cluttered light. Night light pollution creates a problem for clearly viewing the night sky. Planning steps should be made to reduce the impact of street and automobile lights. There is now limited but convincing evidence that moderate sunlight exposure is capable of modulating the immune system and improving health.

25. *The Numinous and noetic experiences* – According to Rudolf Otto, the numinous is something uniquely and "wholly other," whose special character we can *feel*, without being able to give it clear conceptual expression.[36] These patterns can be triggered by breezes in the trees, the smell of fresh earth, a shooting star or the northern lights at night, a rainbow, a view from a mountaintop, or seeing a wild animal in the forest. All of these experiences slow down time and create a heightened presence and conduit moment. Random or non-objective patterns can be soothing and mesmeric, such as watching reflected light or ripples on the surface of the water, changing clouds in the sky, or a seemingly random leaf patterns on the forest floor. Numinous experiences are ineffable and transient, with noetic cognitive content.[37] Noetic experiences relate to the cognitive nature of the mind and the biophilic information that can lead to curiosity, wonder, and imagination. The Celtic notion of *thin places* and Edward Sosa's *Thirdspace* suggests places in which a svelte or thin veil exists between our secular world and the sacred, where numinous experiences can more easily be made.[38] And to Mircea Iliade, the numinous manifests itself, reveals itself, as something different than the profane, and in the context of biophilic design, it saturates us with a deeper grace and sense of awe, and a reverent appreciation of nature.[39]

BIOPHILIC POSITIVE OUTCOMES

Outcome Descriptions

Positive outcomes are a result of experience informed by the biophilic principles and formed by the pattern attributes, which help facilitate greater interactions with the natural environment. In the context of biophilic urbanism there are five outcome categories: climate, sustainability, placemaking, health and wellness, and the numinous. The climate-positive outcomes are a result of larger planning and design measures. The sustainability outcomes are initially a result of planning and design measures, focusing on conservation and on-site renewable resources. The placemaking outcomes entail benefits derived from community building, social interactions, and subsequent biophilic connections. The health and wellness outcomes are experiential in nature manifesting through cognitive functioning, physiological and psychological responses, interacting more frequently with nature and one another, exercising, socializing, and eating healthier, locally grown food. The numinous outcomes are transformative and occur with the extraordinary and profound experiences of nature and the built environment.

1. *Climate-positive outcomes* – are performance-based outcomes that involve carbon sequestering, reducing and/or eliminating fossil fuel consumption, use of on-site renewable resources, and promoting climate-responsive design strategies including site planning for solar access, reducing the heat-island effect, and pedestrianization. They involve awareness of and responses to prevailing climatic and weather patterns, and seasonal and diurnal patterns.

2. *True sustainability outcomes* – are performance-based. They involve overcoming unsustainable consumption patterns and building practices, utilizing on-site renewable energy technologies, creating more durable climate-responsive buildings, planning more densely with greater accessibility, using low-embodied-energy materials, maintaining long-term restorative measures, and designing for passive survivability.

3. *Placemaking outcomes* – are both sustainable and socially based, involving nature-based spatial structures, increased accessibility, pedestrianization, cultural and social engagement and interactions, and community building. Positive spatial identity is a natural consequence of placemaking. The more a community becomes a place, the greater the potential for patterns supporting heritage and sustainable and biophilic behaviors.

4. *Health and wellness outcomes* – are experience-based, involving increased direct and indirect connections to nature and the elements, restorative environments and healthy lifestyles, use of clean natural resources and non-toxic materials, and supporting optimal physiological, psychological, social, nutritional, cognitive, and spiritual wellbeing. Planning and design for air-borne contagions is also a critically important outcome, especially during pandemics.

5. *Numinous outcomes* – are experience-based, involving important agential or transformative dimensions of awe in biophilic design that include sustainability and health and wellness outcomes. Numinous outcomes are important human experiences that are ineffable and transient, and create a sense of clarity. This combination affects the fundamental values that are necessary to drive positive change, and it is through inspired experiences of nature that other outcomes are more easily capable of being achieved.

The design principles of biophilic urbanism can be experienced on multiple levels. The intent of this work is to feature the biophilic attributes in facilitating positive outcomes. As previously mentioned, these include *climate-positive* residential development, maximizing *carbon sequestration*, achieving *true sustainability*, *placemaking* and *community building*, maintaining *high-level wellness*, creating closer *connections to nature*, and encouraging *numinous experiences* and developing a *deeper sense of grace*. It is the scalar integration of the combinator effect of nature, element, form, place, and numinous-based attributes that affords the greatest success.

Mitigating climate change can occur using two main strategies: (1) by reducing emissions from greenhouse gas-producing sources, and (2) by enhancing the sinks that accumulate and store the gasses. The precedents in the following chapters show that the propensity to mitigate climate change includes the preservation of the large areas of forests, pastures, greenways, recreation areas, parks, and meadows that form carbon sinks to absorb carbon dioxide and other contaminants. This is further accomplished by the reduction of automobile use according to a community's size, containment, density, mix of uses, proximities and accessibilities to workplaces, schools, and shopping, and the pedestrian orientation of each community.

Solar access planning is important if stand-alone solar technologies are to be employed on aggregate buildings at the neighborhood and community scales. Both orientation to and clear access to the sun are needed between four and six hours a day – between 9 am and 3 pm in lower-density settings, or 10 am and 2 pm in more dense settings. Solar access is usually used for passive solar heating, domestic hot-water heating, and photovoltaic electricity production. According to "solar envelope" research by Ralph Knowles, solar access can be planned for residential buildings with densities of 50 units per acre (20 units per hectare).[40] Solar energy remains a valuable resource even in climatic contexts where there is a high percentage of cloud cover.

Nature-based climate protection involves a number of conservation, restoration, and improved land-management strategies. The benefits include carbon sequestering, carbon farming, water filtration, flood control, soil health, and increased biodiversity. In contrast, climate change is responsible for cardiovascular mortality, malnutrition from crop failure, and transmission of infectious diseases.[41] Carbon sequestering aims to decrease the atmospheric concentration of carbon dioxide created by energy production, process industry, land-use

2.2
Climate-positive
outcomes (*Source:*
Phillip Tabb)

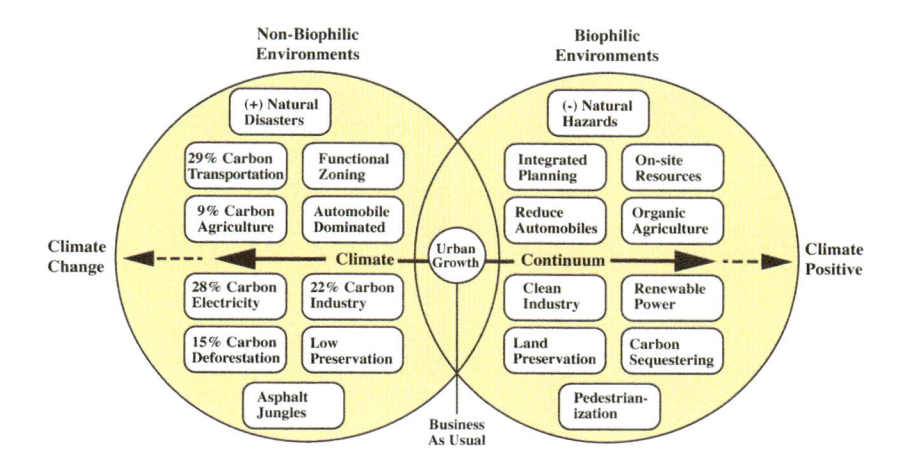

conversion, and soil cultivation. This requires developing low- or no-carbon fuel and sequestering emissions from these sources.

The specific outcomes include carbon sequestering, slowing climate change, pollution reduction, balancing carbon emissions with carbon sinks, mitigating responses to extreme weather and natural disasters, and the movement toward passive survivability. According to Britt Wray, climate change's uncertain status is cause for an increase in psychological impacts such as grief, fear, shock, anxiety, PTSD, and suicidality.[42] Carbon-sequestering strategies include agroforestry, biochar, enhanced gas recovery, and soil carbon sequestration. Figure 2.2 shows the contrast of climate-related outcomes between non-biophilic and biophilic environments.

Sustainability strategies focus on such processes as conservation, preservation, efficiency, low embodied energy, repurposing and recycling, improved accessibility, and use of on-site renewable resources. At the urban design scale, they address the power, transportation, and building energy sectors.[43] They also address conservation and preservation of the natural world. And, according to John Ehrenfeld, unsustainability is a result of the cultural structure of modernity, and "*true sustainability*" is based on living systems.[44] True sustainability goes beyond merely overcoming unsustainability.

Sustainability informed by biophilic urbanism can be further achieved by the close proximity and access to local produce, the vegetated wetland water-waste processes, the use of geothermal heating and cooling systems, water harvesting, and pedestrian access to a variety of mixed uses. By relating directly to nature and the resources it brings to the site, sustainable on-site renewable technologies are possible. The technologies include: organic agriculture; geothermal heating and cooling systems; wind and solar energy for electricity production, heating, cooling, and service hot-water, and natural lighting. At the neighborhood and community scales, solar and/or wind farms can be employed to provide a local renewable energy utility for electricity, such as the 440 acre (178 hectare) solar farm at Babcock Ranch, Florida. There are planning measures that also contribute to greater levels of sustainability including increased accessibility and mix of uses, integrated zoning rather than functional and separated zoning, clustering of end-uses, planning for solar access, smart utility infrastructure, and providing for safe pedestrian circulation and gathering places.[45]

Passive survivability refers to the ability of a building or community to maintain critical life-support functions if utility supplies have been shut off for an extended period of time. Passive survivability was introduced by Alex Wilson in the wake of Hurricane Katrina and was intended for houses, apartment buildings, and emergency shelters.[46] In the context of biophilic urbanism, this concept could be applied to larger scales of resiliency, including neighborhoods and communities. Along similar lines, the Coronavirus pandemic of 2020 required sheltering-in-place, social distancing, self-quarantining, and the wearing of face masks in order to limit the spread of the highly contagious virus. Often essential goods and services were difficult to obtain that included food, sanitation supplies, and household repairs. Passive survivability included shelter from the elements, electricity, clean water and food storage, and access to the Internet. This is a compelling idea in the face of climate change, natural disasters, and increased extreme weather events, including inhospitable temperatures, drought, and even terrorist threats. Passive survivability design strategies are context driven and would include use of on-site renewable energy sources, daylighting, natural ventilation, passive solar heating or heat avoidance, rainwater harvesting or emergency water storage, and back-up power sources. Application of the biophilic urban design attributes would certainly contribute to the design of passive survivability.

The specific outcomes include increased comfort, reduction of greenhouse gas emissions, improved thermal efficiencies, mitigating extreme temperatures, decreased dependence upon fossil fuels, reduction of waste with increased recycling, reduction of embodied energy use, increased density and open space, regenerative and long-term causalities, increased operating efficiencies, utilization of on-site renewable resources, and passive survivability. Figure 2.3

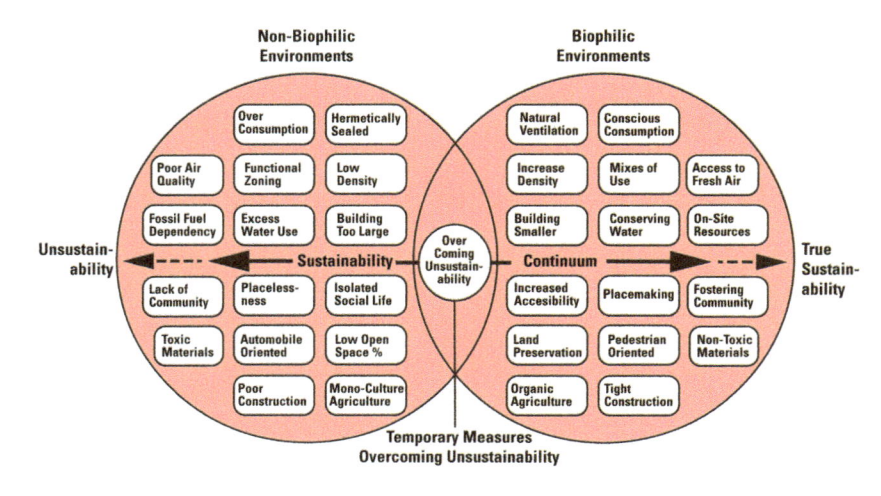

2.3
Sustainability outcomes (*Source: Phillip Tabb*)

indicates a biophilic continuum, with unsustainable practices on one end of the continuum and true sustainable measures on the other.

Placelessness is one of the negative by-products of urbanism. It can occur everywhere, but most often is found in urban areas, particularly those in decline or neglect. Placelessness is pervasive when functioning parts fall into disrepair and decrepitude, and is caused by: changing population and urban migration patterns; zoning and political district restructuring, such as highway insertions through discrete neighborhoods; political disenfranchisement; unemployment; and high crime rates. Placelessness is a geographic territory devoid of four important ingredients necessary for healthy human habitation – diversity, authenticity, meaning, and nature. According to Edward Relph, it is a less authentic attitude that is the "casual eradication of distinctive places and the making of standardized landscapes that results from insensitivity to the significance of place."[47]

Placemaking, as opposed to placelessness, is a positive outcome of biophilic design. It promotes a strong inclusion of nature, supportive spatial structure, diverse mix of uses, integrated circulation networks, pedestrian-oriented outdoor spaces, and people. Placemaking outcomes can be informed by integrating other positive outcomes. The place fosters climate-positive behaviors; sustainability; health and wellness, especially when time is spent outdoors; social interactions; and finally culturally driven numinous experiences. More specifically, overcoming loneliness, aging in place, public safety, and the potential for social interactions are potential placemaking outcomes. Identity and a sense of belonging are also positive consequences of coherent places.

The specific outcomes include an increase in place identity and stewardship, reduction of boredom and loneliness, increase in positive social interactions, nucleation with increased commercial and economic benefits, public safety and communal surveillance, decrease in crime, decreased obesity, and increased exercise. Figure 2.4 is a diagram of the placemaking effects across a place

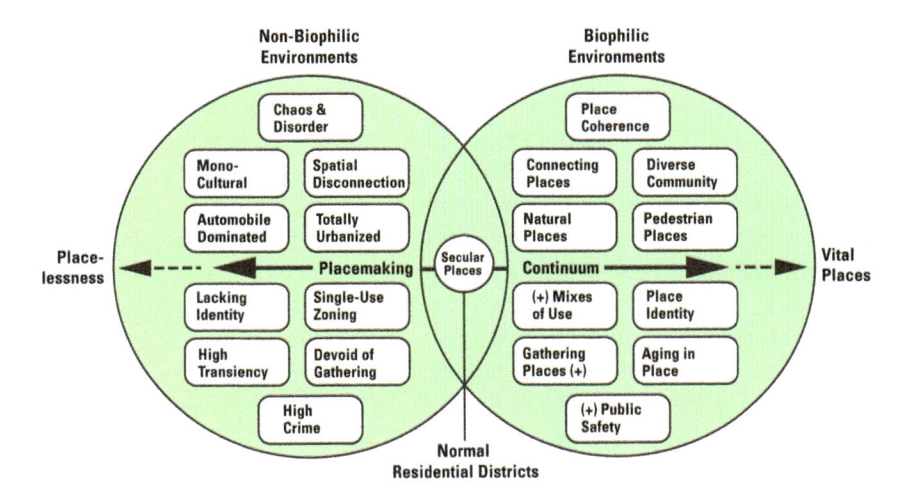

2.4
Placemaking
outcomes (*Source:
Phillip Tabb*)

continuum from placelessness to vital and alive places. The figure shows the contrast of placelessness and placemaking between non-biophilic and biophilic environments.

Research has shown that a disconnection from nature is the cause of increasing health problems: "lifestyles are increasingly characterised by sedentary behaviour, obesity problems, stress, mental ill-health and disconnection from nature."[48] Health and wellness outcomes are present largely because of the integration of the many biophilic pattern attributes, with abundant access to nature, the elements, and fellow residents. According to Halbert Dunn, *high-level wellness* is an integrated, or interrelated, process of maximizing one's potential, balance, and purposeful direction.[49] This includes complete physical, mental, and social wellbeing. High-level wellness is part of a larger wellness continuum beginning with chronic illness, to "*not sick*," and evolving to greater levels of integration and completeness. This certainly can be accomplished within supportive biophilic environments, where there are daily opportunities to connect to nature through the multiple pattern attributes.

According to Colorado State University, the health benefits of interacting with nature include decreasing stress, increasing energy, mental clarity, recovery from fatigue, and increasing hospital recovery rates. Research by Dan Buettner into "*Blue Zones*" revealed there were common lifestyle characteristics that included: stress reduction, less cigarette smoking, moderate caloric intake, moderate alcohol intake, increased social engagement, semi-vegetarian diet, moderate physical activity as an inseparable part of everyday life, and some form of spiritual engagement.[50] A blue zones are specific places in the world where population life-spans are longer than the average including high percentages of centenarians. According to the Centers for Disease Control and Prevention, similar outcomes occur with overcoming high blood pressure, choosing a healthy diet, maintaining moderate weight, engaging in physical activity, not smoking, and drinking limited amounts of alcohol. The CDC also suggests that active living communities, aging in place, and agricultural urbanism can also contribute to healthy environments.[51]

The specific outcomes include stress reduction, lower blood pressure and heart rate, improved circadian system function, and improved concentration and cognitive performance. Walking, for example, increases the flexibility and stability of joints. According to Diane E. Bowler, et al., a meta-analysis provided some evidence of the positive benefits of a walk or run in a natural environment in comparison to a synthetic environment.[52] And recent studies show that people who move to greener urban areas benefit from sustained improvements in their mental health.[53] Figure 2.5 is a diagram of the health and wellness effects across a health continuum from chronic illness to high-level wellness.

Numinous experiences occur through a variety of channels and intimate factors. The natural world is a powerful source of the numinous and sublime encounter with nature, such as viewing a sunrise or sunset, encountering a rainbow, or seeing the Northern Lights. Such experiences are likened to becoming

2.5
Health and wellness
outcomes (*Source:*
Phillip Tabb)

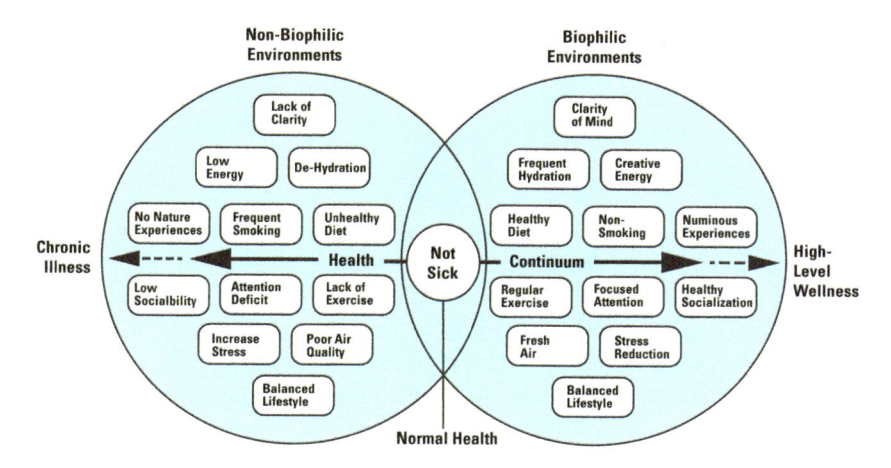

2.5
Health and wellness
outcomes (*Source:*
Phillip Tabb)

aware of a presence that is usually beyond normal perception. Breezes in the trees, light reflecting off of ripples in a river or waves in the ocean, the smell of freshly turned earth, the ebb and flow of the tides, or seeing a wild animal in its native habitat slow time down and create a heightened presence. Numinous experiences can occur within the built environment as well, facilitated by extraordinary architecture, ceremonies and culturally derived events, or through experiences of the arts.

Rudolf Otto divided the numinous experience into three interrelated qualities: the fascinating (*fascinans*) and exuberance; the mysterious (*mysterium*) –that which is hidden from view or knowledge; and the awe-ful (*tremendum*) – that which is fear-inspiring.[54] Some references to awe suggest the complex combination of both fear and reverence. Awe could be likened to Maslow's "*peak experience*" or Russel and Feldman's "*core effect*."[55] Fear is defined by the terrifying sublime, horror, and melancholy. Fear could also be interpreted as an awakening and experience of the vital energies of a place. Emotional responses vary, from pleasant to unpleasant, and arousal from low to high.

In his chapter in *The Idea of the Numinous*, Lionel Corbett identified the four characteristics explained by William James,[56] which describe the biophilic outcomes of the numinous. These transformative experiences: (1) are ineffable – they defy the normal expression of ordinary conceptual language; (2) have noetic and cognitive content – they produce an overwhelming sense of clarity; (3) are transient – usually less than a half hour, but rarely more than a few hours; and (4) produce positive affects – as in being in the grip of a superior power, which can produce healing.

The specific outcomes include stress reduction, increased of presence, positive emotional responses, improved attention and mental alertness, increased opportunities for enhanced perception, becoming more present, insight and spiritual awareness, and feelings of the sublime. Temporal density, for example, is a common characteristic of contemporary culture, which manifests by internalizing too many activities, tasks, ideas, feelings, and considerations in any given moment.[57] The result creates stress. Temporal density can be reduced or eliminated with numinous experiences. The numinous can be elicited by many other experiences as well, such as the performing and visual arts or architecture, and ceremonial experiences.

According to John Carroll, the changeover to an ecological way of living requires a conversion away from the dominant paradigm or value system of our culture to systems that safeguard and realize the regenerative capacities of our natural resources.[58] Through the experience of the numinous, a renewed, reverent, and elevated appreciation of nature occurs. And Carroll goes on to suggest that the conscious development of a sense of connectedness, wholeness, and the cultivation of awe and wonder will further strengthen the principle of right livelihood. First comes sensitivity to the inherent problems and an appreciation of and desire for this right livelihood. Second comes the development of strategies, best practices, and methods designed to realize the most effective planning and design approaches for both new and existing settings. Figure 2.6 is a diagram of the numinous effects across a continuum from profane to charged experiences of awe and the insightful.

The rapid emergence of the Coronavirus has been alarming, and so appropriate mitigation strategies are evolving along with it. Biophilic urbanism can influence health and wellness in every aspect of human life, including specific diseases like Coronavirus. Public health's history reveals the rise of modern city planning around issues raised by infectious diseases, such as cholera, yellow fever, and tuberculosis. Mediation measures to reduce the conduit of spread included the redesign of spatial systems, streets, infrastructure, and sanitation (water and sewage); and the re-evaluation of density. Urban parks emerged as a remediating strategy. Recent research has shown that exercising and contact with nature will reduce stress caused by sheltering-in-place.[59] Varying elements and building types will require differing design approaches. COVID-19 mitigating strategies should occur at three scales: (1) limiting person-to-person transmission

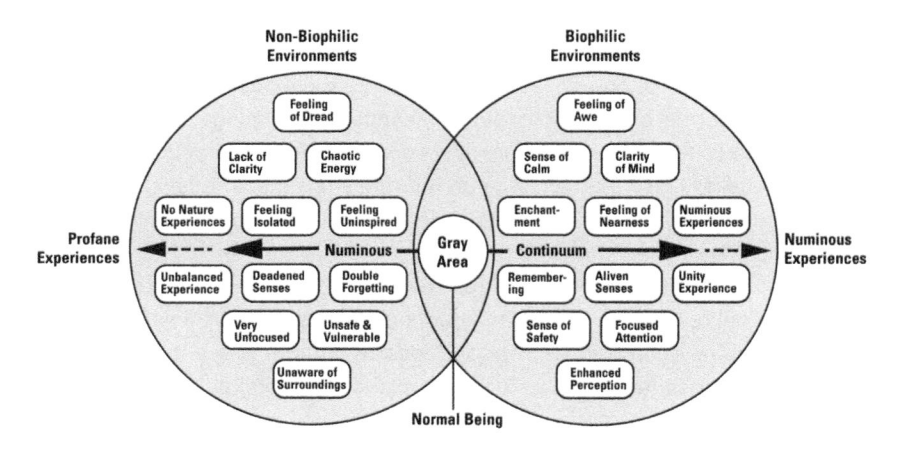

2.6
Numinous
outcomes (*Source:
Phillip Tabb*)

through social distancing and sanitation protocols, (2) community suppression through suspension of mass gatherings and the isolation of high-risk settings, and (3) regional risk reduction by limiting public transportation and place-to-place travel. With COVID-19, the value versus the risks of densification are central to the discussion on urban growth for long-term survival in a pandemic world. This includes decentralizion and spatially accessible distribution of essential services, redefining proximity through technology, and constellating peri-urban areas.

Certain populations are more vulnerable to the disease, including men, adults aged 65 years and older, those predisposed to become ill because of underlying medical conditions, and those living together in confined quarters. According to Jamelle Bouis, African Americans are also vulnerable to the spread of the disease because they are overrepresented in service sector jobs, are more likely to use public transportation to commute to work, and live in denser housing conditions where they are more susceptible to constant human contact.[60] Specific CDC guidelines were distributed to the public in May 2020, and other individuals and businesses have published additional recommendations mainly targeting the planning and design professions. Figure 2.7 shows a street used for social interaction at safe distances. Spatial design measures to reduce significant and moderate spread of the Coronavirus include the following at the building and community scales.

Building Scale

- Homebound living creates the need for the provision of sanctuary spaces for all members of the household, particularly those who telework, zoom meetings, and participate in e-learning.
- Buffer or transition spaces are needed as an interface between visitors and deliveries.
- Providing temporary storage places for deliveries at the door.

2.7
Social distancing
(*Source:
Shutterstock*)

- Immediately inside the dwelling, furnish washbasin and sanitizer if possible.
- Providing sufficient outdoor spaces with access to nature and sunlight for long periods of sheltering-in-place (a plant kingdom attribute).
- Furnishing outdoor spaces with physical distancing markers to accommodate safe social interactions.
- Employing safe distancing of at least 6 feet (1.8 meters) and more depending upon the type of activity, the environment, and duration of time. A sneeze can travel as much as 25 feet (7.6 meters).
- Increasing the capacity of pantries and freezers for sheltering-in-place and self-quarantining.
- Sheltering-in-place and self-quarantining will most likely cause a greater utility demand. Provide passive survivability strategies if possible (on-site kitchen gardens and local agriculture, telecommunications, water, HVAC, and electricity).
- In workplaces, provide spatial opportunities for screening, health checks, sanitation, access to PPE, safe distancing, and isolation of symptomatic individuals.
- Businesses need to address commuting distances, although teleworking at home may eliminate or reduce the need to commute to work.
- Inside the post-pandemic workplace will be the need for health, wellness, and sanitation protocols.
- Providing physical distancing and/or barriers such as sneeze guards or partitions between people in workplaces, indoor and outdoor dining settings, classrooms, and public transport, especially buses, trams, trains, and subways.
- Providing touch-free elevators, public doors, and bathroom fixtures. While studies show that short elevator rides can have low transmission, one should always wear a mask.
- Providing workspaces with PPE cleaning, sanitizing, and disposal capabilities.
- Restaurants should provide delivery, curbside pickup, outdoor physical distancing, and reduced occupancy. Ample supplies of soap and hand sanitizers should be provided in restrooms, and possibly disinfectant spray machines at entrances that sanitize customers before entering. Dining will occur both indoors and outdoors.
- In congregate care facilities, practice every day preventative actions, continuously provide prevention supplies, plan for staff absenteeism, and create isolated places for high-risk residents.
- Improve building air-handling systems to help dissipate aerosols containing Coronavirus droplets by natural ventilation, particle filtration, and UV disinfectant applied to microorganisms.

Community Scale
- Sidewalks should be planned to be wider for safer social distancing, with trees for shading and landscapes for viewing.
- Restructuring public spaces (parks, plazas, promenades, streets, superblocks, and sidewalks) with social distancing markers, prospect and refuge, spatially

separated activity nodes, outdoor dining, natural landscaping, and sanitation protocols.

- Places with larger population densities, such as congregate care, nursing homes and assisted living sites, should provide appropriate safeguards, social distancing, sanitation protocols, and lockdown capabilities, if required.
- In places with tight spaces, such as elevators, entrances, waiting rooms, buses, trams, and airplanes, limit occupancy numbers for safe physical distancing.
- For grocery shopping, use safety precautions when ordering deliveries, reduce shopping trips to grocery stores, and at grocery stores wear masks and gloves, and observe safe distancing and sanitation protocols before and after shopping.[6]
- Faith-based mitigation measures include limiting gathering size, providing outdoor services, marking for physical distancing, and sanitation protocols in restrooms.
- Large-gathering venues, such as sports events, movie theaters, performing arts facilities, or places of worship, should operate only under strict physical distancing protocols.
- Over time, planning should occur for ICU capacities with adequate beds, and ventilators.
- In communities or regions experiencing hotspots, isolate and implement facilities for screening, testing, contact tracing, quarantining, and treatment, and possibly provide a *cordon sanitaire* – a bounding and containment attribute.
- Planning for adaptive reuse and repurposing of existing facilities for COVID-19 patients during epidemic surges, and facilitating rapid-response capabilities for critical equipment and supplies.
- Planning for modular construction and rapidly assembled structures for hospital overloads.
- Creating land-use reforms and pathogen ecology to target the sources of the viruses to reduce risk of pathogen transmission from animals to humans.[61]
- Focusing on in-place and non-motorized connectivity and reduction of between-place transportation, especially between epidemic hotspots.
- Providing travel restrictions, including reduced fights and public transport, and route restrictions, without compromising essential services.
- Poly-nucleation as a planning-scale form of social distancing and passive survivability concept.
- Regionally planning for a network of peri-urban areas with integrated essential services, reducing the need to travel long distances (a systemic constellating urbanism attribute).

The impact of infectious diseases is not new, yet the Coronavirus has presented new challenges in a highly connected global community. It is the intent of this work not only to feature the biophilic attributes in facilitating the five positive outcome categories, but also to include biophilic connections to COVID-19, where applicable. Biophilic urbanism design principles can be experienced on multiple levels. Daily self-care practices and maintenance of physical, mental, social, and spiritual wellness can contribute to navigating through sheltering and quarantining. The spatial structure of architectural and urban spaces can reflect safe distancing modes of mobility. What is demonstrated with each of the case studies that follow is a multi-layered, fully integrated approach to biophilic design that goes beyond what is possible at the single-building scale.

As previously explained, biophilic measures can reduce stress and anxiety and strengthen the immune system during episodes of a pandemic and sheltering-in-place. They involve various levels of interaction with nature and place. They include viewing landscape surroundings, local animals, and natural light, and having direct access to moving water, fresh air, and natural sounds. A safe sense of refuge and prospect are also important. Having fresh food that is locally grown or safely delivered over extended periods of time will contribute to health and wellbeing. Lastly, having safe social interactions with family, neighbors, and friends is desirable. According to Harvard Medical School, ways to boost the immune system include healthy diet, exercise, adequate sleep, and stress reduction – all biophilic outcomes.

With biophilic urbanism, design principles can be experienced on multiple levels. It is the intent of this work to feature the biophilic attributes in facilitating *climate-positive* residential development, maximizing *carbon sequestration*, achieving *true sustainability*, attaining *high-level wellness,* creating closer *connections to nature*, developing a *deeper sense of grace*, and responding to *infectious diseases*. What is demonstrated in each of the precedents and case study that follow is a multi-layered, fully integrated approach to biophilic design that goes beyond what is possible at the single-building scale. It is the scalar integration of the combined pattern attribute categories – nature, element, form, place, and numinous – that affords the greatest success.

Outcome Research Sources

Biophilic outcomes derive from many research and academic sources in the fields of climate change, sustainability, place and placemaking, health and wellness, and the numinous. It is the function of this section to direct the outcome finding of this work to the source of scientific and academic research, scholarly articles, and seminal publications behind the selected outcomes. For full referencing, refer to the notes at the end of this chapter.

Climate-Positive Outcomes

- Carbon sequestering – NIH (2020)[62]
- Afforestation/reforestation/carbon farming – Mary Hoff (2017)[63]
- Greenhouse gas reductions – NIH (2019)[64]
- Climate resiliency – C.S. Holling (2009)[65]
- Climatic design – Victor Olgyay (1963)[66]

Sustainability Outcomes

- Energy conservation – Department of Energy[67]
- Utilization of renewable energy – NIH (2019)[68]
- True sustainability – John Ehrenfeld (2008)[69]
- Transportation use reductions – C2ES (1998)[70]
- Water–waste – Nancy Jack Todd and John Todd (1993)[71]
- Site planning for solar access – US Department of Housing and Urban Development (1980)[72]
- Passive survivability – Alex Wilson (2005)[73]
- Sustainable materials – McDonnough and Braungart (2002)[74]
- Embodied energy – David Benjamin (2018)[75]

Placemaking Outcomes

- Central place theory – Walter Christaller (1923)[76]
- Place identity – Perkins and Thorns (2012)[77]
- Overcoming placelessness – Edward Relph (1984)[78]
- Community building – Robert Putnam (2000)[79]
- Genius loci – Christian Norberg-Schultz (1984)[80]
- Pedestrianization – Chris van Uffelen (2015)[81]

Health and Wellness Outcomes

- Nature-deficit disorder – Richard Louv (2008)[82]
- Stress reduction – Brown, Barton, and Gladwell (2013)[83]
- Cognitive activity – Valtchanov and Ellard (2015)[84]
- Health effects of physical activity – Warburton, Nicol, and Bredin (2006)[85]
- Walking in nature – Barton, Hine, and Pretty (2008)[48]
- Physiological effects of wood – Ikei, Song, and Miyazki (2016)[86]
- Increased health recovery times – Roger Ulrich (1984)[87]
- High-level wellness – Halbert L. Dunn (1971)[88]
- Immune function – Harvard Health Publishing[89]
- Mood enhancement – Bower, Buyung-Ali, Knight, and Pullin (2010)[90]
- Responses to COVID-19 – Prem Chandavarkar (2020),[91] and CDC (2020)[92]

Numinous Outcomes

- Reduction of temporal density – John Steele (1985)[93]
- Euphoric and numinous experiences – Lionel Corbett (2006)[94]
- Insights and understandings – Rudolf Otto (1950)[95]
- Thin places – Edward William Soja (1996)[96]
- Charged places – Michael Brill (1985)[97]
- Spirit of place – Mircea Iliade (1959) and Belden Lane (2001)[98]
- Awe and inspiring energy – Bethelmy and Corraliza (2019)[99]

In Part 2, which follows, Chapters 3 to 8 present six biophilic urbanism precedents that illustrate the application of the biophilic principles and key patterns attributes.

They increase in scale from a small fortress to an island city. They are: (1) Castello di Gargonza – a medieval fortified castle-village turned into a hospitality retreat; (2) Google Headquarters, Mountainview, California – Googleplex (an existing campus) and Charleston East (a new biophilic mixed-use workplace); (3) Helsinge Haveby, Denmark – a regenerative net-zero planning concept now being realized; (4) Kronsberg District, Germany – a district planned for the European Expo 2000, addressing sustainability and housing shortages; (5) Pontevedra city center, Spain – a pedestrian car-free city center supporting biophilia; and (6) Singapore Park Connector Network – a continuous 186 miles (300 kilometer) green corridor that encircles the city and connects park neighborhoods.

NOTES

1. Phillip James Tabb, *Serene Urbanism: A Biophilic Theory and Practice of Sustainable Placemaking* (London, UK: Routledge, 2015). p 61.
2. Lionel Corbett, "Varieties of numinous experiences: the experience of the sacred I the therapeutic process," in Ann Casement and David Tacey (eds.) *The Idea of the Numinous: Contemporary Jungian and Psychoanalytic Perspectives* (London, UK: Routledge, 2006). pp 53–55.
3. Constantinos Doxiadis, *Ekistics: An Introduction to the Science of Human Settlement* (London, UK: Hutchinson & Company, 1968).
4. Christopher Alexander, Sara Ishikacca, and Murry Silverstein, *A Pattern Language: Towns, Buildings, Construction* (New York, NY: Oxford University Press, 1977).
5. Michael Brill, *Using the Place-Creation Myth to Develop Design Guidelines of Sacred Space* (Champagne-Urbana, IL: Council of Educators in Landscape Architecture, 1985).
6. Michael Brill, *The Mythic Consciousness as the Eternal Mother of Place-Creation* (Buffalo, NY: BOSTI, 1986). This work was done with a two-year National Endowment of the Arts grant.
7. Stephen R. Kellert, Judith H. Heerwagen, and Martin Mador, *Biophilic Design: The Theory, Science, and Practice of Bringing Building to Life* (New York, NY: John Wiley & Sons, Inc., 2008).
8. Timothy Beatley, *Biophilic Cities: Integrating Nature into Urban Design and Planning* (Washington, D.C.: Island Press, 2011).
9. Terrapin Bright Green, *14 Patterns of Biophilic Design: Improving Health and Wellbeing in the Environment* (online: https://www.terrapinbrightgreen.com/reports/14-patterns/, 2014).
10. Phillip Tabb, *Serene Urbanism: A Biophilic Theory and Practice of Sustainable Placemaking* (London, UK: Routledge, 2015). pp 214–216.
11. Mark Holland and Janine de la Salle, *Agricultural Urbanism: Handbook for Building Sustainable Food & Agriculture Systems in 21st Century* (Winnipeg, Canada: Green Frigate Books, 2010).
12. Prem Chandavarkar, *The Corvid Pandemic: Seven Lessons to be Learned for a Future* https://medium.com/@premckar/the-covid-pandemic-seven-lessons-to-be-learned-for-a-future-81792f7f175 (accessed May 4, 2020).
13. Center for Disease Control, About Pets & People https://www.cdc.gov/healthypets/health-benefits/index.html (accessed May 2, 2020).
14. Jane Jacobs, *The Life and Death of Great American Cities* (New York, NY: Vintage, 1992).

15. John Steele, *Geomancy: Consciousness and Sacred Sites* (New York, NY: Trigon Communications, 1985).
16. Haleh Moghaddasi and Phillip James Tabb, material discussed together while I was Chair of her PhD committee at Texas A&M University, 2018–2019 for research in the area of net-zero developments.
17. Abby Phon, "10 Reasons Why You Should Drink More Water," https://abbyphon.com/10-reasons-drink-water/ (accessed January 22, 2020).
18. Phillip James Tabb, *Celestial Moments in Architecture: The StarHouse* (Trinity College, University of Toronto: ACS6 Symposium, 2014).
19. David Malin, *The Invisible Universe* (New York, NY: Bullfinch Press, 1999).
20. Jay Appleton, *The Experience of Landscape* (New York, NY: John Wiley & Son, Inc., 1975).
21. Konrad Lorenz, *King Solomon's Ring* (London: Methuen, 1964).
22. Stephen R. Kellert, Judith H. Heerwagen, and Martin Mador, *Biophilic Design: The Theory, Science, and Practice of Bringing Building to Life* (New York City, NY: John Wiley & Sons, Inc., 2008).
23. Stan Allen and Marc McQuade (eds.), *Landform Building: Architecture's New Terrain* (Baden, Switzerland: Lars Müller Publishers, 2011).
24. Serge Chermayeff, *Community and Privacy Toward a New Architecture of Humanism* (New York City, NY: Doubleday Publishers, 1963).
25. Gordon H. Orians and Judith H. Heerwagen, "Evolved Responses to Landscapes," in Jerome H. Barlow, Leda Cosmides, and John Tooby (eds.) *The Adapted Mind: Evolutionary Psychology and the Generation of Culture* (New York, NY: Oxford University Press, 1992). p 560.
26. Mircea Eliade, *The Sacred and the Profane: The Nature of Religion* (Orlando, FL: Harcourt Brace, 1959). p 11.
27. Michael Brill, *The Mythic Consciousness as the Eternal Mother of Place-Creation* (Buffalo, NY: BOSTI, 1986).
28. Terrapin Bright Green, *14 Patterns of Biophilic Design: Improving Health and Wellbeing in the Environment* (online: https://www.terrapinbrightgreen.com/reports/14-patterns/, 2014) (accessed December 15, 2019).
29. Christopher Alexander, Sara Ishikacca, and Murry Silverstein, *A Pattern Language: Towns, Buildings, Construction* (New York, NY: Oxford University Press, 1977).
30. Michael Pawlyn, *Biomimicry in Architecture* (London: RIBA Publishing, 2011).
31. Robert Putnam, *Bowling Alone: The Collapse and Revival of American Community* (New York, NY: Simon & Schuster, 2000).
32. Heather K. Stuckey, DEd and Jeremy Nobel, MD, MPH, *The Connection Between Art, Healing, and Public Health: A Review of Current Literature* https://www.ncbi.nlm.nih.gov/pmc/articles/PMC2804629/#bib2 (accessed March 10, 2020).
33. Roger Shepard, "Perceptual Organization of Colors: An Adaptation to Regularities of the Terrestrial World?" in Jerome H. Barlow, Leda Cosmides, and John Tooby (eds.) *The Adapted Mind: Evolutionary Psychology and the Generation of Culture* (New York, NY: Oxford University Press, 1992). p 496.
34. Christopher Day, *Places of the Soul: Architecture and Environmental Design as a Healing Art* (Wellingborough, UK: The Aquarian Press, 1990).
35. John Lobell, *Between Silence and Light: Spirit in the Architecture of Louis I. Kahn* (Boulder, CO: Shambala Publications, Inc., 1979).
36. Rudolf Otto, *The Idea of the Holy* (Oxford: Oxford University Press, 1950). p 5.
37. Lionel Corbett, "Varieties of numinous experiences: the experience of the sacred in the therapeutic process," in Ann Casement and David Tacey (eds.) *The Idea of the Numinous: Contemporary Jungian and Psychoanalytic Perspectives* (London, UK: Routledge, 2006). p 54.

38. Edward W. Soja, *Thirdspace* (Malden, MA.: Blackwell, 1996).
39. Mircea Eliade, *The Sacred and the Profane: The Nature of Religion* (Orlando, FL: Harcourt Brace, 1959). p 11.
40. Ralph Knowles, *Sun Rhythm Form* (Cambridge, MA: MIT Press, 1981).
41. Julia Africa and Judith Heerwagen, *Loftness and Balagras, Biophilic Design and Climate Change: Performance Parameters for Health* (2019) https://www.researchgate.net/publication/331883116_Biophilic_Design_and_Climate_Change_Performance_Parameters_for_Health (accessed February 14, 2020).
42. Britt Wray, *How Climate Change Affects Your Mental Health* (TED Talk 2019), https://www.ted.com/talks/britt_wray_how_climate_change_affects_your_mental_health/footnotes (accessed April 24, 2020).
43. Haleh Moghaddasi and Phillip James Tabb, material discussed together while I was Chair of her PhD committee at Texas A&M University, 2018–2019 for research in the area of net-zero developments.
44. John R. Ehrenfeld, *Sustainability by Design* (New Haven, CT: Yale University Press, 2008). pp 175 and 178.
45. Susan Owens, *Energy Planning and Urban Form* (London: Pion, 1986).
46. Alex Wilson, Passive Survivability: A new Design Criterion for Buildings https://www.buildinggreen.com/feature/passive-survivability-new-design-criterion-buildings (accessed January 12, 2020).
47. Edward Relph, *Place and Placelessness* (London: Pion Ltd., 1984).
48. Joanna Barton, Rachel Hine and Jules Pretty, *The health benefits of walking in greenspaces of high natural heritage* value https://www.tandfonline.com/doi/full/10.1080/19438150903378425 (accessed January 12, 2020).
49. Halbert L. Dunn, *High Level Wellness* (Arlington, VA: Beatty, 1971).
50. Dan Buettner, *The Blue Zones: 9 Lessons Learned from the People Who've Lived the Longest*, 2nd edition (Washington, DC: National Geographic, 2012).
51. Center for Disease Control, *Evidence Summary: Control High Blood Pressure*, https://www.cdc.gov/sixeighteen/bloodpressure/index.htm (accessed March 21, 2020).
52. Diane E. Bowler, Lisette M. Buyung-Ali, Teri M. Knight, and Andrew S. Pullin, 2010 https://bmcpublichealth.biomedcentral.com/articles/10.1186/1471-2458-10-456?dom=prime&src=syn (accessed February 13, 2020).
53. Ian Alcock, Mathew White, Benedict Wheeler, Lora Fleming, and Michael Depledge, *Longitudinal effects on mental health of moving to greener and less green urban areas* https://pubs.acs.org/doi/abs/10.1021/es403688w?cookieSet=1 (accessed January 12, 2020).
54. Rudolf Otto, *The Idea of the Holy* (Oxford: Oxford University Press, 1950). p 5.
55. Lionel Corbett, "Varieties of numinous experiences: the experience of the sacred I the therapeutic process" in Ann Casement and David Tacey (eds.) *The Idea of the Numinous: Contemporary Jungian and Psychoanalytic Perspectives* (London: Routledge, 2006). p 54.
56. Lisbeth C. Bethelmy and Jose A. Corraliza, *Transcendence and Sublime Experience in Nature: Awe and Inspiring Energy* https://www.ncbi.nlm.nih.gov/pmc/articles/PMC6424873/#!po=70.4545 (accessed August 6, 2020).
57. Phillip James Tabb, *Elemental Architecture: Temperaments of Sustainability* (London: Routledge, 2019). p 118.
58. John E. Carrol, *Sustainability and Spirituality* (Albany, NY: State University of New York Press, 2004).
59. Jared Green, *Amid the COVID-19 Pandemic, Take Time to Reconnect with Nature* https://dirt.asla.org/2020/03/20/amid-the-covid-19-pandemic-take-time-to-reconnect-with-nature/ (accessed June 10, 2020).

60. Jamelle Bouel, *Why Coronavirus is Killing African-Americans More Than Others* https://www.nytimes.com/2020/04/14/opinion/sunday/coronavirus-racism-african-americans.html (accessed June 2, 2020).

61. *'Major gaps' in understanding how land-use changes affect spread of diseases*, University of Exeter, June 3, 2020 https://www.sciencedaily.com/releases/2020/06/200603100519.htm (accessed July 3, 2020).

62. Mary Hoff, *To Avoid Climate Catastrophe, We'll Need to Remove CO2 from the Air: Here's How*, https://ensia.com/features/sequestration/ (accessed January 14, 2020).

63. Qian Xu, Yuxiang Dong, and Ren Yang, *Influence of different geographical factors on carbon sink functions in the Pearl river Delta*, https://www.ncbi.nlm.nih.gov/pmc/articles/PMC5427894/ (accessed March 19, 2020).

64. National Institute of Health, *Greenhouse Gas (GHG) Reduction*, https://nems.nih.gov/sustain/Pages/Greenhouse-Gas-Reduction.aspx (accessed January 14, 2020).

65. Lance Gunderson, Craig Allen, and C.S. Holling (eds.), *Foundations of Ecological Resilience* (Washington, DC: Island Press, 2009).

66. Victor Olgyay, *Design with Climate: Bioclimatic Approach to Architectural Regionalism* (Princeton, NJ: Princeton University Press, 1963).

67. Department of Energy, Energy Savings Performance Contract ENABLE Energy Conservation Measures, https://www.energy.gov/eere/femp/energy-savings-performance-contract-enable-energy-conservation-measures (accessed February 5, 2020).

68. National Institute of Health, *Clean and Renewable Energy*, https://nems.nih.gov/sustain/Pages/Clean-and-Renewable-Energy.aspx (accessed January 14, 2020).

69. John R. Ehrenfeld, *Sustainability by Design* (New Haven, CT: Yale University Press, 2008). pp 175 and 178.

70. Center for Climate and Energy solutions (C2CS), *Reducing Your Transportation Footprint* https://www.c2es.org/content/reducing-your-transportation-footprint/ (accessed March 10, 2020).

71. Nancy Jack Todd and John Todd, *From Eco-Cities to Living Machines* (Berkeley, CA: North Atlantic Books, 1993).

72. US Department of Housing and Urban Development, *Site Planning For Solar Access: Guidelines for Residential Developers and site Planners* (Washington, DC: US Government Printing Office, 1980).

73. Alex Wilson, *Passive Survivability: A New Design Criterion for Buildings* https://www.buildinggreen.com/feature/passive-survivability-new-design-criterion-buildings (accessed January 12, 2020).

74. William McDonnough and Michael Braungart, *Cradle to Cradle: Remaking the Way We Make Things* (New York, NY: North Point Press, 2002).

75. David Benjamin, *Embodied Energy and Design: Making Architecture Between Metrics and Narratives* (Zurich: Lars Muller Publishers, 2018).

76. *Central Place Theory by Walter Christaller*, 1933 https://planningtank.com/settlement-geography/central-place-theory-walter-christaller (accessed February 13, 2020).

77. Harvey Perkins and David Thorns, *Place, Identity and Everyday Life in a Globalizing World* (New York, NY: Palgrave Publishers, 2012).

78. Edward Relph, *Place and Placelessness* (London: Pion Ltd., 1984).

79. Robert Putnam, *Bowling Alone: The Collapse and Revival of American Community* (New York, NY: Simon & Schuster, 2000).

80. Christian Norberg-Schultz, *Genius Loci: Towards a Phenomenology of Architecture* (New York, NY: Rizzoli, 1980).

81. Chris van Effelen, *Pedestrianization Zone: Car-Free Urban Spaces* (Salenstein: Braun Publishing AG, 2015).

82. Richard Louv, *Last Child in the Woods: Saving Our Children From Nature-Deficit Disorder* (New York, NY: Algonquin Books, 2008).

83. Daniel Brown, Jo Barton, and Valerie Gladwell, *Viewing Nature Scenes Positively Affects Recovery of Autonomic Function Following Acute-Mental Stress* https://www.ncbi.nlm.nih.gov/pmc/articles/PMC3699874/ (accessed March 12, 2020).

84. Deltcho Valtchanov and Colin Ellard, Cognitive and affective responses to natural scenes: Effects of low level visual properties on preference, "Cognitive load and eye-movements," https://www.sciencedirect.com/science/article/abs/pii/S0272494415300220 (accessed January 12, 2020).

85. Darren E.R. Warburton, Crystal Whitney Nicol, and Shannon S.D. Bredin, *Health benefits of physical activity: the evidence* https://www.ncbi.nlm.nih.gov/pmc/articles/PMC1402378/#__ffn_sectitle (accessed January 12, 2020).

86. Haumi Ikei, Chorong Song, and Yoshifumi Miyazaki, *Physiological effects of wood on humans: a review*. Online publication, 2016: https://jwoodscience.springeropen.com/track/pdf/10.1007/s10086-016-1597-9 (accessed December 10, 2019).

87. Daniel Brown, Jo Barton, and Valerie Gladwell, *Viewing Nature Scenes Positively Affects Recovery of Autonomic Function Following Acute-Mental Stress* https://www.ncbi.nlm.nih.gov/pmc/articles/PMC3699874/ (accessed March 12, 2020).

88. Halbert L. Dunn, *High Level Wellness* (Arlington, VA: Beatty, 1971).

89. John Steele, *Geomancy: Consciousness and Sacred Sites* (New York, NY: Trigon Communications, Inc., 1985).

90. Harvard Health Publishing, *How to boost your immune system* https://www.health.harvard.edu/staying-healthy/how-to-boost-your-immune-system (accessed March 21, 2020).

91. Prem Chandavarkar, *The Covid Pandemic: Seven Lessons to be Learned for a Future* https://medium.com/@premckar/the-covid-pandemic-seven-lessons-to-be-learned-for-a-future-81792f7f175 (accessed May 4, 2020).

92. Center for Disease Control, *Guidelines for Opening Up America Again* https://assets.documentcloud.org/documents/6889330/Guidance-for-Opening-Up-America-Again-Framework.pdf (accessed May 22, 2020).

93. Diana Bower, Lisette Buyung-Ali, Teri Knight, and Andrew Pullin, *A Systematic Review of Evidence for the Added Benefits to Health of Exposure to Natural Environments* (2010), https://bmcpublichealth.biomedcentral.com/articles/10.1s186/1471-2458-10-456 (accessed January 13, 2020).

94. Lionel Corbett, "Varieties of numinous experiences: the experience of the sacred I the therapeutic process," in Ann Casement and David Tacey (eds.) *The Idea of the Numinous: Contemporary Jungian and Psychoanalytic Perspectives* (London: Routledge, 2006).

95. Rudolf Otto, *The Idea of the Holy* (Oxford: Oxford University Press, 1950).

96. Edward W. Soja, *Thirdspace* (Malden, MA.: Blackwell, 1996).

97. Michael Brill, *Using the Place-Creation Myth to Develop Design Guidelines of Sacred Space* (Champagne-Urbana, IL: Council of Educators in Landscape Architecture, 1985).

98. Christian Norberg-Schultz, Genius Loci: Towards a Phenomenology of Architecture (New York, NY: Rizzoli, 1980). *Belden Lane, Landscapes of the Sacred: Geography and Narrative in American Spirituality* (Baltimore, MD: Johns Hopkins University, 2001).

99. Lisbeth Bethelmy and Jose Corraliza, *Transcendence and Sublime Experiences in Nature: Awe and Inspiring Energy* https://www.researchgate.net/publication/331712038_Transcendence_and_Sublime_Experience_in_Nature_Awe_and_Inspiring_Energy (accessed January 14, 2020).

Part 2 PRECEDENTS

PRECEDENT STUDIES

It is important to view the biophilic principles and pattern attributes as actionable planning and design guidelines represented within actual demonstration projects. To do so, six precedents are explored worldwide in Italy, the United States, Denmark, Germany, Spain, and the Republic of Singapore. They provide varying examples and contexts, each with the integration of differing sets of pattern attributes and intended outcomes. Some represent completely new construction, while others are insertions into existing urban environments. Some focus on residential development, others focus on commercial, destination resort, or recreational uses. This work does not address larger cities and metropolitan areas; it features more manageable community-sized examples. The structure of the analysis begins with backgrounds and descriptions of the design, followed by an explanation of the most prevalent pattern attributes, and ends with associated positive outcomes.

The purpose of the analysis of the six precedents is to explain projects worldwide that clearly demonstrate effective biophilic strategies. Each has unique planning and design measures that contribute to its success. Taken together, they present a comprehensive set of guidelines and measures suggesting a combinatory effect and full range of designs informing Biophilic Urbanism. The exploration of each of the precedents will contain the location, history, main features of the project, a land use program summary, an analysis of the masterplan or site plan, the articulation and listing of the primary biophilic pattern attributes, and a summary of their positive outcomes. Outcomes have been obtained through "actualistic" observations, literature searches, and masterplan analyses. The six precedents are as follows:

- *Castello di Gargonza* – A 13th-century historic and car-free fortified hamlet in Tuscany, Italy is revitalized into a hospitality destination.
- *Google Headquarters* – The existing and a new facility under construction in Charleston East, California include progressive work environments and an innovative biophilic biome.
- *Helsinge Haveby village* – A biophilic neighborhood cluster concept being realized in Helsinge, Denmark is based on regenerative concepts of biophilic urbanism applied to an agrihood.

- *Kronsberg District* – The Expo 2000 Kronsberg District in Hannover, Germany is oriented toward sustainability and to address Hannover's affordable housing shortage.
- *Pontevedra city center* – A vibrant automobile-free historic city center in Pontevedra, Spain contains biophilic features and pedestrianization.
- *Park Connector Neighborhood, Singapore* – 186 miles (300 kilometers) of park connectors and park neighborhoods existing throughout the island city of Singapore.

3 CASTELLO DI GARGONZA

CASTELLO DI GARGONZA

Background and History

About 16 miles (25 kilometers) from Cortona, Italy as the crow flies, and a great deal further by car, is the little *borgo* of Gargonza, just up the secluded Apennine hill from Monte San Savino. More as a castle whose walls contain a perfectly preserved 13th-century hamlet, Castello di Gargonza is a 1,235-acre (500-hectare) estate that has a dominating prospect above the Val di Chiana from the center of its wooded site.[1] It was known as an agricultural community dedicated to cultivating the forest as well as wool production. Later it became a share-croppers' farm with 33 farmers' homes. It was also an outpost settlement a day's horseback ride from Siena. The hamlet had a parish church, school, olive oil mill, stables, and bread ovens. It is reported that due to a shift in power Dante Alighieri and other Florentine exiles fled to the hamlet in about 1302 in the wake of the trouble between the Guelphs and the Ghibellines.[2] The village proper is surrounded by tapered stone walls and cypress trees.

By 1972, the castle had fallen to decay and was abandoned. It was restored by Conte Roberto Guicciardini Corsi Salviati with sensitivity toward retaining its original character and integrity. It was no longer a community of farmers, but rather a "*community of travelers*."[3] It was revitalized into a destination hospitality resort and corporate retreat that benefits from biophilic design attributes. Gargonza receives 1,800 visitors annually. The 23 tiny cell-like peasants' cottages can accommodate 80 guests, while the small inn holds another 14. The cottages and inn have now been converted into self-catering retreats and accommodate conference guests. The climate of Castello di Gargonza is temperate; temperatures are mild, typically not exceeding 85 °F, and rarely fall below freezing.[4]

Castello di Gargonza offers a swimming pool, a restaurant, and meeting rooms. They have skillfully featured and maintained the authentic character of the original antique village. Even today, the village residences consist of apartments, bed and breakfasts, and conference facilities equipped with comforts of medium- and high-level tourist facilities. They are also connected to the circuit of historical-tourist brands of Europe. The village homes maintain the names

3.1
Aerial view
of Castello di
Gargonza (*Source:
Phillip Tabb*)

of the original inhabitants: Fattore, Niccolina the seamstress, and Celso the gamekeeper.[5] The restaurant is located just outside the Gargonza village walls, near the swimming pool. Its location has views of Gargonza's woods and Val di Chiana. Surrounding the castle are walking paths and bicycle trails. The aerial view in Figure 3.1 shows the coherent village form within its wooded site.

The hamlet of Gargonza is completely car-free. Though vehicles are able to drive around the exterior of the outside walls to the main entrance for deliveries and drop-off, there are only stone and gravel footpaths inside. The central plaza is located near the northwest boundary wall and is defined by the Romanesque church of St. Tiburzio and Susanna, the castle tower, the hotel reception, and several of the attached cottages. In the center of the plaza is a small village green with stone pavers in it and surrounding a stone well. Spread throughout the village are gardens, stands of cypress trees, and green areas. There is a vegetable garden along the northeastern edge within the fortified walls, and stands of cypress trees line the southwestern side of the village. While the center of the village is quite dense, the village is generally punctuated by many varying green areas, and open spaces. Refer to Figure 3.2 for the center well below the tower.

The La Torre di Gargonza Restaurant is the crown jewel of Castello di Gargonza, open for guests of the bed and breakfast, Castello's vacation apartments, and external clients. It is family-owned and located within a separate building outside of the fortified hamlet, affording easy access to service vehicles and to visitors who only want to dine at the restaurant. The stone and wood interior has a high vaulted ceiling and the dining areas are surrounded by large windows with commanding views of the surrounding forests and hills. There

3.2
Gargonza center
well (*Source: Phillip Tabb*)

is a large protected terrace that accommodates up to 170 guests and boasts breathtaking views that are framed by the cypress trees. The menu consists of authentic traditional Tuscan cuisine and local wines.

In their book *Chambers for a Memory Palace*, architects Donlyn Lyndon and Charles Moore developed a series of what they called thoughtful architectural devices that contributed to a place's memorable qualities. They both had visited Gargonza multiple times and were familiar with its charm. These devices or themes were remarkably similar to many of the biophilic pattern attributes. In describing Gargonza they explain that the tower "takes claim to the surroundings," that the outer stone walls "circumscribe and define the territory," and that there is a "straight-arrow vista" from the plaza east to the Val di Chiana.[6] Their themes included:

- Axes that reach – Axes reach across space to connect or draw together important points within a place.
- Orchards that measure – Orchards represent orderly rows of trees, which modulate a field of space.
- Platforms that separate – Platforms form a stage, which is a space apart from a larger place.
- Borders that control – Borders distinguish inside from outside and make clear where we are and dwell.
- Openings that frame – Openings, which include passages, doorways, and gates, cultivate expectations of the places that lie beyond.
- Roofs that encompass – Roofs encompass, shed and keep the weather away, but also reflect the heavens and tell us how big the place is.

- Markers that command – Monuments, towers, obelisks, pyramids, and the like command attention and mark a center.
- Light that plays – space and form are understood in light, which clarifies them. This can clearly be seen in the aerial view in Figure 3.1.

In the center, there are seven what they call function rooms of varying sizes from 350 to 1,668 square feet (32 to 155 square meters) that host amenities for weddings, conferences, and other business or social gatherings. Originally these spaces were used as an olive mill, cellars, and stables for animals. The 23 cottages are small and vary in configuration as they were constructed organically throughout the hamlet. Today, the cottages are fully equipped with linens, blankets, towels and dishes, and open stone fireplaces. There are no dishwashers, but there is an array of culinary equipment, enough to prepare espressos and pasta and other typical meals. Walls are whitewashed plaster, floors are terracotta-tiled, and ceilings are typically exposed hewn chestnut rafters and wood decking. The exterior facades have been kept intact, as have the interiors. Cottages vary in size somewhat, from one and two bedrooms to four bedrooms. The country house just outside the walls can accommodate ten guests. From a biophilic point of view the cottages are perfect refuges, made from natural materials, having indoor–outdoor spaces, and being humanly scaled and near gardens. While the cottages do not have televisions, they do have Wi-Fi and are pet friendly. Refer to Figure 3.3 for images that depict the character and scale of the cottages. Castello di Gargonza is a good example of biophilic urbanism because it is engulfed in nature: it is completely surrounded by the commanding estate, and the nooks and crannies of its urban structure are infused with nature.

Analysis of the Masterplan

Castello di Gargonza is accessed by a single road that winds through the forest, arriving at the parking lot, drop-off, restaurant, and recreational facilities. Stone walking paths circumambulate the tapered foundation walls, which in some places are two or more stories in height. The main gate and entranceway are located on the northern side of the walled-in enclosure. The entrance leads to a small plaza

3.3
Natural materials: (a) cottage entry stair, (b) cottage covered terrace (*Source: Phillip Tabb*)

and village green with a well in the center. These are beneath the overwatch of the crenellated castle tower. The center of the village is eccentrically nucleated and located near the northern end of the hamlet. It is organized by a cobblestone rectangular grid that fragments at the perimeter allowing for a more informal serrated geometry producing intimate private terraces, courtyards, and gardens. The fortified hamlet is rather small, measuring approximately 315 by 415 feet (96 x 126 meters), and its egg- or heart-shaped form encompasses nearly 3 acres (1.2 hectares) of land within the overall forested estate. With 23 cottages, the density equates to approximately 7 du per acre (17.5 du/ha). There is a patchwork of greenery and gardens, while the perimeter is generally filed with trees and gardens. Buildings occupy only the north and northwest sides of the perimeter. From behind the boundary walls are clear views to the east and to the valley below. Refer to Figure 3.4 for an analysis of the estate and hamlet masterplan.

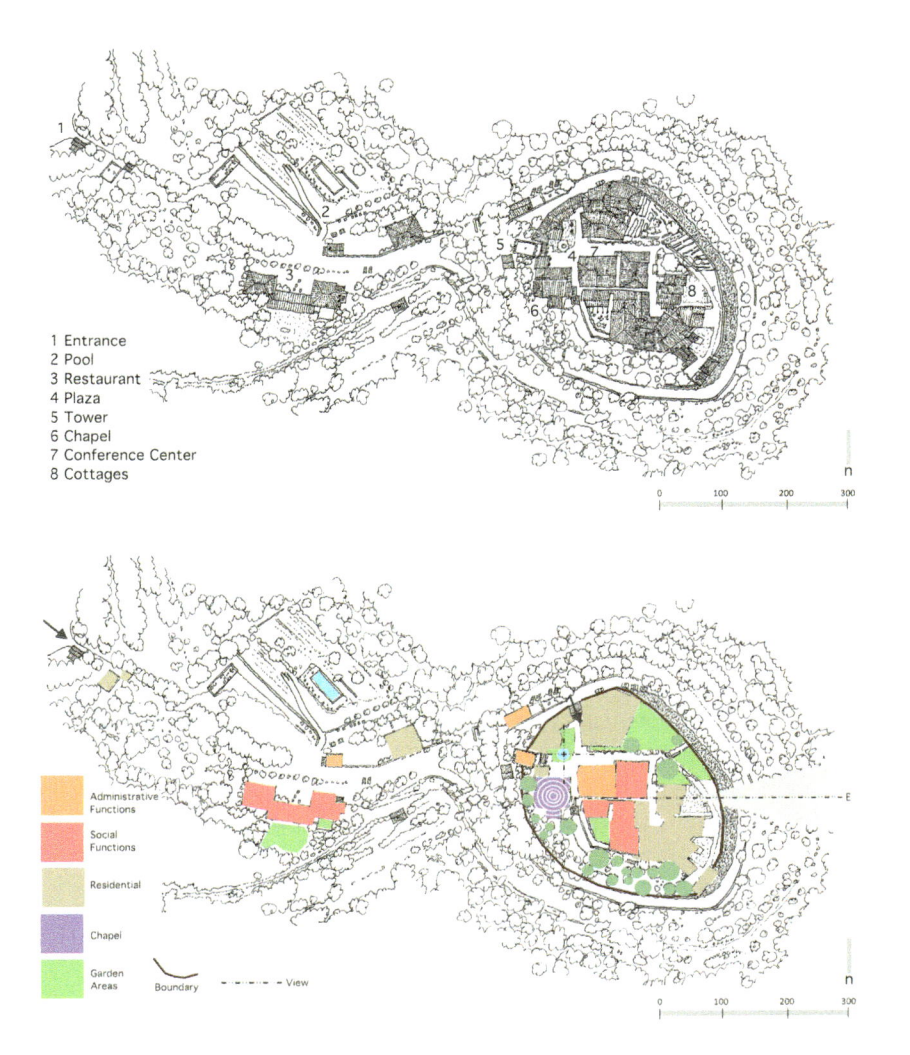

1 Entrance
2 Pool
3 Restaurant
4 Plaza
5 Tower
6 Chapel
7 Conference Center
8 Cottages

3.4
Gargonza masterplan analysis: (a) base map, (b) biophilic patterns (*Source: Phillip Tabb*)

Administrative Functions

Social Functions

Residential

Chapel

Garden Areas

Boundary

— — — — View

Primary Pattern Attributes

Since the fortified hamlet is small, it is easy to find the close-knit integration of many biophilic pattern attributes. They are completely encompassing and permeate within the site. Castello di Gargonza is a destination upon a hill surrounded by forests and has direct access to nature. There is a powerful sense of place due this hilltop location and the strong defining form of the castle walls. Castello di Gargonza integrates most of the archetypal placemaking characteristics, such as an identifiable center, differentiated boundary, clear internal spatial order, the vertical placemarker of the tower's rise, the groundedness provided by the stone tapered foundation's retaining walls, directional and prospect views, and the many nature elements within.[7] A primary objective of a hospitality destination like Castello di Gargonza is to support health and wellness outcomes in intimate, sustainable, and environmentally conscious ways. Because Gargonza is a community of travelers and hosts so many weddings, it is an indication of the numinous at play. An outline of many of the biophilic pattern attributes follows:

- The plant world within a forest (cypresses, olive trees, fig trees, lemon trees, holm oaks) and gardens.
- The cottages and hamlet are pet-friendly, woods have deer, wild boar, pheasants, local birds, and there is horseback riding nearby.
- Plentiful views and vistas of nature and dominant view of the Val di Chiana to the east.
- Sensory connections (gardens and restaurant).
- Wood-burning fireplaces within cottages.
- Earth is represented by all the stone and particularly the tapered boundary walls.
- Isolated location affords access to fresh air (car-free environment).
- Integrated water features (center well), and swimming pool.
- Prospect is to Val di Chiana and refuge within the medieval walls and cottages.
- Encouraging indoor–outdoor activities, outdoor rooms, patios, balconies.
- Spatial structure is contained and fortified, with an internal rectangular grid.
- Eccentric centering occurs with the main plaza, chapel, and tower.
- Bounding characteristics are strong, with the completely surrounding fortified medieval stone wall.
- The fortified hamlet is oriented to the east toward views of the Val di Chiana.
- The topography slopes downhill around castle walls, with flat terrain within the walls.
- Native natural materials (stone, brick, stucco, chestnut wood, tile).
- Form language is medieval with touches of the newly acquired contemporary, and it is highly integrated and place-oriented.
- Community and work-related (conference center) cultural and social activities.

- Integration of art and woodcraft, artists in residency program, and the ecclesiastical artwork found within the chapel.
- Exposure to living color in flowering plants, and in the natural colors of wood, stone, and clay tile.
- Experience of four seasonal transformations.
- Experience of light in all forms.
- Potential for numinous experiences through nature, dining, or social events.
- The cottage placements offer ample social distancing and access to nature.

Positive Outcomes

Climate neutrality is supported by the pedestrianization of the village even though there is only automobile and bus access to the site. Because of the large number of trees, carbon sequestering is abundant. Sustainability is difficult to achieve in older, historic structures, but renovations have tightened up the cottages, reducing energy demands for heating. Embodied energy and resources were reduced by preserving the existing structures. Pedestrianization is another sustainability measure, even though it was originally planned that way. Once you arrive at Gargonza, there is no need to use the car because everything is within walking distance. Placemaking is a major feature of the village, supported by its fortification, materiality, history, and human scale. It has a strong center and boundary, and there is a powerful sense of place.[8] Health and wellness outcomes are plentiful, which is often characteristic of hospitality places. Because hospitality places are comforting, bright, elegant, and personal, stress reduction, improved productivity, increased energy and creativity, and improved

3.5
Gargonza lemon tree garden (*Source: Phillip Tabb*)

cognitive abilities are common outcomes. The first component of the health-scapes model includes the environmental dimensions that serve as the stimuli for generating customer responses, and this is certainly present at Gargonza.[9] The inclusion of fresh, wholesome food also contributes to positive health and wellness outcomes. The opportunity for numinous experiences is also present through weddings, social gatherings, and church services, the calm of the natural environment, and the cuisine. The atmosphere is quietly inspiring. The flickering lights from across the valley, within the forest, and toward the clear night sky are numinous. Figure 3.5 shows the richness of the lemon tree garden. The primary contribution to biophilic urbanism is Gargonza's complete form and placemaking characteristics, with clear center, boundary, internal spatial order, prospect and refuge, and involvement with nature.

NOTES

1. City of Gargonza, *Castello di Gargonza: A medieval village in Val di Chiana*, https://www.dimorestoricheitaliane.it/en/dimora/castello-di-gargonza/ (accessed January 15, 2020).
2. Constance Rosenblum, *Living the Life of a Tuscan Village*, https://www.nytimes.com/1985/10/20/travel/living-the-life-of-a-tuscan-village.html (accessed January 25, 2020).
3. Castello di Gargonza History, http://www.gargonza.it/history_gargonza.html (accessed January 26, 2020).
4. Gargonza, Provence of Arezzo, Italy: Weather Averages https://www.google.com/search?client=safari&rls=en&q=gargonza+climate&ie=UTF-8&oe=UTF-8 (accessed January 29, 2020).
5. Castello di Gargonza, https://www.histouring.com/en/historical-places/castello-di-gargonza/ (accessed January 25, 2020).
6. Donlyn Lyndon and Charles Moore, *Chambers for a Memory Palace* (Cambridge, MA: MIT Press, 1994).
7. Phillip James Tabb, *Serene Urbanism: A Biophilic Theory and Practice of Sustainable Placemaking* (London: Routledge, 2017). p 72.
8. Phillip Tabb, "Secular Sacredness in Place Creation: A Case Study land Analysis of Serenbe," in T. Barrie, J. Bermudez, and P. Tabb (co-eds), *Architecture, Culture, and Spirituality* (London: Routledge, 2015). pp 190–191.
9. *Hospitality Healthscapes: The New Standard for Making Hospitals More Hospitable* https://www.bu.edu/bhr/2017/06/07/hospitality-healthscapes/ (accessed January 25, 2020).

4 GOOGLE HEADQUARTERS

GOOGLE HEADQUARTERS

Background and History

Google was cofounded in 1998 by Larry Page and Sergey Brin. The number of Google offices located around the world has increased as its global influence has exploded. The aggregate companies represent approximately 11.2 million square feet of building space.[1] The Google purpose is to organize the world's information and make it universally accessible, and this mission contributes to its leading culture. Google workspaces typically encourage "*casual collision;*" there are abundant common areas for collaboration, unconventional workspace environments, an atmosphere of innovation, dog friendly spaces, hackable spaces, and in the New York office they employ the "*150 feet from food*" rule.[2] There is a commitment to wellness, so there is encouragement for exercise, use of recreational facilities, provision of healthy food, and access to nature. And there is a culture of work–life balance, which in addition to an emphasis on wellbeing includes employee retention and long-term engagement, supportive leadership, and happiness impacts at work.[3] In addition, it was the intention of the founders to promulgate features in the workspaces that promote efficiency, good feelings, and environmental awareness. Steven Levy, in his book *In the Plex*, describes Google's offices and performance principles:

> "Google offices appeared to be a geek never-never land for unspeakably brainy Lost Boys (and Girls)."[4]
>
> "Being truly Google goes beyond the walls with bright colors and liberally disturbing lava lamps. A Googley space is one that reflects – and supports – our employees. We are a diverse team of committed, talented, smart, thoughtful, hard-working individuals. Our core values should be manifested in our work environment."[5]

The Googleplex (combining Google and complex) in Mountain View, California is a complex of buildings that house 2,000,000 square feet (185,806 square meters) of office space, and the playful interiors were designed by architect Clive Wilkinson.

It was acquired from Silicon Graphics, Inc. (CGI) in the early 2000s and now consists of a complex of six buildings surrounding an outdoor common and spacious dining patio. The campus became a vibrant density of 8,000 people. In 2007, 9,212 solar photovoltaic panels were installed on the rooftops spanning about four acres across four main buildings at the Googleplex campus, generating 1.6 megawatts of electrical power. Google moved into the 1900, 1950, and 2000 Charleston Road facilities located directly west of the Googleplex in 2008.

The latest Google Headquarters (and Alphabet), called Charleston East is being constructed north of Mountainview and next to their current campus, "Googleplex." This biophilic precedent will include both campuses and Charleston Park between them. The existing Googleplex, including Building 1900, expresses many of the biophilic attributes, and the Charleston East pushes the envelope of biophilic design. Designed by the Bjarke Ingels Group and Thomas Heatherwick, the new campus is being constructed on 18.6 acres (7.5 hectares) of land with a two-story structure comprising 595,000 square feet (55,277 square meters), and will house up to 2,700 Google employees. The facility is Google's first purpose-built office building, advancing their innovation in its workplace design and their commitment to biophilic principles.

The large, hanger-like canopy spaces allow for flexibility and changes within the work environment enhancing connections with nature, including a vast amount of natural light and ventilation, views and access to plants and landscaping elements, and a giant tent-like roof structure with integrated photovoltaic panels. The roof canopy will capture water for reuse and hold solar panels that will create an additional four megawatts of power. There is also a blurring of inside and outside, an important biophilic pattern attribute. There is a strong commitment to the surrounding community with the creation of a new "front door," and offering a wide range of amenities to both neighbors and employees. Google is experimenting with biophilic design to support wellness, reduce stress, and boost employee productivity and satisfaction. Figure 4.1 is an aerial view of the original Googleplex adjacent to the Charleston East facility showing the exterior commons and the rooftop photovoltaic arrays.

The work environment is flexible and changeable, and Google likens its architecture to software, imagining a building that can be continually shaped and updated just like the latest applications. To Danish architect Bjarke Ingels, it is a dynamic environment "open for interpretation and cross-pollination."[6] There is a diversity of space types from intimate contemplative workspaces to small informal group interaction spaces, and from social gathering spaces to larger events spaces. The workplace is intended to be a culture with "perks and overloaded with intellectual stimulation."[7]

The Charleston East facility supports working in nature, which is at the core of the design, with images showing the office modules draped with vines and climbing plants, and Googlers working outside on laptops beneath trees. The ambiguous inside and outside forms strong connections to nature, which is an important biophilic pattern attribute. The enclosing membrane is a greenhouse-like

4.1
Aerial view of
the Googleplex
in Mountainview,
California (*Source:
Alamy Stock*)

glass fabric draped over supporting structures. It regulates indoor climate and protects from inclement weather, providing summer shading, air quality, and sound control, and the entire roof can produce electricity. Refer to Figure 4.2, which shows biophilic characteristics of integrated nature, socializing, and outdoor spaces at the Googleplex in Mountainview. Plant life and social spaces are plentiful.

While the other precedents represent larger urban contexts, the Google Headquarters is an incubator and catalyst impacting the larger community within which it exists. Additionally, it represents the new paradigm and landscape for work environments. It is far more inclusive of the needs of contemporary culture. Productive employment, exercise, wellness, daycare, massages, laundry, recreation, entertainment, organic gardening, dining, and community engagement are among the included functions. Works of art are an integral part of the campus. Even Burning Man is promoting competitions to create significant exterior art

4.2
The Googleplex:
(a) inner commons,
(b) outdoor seating
(*Source: Alamy
Stock*)

installations on the campus designed to further engage the community.[8] The new facility is an expression of several of Google's management goals: to assert transparency, to enhance communication, and to have fun. The Googleplex does all three of these.

The new Charleston East headquarters was grounded in the core principles of the Ingels Group, reflecting a high-technology workspace of innovation with bold and progressive architecture. The innovative strategies for the new complex include a tent-like, hanger-like volume or biodome with metal roofs composed of slightly concave square and triangular canopies. The form is in part inspired by the adjacent two white peaks of the Shoreline Amphitheater to the north of the site. They will be sheathed in photovoltaic electric cells, and will allow daylight through gaps between the canopies, which are characterized as "smile shapes," and assembled with glass coupled with automated shading devices.[9] Beneath the canopies are several structures housing workspaces, laboratories, cafes, and an events space. Google provides a colorful fleet of 1000 bicycles. They are harvesting their own honey, and a shipping container has been repurposed for hydroponic growing.[10] The innovative interior spaces reflect the founders' vision of a sustainable Montessori-inspired freedom to pursue personal interests, innovative ideas, and the territory outside the box. The biome is a perfect reflection of this vision. Google is also developing similar biomes at the Bay View site located several blocks from the Charleston East facility. Bay View is reported to have the largest ground-sourced heat pump system in North America.[11]

In an attempt to respond to criticism from the nearby community of Mountain View, automobile traffic and parking were de-emphasized and replaced with pedestrianization, biking, and bussing. Certain portions of the facility were designed to be accessible to the public, with a pathway going through the building that will create more opportunities for employees and visitors to walk around Google's campus. With an openness toward the community, the concept is intended to become a remarkable cultural and landscape destination. The ground level will include some retail, a 2 acre (1 hectare) public plaza on the southeast corner of the site that will be reserved for public events, allowing food trucks, live music, or tech exhibits. Also planned are a public park, an indoor green loop with art installations, and a fitness trail system that connects to the surrounding community. While Google plans to cut down nearly 200 trees to make way for the project, it intends to plant nearly 400 new ones, adding native species to the area – a commitment to habitat restoration. In 2017, the project was unanimously approved by the Mountainview City Council. Refer to Figure 4.3(a) showing the structural framing of the biome under construction, and to Figure 4.3(b) showing an aerial view of the nearly completed biome canopy.

A few non-locally native Redwood trees were removed from the site and are being replaced with locally native trees and plants that will help re-establish a mix of riparian forest and oak woodlands. Redwoods are native north of the Google

4.3
Charleston East
biome: (a) biome
under construction
(*Source: Wikimedia
Commons*),
(b) biome canopy
(*Source: Getty
Images*)

site and in the nearby mountains. The addition of trees contributes to carbon sequestering. As can be seen from the masterplan analysis, Figure 4.4(b), trees are planted in street medians, along sidewalks, and around the various buildings. Google is committed to resilience in response to climate change, which is evident in the new Charleston East facility. They are committed to reaching carbon neutrality and 100 percent renewable energy by 2030. In 2015, they developed a set of climate resilience principles as follows:[12]

- Resilience response to specific regions.
- Resilience response to varying scales (building, campus, district, and region).
- Well-designed, -constructed, and -managed systems.
- Integrated linkages and optimized infrastructure.
- Incorporation of redundancy in response to disruption.
- Diversity and complexity in the network systems.
- Inform and engage people to support the principles.

Analysis of the Masterplan

The masterplan includes the existing Googleplex, Building 1900, and the new Charleston East facility. It includes the open spaces between them. While the headquarters' complexes are primarily architectural facilities, their urban connections include a commitment to reducing the impact of the automobile, and an interest in engaging with the surrounding community of Mountainview and commitment to restoring the natural environment that surrounds and is included within it. The Googleplex's complex facades, the commons, gardens, and amphitheater illustrate Google's commitment to sustainability. There is a figure–ground relationship between the original Googleplex and the Charleston East campus. The former is a random composition of building forms creating a large void-like green internal street within its center. The latter is a singular structure placed and rotated slightly in the center of its site with the green loop occurring around the perimeter. In contrast to the original Googleplex, it is an object building with a pin-wheel internal spatial order for primary circulation. The rotation of the biome aligns with the diagonal geometry introduced by the Googleplex forms. Parking occurs beneath the building. The public plaza is located in the northeast corner

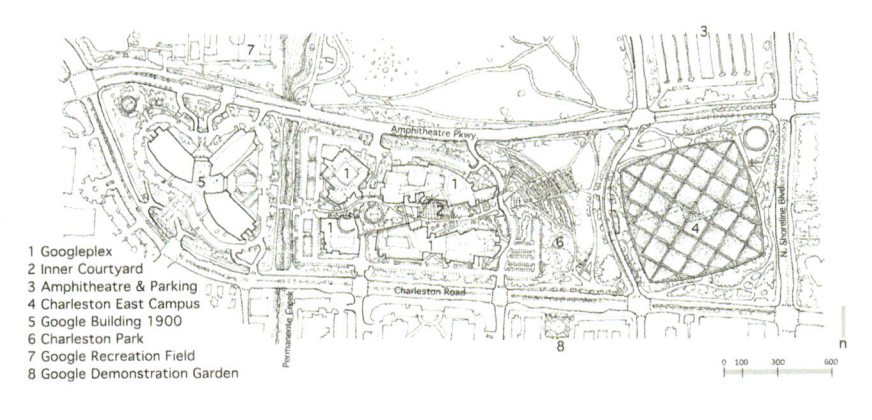

1 Googleplex
2 Inner Courtyard
3 Amphitheatre & Parking
4 Charleston East Campus
5 Google Building 1900
6 Charleston Park
7 Google Recreation Field
8 Google Demonstration Garden

4.4
Google masterplan analysis: (a) base map, (b) biophilic patterns (*Source: Phillip Tabb*)

of the site. The main structure is connected to a park west of the Googleplex. Refer to Figure 4.4 for the Google masterplan base map and an analysis of the Googleplex, Building 1900, and Charleston East masterplan.

Primary Pattern Attributes

Biophilic design is not new to Google.[13] Their 237,198 square foot (22,036 square meter) Chicago facility incorporates many patterns that include varying types of natural light, places of refuge, direct visual connections to nature, and an internal video wall with undulating patterns of nature. The new 330,000 square foot (30,658 square meter) Boulder, Colorado campus offers wonderful views of the Colorado Front Range, defines a natural courtyard, has tremendous spatial variety, has an abundance of natural light, has its own pizza oven and indoor fire pits, and incorporates natural reclaimed material features and birch-tree columns. In the Zurich, Switzerland campus, "Zooglers" have abundant views of nature and the cityscape, outdoor gathering spaces, and inside aquariums, and employees are extremely international. What's not to like about Fondue Fridays?

At the Googleplex, the pattern attributes are oriented inward to the campus commons and programed spaces within the buildings. In the new Charleston

East project biophilia was also an important design determinant for the new headquarters, from the technological innovations to the sustainable strategies. Since the facility is in construction, no real data exists relative to the effects of the biophilic pattern attributes. Views of nature and the plant world are extremely important, as are the multi-sensory experiences that result from direct contact with them. Similarly, prospect and refuge are important for creating a vital and productive work environment. Because of the unique biome design, the pattern attribute of inside–outside is an integral part of the building design. The overall form supports spatial variety, flexibility, and community engagement, and creates a natural analog. The integration of public art throughout the campus will provide visual interest and meaning, and reflects our evolving culture and collective memory. Natural light is ubiquitous, and research shows us that it will contribute to productivity, to health and happiness in the workplace environment, and to numinous experiences as well. Charleston Park also plays an important biophilic function as an important natural transition between the two facilities. An outline of many of the biophilic pattern attributes for both facilities follows:

- Connections to the plant world, outdoor amphitheater at Charleston Park, dining areas, healthy food, intimate landscape gardens (climbing vines and green loop), and the Google Demonstration Garden.
- Plentiful views and vistas of nature, the lake, and cityscape.
- Sensory connections, especially visual and olfactory experiences.
- Fire (photovoltaic electricity production at both campuses).
- Charleston East employs a ground-sourced heat pump.
- Access to fresh air, commitment to walking, bicycling.
- Integrated water features; pond, Googleplex is adjacent to Permanente Creek, and Charleston East will employ water harvesting.
- Interior structure for prospect and biome refuge, and views to the commons and natural areas of the site.
- Encourages indoor–outdoor activities, especially through the function of the Googleplex commons.
- Spatial structure is composed of a complex of exterior spaces and interconnectedness among the various buildings, and the biome has a pin-wheel internal circulation order with gridded quarter sections that are variable, open, flexible, and cross-pollinating.
- Centering in the Googleplex commons, and by a catalyst for and "front door" to Charleston East.
- Bounding characteristics of the Googleplex's positioning of building elements, the biome, and perimeter green loop and streets.
- Selective natural materials, cradle-to-cradle building materials, or products with high recycled and reclaimed content.
- The form language of the Googleplex is complexity like a giant geode, and the form language for Charleston East is a natural analog of a geological

structure in nature as expressed in the large canopy covering the facility being reflective of the Shoreline Amphitheater.

- Community- and work-related recreational, culinary, cultural, and social activities.
- Integration of public works of art throughout both campuses.
- Exposure to living color expressed both indoors and outdoors.
- Experiences of seasonal transformations, and campus expansions over time.
- Experiences of light in all forms, especially on the second-level mezzanines beneath the canopy.
- Potentials for numinous experiences (individual and group).
- During the pandemic, Google announced a work-at-home policy until the middle of the summer 2021.

Positive Outcomes

Google employees in 2019 petitioned the company to publish a climate action plan that committed to zero emissions by 2030. Because the Charleston East Google Headquarters is in construction phase, there is no empirical evidence of positive outcomes. However, on analyzing the site plan, building images, and development goals, positive outcomes can be speculated. Google was ranked by *Fortune* magazine in 2009 as the best place in the US to work,[14] and in 2019, Google received honors for being the best employer for new graduates, for diversity, and for women. For a company that values creativity, wellness, productivity, and retention, it is clear to see why biophilic principles are important in its designs.

Climate neutrality is supported through pedestrianization and emphasis on alternative modes of transportation such as walking, bicycling, electric scooters, and electric cars, with off-site parking, and commuter busses. The promise of the ring loop of native trees will add to carbon sequestering. Sustainability will occur with utilization of on-site resources, mainly natural light, passive solar heating, solar photovoltaic electricity, and stormwater storage and rainwater harvesting. Charleston East is slated for LEED Platinum, when completed. Placemaking will occur as it becomes an exemplary work environment and destination facility. It will be open to the neighboring community, where cultural activities and social interactions can occur. The variable spatial environment and use of natural materials will also contribute to positive outcomes. Health and wellness outcomes include stress reduction; improved productivity; and increased energy, creativity, and cognitive abilities. Google has supported a telework process and ordered a stay-at-home order in response to the Coronavirus for its employees worldwide through the summer of 2021. In addition, they have place restrictions on travel, events, and face-to-face meetings. The numinous experiences found at Google will most likely derive from the extraordinary architecture and its enabling connections to nature. The primary contribution to Biophilic Urbanism is its progressive and biophilic interiority, the biome shell and its integration with

4.5
Interior lobby
of building
1900 (*Source:*
Shutterstock)

renewable energy sources, and the commitment to community engagement with the place. Refer to Figure 4.5 for the lobby interior of Building 1900 showing natural light, green walls, and slide.

NOTES

1. *Alphabet, Inc. – Climate Change* https://services.google.com/fh/files/misc/alphabet-2019-cdp-report.pdf (accessed February 12, 2020).
2. *What can we learn from Google's offices about workspace design?* https://www.workspacedesign.co.uk/what-can-we-learn-from-googles-offices-about-workplace-design/ (accessed January 24, 2020).
3. Laszlo Bock, *Google's Scientific Approach to Work-Life Balance (and Much More)* https://hbrascend.org/topics/googles-work-life-balance/ (accessed February 10, 2020).
4. Steven Levy, *In The Plex: How Google Thinks, Works, and Shapes Our Lives* (New York, NY: Simon & Schuster, 2011). p 123.
5. Steven Levy, *In The Plex*, (New York, NY: Simon & Schuster, 2011). p 130.
6. Bjarke Ingels Group and Heatherwick Studio, *Google Charleston East Campus will become reality by 2019* https://aasarchitecture.com/2018/04/google-charleston-east-campus-will-become-reality-2019.html/ (accessed January 8, 2020).
7. Steven Levy, *In The Plex*, (New York, NY: Simon & Schuster, 2011). p 133.
8. Burning Man, *The Culture: Burning Man Arts*, https://burningman.org/culture/burning-man-arts/civic-arts-program/charleston-east-plaza/ (accessed January 8, 2020).
9. Geraldine Chua, *Google is changing the sustainable office game* https://www.architectureanddesign.com.au/sustainability-awards/google-is-changing-the-sustainable-office-game# (accessed March 13, 2020).
10. Bjarke Ingels Group and Heatherwick Studio, *Google Charleston East Campus will become reality by 2019* https://aasarchitecture.com/2018/04/google-charleston-east-campus-will-become-reality-2019.html/ (accessed January 8, 2020).
11. Google's New Office Will Be Heated And Cooled By The Ground Underneath https://www.fastcompany.com/40484709/googles-new-office-will-be-heated-and-cooled-by-the-ground-underneath (accessed January 21, 2020).

12. CDP, *Alphabet, Inc. – Climate Change 2019* https://services.google.com/fh/files/misc/alphabet-2019-cdp-report.pdf (accessed March 18, 2020).
13. Nick Bastone, *Here's a Look at 10 Ways Google Tries to Make its Campuses Around the World More Sustainable* https://www.businessinsider.com/google-campus-sustainability-2019-4 (accessed January 4, 2020).
14. Joshua Cook, *How Google Motivates their Employees with Rewards and Perks* http://hubpages.com/business/How-Google-Motivates-their-Employees-with-Rewards-and-Perks (accessed January 16, 2020).

5 HELSINGE HAVEBY (GARDEN VILLAGE)

HELSINGE HAVEBY

Background and History

Helsinge Haveby is a garden city concept that won first prize, at "the village of tomorrow" competition. The project, Helsinge Nord Udviklinngspan, was sponsored by the Gribskov Municipality in 2016. EFFEKT, karres+brands, Atkins, and CFBO were the designers. The term "*haveby*" means garden city. The project was a visionary design for a new residential development located in Helsinge, Denmark, and is located about 30 miles (48 kilometers) north of Copenhagen. It is oriented towards a self-sufficient constellation of neighborhood clusters with local food and energy production. According to EFFEKT, many young families desire to move to the countryside to be closer to nature, enjoy fresh air, make the most of affordable living, and to provide a better environment for their children. The new garden city at Helsinge transforms traditional monocultural agriculture fields into a diverse mix of housing clusters among wetlands, meadows, orchards, and agroforestry.[1] The new neighborhoods enable future residents to lead more sustainable lifestyles with higher degrees of self-sufficiency and reduced of carbon emissions. They will be able to do this without relinquishing the same services, amenities, and freedoms found in the urban life of cities. Construction is scheduled to begin later in 2020.

The project is designed to be highly biophilic because of its intentional connections to nature. The masterplan was developed along three primary themes: (1) creation of a robust sustainable design integrated into the natural environment, (2) creation of community fostering a strong sense of identity, and (3) creation of affordable lifestyles with provision of affordable homes.[2] According to the institute, YouGov, made for the Homeowners Knowledge Database, Bollus, their analysis showed that every fifth person living in the city today plans to live in the countryside in 2030 – calling for a better, healthier living environment, greater community building, and affordability.[3] This suggests that new models are needed, especially for multiple-use, single-family attached residential development. Helsinge Haveby is regenerative; as in biology, it supports the process of renewal, restoration, and new growth. It is an integrated

5.1
Helsinge Haveby,
Denmark (aerial
image) (*Source:
EFFEKT Architects*)

and resilient development, and an experimental model neighborhood. Refer to Figure 5.1 showing an aerial rendering of the project.

The design features a network or constellation of neighborhood clusters or "*agrihoods*," a term intended to describe identifiable housing groupings sharing common open spaces. The plan allows for a lush landscape, orchards, wetlands, integrated with food production based on field farming, permaculture, and agroforestry. Janine de la Salle and Mark Holland posit in their book on *Agricultural Urbanism* that food production becomes the catalyst for community formation.[4] The clusters will be developed as 25 small neighborhoods, each with its own characteristics inspired by the qualities of its location. They will be formed around a natural feature, such as a pond, green, square, or outdoor recreation area, where public life can unfold and flourish. With 700 dwelling units, each cluster averages between 25 and 30 homes. All homes have direct access to the outdoor natural areas of the site, or what is referred to as the "*first row*" to nature.

Both the neighborhood clusters and residential housing typologies vary throughout the development. Social diversity is important and to this end, the clusters differ in form, materiality, sizes, and types of ownership. Biodiversity is also important. Individual residences are encouraged to have kitchen gardens and two direct outdoor spaces or rooms. The residential architecture is typically contemporary Danish vernacular, using natural materials coupled with glass conservatories. While designing for sustainability has proven successful in individual single-family buildings, grouping together into neighborhoods makes even more sense because there can be more shared resources and potential efficiencies. The concept of a "*super cluster*" relates to the multiplication of neighborhood cells found at Helsinge Haveby. They are designed to be different, yet it is anticipated that residents share common values regarding food

5.2
Helsinge Haveby
food and social hub
(*Source: EFFEKT
Architects*)

production, sustainability, climate neutrality, and preservation of nature. This "integrated neighborhood" approach represents an emerging vision for residential development.

A food hub is centrally located within the masterplan and provides a meeting place for residents and visitors. This becomes a destination and place marker not only for local residents, but functions as a "*front door*" for visitors and the surrounding city of Helsinge. The Hub will provide social programs and food-related activities, including a farmer's market, farm shop, restaurant, common kitchen, nursery and kindergarten, recreation, and garden selling local produce. The proximity to the food production can help eliminate food waste and lower the general energy consumption. Breaking bread together and working together to accomplish shared goals are great ways to get to know neighbors at a deeper level and develop camaraderie.[5] Refer to Figure 5.2 showing the food hub, outdoor communal activities, and inside dining area.

The 173-acre (70-hectare) site is located on the north side of the city of Helsinge along Helsingervej Road. It is located approximately one-half mile (0.8 km) from the city center. The site is surrounded by farmland on the northeast and west sides. The Højbogård café is located adjacent to the site within walking distance to the northwest. The masterplan is designed for 700 residential dwelling units, which gives a gross density of four dwelling units per acre (10 du/hectare). The site is connected to Copenhagen via Route 16, or the Copenhagen-to-Tisvilde railway. It takes about 42 minutes to drive to Copenhagen by car; the train takes a little over an hour. A bus line also connects the two cities. It is clear that Helsinge Haveby can be an in-place local community, and/or it can function as a commuter residential district.

The climate of Helsinge is characterized by comfortable and partly cloudy summers; the winters are long, very cold, and mostly cloudy; and it is windy year round. Over the course of the year, the temperature typically varies from

29 °F to 70 °F and is rarely below 16 °F or above 79 °F.[6] The average percentage of the cloud cover is significant, with seasonal variations. Rain falls throughout the year in Helsinge. The growing season typically lasts for 6.4 months (194 days).[7] Climate-oriented architectural designs focus on underheating during the cold winters, mild but constant rain, and variable cloud cover. Conservatories attached to the dwellings for passive solar heating, buffering, and planting are a good climatic design approach. Dwellings are relatively compact, two-story structures with steep gable roofs. This concept can adapt to varying regional contexts with climate-driven architectural languages and associated regenerative technologies. Depending upon the climatic location of these villages, as much as 50 to 100 percent of the necessary food and water can be obtained on site.

Sustainable on-site resources are important. The development includes provision for photovoltaic electricity production, passive solar heating, geothermal heating, and electric vehicle charging stations. Water will be collected, cleaned, and re-introduced into the system. Helsinge is designed to reduce CO_2 emissions and fossil fuel consumption, and to respond to the scarcity of natural resources, including food. Technologies planned for the Helsinge Haveby are already available and in common use. The greenhouse architecture is a good fit for the temperate climate zone, characterized by cold winters and overcast skies, as large conservatory glass areas are unlikely to overheat. The primary planning and design features of the project include:

- New train station with connection to Copenhagen with a 55 minute travel time.
- Bridge connecting the new neighborhood with the recreation areas and city of Helsinge on the other side of the main road.
- Food hub with local restaurant and farm shop for distribution of locally grown produce.
- Social clusters with smaller private outdoor spaces directly connected to nature integral to each house.
- Universal access to community services – Access by bicycle or walking to community services and the food hub.
- Human scale humane places – Environment scaled for cultural activities and interaction.
- Multiplication of the cluster planning pattern to 25 individual placemaking sites.
- The concept of circular flows – economically, socially, and environmentally.
- Variety of recreational activities along the new open spaces and system of paths.
- Diverse natural surroundings including forest gardens, fruit gardens, kitchen gardens, and high levels of biodiversity.
- Sunspaces and conservatories are used for passive heating and household agriculture.

- The 25 clusters offer opportunities for sheltering-in-place and quarantining, if required.
- On-site resource utilization and self-sufficiency.
- Incorporation of biophilic planning and design patterns in creating the site plan.

The physical elements of the design include a new train station, the food hub, bridges from the main development to the recreation areas, and the 25 clusters. The new train station is located on the northeastern edge of the site and connects to the coast to Copenhagen. The natural elements include organic farms and gardens, biodiverse landscaping, wet areas, meadows, forest gardens, fruit orchards, and animal husbandry. The in-between spaces function as common areas used for recreational purposes and agriculture. There are two primary circulation systems. A main automobile distribution street branches to connect to each neighborhood cluster, and that, in turn, connects the entire village to the street system of Helsinge. In addition, a pedestrian network independent of automobile roads also connects each of the clusters and bridges over Helsingervej Road, giving easy access to the recreation area to the south. These design measures contribute to a biophilic focus, including accessible engagements with nature, on-site food production, experiences of the elements, responses to climatic changes and ecological flows, and social interactions. The nucleated planning diagram nests within public spaces, food production, and community programs, with individual interconnected dwelling-greenhouses. Refer to Figure 5.3 for an image that shows the character of a cluster center with bonfire, social spaces, and individual residential building outdoor spaces.

5.3
Helsinge Haveby
cluster center
(*Source: EFFEKT
Architects*)

Analysis of the Masterplan

The Helsinge project currently occupies one site – a five-sided polygonal agricultural field of approximately 173 acres (70 hectares) of land – and it is adjacent to the city of Helsinge recreation site, Helsinge Fodbold Kunststofbane, of approximately 25 acres (10 hectares). To the west and northwest of the main site are agricultural fields with a couple of small farm-house clusters, to the northeast is a landscape buffer and the proposed train station, to the southeast is the main access road and recreation site, and to the south is a housing development. The overall plan is a horizontal scheme with one- and two-story attached buildings, densely clustered. The design is organized with an organic series of 25 interconnected sub-neighborhood clusters ("*agrihoods*") surrounded by open space and agricultural fields. The cluster centers contain additional shared open space, natural features, or rec-reational functions. The plan in many ways functions similarly to co-housing also developed in Denmark in the 1970s with its individual housing units and common center. And according to Corinne McLaughlin and Gordon Davidson, community living teaches us first-hand the reality of the interdependence of all life, certainly an integral notion of the Biophilic Hypothesis.[8] And accord-ing to Dorit Fromm, the common house, which is similar to the food hub at Helsinge Haveby, is the community face or front door, and should be near the entrance to the community, should not be dominated by cars, should have an equivalent outdoor area for social gatherings, and should have a welcoming architectural language.[9] The seamless automobile and pedestrian networks create high connectivity within the community. These measures for the food hub are found within the masterplan. Refer to Figure 5.4 which shows the base map and biophilic patterns incorporated into the masterplan. Note the large areas of greenspace, farmland, and reforestation woven throughout the design.

Primary Pattern Attributes

There are multiple opportunities for residents to interact directly with nature in the Helsinge garden village. First, most residences are equipped with isolated gain passive solar houses and conservatories filled with plants and views to the outside, thereby supporting fluid inside–outside connections. Second, the residences are planned with two outdoor spaces to be embedded adjacent to forested and vegetated landscapes. Third, the residential clusters are conveni-ently connected to the food hub located near the center of the village where social interaction occurs. Clusters have a clear boundary and their centers vary affording individual identity. And fourth, the village is easily connected to the city of Helsinge and to the center of cultural activities found in Copenhagen. The closed loop of the food-production system is analogous to the broader ecological flows and biological systems within which the garden village exists. The local food hub is a place for homeowners' exchange and socialization. The food systems are managed, so community members do not necessarily have

5.4
Helsinge Haveby
masterplan
analysis: (a) base
map, (b) biophilic
patterns (*Source:
Phillip Tabb*)

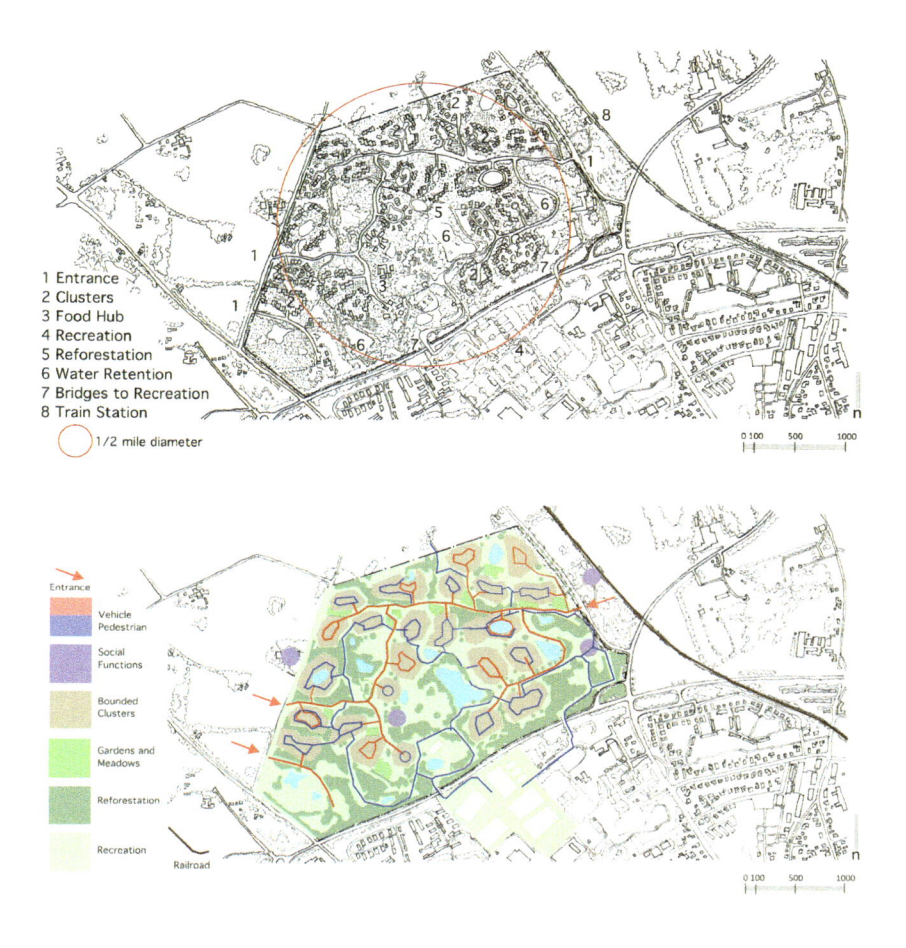

1 Entrance
2 Clusters
3 Food Hub
4 Recreation
5 Reforestation
6 Water Retention
7 Bridges to Recreation
8 Train Station

1/2 mile diameter

to become farmers to live there. An outline of many of the biophilic pattern attributes follows.

- Connections to the plant world (farms, meadows, orchards, gardens, riparian areas, marshes, and green roofs).
- Connections to household pets, animal husbandry, and wild animals typically found in Denmark (red, roe, and fallow deer; squirrels, foxes, hares, swans, geese, and oystercatchers).
- Plentiful views and vistas to nature, especially into the agricultural fields and cluster centers.
- Sensory connections common to a rural agrarian environment.
- Solar energy, biomass incineration, geothermal heating and cooling, microgrid.
- Direct connections to earth through farming, gardening, and recreation.
- Access to fresh air within dwellings and in the abundant outdoor areas.
- Access and views to water (reservoirs, ponds), composting, waste recycling.

- Dwellings are oriented to cluster centers and to solar access.
- Dwellings are designed for prospect and refuge (views to common areas, refuge within homes).
- Strong indoor–outdoor connections, greenhouses, and outdoor rooms.
- Village has the food hub as center, cluster centers, polynucleated.
- The spatial structure is organic, informal, and free-flowing throughout the site.
- Bounding characteristics of sub-neighborhood clusters, and roadways around the entire development.
- Abundant natural materials; most buildings are built with wood.
- Observation of ecological processes; "*living machine*."[10]
- Provision of cultural and social activities, especially in cluster centers and the food hub.
- The urban form language is progressive rural, and the architecture is conservatory-vernacular, solar-greenhouse oriented, simple iconic forms.
- Exposure to living color through the plant world.
- Experiences of seasonal transformations.
- Experiences of light in all forms, especially diffused greenhouse light.
- Potentials for numinous experiences through the food production cycle and community social and cultural activities.

Positive Outcomes

The Helsinge garden village is in concept stage and its realization has not occurred, so no empirical evidence of positive outcomes is yet available. However, positive outcomes can be speculated with analysis of the masterplan. Climate neutrality will likely result because of the high degree of pedestrianization, and carbon sequestering due to the large amount of farmland and forests. Sustainability is central to the concept and will occur through renewable low-emissions energy technologies, closed-loop water–waste system, passive solar greenhouse architecture, and tight construction methods. It should be noted that the high-glazed greenhouse architecture functions better in climate zones where there is a large percentage of cloud cover and colder temperatures, otherwise they would overheat. Placemaking occurs through a shared identity and world view and commitment to an agriculture-centered lifestyle. The pedestrianization lends itself to increased social contact. This outcome is projected to be one of the distinguishing characteristics of the development. The sub-neighborhood clusters have strong placemaking patterns, as demonstrated by identifiable centers, clear boundaries, and strong sense of place. Health and wellness outcomes will likely result from the nature-based lifestyle, pedestrianization, encouraged socialization, easy access to nature, and nutritious on-site food production and the activities of the food hub. During times of global pandemics, individual dwellings and clusters can function as sequestered places. Denmark is experiencing relatively

5.5
Helsinge Haveby
moments (*Source:
EFFEKT Architects*)

low COVID-19 numbers as of early September 2020 with less than 19,000 cases and 630 deaths.[11]

The numinous outcomes may occur through the direct connections to nature and the cultural and social activities of the clusters and community. The primary contribution to Biophilic Urbanism is this garden village's comprehensive and integrative qualities, the focused food systems, its closed-cycle renewable utility network, and the multiplication of residential clusters. Taken together, these mean it is designed to reduce CO_2 emissions and fossil fuel consumption, and to respond to the scarcity of natural resources, including food. Its "integrated multiplication of neighborhoods" represents a new vision for residential development. Refer to Figure 5.5 that shows a pastoral scene with pond, natural landscaping, and simple Danish contemporary vernacular homes. This image truly expresses a biophilic moment.

NOTES

1. EFFEKT, *Helsinge Haveby, Village of Tomorrow* https://www.effekt.dk/hno (accessed March 5, 2020).
2. Thomas Wagner, *The New Economy* https://medium.com/global-design-futures/new-economy-e70196864e4 (accessed March 6, 2020).
3. YouGov, made for the Homeowners Knowledge Database, Bollus https://www.karresenbrands.com/project/helsinge-nord (accessed March 10, 2020).
4. Janine de la Salle and Mark Holland, *Agricultural Urbanism: Handbook for Building sustainable Food and Agriculture Systems in 21st Century Cities* (Winnipeg, CA: Green Frigate Books, 2010).
5. Mountain View Cohousing Community http://mountainviewcohousing.org (accessed March 5, 2020).
6. Weather Spark, Average Weather in Helsinge, Denmark https://weatherspark.com/y/74064/Average-Weather-in-Helsinge-Denmark-Year-Round (accessed March 6, 2020).
7. Ibid.

8. Corine McLaughlin and Gordon Davidson, *Builders of the New Dawn: Community lifestyles in a Changing World* (Walpole, NH: Stillpoint Publishers, 1985).

9. Dorit Fromm, *Collaborative Communities: Cohousing, Central Living, and Other New Forms of Housing with Shared Facilities* (New York, NY: Van Nostrand Reinhold, 1991).

10. John and Nancy Todd, *From Eco-Cities to Living Machines* (Berkeley, CA: North Atlantic Books, 1994).

11. Worldometer, *COVID-19 Coronavirus Pandemic*, https://www.worldometers.info/coronavirus/#countries (accessed September 8, 2020).

6 KRONSBERG DISTRICT

KRONSBERG DISTRICT

Background and History

Kronsberg District was originally planned to demonstrate sustainable principles for the Expo 2000 World Exposition, held in Hanover, Germany. The motto for the Fair was "*Humankind – Nature – Technology*," which guided the exemplary planning approach to Kronsberg.[1] The District site conformed to the regional planning principle to encourage growth along transit lines and to create stops that would function as catalysts for housing concentrations and mixed-use development. The development goal was to accommodate growth, improve quality of life, and preserve the natural environment. The site is along the low Kronsberg Hill, 1.2 miles (2 kilometers) wide and 3.7 miles (6 kilometers) along the north–south direction. The new district was ultimately planned for 6,000 dwelling units with 64 percent green space and a density of 18 du/ac (45 du/ha) on 2,965 acres (1,200 hectares). The proportion of open space in the Kronsberg District was raised by 5–10 percent compared to conventional urban planning in Germany.

There are three main tram stops along the eastern edge of the community along the D-Sud (south) light rail. The community employs three wind turbines and a 45-kW photovoltaic system providing 72 percent of the electricity supply, and two combined heat and power systems to make up the rest of the power needs. Kronsberg is known for its "*super-blocks*," which are biophilic neighborhoods. There are tree-lined streets and front gardens along the outside of the blocks and protected natural interiors on the inside, including playgrounds, schools, water features, and landscaped spaces. The primary biophilic outcomes are oriented toward climate change mitigation, automobile and emissions reductions, the use of on-site resources, and pedestrian placemaking. In developing the project, Hanover's primary goals were city as garden and city as social habitat: thus, planning took place in terms of eco-compatibility.[2] Figure 6.1 shows an aerial view of the Kronsberg District from the northeast.

The super-blocks occur within the overall meshed rectangular grid, and vary slightly in size. Dimensions for block widths are generally the same, while

6.1
Kronsberg District
aerial view
(*Source: Alamy Stock*)

lengths tend to vary. Typically they measure between 300 by 500 feet on a side (90 by 150 meters), and the area is between 2 and 4 acres (0.8 and 1.6 hectares). The blocks have a density gradient from five-story buildings along the tram line on the west side to two-story terraced buildings along the agricultural east side. Approximately half of the plan incorporates the super-blocks. Architecturally, about a half of the block perimeter is bounded by a five-story apartment building, and the other half of the block has smaller-footprint four-story buildings. Together they define a large interior neighborhood park and courtyard of varying designs and functions. These interior parks vary in size, but average between 1 and 1.5 acres (0.4–0.6 hectares). Each of the super-block interiors varies, from manicured landscapes and water collection and storage to recreational spaces and daycare centers.

Each neighborhood is made up of eight residential blocks that are grouped around a central park. The blocks are uncommonly large in order to allow adequate green space for both private and shared gardens, on-site water retention and absorption, and large open spaces for unstructured play. Throughout the district, there are 80 different tree types. Tree plantings vary along differing street orientations, giving a more refined sense of identity. Along north streets are sycamore trees and along the south are ash trees. East streets have both the smaller lime trees and larger maple trees, and west streets have the lime and ash trees. Additionally, there are five linear transverse green corridors that connect residential areas with the hilltop and park. They not only provide further introduction of nature within the district, but also function as neighborhood boundaries and rainwater management systems.[3] The use of the regional tram line, electric vehicles, car-sharing, and small electric trollies further reduces greenhouse gas emissions. It is the combination of these green strategies that contributes to the ecological balance and biophilic experience of the place.

The Kronsberg-Nord district contains a kindergarten and youth center as well as a block of *Passivhaus*-style row houses. The central district square, designed in consultation with Kronsberg residents, is located at the southwestern edge of this neighborhood, directly adjacent to Kronsberg-Mitte. The public square is bounded by the KroKuS arts and community center, a center for social services, a health center, an ecumenical church with shared meeting spaces and apartments, a youth center, and a variety of shops with housing above. The smaller of two combined heat and power (CHP) district heating plants is located in the cellar of one of the apartment blocks at the northwestern edge of the neighborhood. The Kronsberg-Mitte neighborhood includes two children's daycare centers, one placed in its large central park, the other adjacent to the Kronsberg nature reserve at the southeastern edge of the neighborhood. A comprehensive high school for all the neighborhoods' children anchors the southwestern edge of this neighborhood, directly adjacent to the district's largest CHP plant.[4] Refer to Figure 6.2, which illustrates the interior of one of the super-blocks and space-defining buildings.

Sustainability was a primary consideration for Kronsberg. Renewable technologies, water and waste management, greenhouse gas reduction, soil restoration, and pedestrianization were all addressed in the development. Photovoltaic electricity production is distributed throughout. Rainwater harvesting typically occurs within the open-space interiors of the super-blocks. Rainwater in built-up areas is absorbed, collected, and released gradually. The

6.2
Kronsberg super-block interior park
(*Source: Gary J. Coates*)

Kronsberg goal of energy efficiency optimization was to reduce CO_2 emissions by at least 60 percent compared to current standards for conventional residential buildings. Water was an important consideration in the overall design, and the aim was to preserve the water balance after development to resemble that in the undeveloped site. Site-produced rainwater infiltrates to ponds, soakaway systems, and grass hollows, and permeable surfaces drain directly into the ground. Figure 6.3 shows super block interior landscapes.

Energy was a primary concern and is supplied from three sources: CHP, on-site renewable solar photovoltaic, and wind turbine systems. The development employs two district heating and power systems for all buildings. They are designed to operate at between 80 and 95 percent efficiency. The discharged combustion gases produced by the CHP system pass through a three-way catalytic converter before being emitted into the air. Solar power is with stand-alone systems and solar district heating. There are two wind turbines, of 1.5 and 1.8 megawatts of energy output respectively. Energy demand reductions were in part accomplished through low-energy building construction.

Dwellings vary in type and size. Dwelling types are based on the desire for flexibility in response to changing needs and the desire for social diversity. Dwelling sizes are relatively modest, from 1000 to 1500 square feet (100 to 150 square meters), and contain from one to more than four room units. Additionally, there are 32 terraced houses arranged in four rows with eight attached dwellings each. These were conceived as passive houses that were super-insulated with pre-heating augmenting the balanced ventilation system. "Habitat" was a residential project intended to promote the multicultural coexistence of both Germans and migrants. There were 53 flats constructed in 3½-story buildings, creating an internal courtyard and tenants' gardens. There was a concerted effort to provide for a diversity of residents, such as families, children, the elderly, and those of different ethnic origins. Interestingly, spectacular one-off architectural projects were forbidden. Instead, functional projects at the neighborhood and community scale were considered a higher priority. A majority of the dwelling units are rented. Kronsberg's ambition is to develop the highest possible quality of life using natural resources sparingly.

6.3
Kronsberg super-blocks: (a) interior lawns and apartment blocks, (b) pedestrian circulation and rainwater swale (*Source: Gary J. Coates*)

Analysis of the Masterplan

The masterplan follows consolidated and fixed regional planning rules, providing for the development of dense residential settlements along local public transport lines. The overall masterplan can be described by the zoning of three distinct layers: (a) the tram line, (b) the compact urban district, and (c) the common natural lands. The urban portion of Kronsberg is defined by two neighborhoods each organized by a gridded fabric of square, rectangular, and trapezoidal blocks running parallel with the tram line to the west and the common open lands to the east. A district center occurs between the two neighborhoods and provides central functions, including facilities for commercial, cultural, religious, healthcare, and community services. Block sizes and shapes vary a little. The grid layout of the blocks, the avenue-like streets, and the open-space planning unite many different construction forms and architectural styles in a harmonious townscape. The size of the built portion is nearly a mile by a third of a mile (1.5 x 0.5 kilometers). Running along the entire western edge of the District next to the tram line is a one-sided zone with mixed commercial below and residential above. In the center of this zone is the district central square with tram stop. Both the central square and commercial street are served by a boulevard for access, service, and local parking.

Access to all the residential blocks is provided by the grid of narrow tree-lined streets, designed to allow access for local traffic to all dwelling units. The wider north–south avenues running parallel to the tram line connect residents to double-loaded street-tree-shaded parking areas, and along the super-blocks. Most do not pass through the entire district. Mid-street pinch-points and on-street parking assist in traffic calming. The narrower east–west streets are on a gradient of an average of 5 percent, running from the tram line uphill to the nature reserve, and they do connect directly for pedestrian and bicycle access. As can be observed from the masterplan, automobile parking has minimal impact on the community along designated streets and in decentralized locations. It was anticipated that residents would utilize joint car use, on-street parking, underground parking, and hillside parking; and that, due to the pedestrian nature of the district and close proximity to the tram, automobile ownership would lessen. To help ameliorate the situation, parking ratio requirements were reduced from 1.0 to 0.8 parking places per dwelling, and 0.2 for public parking on streets.[5] The goal was to spread the transportation modalities equally between pedestrians, bicycles, buses, trams, and private automobiles. The built portions fit within a one-half mile (0.8 kilometer) radius, which is recommended for a pedestrian-oriented development.

Kronsberg was planned to address Hanover's housing shortage and to be located along a commuter train line. When complete, it is planned to have a density of 18 dwelling units per acre (42 per hectare), with 6,000 total projected dwellings.[6] Apartments make up the majority of housing types, and are designed to be light, airy, space-saving, and well fitted. The compactness and density of the built portions of the district lend efficiency to the use of combined heat and power with district distribution. The first gas-powered CHP plant is located at the edge of the district, and provides electricity and waste heat for domestic hot water and base-load heating. According to Tim Beatley, Kronsberg has one of the largest centralized solar hot-water heating systems in a residential development.[7] Solar-heated water is partially stored underground in a 3,500 cubic yard (2,700 cubic meter) storage tank. The majority of Kronsberg's electricity is supplied by wind power. The masterplan of Kronsberg followed the *Hannover Principles* written by William McDonough and Partners and their recommendations for sustainable design.[8] Refer to Figure 6.4 for the base map and layers of biophilic patterns found within the masterplan.

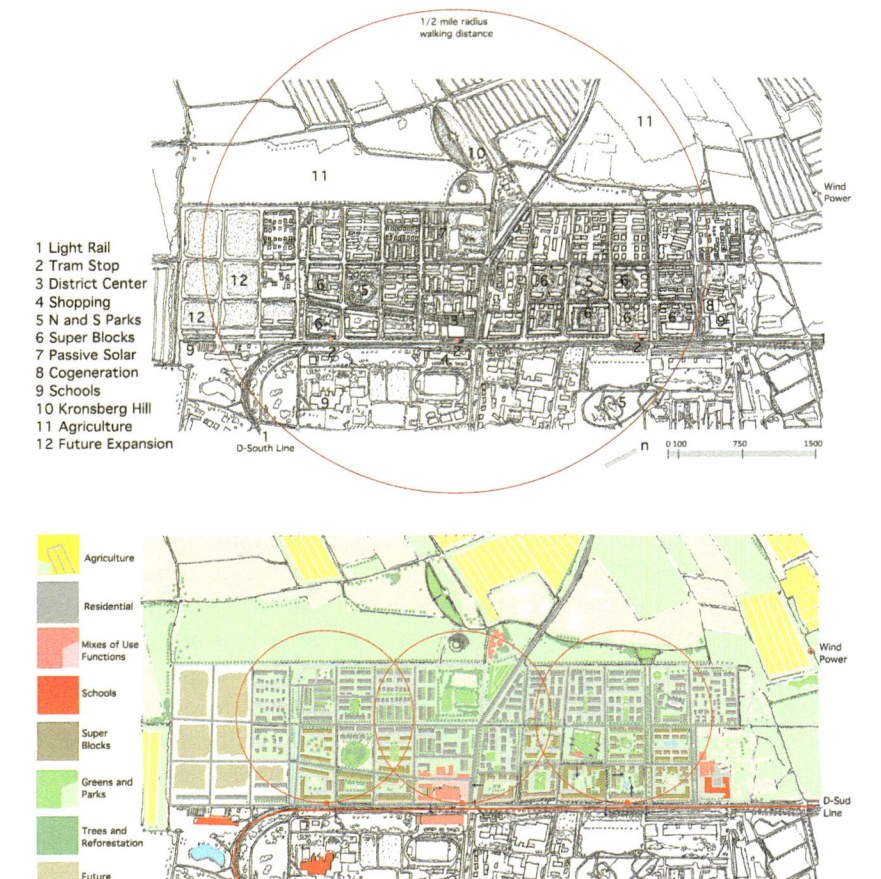

1 Light Rail
2 Tram Stop
3 District Center
4 Shopping
5 N and S Parks
6 Super Blocks
7 Passive Solar
8 Cogeneration
9 Schools
10 Kronsberg Hill
11 Agriculture
12 Future Expansion

6.4 Kronsberg masterplan analysis: (a) Kronsberg base map, (b) Kronsberg biophilic patterns (*Source: Phillip Tabb*)

Primary Pattern Attributes

There are a host of biophilic principles and pattern attributes operating within Kronsberg. Due to the amount of natural land to the east, there are opportunities to engage with nature, and the farm allows interaction with the farm animals. All the elements are present within the District. The renewable technologies connect to natural on-site resources and attributes of wind (air), sun (fire), stormwater and rainwater harvesting (water), and agriculture (earth). Water features are used throughout the District. The structure and square-gridded plan allow connections to the intensity of the higher density to the west and the openness of the pastoral landscape to the east. The street grid (spatial order) also accommodates the dominant orientation of solar energy to the south. Form characteristics include fabric structures, density gradients, spatial hierarchies, and the super-block designs. Bounding occurs with the super-block-defining buildings and their green inner courtyards. Further, these super-blocks create identity, prospect and refuge, direct access, and safe outdoor environments. From the two-to-five-story residential buildings there are multiple views to the natural and social spaces. The centrality of the public plaza provides easy access and support for social diversity and community gathering. Both natural and social connections offer opportunities for numinous experiences. An outline of many of the biophilic pattern attributes follows.

- Connections to the plant world – streetscapes, green corridors, drainage channels, green perimeter, grassy swales, and agriculture, and nearly every home has a private outdoor space.
- Connections to animal husbandry at the farm, pet friendly.
- Plentiful views and vistas to nature (large courtyards in super-blocks and to agriculture).
- Sensory connections, especially to landscaped areas and farm.
- Connections and responses to local ecology and natural hydrological flows down from the organic farm.
- Fire (wind, biomass, and photovoltaic electricity production).
- Access to fresh air due to pedestrianization.
- Integrated water features, swales, soakaway hollows, and gravel-filled trenches to infiltrate.
- Rainwater runoff, and rainwater harvesting.
- The design is oriented to the tram line, the hill, and to solar access.
- The design is responsive to topography from tram to hill.
- Prospect occurs at the edges of the District overlooking tram line and agricultural land, and refuge occurs within the super-blocks.
- The super-blocks and buildings encourage indoor–outdoor activities and views.
- Spatial structure is rational, hierarchical, and transected, highly connected within by vehicle routes and pedestrian pathways, and connected to Hanover by tram.

- Centering with central plaza and gathering space.
- Bounding characteristics with the sharp grid edge perimeter, surrounding green zones, and the super-block forms with interior and outdoor spaces.
- Selective natural materials, including impervious street cover.
- The form language is contemporary and varies along the urban-to-rural transect.
- Provision of cultural and social activities at the district center and in super-blocks.
- Exposure to living color in both natural and urban areas.
- There are experiences of seasonal transformations.
- There are experiences of light in all forms.
- Super-blocks offer safe connections to nature, and medical facilities are within walking distance (pandemics).
- There are potentials for social and natural numinous experiences.

Positive Outcomes

The compact community plan has produced opportunities and positive outcomes for biophilic urban experiences. Climate change in the Hanover region has resulted in longer summer days of dry heat, which is exacerbated by denser areas and the heat island effect.[9] While the District is quite dense, there exists a large percentage of open space, affording multiple connections to nature and access to the integrated agriculture. The automobile-free green super-block courtyards are safe and provide direct access to nature. Figure 6.5 shows sheep roaming below Kronsberg Hill. This commitment to greenspace coupled with the pedestrianization of the community contributes to climate neutrality. All residents are within a one-third mile of a tram stop.[10] Sustainability is a major goal of the community and occurs in multiple ways. Building fairly small dwelling units reduces

6.5
Kronsberg Hill
and farm animals
(*Source: Alamy
Stock*)

energy demand. The on-site energy resources of wind power and solar power are renewable. Transportation energy use is reduced through the pedestrianization of the District and direct access to public transit. Public spaces and common lands provide opportunities for positive social interaction and enriched placemaking. Health and wellness outcomes occur through nutritious on-site agriculture, increased exercise, improved air quality, and direct access to nature. The super-blocks within the context of COVID-19 function as contained outdoor spaces, and with safe distancing and sanitation protocols can contribute to health and wellness. As of the beginning of September 2020, Germany has more than 250,000 cases and 9,400 deaths.[11] The primary contribution to Biophilic Urbanism is Kronsberg District's density and super-block designs, with their connections to nature, mass transit, pedestrianization, and renewable energy systems.

NOTES

1. Eva Hootz and Karl Johaentges, *Living on Kronsberg* (Hannover, Germany: City of Hannover, 2000).
2. Harrison Fraker, *The Hidden Potential of Sustainable Neighborhoods: Lessons from Low-Carbon Communities* (Washington, DC: Island Press, 2013). p 80.
3. Madeleine Granvik Dorita Wlodarczyk and Lars Ryden, "Building a sustainable neighborhood: Kronsberg", In Lars Rydén (ed.), *Building and Re-building Sustainable Communities: Reports from the Superbs project* (Uppsala, Sweden: Baltic University Press, 2003). pp 26–34.
4. City of Hanover, *Hannover Kronsberg Handbook: Planning and Realisation* (Hanover, Germany: City of Hanover, 2002). p 16.
5. Harrison Fraker, *The Hidden Potential of Sustainable Neighborhoods: Lessons from Low-Carbon Communities* (Washington, DC: Island Press, 2013). p 133.
6. Gary Coates, *The City as Garden: A Study of the Sustainable Urban District of Kronsberg (Hannover), Germany* https://www.academia.edu/8041051/The_City_as_Garden_A_Study_of_the_Sustainable_Urban_District_of_Kronsberg_Hannover_Germany (accessed January 6, 2020).
7. Tim Beatley, *Native to Nowhere: Sustaining Home and Community in A Global Age* (Washington, DC: Island Press, 2005).
8. William McDonough and Partners, *The Hannover Principles: Design for Sustainability* (Hanover, Germany: City of Hanover, 1992). pp 76–77.
9. State Capital Hannover, *Living with Climate Change – Hannover Adapts* 53+ Living+with+climate+change+-+Hannover+Adapts.pdf, (Hannover, Germany: Capital City Hannover, 2017). (accessed February 12, 2020).
10. Douglas Farr, *Sustainable Urbanism: Urban Design with Nature* (Hoboken, NJ: John Wiley & Sons, 2008).
11. Worldometer, *COVID-19 Coronavirus Pandemic*, https://www.worldometers.info/coronavirus/#countries (accessed September 8, 2020).

7 PONTEVEDRA CITY CENTER

PONTEVEDRA CITY CENTER

Background and History

Pontevedra is a city located in the northwest of the Iberian Peninsula in Spain, and has a long history of maritime trade. It sits within a coastal region with a humid oceanic climate. While temperatures are mild, Pontevedra receives on average about 67 inches (1,700 mm) of precipitation each year.[1] It has an abundance of natural beauty consisting of mountains, green hills, rivers, lakes, estuaries, and seashores. About half of the city center perimeter is bordered by the river Lerez. The name Pontevedra derives from the ancient Galician meaning "old bridge." It is known for its history and art and was considered a fishing and craft city. Galicia's second city, it is considered "the Good City,"[2] and has a current population of 83,029 inhabitants. Pontevedra is considered to have a humid oceanic climate. By the end of the 1990s, Pontevedra was dominated by automobile traffic and congestion, especially within the historic city center not designed for it, and it was considered dirty and dangerous. As a result, it was in severe decline, with people fleeing the center. In 1999, the new mayor, Miguel Anxo Fernandez Lores, proposed the program to eliminate automobiles within the city center. It is within this context that biophilic design principles and pattern attributes were able to flourish and inform the redistribution of public space. Transportation remains an important urban issue for most communities. Excessive automobile use creates long commute distances, congestion, pollution, noise, and injuries, and stifles social interaction.

Pontevedra is recently known for its aggressive urban planning strategy of pedestrianization of its historic city center and creating an automobile-free environment. Automobile-free urban zones are not new. Take for example Venice, which is completely car-free except for the bus station. Giethoom, Netherlands, with a population of 2,620 people, is known as the "Venice of the Netherlands," with its automobile-free pedestrian district, boat-filled waterways, footpaths, and bicycle trails. The entire town of Houten, the Netherlands is known for its accessibility to the railway, green and water zones throughout the city, and cycling

7.1
Pontevedra,
Spain, city center
aerial view
(*Source: Alamy
Stock*)

network. Car-moderate environments can be found in Cinque Terre, Italy because of the difficult terrain. Liege, Belgium has one of the oldest car-free historic city centers. Zermatt and Bettmeralp, Switzerland are alpine resorts where the entire town is automobile-free. The medieval core of Zurich, Switzerland is car-free. Helsinki is developing a "mobility-on-demand" service that will bring together carpools, buses, taxis, bikes, and ferries – all to prevent anyone from needing to drive a car in the city center by 2025. Countless numbers of eastern and western European cities have car-free areas designated within their older city centers. In Asia, many island cities and inland city centers are car-free. And in the United States, ski resorts, main streets and pedestrian malls have transformed into automobile-free zones. Refer to Figure 7.1 for an aerial view of the city center of Pontevedra.

Pontevedra was a city with narrow streets invaded by traffic, and city squares were more like parking lots. It was in 2000 that the 75 acres (30 hectares) of Pontevedra's historic center and its public spaces was freed by the pedestrianization process. The plan incrementally limited the use of automobiles and service vehicles and reduced speed limits. One can cross the entire city center in 25 minutes. The purpose was to make the city more accessible, especially to the most vulnerable, senior citizens, children, and those who are handicapped. As Pontevedra's cultural councilor, Carmen Fouces, said, "It is like building a nest."[3] Traffic that had traveled through the city instead of around it, and those looking for parking spaces, were now diverted. A few parking spaces are sprinkled throughout the central area that can be used for five minutes for drop-off and pickup, for residents with a private garage, and for delivery services and emergencies. The city estimates that car use has dropped by 77 percent and CO_2 emissions by 66 percent.[4] Visitors can park near the perimeter in underground

7.2
Pontevedra central
plaza (*Source:
Alamy Stock*)

parking garages directly beneath the Alameda (town square), beneath the Plaza de la Libertad or Plaza Barcelos, in parking lots at Zona Monumental and Campolongo, or at the Mercado de Pontevedra. Refer to Figure 7.2 for inner city social gathering space.

Pedestrianization occurs in two zones – a car-free zone and a traffic-calming zone. The land use for the car-free zone provides a mix of uses, including shopping, education, medical, and leisure for the people.[5] The car-free zone reduces vehicle traffic by 97 percent and the traffic-calming zone by 77 percent.[6] The streets are now crowded with people walking their dogs, pushing baby strollers, heading to work, shopping, or simply sitting and people-watching. The city center also adopted a pedestrian and bicycle integration policy. Pontevedra has picturesque public squares, where everyone strolls in the evenings. When the weather is cold, nothing beats stopping at a street vendor for a still-hot packet of fresh roasted chestnuts. The Mercado Municipal de Abastos and Mercado Municipal de Tomnino contain sites for the farmers' markets. The Mercado Municipal market's two stories display Galician products including the famous tetilla cheese, tarta de Santiago (almond tart), and orujo (a typical Galician liquor). The markets now activate the adjacent plazas, house high-quality fresh produce, host wine tastings, and become thematic markets throughout the year. Not only has this created a more enjoyable place in which to live, but the air is cleaner and the city's carbon dioxide emissions are significantly lower. Fewer than 10 percent of automobiles can enter the city center.

They found that prior to pedestrianization, 60 percent of the traffic was concerned with looking for parking places. Now people walk. Family-centered services have moved from outside to within the city center. Schools, maternity and pediatric services, libraries, cultural activities, and children's boot camps have either remained or have been relocated into the city center. The Plaza da Ferrería is Pontevedra's main town square and it is surrounded by some of the best cafes and restaurants around. It is also the liveliest place in the city center, always full of local residents chatting and eating, with free-ranging children playing about. The transformation is gradual and ongoing. Pontevedra has continued to expand the pedestrian area from the center to the outskirts, liberating another 166 acres (67 hectares) previously dominated by cars. The Old Town is now a UNESCO World Heritage Site, containing Romanesque, Gothic, Renaissance, Baroque, and Neoclassicist architecture. The image of the Plaza de la Lena, where the firewood trade occurred, illustrates the spatial character of Pontevedra's historic roots. Refer to Figure 7.3(a) for the Plaza de la Lena for freco dining and 7.3(b) for the pedestrian walking map.

There are many green and social gathering areas within the city center, including the tree-lined pedestrian streets, the Alamedia (or town square), Gardens de Eduardo Vincenti, Gardens de Castro Sampedro, the Plaza de Mugrtago, Plaza de Gali, Plaza da Pedreira, Plaza de Galicia, Plaza da Ferrara, the Plaza de Espana (the main pedestrian square where large concerts occur), the sports field at the Pista de Atletismo (athletic track), and the numerous private courtyard gardens. Running along the entire southern edge of the city center is the Rio Gofos, a small tributary of the Lerez river. Not far from the city center to the west and north, solitude can be found along the tranquil Lerez; there is a small sandy beach, and a pedestrian suspension footbridge leading to the incredible Parque Illa das Esculturas (Island of Sculptures). This contains 17 acres (7 hectares) of parkland and eucalyptus trees, with riparian vegetation and aquatic fauna. Most importantly there are 12 large-format contemporary granite works of art, including a labyrinth and a museum. The island was originally

7.3
Pontevedra pedestrianization: (a) Plaza de la Lena (Firewood Square) (*Source: Alamy Stock*), (b) Pontevedra Metrominuto (*Source: City of Pontevedra, Spain*)

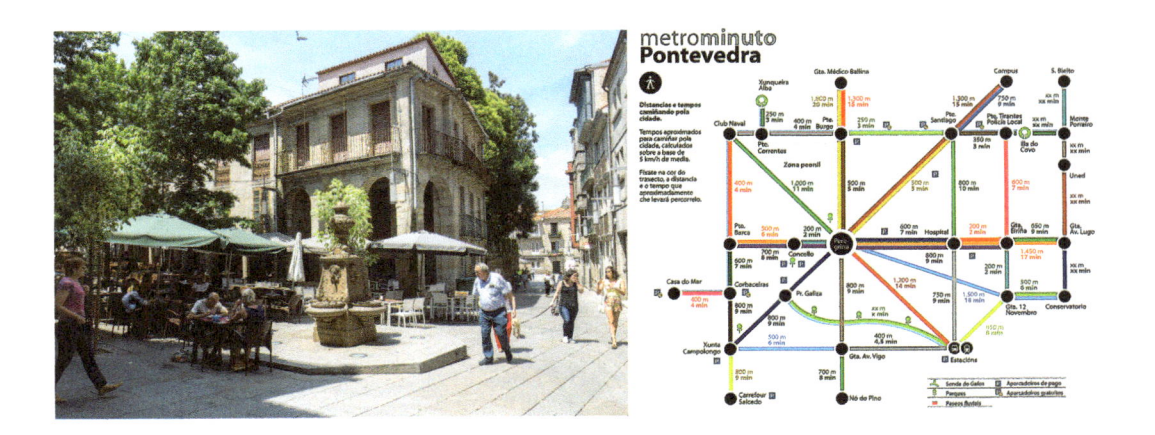

called the Isle of Xunquelra Lerez, but since 1999 it has gained community importance because of its transformation into a park and outdoor museum with the theme "the relationship between man and his environment." That is certainly a biophilic notion.

Pontevedra has changed its car-dominated street system into one that is safer and supports a pedestrian environment. It has also been able to advance a biophilic agenda. This single planning strategy has activated a number of biophilic patterns. Most importantly, it has empowered people to safely navigate, congregate in, and enjoy the urban outdoors. It has become a safe place for children and their caretakers.[7] As a consequence, Pontevedra published a pedestrian-oriented streetscape map – what they call "*Metrominuto*" (meaning "meter-minutes") map – that is like a subway map. It delineates walking times, connections and transfer points throughout the city center with "*móvete coa túa propia enerxía*" ("move with your own energy") as its tagline.[8] Walking times are calculated on average at approximately 2.5 miles per hour (4 km/h) calculated at 3.3–4.0 feet per second (1.0–1.2 meters per second).[9] These walking speeds represent an average from an entire population of people, including children and elderly. From each of the four corners to the center takes about 15 minutes. And the Plaza de Verdura is a frequented tourist destination because of the bars, outdoor dining, and canopy of trees. Refer to Figure 7.4 for the Plaza de Verdura.

Population and birth rates within the city center have increased over the two decades of pedestrianization, as the number of children has increased by 8 percent. The "work–family" urban model is tremendously beneficial. Pontevedra has been awarded several international awards for its urban quality and quality of life, accessibility, and urban mobility policy. These include the international

7.4
Plaza de Verdura, Pontevedra (*Source: Alamy Stock*)

European prize "Intermodes" in Brussels in 2013, the United Nations Habitat prize in Dubai in 2014, and the "Excellence Prize" of the Center for Active Design in New York City in 2015.

Analysis of the Masterplan

The masterplan of the Pontevedra city center shows that it is bounded by the Lerez river and automobile roadways (Av. De Uruguay, Av. Das Corvaceiras, Av. Marin, and Av. De Buenos Aires) on the west and north, and roadways (Av. De Maira Vicoria Moreno, Rua Eduardo Pondal, and Rua Jose Malvar Figueroa) to the east and south.[9] The overall shape is organic, non-Euclidian, and currently defined by the river and circumferential roads around the center. The average travel budget (or the Marchetti constant) of one hour's travel time per day is challenged by pedestrianization and walking cities like Pontevedra.[10] The travel time per day is more likely to be minutes than hours. In fact, in Pontevedra, one can traverse the entire city center on foot in 25 minutes. The city center provides over 1,600 free parking spaces along its perimeter so that drivers can leave their cars there and enter without them.[11] The parks and gardens form a patchwork throughout the city center. Many streets within the center that do allow cars have taken the counterintuitive step of removing sidewalks entirely to imply that streets are for pedestrians first.

The street structure is medieval with its partially radial and fractured or random grid. Due to its density of built form, the city is primarily a fabric of solids and voids. It is the negative space or voids in the streets, plazas, and parks that renders Pontevedra a biophilic urban place. Typically, cafes and restaurants spill out into the pedestrian spaces protected by canopies or awnings. Pontevedra is the second-largest city in Galicia in terms of green areas per square mile per capita. Of note are the Park of the Palm Trees, Barcelona Park, Rosalia de Castro Park, the Park of the Island of Sculpture, and Galos River Park. They are public spaces supporting a rebirth of nature and revitalized social interaction. Refer to Figure 7.5, which shows the base map and layering of biophilic attributes throughout the city center.

Primary Pattern Attributes

The transformation of the Pontevedra city center reflects a number of biophilic pattern attributes. Positive outcomes can be speculated from published material, photographs, and site observations. Carbon neutrality is approximated with the pedestrianization of the city center. It reflects a temporal and transformative processes that has occurred over the last two decades that produces a quieter and less polluted public environment.

Placemaking has certainly intensified with an increase of population and safety (an increase of 12,000 new residents), and a decrease in noise, crime, and environmental dereliction. The increase in pedestrians has contributed to an increase in commercial activity and social interaction. The city is now truly a center because the elimination of automobiles has created a welcome sense of place. It encourages greater indoor–outdoor interconnections because there

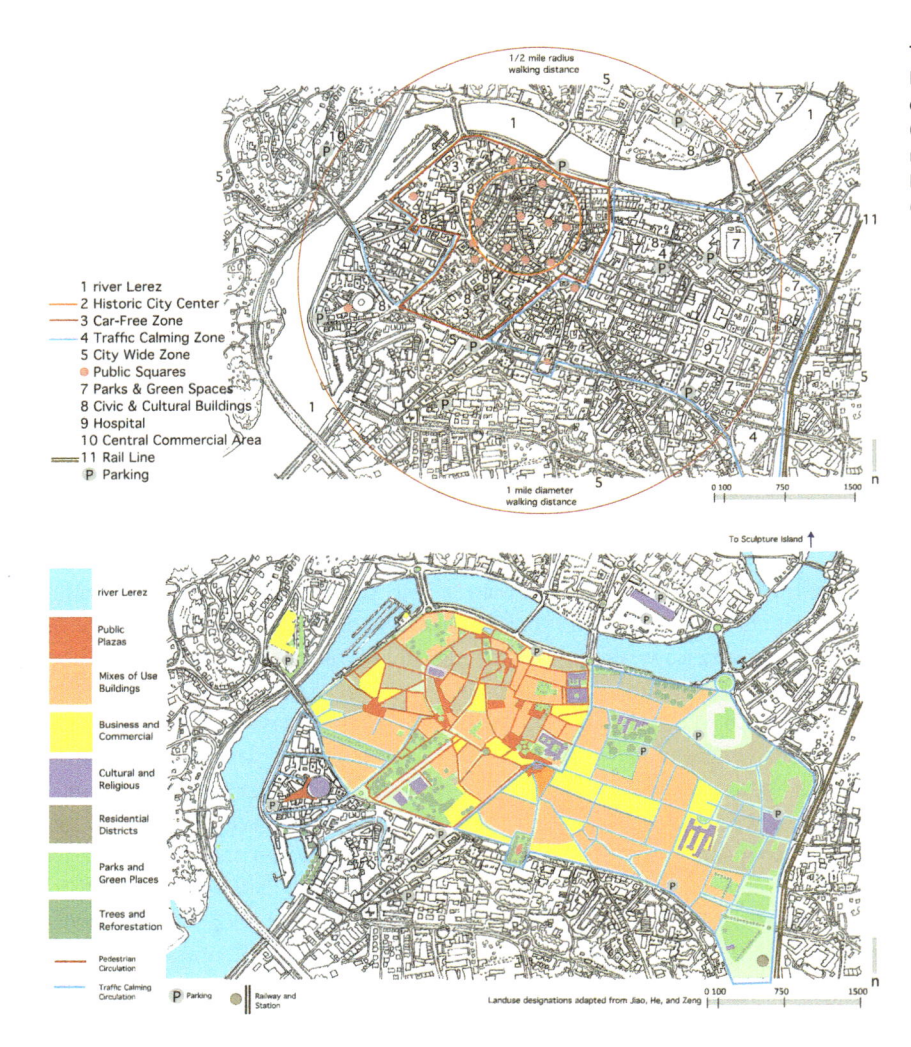

7.5
Pontevedra city
center analysis:
(a) Pontevedra base
map, (b) Pontevedra
biophilic patterns
(*Source: Phillip
Tabb*)

are reasons to go outdoors and places that support outdoor activities (seating areas, people-watching, water features, outdoor cafes, and markets). Cultural, social, and historic activities contribute to social cohesion, identity, and place-boundedness. Within the city center there is a greater opportunity to connect directly with nature (plants and animals) and enjoy the outdoors. An outline of many of the biophilic pattern attributes follows:

- Connections to the plant world (river walk, gardens, streetscapes, and urban parks), and 25 miles (40 kilometers) of foot and cycling paths along the Lerez river.
- Plentiful views and vistas of nature and urban spaces.
- Sensory connections, especially gastronomy with so many outdoor cafes and restaurants.
- Access to fresh air, and a 70 percent greenhouse CO_2 reduction.

- Integrated water features, access to Lerez river and numerous fountains, wastewater discharge eliminated in river.
- Encouraged indoor–outdoor activities as shops and restaurants spill out into public spaces.
- Spatial structure is based on existing street grid and plaza and parks that are automobile-free.
- Spatial structure also follows the "avoid/reduce, shift/maintain, improve" (A-S-I) approach to transportation emissions reduction.
- Centering by renewing the historic center as a revitalized destination, and Pontevedra's main square, Plaza de la Herreria (Blacksmith's Square).
- Bounding with Lerez river, peripheral automobile road and car-free historic area.
- Selective natural materials, stone pavers, and extensive landscaping.
- Provision of religious, cultural, commercial, and social activities.
- The form language is historic and human-scaled, with Romanesque, Gothic, Renaissance, Baroque, and Neoclassicist architecture.
- Prolific integration of public works of art (Sculpture Island).
- Exposure to living color found in both the natural and built environments.
- Experiences of urban and seasonal transformations, urban transformation to car-free.
- Experiences of light in all forms, especially pools of light in public plazas.
- There are numerous open and green spaces, and there are a dozen clinics and hospitals in the central area in the event of pandemics.
- Potential for numinous urban experiences, especially culturally and socially driven.

Positive Outcomes

The Galician strategy for mitigating climate change is to reach the EU 2050 goal with a focus on climate awareness, decarbonization, and transition to renewable energy sources.[12] The pedestrianization has produced opportunities and positive outcomes for biophilic urban experiences. Climate-neutral outcomes include carbon sequestering, and reductions in pollution and greenhouse gas emissions. An increase in the greening of spaces and the introduction of more porous flagstone ground surfaces have resulted in greater carbon sequestering. Vehicle use has dropped by 77 percent, with emissions down by 66 percent.[13] Pontevedra is the perfect size for pedestrianization, as one can walk across the entire city in 25 minutes. Sustainability outcomes include lower transport energy consumption due to the pedestrianization and the rebirth of destination mixed uses, such as markets, cafes, urban services, and an increase of population density. The revitalization of an existing place also supports sustainability and a strong sense and pride of place. Pontevedra is an inclusive social city that allows people with a physical disability to move smoothly throughout the city.[14] Schools are located close to the southern boundary of the car-free zone and bus stops are out of the car-free area. Refer to Figure 7.6 for the Herreria Square in the center of the city.

7.6
Herreria Square,
Pontevedra (*Source: Getty Images*)

Cultural, social, and historic activities have increased dramatically. Since pedestrianization started in 2000, the population of children's ages, up to 14 years old, also increased by 8 percent. Health and wellness outcomes include increased access to fresh air, more physical activity by being outdoors and walking, and an increase in frequency and quality of experiences of nature and interactions with fellow residents. The city center is safer. There are no traffic fatalities, and crime rates are lower. Health and wellness benefits from walking include burning calories, strengthening the heart, lowering blood sugar, easing joint pain, boosting energy, and improving mood.[15] During the Coronavirus pandemic, it has been beneficial to experience the outdoors through safe distancing in the wide pedestrian streets and numerous parks and plazas. Numinous outcomes come in the form of cultural and intimate natural moments found in the pedestrianized area of the central city. The primary contribution to Biophilic Urbanism is its focus on pedestrianization; revitalization of its streets, parks and plazas; and the social, cultural, and historic activities. Spain's infection rate of the Coronavirus in 2020 rose exponentially in the months of March and April, surpassing Italy. By May and June the number of cases began leveling. As of early September 2020, the number of cases and deaths are more than 543,000 and 29,000 respectively.[16]

NOTES

1. Climate and Weather of Pontevedra http://www.iberianature.com/material/Spain_climate/pontevedra_climate.htm (accessed February 11, 2020).
2. Pontevedra Wikipedia entry: https://en.wikipedia.org/wiki/Pontevedra (accessed January 24, 2020).

3. Jaime Velazquez, *What happens to Kid Culture When You Close the Streets to Cars* https://www.citylab.com/design/2018/11/car-free-pedestrianization-made-pontevedra-spain-kid-friendly/576268/ (accessed January 7, 2020).
4. Will Doig, "Spain's Happy Little Carless City" https://reasonstobecheerful.world/spains-happy-little-carless-city/ (accessed January 17, 2020).
5. Jiacheng Jiao, Sheng He, and Xiaochen Zeng, "An Investigation into European car-free development models as an opportunity to improve the environmental sustainability in cities: The case of Pontevedra" https://uniqueca.com/archives/proceedings/HUSO2019.pdf#page=84 (accessed March 28, 2020).
6. Council of Pontevedra, "Pontevedra: Fewer Cars, More City" http://www.pontevedra.gal/publicacions/fewer-cars/files/assets/common/downloads/publication.pdf (accessed April 15, 2020).
7. Chris van Uffelen, *Pedestrian Zones: Car Free Spaces* (Salenstein, CH: Braun Publishing, 2015).
8. El ejemplo de Pontevedra metrominuto Pontevedra https://nuevecuatrouno.com/2016/02/17/el-ejemplo-de-pontevedra/ (accessed January 24, 2020).
9. "Reclaiming the streets: the increasing trend of pedestrianisation around the world" (2018) https://www.rapidtransition.org/stories/reclaiming-the-streets-the-increasing-trend-of-pedestrianisation-around-the-world/ (accessed March 13, 2020).
10. Marchette constant: https://en.wikipedia.org/wiki/Marchetti%27s_constant (accessed January 15, 2020).
11. Letivia Perez, *Pontevedra City Guide: an easy guide for a visit to Pontevedra city and its surrounding area* (Pontevedra, Spain: Independently Published, 2020).
12. 18th European Week of Regions an Cities, *European Regions Fighting Climate Change: the Galician Contribution* https://europa.eu/regions-and-cities/programme/sessions/570_en (accessed February 11, 2020).
13. Jaime Velazquez, (see note 3).
14. *Pontevedra: a city model focus on people* (accessed March 10, 2020).
15. Meghan Rabbitt, *11 Biggest Benefits of Walking to Improve Health, According to Doctors* https://www.prevention.com/fitness/a20485587/benefits-from-walking-every-day/ (accessed February 6, 2020).
16. Worldometer, *COVID-19 Coronavirus Pandemic*, https://www.worldometers.info/coronavirus/#countries (accessed September 8, 2020).

8 SINGAPORE PARK CONNECTOR NEIGHBORHOOD

SINGAPORE PARK CONNECTOR NEIGHBORHOOD

Background and History

Singapore is a diamond-shaped island about 85 miles (137 kilometers) north of the equator. It measures 31 miles (50 kilometers) from east to west, and 17 miles (27 kilometers) north to south. In the late 14th century it was inhabited by fishermen and pirates. Two-thirds of the island is less than 50 feet (15 meters) above sea level. Singapore experiences an equatorial climate and is in the equatorial monsoon region of Southeast Asia. A majority of the urban density is situated along the southern portion of the island. Natural gas produces approximately 95 percent of the electricity (having switched from oil in 2000). Singapore currently has plans to develop electricity from solar power and waste-to-power energy.

Since 1965, Singapore has envisioned itself as a garden city, a process which initially took the form of a tree-planting initiative and national parks system. Later the vision of a garden city changed from a "garden in the city" to a "city in a garden," bringing gardens, natural green spaces, and biodiversity to every resident. With this conceptual shift, the Singapore Park Connector Network (PCN) was created and today is an innovative "green matrix." It provides recreational and green spaces along underused land and existing infrastructure, along roads, canals, and railroads. The park connectors are linear landscapes that connect major neighborhood parks to residential areas. As part of the overall Concept Plan for Singapore, the PCN has played a pivotal role in creating a city oriented to "live, work and play" and cultivating the city's image as a model for Biophilic Urbanism, healthy infrastructure, and as a premier horticulture hub. It is an exemplar of "livable density." Another green strategy is the planting of continuous tree canopies above all major roads. Given the fact that Singapore has a similar population density to Hong Kong, approximately 3,142 people per square mile or 8,137 per square kilometer), the PCN is a welcome addition to urban living.[1] One of its conservation measures is to create new parks and connectors for new development that disrupts natural areas. Refer to Figure 8.1 for an aerial view of the Gardens by the Bay overlooking the Central Business District of

8.1
Singapore
aerial view
(*Source: Alamy
Stock*)

Singapore. The evolution of Singapore's leadership in biophilic urbanism has occurred in three stages.

- Singapore as garden city – by creating nature-accessible parks and recreation spaces and community programs.
- Singapore in a garden – further enhancing natural experiences in daily life, conservation practices, and supporting community stewardship.
- Biophilic Singapore in a garden – developing world-class gardens, enriched biodiversity, and the enhancement of the nature–people relationship through the PCN.

The PCN ties together six loops with a network of jogging, cycling, skating, and walking pathways. The first leg of this program, Kalling Park Connector, was completed in 1992. The latest leg, the Eastern Coastal Loop was completed in 2007. The program created a linear urban network capable of utilizing existing greenery, providing improved conservation, recreation space, a habitat for wildlife, greater access and linkages to other urban districts, and a contribution to a stronger sense of place. The result is a park connector 186 miles (300 kilometers) in length. A fair number of genuinely native animals and plants have managed to adapt to the urban environment.[2] Surveys of various Park Connectors have cataloged a total of 90 species of birds, including the white-throated kingfisher, grey heron, and scaly breasted munia; 57 species of butterflies like the common mime; and 22 species of dragonflies. Rather than nucleated designs seen in previous examples, the Singapore Park Connector is an example of an infrastructure network using biophilic principles. According to Poon Hong Yuen, many of the linkages occur on very narrow land unusable for any other purpose, and they often visually borrow from adjacent greenery.[3] This works both ways: from residential developments adjacent to the PCN looking at greenery, or from the PCN overlooking nearby natural or water-related landscapes.

The Eastern Coastal Loop is 26 miles (42 kilometers) long, and seamlessly connects to the city center and to exciting places adjacent to the southern and eastern coasts. Along the way there are plenty of rest stops, food outlets, playgrounds, water sports such as canoeing and yacht-surfing, beaches, and wildlife to enjoy. This loop also includes the three Gardens by the Bay, which occupy 250 acres (101 hectares) of reclaimed land, and contain more than 1,500,000 plants. They represent Singapore's premier outdoor recreation space and serve as Singapore's national icon.

The Northern Eastern Riverine Loop is 16 miles (26 kilometers) of relatively flat terrain and rustic landscapes good for cycling. It is one of the less-traveled loops and is considered one of the most scenic. With its stretches of coastline, canals, waterways, and wetlands, it features an abundance of wildlife, greenery, and birds like kingfishers and herons, as well as exotic fruits such as lychees and sweetsops.

The Central Urban Loop is 22 miles (36 kilometers) in length is one of the larger loops, and is known for its charming neighborhoods, lush greenery, recreational options, playgrounds, wide open spaces, wildlife, and the Kallang river. The loop gives direct access to the popular Punggol Park, Bishan-ang Mo Kio Park, and Ang Mo Kio Town Garden, as well as loops within the network. It encompasses multiple central city housing estates.

The Northern Explorer Loop is 16 miles (25 kilometers) in length. The terrain is hilly and undulating, and features nature areas and the woodlands waterfront. It links four estate districts together. There are scenic areas, especially around the Lower Seletar Reservoir where there are also fish and crab farms, and views of Singapore's longest coastal jetties. And to the south is Singapore Zoo, which is considered one of the world's best rainforest zoo environments with its "open concept." It houses 2,400 specimens and more than 300 species.

The Western Adventure Loop is 12 miles (20 kilometers) in length, made up of more rugged natural trails. Included in this network are the Singapore quarry, a dairy farm, and nature parks. Set within a rustic environment is the 156-acre (63-hectare) Dairy Farm Nature Park that offers many recreational amenities and activities. The park no longer has dairy cows, but does include the Wallace Education Centre. At the southwestern end of the park is the Singapore quarry, providing scenic views.

The Southern Ridges Loop runs a little over 6 miles (10 kilometers) and is a lightly traveled and pram-friendly loop. It features a ribbed pedestrian bridge between two hilltops and picturesque views. This loop contains themed gardens, with landscape designs, and forest walks. It is known for the Henderson Waves, its iconic nearly 900-foot (274-meter) pedestrian bridge which literally undulates across the forested landscape. The Southern Ridges Loop is home to a wide variety of flora and fauna and is one of the best spots in Singapore to enjoy panoramic views of the city, harbor, and the Southern Islands.

According to Peter Newman, "As biophilic urbanism in Singapore spreads and matures into a more complete coverage of the urban environment, it can be expected that local biodiversity will rise."[4] The project was initially intended to protect natural landscapes, heritage spaces, and increase ecological resilience. There are plans to increase the recreational corridors to nearly 250 miles (400 km) in the next fifteen years. According to Peter Newman,

> "creating a continuous tree canopy above all major roads is the backbone of the 'city in a garden' vision. The Streetscape Greenery Master Plan (SGMP) is concerned with extending the local identity of an area to create a sense of place in the physical landscape to the stretch of road that spans the area, with the aim to create a 'seamless green mantle' throughout the island."[5]

Biophilic architecture and landscape architecture also play an important role in Singapore's efforts to become greener. The Marina Barrage forms one of the largest freshwater reservoirs in the world on reclaimed land, preventing flooding. Atop of the pump house is a green roof used for recreational purposes including kite flying. Singapore Botanic Gardens is a UNESCO heritage Site and houses 60,000 plants including orchids. In the Bay South Gardens are 18 solar-powered "*supertrees*" comprising a human-made forest. The trees vary in height from 82 to 164 feet (25 to 50 meters). Several of the supertrees are connected with bridging "skywalks." In Horticulture Park, there are experimental green walls. A Newton Suite designed by WOHA in 2007 has a 36-floor green wall with green terraces every four floors and views of the city's nature reserves. The Oasia Hotel, also designed by WOHA, is a high-rise structure with a mesh exterior fabric envelope of glass and 1,793 planter boxes, which provide 60 percent shade on the facades. Marina Bay Sands and Skypark, designed by architect Moshe Sofdie and built in 2010, is another iconic landmark with 360-degree panoramic views of Singapore's skyline and city below.

Taken together, the greening strategies combine to reinforce the concept of Singapore as a city in a garden – a powerful biophilic and placemaking strategy. This occurs at the building, street, neighborhood, city, and island regional scales equally. Placemaking occurs with the intimate knowledge of and interaction with the local environment, natural ecological processes, and its inhabitants. It becomes a pathway for self-understanding and a sense of belonging. Other biophilic strategies are also being implemented, including strengthening the conservation of wetland biodiversity in northwestern Singapore, and the protection of habitats, including mangroves, freshwater marshes, and mudflats. Refer to Figures 8.2 and 8.3, which show images within two of the park connectors.

Analysis of the Masterplan

The masterplan is composed of an island-wide connector loop that links together six smaller neighborhood park loops, all of which provide convenient access to Singapore's increasing population. The plan places a large natural imprint upon the entire city and contributes to its robust green agenda. The overall plan

8.2
Singapore Bukit
(Hill) Timah Public
Nature Park
(*Source: Alamy
Stock*)

suggests four broad concentric rings of land uses. As an island, the outer perimeter consists of water, coastline, and coastal development. To the north is the Strait of Johor, and to the south is the Strait of Singapore. To the west are lands dedicated to farms and the army. And to the east are the naval port and airport. Next is the Parks Connector Neighborhood ring, which weaves between the city and the coast. The next ring occupies the portion of the island center, the large park, central catchment area, water reservoirs, and a majority of the built environment. And finally, the innermost ring contains the large parkland, nature reserves, zoo, and reservoirs and central water catchment. A majority of the

8.3
Singapore Bukit
(Hill) Batok
(*Source: Wikimedia
Commons*)

8.4
Singapore
masterplan
analysis: (a) Park
Connector
Neighborhood
base map,
(b) Park Connector
Neighborhood
biophilic patterns
(*Source: Phillip
Tabb*)

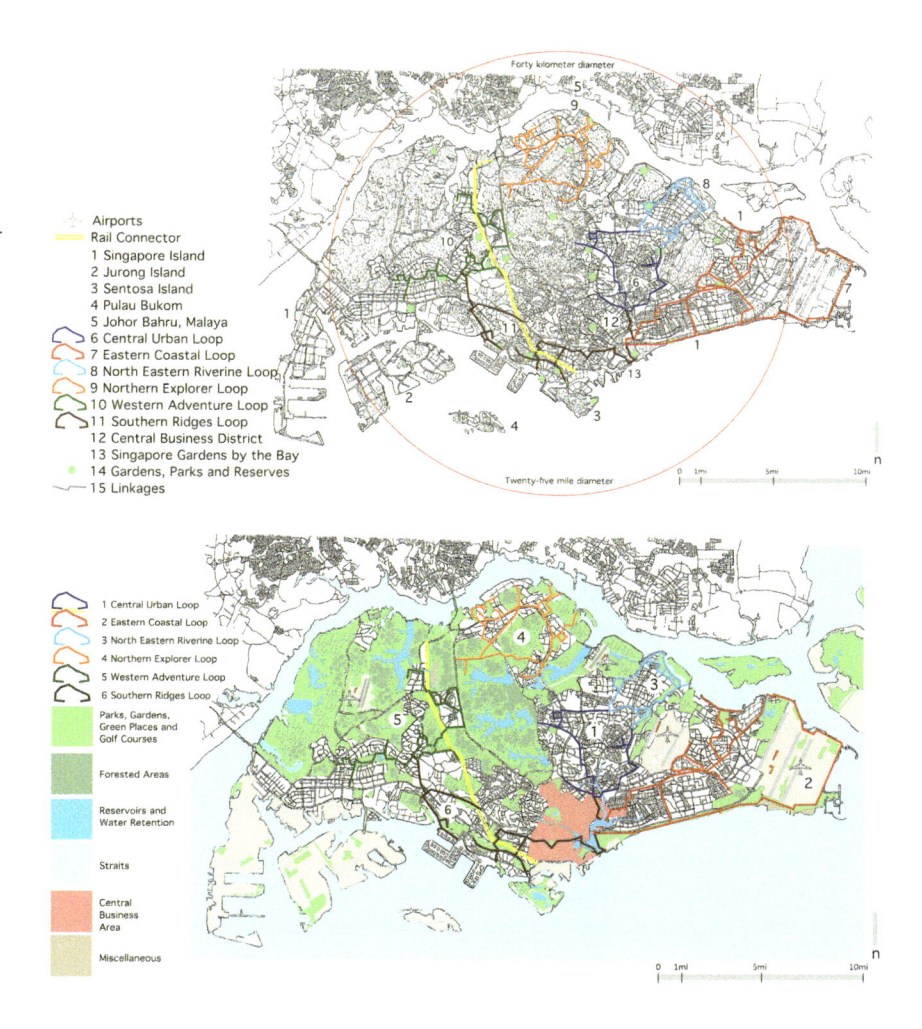

urban development occupies land along the southeast, south, and southwest areas of the island, while the north and northwest remain more natural with water inlets and woodlands. There are two major MRT routes, the east–west line and the northern loop line. The PCN is composed of three interrelated systems: (1) loops which encircle parks, (2) links which connect park loops to one another, and (3) park connectors which extend out into surrounding neighborhoods or complete loops.[6] Refer to Figure 8.4 that shows the base map and masterplan of the loops, links, and connectors.

Primary Pattern Attributes

There are a host of biophilic principles and pattern attributes operating within the Park Connector Neighborhood. The pattern attributes that are most present are in the human–nature connection, with abundant connections to and direct experiences of the natural environment replete with manifestations of plants, animals, water features, geography, and seasonal changes. The visual and sensory connections occur everywhere along the PCN. There is a concerted effort to connect the resident population to the local plants and animals found along the various connectors and loops. Intimate views and larger vistas are plentiful as one walks or rides along the trails. Sensory experiences occur along the connector walks and within the six parks, including areas for casual outdoor dining. In terms of Singapore's temporal transformative processes, according to Dr. Lena Chan, "A city does not turn biophilic on a planned day. Like all things natural, it evolves."[7] An outline of many of the biophilic pattern attributes follows.

- Connections to the plant world and forest bathing (green connectors, loops, tree canopies, supertrees, gardens, medicinal plants, and abundant flowers).
- Connections to wildlife found abundantly throughout the PCN: at one time the Brahman cow, along with 80 other species of mammals, 395 species of birds, 110 species of reptiles, 30 species of amphibians, and others (fish, crabs).[8]
- Plentiful intimate views and broad vistas to nature.
- Sensory connections (especially visual, auditory, olfactory, and gastronomic).
- Singapore is slowly developing solar energy for electricity.
- Access to fresh air (forest-enriched, coastal).
- Access to regional and local water features.
- Responses to naturally occurring topographical changes.
- Encourages indoor–outdoor activities throughout the parks network.
- Spatial structure is natural and organic (free-flowing).
- Centering by reinforcing the concept of a city in a garden, the downtown core ("the city"), and neighborhood parks within the loops.
- Bounding characteristics of the loops around neighborhood parks.
- Natural materials are abundant (nature, benches, bridges).
- Exposure to natural ecological, geographical, and biological processes.
- Provision of recreational, cultural, and social activities.
- The form language is natural.
- Exposure to living color, especially in the plant world.
- Experience of seasonal transformations.
- Experience of light in all forms (especially natural, pools, and flickering).
- The numerous parks and extensive networks provide great relief during the Coronavirus pandemic.
- Potential for numinous experiences from connections to nature, sensory experiences, and medicinal plants.

Positive Outcomes

The primary positive biophilic outcomes derive from direct contact with nature, which promotes healthier lifestyles and sustainable transportation. In addition, preserving the enormous parkland contributes to a positive climate reduction of carbon dioxide and the production of oxygen. Carbon sequestering is a natural by-product of the effort to preserve flora and fauna. According to Richard T. Corlett et al., climate change in Singapore will gradually increase temperature, rainfall, sea level, and ocean acidity, and will affect native plants and animals.[9] Because Singapore is a disadvantaged renewable energy supplier, its focus on climate change mitigation is on energy efficiency and cleaner energy production. And placemaking is abundantly present, with the generous amount of outdoor recreational and social activities, the bounding nature of the larger ring connector, and by truly making Singapore a "city in the garden." Physical activity, contributing to health and wellness outcomes, was cited as a beneficial experience because of the PCN's connectivity and pleasant connections to nature. Surveys conducted by the National Parks Board show that residents are not only using the PCN for recreation, physical activity and commuting, but also for social gatherings.

Biodiversity and regeneration are also outcomes of this primarily natural environment. Numinous experiences abound, with nature's beauty and inspiration found in the Park Connector Neighborhood. According Dr. Lena Chan, biophilic cities will most likely be different depending upon the kinds of species that thrive there, as well as their unique cultural factors.[10] Singapore's food culture is closely linked to its neighbors. Malaysian, Chinese, Indonesian, Indian, Thai, Vietnamese and even British influences have made Singapore a gastronome's delight. In Singapore, certain plants are considered sacred, including tulsi or holy basil, and vishnuism, among others.[11] It should be noted that in a study by the University of Southern California, researchers found that extraversion and emotional stability increased subjective well-being, positive affect and life satisfaction, and decreased stress and negative affect. Yet, their findings did not reveal significant positive outcomes in the nature–wellbeing relationship,

8.5
Singapore Gardens by the Bay (*Source: Alamy Stock*)

probably due to Singapore's more humid and warmer climate.[12] During the Coronavirus pandemic, Singapore initially instituted strict lockdown and aggressive contact-tracing measures. By the end of April 2020, however, the number of cases rose dramatically within the overcrowded foreign migrant worker dormitories. As of the beginning of September 2020, the number of cases was over 57,000, with 27 deaths.[13] This is a remarkably low number of fatalities as compared to other countries. Singapore's primary contribution to biophilic urbanism is the comprehensive and integrative qualities of the park system, and the focus on bringing nature to everyone in the city. Refer to Figure 8.5, which shows an aerial view of the Gardens by the Bay with its beautiful supertrees.

NOTES

1. Macrotrends, *Singapore Population Density 1950-2020* https://www.macrotrends.net/countries/SGP/singapore/population-density (accessed September 7, 2020).
2. Peter K.L. Ng, Richard T. Corlett, and Hugh T.W. Tan, *Singapore Biodiversity: An Encyclopedia of the Natural Environment and Sustainable Development* (Singapore: Raffles Museum of Biodiversity Research, 2011).
3. Poon Hong Yuen, *Park Connectors: Living Large in Small* Spaces https://www.clc.gov.sg/docs/default-source/urban-solutions/urb-sol-iss-2-pdfs/case-study-singapore-park-connectors.pdf (accessed January 5, 2020).
4. Peter Newman, *Biophilic Urbanism: A Case Study on Singapore* https://www.tandfonline.com/doi/pdf/10.1080/07293682.2013.790832 (accessed January 2, 2020).
5. Peter Newman and Isabella Jennings, *Cities as Sustainable Ecosystems: Principles and Practices* (Washington, DC: Island Press, 2008).
6. Peter K.L. Ng, Richard T. Corlett, and Hugh T.W. Tan, *Singapore Biodiversity: An Encyclopedia of the Natural Environment and Sustainable Development* (Singapore: Raffles Museum of Biodiversity Research, 2011). p 154.
7. Wildlife of Singapore https://en.wikipedia.org/wiki/Wildlife_of_Singapore (accessed January 21, 2020).
8. *Is Singapore a biophilic city?* https://www.ura.gov.sg/Corporate/Resources/Publications/Skyline/Skyline-Issue10/Biophilic-city (accessed January 21, 2020).
9. "Climate Change and Biodiversity in Singapore," in Peter K.L. Ng, Richard T. Corlett, and Hugh T.W. Tan (eds.) *Singapore Biodiversity: An Encyclopedia of th Natural Environment and Sustainable Development,* (Singapore: Editions Didier Millet, 2011), p 114.
10. *Is Singapore a biophilic city?* https://www.ura.gov.sg/Corporate/Resources/Publications/Skyline/Skyline-Issue10/Biophilic-city (accessed January 21, 2020).
11. L.E. Saw, Felix K.S. Lim, and Luis R. Carrasco, *Happiness Does Not Hold in a Tropical City-State* https://journals.plos.org/plosone/article?id=10.1371/journal.pone.0133781 (accessed January 24, 2020).
12. Worldometer https://www.worldometers.info/coronavirus/ (accessed June 20, 2020).

Part 3 CASE STUDY

9 SERENBE COMMUNITY

SERENBE COMMUNITY

Serenbe Community is a biophilic residential development located southwest of Atlanta, Georgia. Existing within Serenbe are the biophilic principles and attributes found in the planning, architecture, and landscape architecture of the community. The name, *Serenbe*, combines the terms "*serene*" and "*being*," suggesting the essential connections to a vital natural environment.[1] Serenbe was initially described as a community among the trees and now is being considered one of the first truly biophilic residential developments. Serenbe received the inaugural Sustainability Award from the Urban Land Institute in 2008 and is considered an exemplar of land preservation, creative mix of uses, density, agrarian urbanism, connectivity and walkability, wellness and active living, green architecture and construction practice, and their association with biophilia. The initial goals for the project included land preservation, a sensitivity to the existing environment, community formation, integration of the arts, diversity of inhabitants, inclusion of sacred geometry, and a demonstration as a model intentional environmentally oriented development.

Metro Atlanta is the ninth-largest metropolitan area in the United States, with a population in 2018 of 5,949,951.[2] Most of the surrounding land encircling Atlanta has been developed, except for a southwestern strip that includes most of South Fulton County. This land area covers approximately 40,000 acres (16,200 hectares), about the size of the Napa Valley, and is bounded by Interstate Highway 85 and the Chattahoochee River. Located within an hour's drive of downtown Atlanta and a little over 20 minutes to Hartsfield–Jackson International Airport (America's busiest airport), Serenbe is both connected to larger urban amenities and sited in a natural rural setting. As such, it is considered a peri-urban development – an interface between hinterland and urban areas.

The City of Chattahoochee Hills was incorporated in 2007 to municipalize the southern part of the county, and to allow local residents to have local control of zoning. It comprises an area of 37,473 acres (152 square kilometers). The Chattahoochee Hill Country underwent a planning charrette in 2004 when its conventional zoning was changed by an overlay district allowing for the transfer of density rights (TDR). As a consequence of this planning work, three villages were identified as receivers of this transfer of density where three-to-four villages could accommodate as many as 30,000 dwellings. Simultaneously, this allowed for greater protection of the already open space existing there. Serenbe can be seen located along the south edge of Chattahoochee Hills along the Fulton/ Coweta County line, and is being created as a model for biophilic development under these new zoning opportunities. Greater land preservation, community-building, health and wellness, agri-settlement, and sustainability are intended outcomes of this kind of process. According to Steven Cover, who was the Fulton County Planning Director, "One of Serenbe's goals was to concentrate development and preserve as much open space as possible. Today, Serenbe has preserved over 70 percent of its land for permanent open space – a truly remarkable planning feat, and a reflection of a superior community design."[3]

Serenbe is composed of a constellation of hamlets where the non-residential land uses are themed or given different focuses. Selborne is oriented toward the arts (culinary, visual, and performing); Grange is concerned with agriculture and equestrian activities; Mado, meaning *all things in balance*," is oriented to health and wellness; Spela is oriented to family and play and has a large 400 by 400 foot (122 by 122 meter) park in the middle of it; and the Education Hamlet is oriented to schools, study-away, and continuing education. As of 2020, Serenbe has a population of 850 residents. The final build-out for Serenbe is planned for 1,800 dwelling units on 1,200 acres of land.

Construction of the infrastructure and first home in Selborne hamlet began in 2004, and it is now nearly built out. What can clearly be seen is the sensuous omega form with its double-loaded spatial structure, and large areas of forest protected within the omega and surrounding the built portions. The spatial organization allows each home to front onto the omega street where social interaction largely occurs, and to back onto the forest edge with both visual and physical access. Biophilic Urbanism is certainly an outgrowth of these applications of biophilic principles. Where Serenbe differs from other residential development is by integrating all of the biophilic pattern attributes on varying levels within a given setting, from building interiors to urban infrastructure. It addresses the power, transportation, and building sectors in an attempt to create climate-positive, true sustainability, placemaking, health and wellness, and numinous outcomes.

The design for Serenbe was inspired by the characteristics of English villages and serene urbanism, utilizing the best qualities of both the natural landscape and urban amenities. English villages and hamlets possessed organic and informal site-fitted forms, especially in relation to natural features – undulating topography, adjacencies to rivers and streams, and sunlight. The Serenbe development grew from what the land had to offer: a set of rolling hills and valleys that formed a pattern of natural habitable places. What emerged was a constellation of interconnected omega-shaped hamlet sites that were fitted into the gently defined valley–hill interfaces. As a consequence, five hamlet sites were identified and connected to the serpentine road. Refer to Figure 9.1 illustrating the 2019 masterplan in color.

9.1
Serenbe
masterplan, April
2019 (*Source: Phillip
Tabb*)

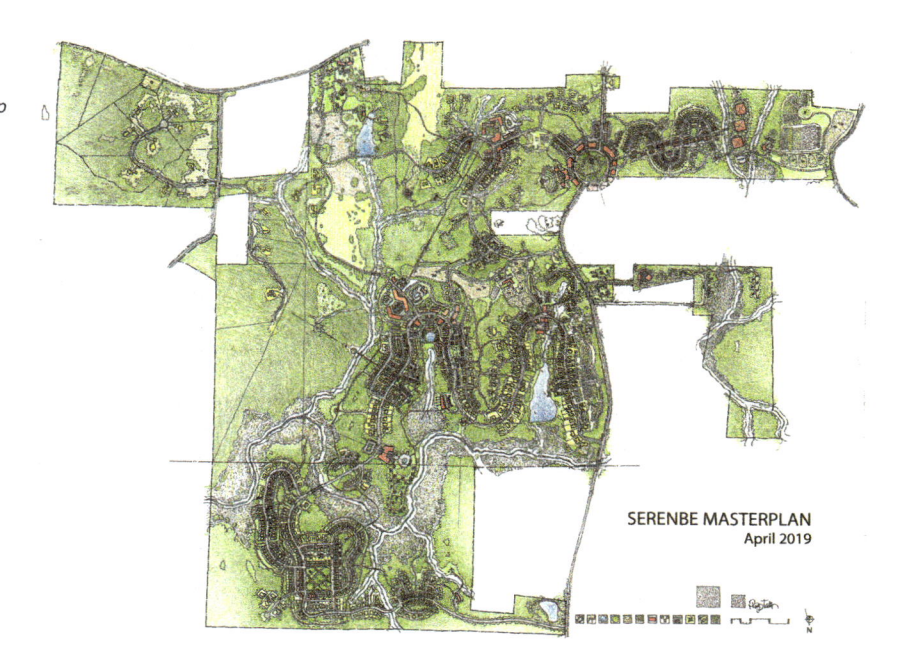

SERENBE MASTERPLAN
April 2019

THE SETTLEMENT FORM

The Thorburn transect was an observation of English village entrance roads by Andrew Thorburn in 1971. It was seen as a spatial organization of varying building densities and landscape distributions in English villages. Density increases as the rural road approaches the village center. Buildings are placed closer to the road and closer to one another. In contrast the landscape does the reverse, with buffers between the road and dwellings at the perimeter. Then they progress to the center with mature trees along paths and walled-in gardens, and in Serenbe connections to the omega center occur at the apex. Planned for the centers or omega apex are public "outdoor rooms" defined by attached buildings and landscapes. This transect has been applied to Selborne, Grange, Mado, and Spela hamlets.

The curvilinear hamlet forms resemble omega or horseshoe shapes and are characteristic of this particular typology. The hamlet forms are not a "U" shape, but an "Ω" shape. This creates slightly greater enclosure and supports greater containment. Simultaneously, the open ends of the omega allow for natural eco-logical flows—solar energy, water, clean air, resident animals, and people.[4] At the ends the omega shape slowly opens outward to create both a sense of entry and of exit, with connections to the neighboring hamlets. At the top or apex of each omega form are a collection and an intensity of mixed-use activities. They give a particular focus and identity to each hamlet – the arts, agriculture, health and well-ness, family and play, and education. The hamlets are connected by a serpentine road system that closely follows the contours and shapes of the natural landform. Refer to Figure 9.2, which is an aerial view of the omega form of Selborne Hamlet.

9.2
Selborne hamlet
aerial view
(*Source: Serenbe
Development*)

Intentional planning decisions were made to reinforce the Thorburn rural-to-urban transect. Selborne Lane, which connects the Inn at Serenbe to Selborne Hamlet, is a curving gravel and dirt road with no curbs or sidewalks. As it enters the Selborne Hamlet, the road surface changes to asphalt paving with bioswales and no curbs. The houses on both sides are on estate lots set back from the road with existing pines acting as natural landscape filters. Further into the hamlet, a cobblestone walkway and traffic calmer crosses the road indicating another transition along the transect. From this point on, the street has granite curbs and sidewalks on both sides, parking on one side, and is tree-lined, with cottage houses closer to one another and closer to the street. Also at these street crossings are traffic calming bumps and night streetlights that indicate the points of crossing. At the beginning of the circular apex another crosswalk appears and from this point to the center are attached buildings that align along a widened sidewalk with townhomes, live–work units, commercial businesses, and parking on each side of the street. Outdoor dining occurs near the apex, and Selborne Green indicates the center or top of the omega form of the hamlet. Exterior building materials change along the transect from predominantly wood at the edge to brick and stone at the center. Refer to Figure 9.35(b), which explains the Thorburn Transect and to Figure 9.1 for an aerial view of the Selborne Hamlet where the transect can clearly be seen.

THE HAMLETS

A charrette was organized in 2002 to focus on further developing the design for Selborne Hamlet and the Crossroads. The Thorburn transect was used to establish plot locations and sizes, the density gradient, and the location of non-residential uses. While the theme was "the arts," it was the culinary arts that contributed the most, especially in the early days of development, with the introduction of the Blue Eyed Daisy and Hil restaurants. Selborne Hamlet is approximately 30 gross acres (12 hectares) in area including the open-space center, and accommodates 120 dwelling units. The hamlet is oriented on a north–northeast and south–southeast axis. This coincides with the overall geology of the Piedmont region it is a part of. The interior of the omega-shaped hamlet contains a small stream and densely forested pedestrian area.

The second hamlet is called Grange and is approximately 50 gross acres (20 hectares) in size including the center open space and lake, and it is 750 feet (229 meters) wide from the centerlines of omega road. The hamlet is oriented toward more pragmatic matters of the land and community including the equestrian center, Montessori elementary school, and the general store. In the center of the hamlet is a 5-acre (2-hectare) lake that provides a focus for activity and a tranquil view. Planned at the apex of the omega road are more commercial uses, a restaurant, and a few related shops. Grange is planned to have 164 dwelling units. An important part of the Grange hamlet are the Serenbe Farms located on land adjacent to the east omega leg. Initially planned to have about 25 acres (10 hectares), Serenbe Farms uses approximately two-thirds of the available land while the other third is used for crop rotation, construction materials, staging, and storage. It is a certified organic farm with more than three 350 varieties of vegetables, herbs, flowers, fruits, and mushrooms. All the produce is distributed within a 40-mile (64-kilometer) radius through a community-supported agriculture program. Refer to Figure 9.3 for an aerial view of Grange hamlet and Serenbe Farms.

The Mado charrette in April of 2007 was specifically targeted to the development of the third hamlet form and its theme of health and wellness non-residential functions. In the center of the hamlet is an existing natural wetland

9.3
Grange hamlet and
Serenbe Farms
aerial view
(*Source: Serenbe Development*)

and the 100-year flood plain, part of the Cedar Creek basin. The eastern leg of the omega is on fairly sloping forested land, while the west leg is on relatively flat land which is easier to develop. The name "Mado" comes from the Creek Nation Native American meaning "things in balance," which seemed a fitting name for a focus on health and wellness.[5] Consequently, and following this focus, a cluster of activities was determined and dispersed throughout the fabric of the hamlet plan. Mado is approximately 55 gross acres (22 hectares) including the open-space center and wetlands, and it is 700 feet (213 meters) wide from the centerlines of each leg of the omega road. Planned for 550 dwelling units, Mado is a unique blend of residential dwelling types and health and wellness functions. Refer to Figure 9.4, which show two views of Mado currently being developed.

According to landscape architect Alfie Vick, the Mado food forest and medicinal garden is a food-producing public garden that reflects the structure and diversity of the native piedmont forest.[6] The garden is focused on balance and wellbeing; all the plants are either edible or medicinal, many of them are both. Additionally, the garden is designed to engage residents who live adjacent to it. It is universally accessible, safe, and attractive with several spaces that encourage social interaction. Most of the vegetation is native, creating a food forest that is a microcosm of the surrounding natural ecosystems.

The Spela Hamlet occupies the southernmost lands in Serenbe and is in Coweta County, rather than Fulton County where the rest of Serenbe is based. This is seen as a benefit of lower property taxes and better public schools. The name derives from the Swedish word meaning "play." The charrette took place in 2018 and focused on a family-oriented scheme surrounding a large central park. The park is naturally wooded with varying topography, and is 400 by 400 feet (122 by 122 meters) in size. The park is intended to accommodate outdoor recreational activities, such as a treehouse, zip-lines, picnic areas, children's gardens, dogs park, and an outdoor coffee bar. Two sides of the park are lined with wide pedestrian walkways and townhomes. The other two sides have electric cart parking. The Spela site does not follow the omega geometry, but rather is site-fitted around the central park with views and connections that open to the forest land surrounding it. There are several neighborhood clusters, each of which focuses on internal greenspaces. Spela is planned to have 320 dwelling units.

9.4
Mado aerial views:
(a) west leg of
Mado hamlet,
(b) the healing
garden
(*Source: Serenbe
Development*)

The Education Hamlet is still in the planning process and has not yet been named. The site for this hamlet is generally located along Atlanta Newnan Road to the northeast of the other Serenbe hamlets, and it has fairly easy access to them. The site is relatively level along the road, but then dramatically slopes downhill from west to east down to a streambed below. The exact size and location of this property is still undetermined, making any design somewhat speculative. Its accessible and visible location along Atlanta Newnan Road suggests a larger number of non-residential functions that might not be appropriate for the more intimate omega hamlets. Additional purposes that are being considered for this hamlet include a small grocery store, restaurant/cafe, conference-hotel, charter school, bank, post office, fire station, retail shops, and office space. There was even a discussion about including a small gasoline and electric car charging station. Adjacent to the hamlet is space allocated for higher educational facilities for on-site classes where students could learn about Serenbe within a living–learning environment, work on planning and architecture projects, spend time at Serenbe Farms, and construct some permanent works for the community, such as bridges, benches, shelters, and other small structures. The five hamlets:

- Selborne Hamlet – is oriented toward the arts (culinary, visual, and performing), and includes the Crossroads. Selborne Hamlet is approximately 35 gross acres (14 hectares) and 100 dwelling units, and Crossroads is 5 acres (2 hectares) and 24 dwelling units.
- Grange Hamlet – is oriented toward agriculture and is approximately 75 gross acres (30 hectares) and includes Serenbe Farms, Grange Lake and Swan Ridge, and 164 dwelling units.
- Mado Hamlet – is oriented toward health and wellness and is approximately 75 gross acres (30 hectares) including the interior wetlands, and is planned for 575 dwelling units.
- Spela Hamlet – is oriented toward play and is approximately 80 gross acres (32 hectares) and is planned for 320 dwelling units.
- Education Hamlet – is oriented toward education and outreach and is approximately 50 gross acres (20 hectares), planned for 500 dwelling units.

CONSTELLATING URBANISM

The combination of the five hamlets and Crossroads clusters evolve as proximate urban areas creating the larger development whole and sphere of influence, which is referred to as Serenbe Community. Rather than develop a single form growing by addition, Serenbe has grown incrementally through a process of multiplication. This process is called "*constellating urbanism*."[7] Commonly applied to human systems, such as families or organizations, there is usually a hidden dynamic at work. Systemic Constellation Theory, originally developed by psychotherapist Bert Hellinger for family dynamics, suggested that independent yet interconnected parts of a system create a combination of actions affecting

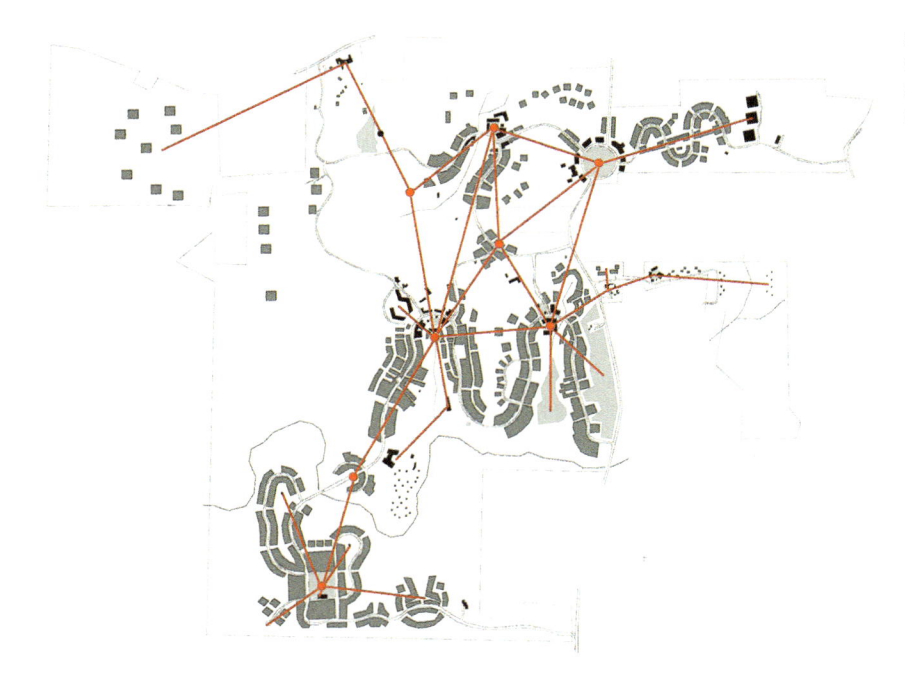

9.5
Constellating
Serenbe hamlets
(*Source: Phillip Tabb*)

the collective whole. For Serenbe, this means that the interrelated hamlets, and the individual placemaking practices they employ, can support even greater constellating, synergetic, and programmatic relationships. This is a kind of development process that allows for adaptation to market preferences, economic pressures, the introduction of greater levels of sustainable technologies, the creation of additional housing or non-residential types, and the inclusion of more community-wide activities.

The masterplan for Serenbe supports the concept of development by multiplication and takes it even further through the theming of the hamlet apex mix of uses. The differences established by the themes create an interdependence. When taken together, they form a land use constellation. And finally, for Serenbe, the constellation is the atmosphere of the place, the residents, the sense of community, and those who dwell there. The major non-residential functions that are of use to the entire community are indicated at the apex of each hamlet in the constellation in Figure 9.5.

THE BIOPHILIC PRINCIPLES

The design for Serenbe follows many important biophilic principles, where biophilic form-making and place-making, and connections to nature, the elements, and the numinous, are important. At the planning scale, Serenbe situates residents so they have direct connections to nature, creating source experiences. This "front door to nature" planning approach was selected to amplify biophilic principles and demonstrate an inclusive, comprehensive, and integrated approach to residential development. An initial design intention was to position every house adjacent to some form of open space: forested hamlet center, meadow, Serenbe Farms, tributary, or pond. The biophilic attributes that inform the masterplan from Serenbe are clearly evident.

The design for Serenbe grew out of an organic and incremental land planning process and is difficult to describe and label. It had elements from English villages, the New Urbanism, peri-urbanism, conservation communities, sustainable urbanism, agricultural urbanism, and wellness communities. Throughout its 20-year evolution Serenbe has been inclusive of all these characterizations, yet none of them were broad enough or aggregated enough to provide a full conceptual umbrella that was comprehensive enough to fully describe it. In the end, Biophilic Urbanism seemed to best capture the nature of Serenbe and all its integrated characteristics. The Serenbe Biophilic Institute was established in 2013 and formed as a charitable organization to promote this concept. Each year there is a biophilic leadership summit held in Serenbe where industry professionals and thought leaders discuss biophilic architectural and urban examples and future directions in the field. Following is a list of the development goals initiated at the beginning of the planning process in the first thought leader meeting, held in September of 2000.[8]

- Focus on the essence of community formation and the interaction of residents to foster development of their potential.
- Respect for and integration of the cultural history of the surrounding area, that is, agriculture.
- Preservation of permanent open space (forests and pastures).
- Age diversity of inhabitants, from children to seniors.
- Economic diversity of inhabitants.
- Economic sustainability of the development effort.
- Environmental sustainability of all aspects of the development.
- High-tech, connected development to allow integration of Serenbe with the world at large (at minimal environmental impact).
- Music, arts, and crafts as a theme for the development.
- The use of land trusts to achieve the desired character of the community.
- The development as a living laboratory.
- Integration of design across disciplinary, infrastructure, and philosophical dimensions.
- Inclusion of sacred geometry informing the planning process.

Another important design principle across all scales of development was that some form of shared or non-residential land use was achieved. This shared form of land use planning would vary depending upon residential numbers. For example, at the dwelling scale having a shared driveway could reduce costs; at the cluster scale a shared green, parking area, or central mail collection was contemplated; at the hamlet scale having a restaurant was important to serve as a community gathering place; and at the entire community scale having access to the open space. This non-residential land use pattern was fractalized throughout the development at these various scales.

SERENBE BIOPHILIC PATTERN ATTRIBUTES

Serenbe is considered a biophilic community, which is due in part to its proximity to an abundant amount of natural open space. All 25 pattern attributes are abundantly present in Serenbe, occurring at the individual building, landscape, street, hamlet, open space, and community scales. As a model, it can be applied to all of Chattahoochee Hills as a regional strategy. Not only are they present individually, but they also unite to create combinatory synergetic effect across the scales of the entire community. Each of the patterns is individually shown on 25 masterplan drawings. They are illustrated using on-site photographs of both the natural and built environments, and they are described in the ways they exist in Serenbe on their various scales. While the patterns are described in Serenbe site- and context-specific terms, they are intended to be applied across more varied contexts – both geographic and along the urban-to-rural transect. The climatic, sustainable, placemaking, health and wellness, and numinous outcomes are also described for each pattern attribute when applicable.

References have been made in the descriptions of the patterns concerning responses to the Coronavirus. Not all pattern attributes are applicable to mitigation strategies. During the most intense months of the first wave of the pandemic (March, April, and May) in the United States, the state of Georgia relaxed stay-at-home policies and opened the economy early. As a result, case numbers and reported deaths were relatively high compared to other states. For most of this time, Georgia was 11th in the nation. In the second wave (June, July and August), Georgia moved up to 5th nationally. In Serenbe there were only a couple reported cases, which is in part due to its lockdown, remote location, and relief in access to nature.

Following is the series of 25 pattern attributes applied to the case study of Serenbe. A masterplan drawing accompanies each pattern attribute indicating its location in the plan and the extent to which the pattern is present. An image of a natural example of each pattern is shown juxtaposed with one occurring within the built environment. For example, the pattern attribute for living color is shown with photographs of the wildflower meadow and the colorful community swimming pool. These pattern attributes and outcomes have been identified through actualistic masterplan analyses and in-depth, on-site empirical observations. The purpose of this deep dive into the biophilic analysis was to illustrate the full extent to which biophilic urbanism can be realized throughout the various scales in a single residential development. A base map indicates the location of each pattern and the kind of attribute within the community. Figure 9.6 shows the hand-drawn base map used in the analysis of the Serenbe biophilic pattern attributes.

9.6
Serenbe base map
(*Source: Phillip Tabb*)

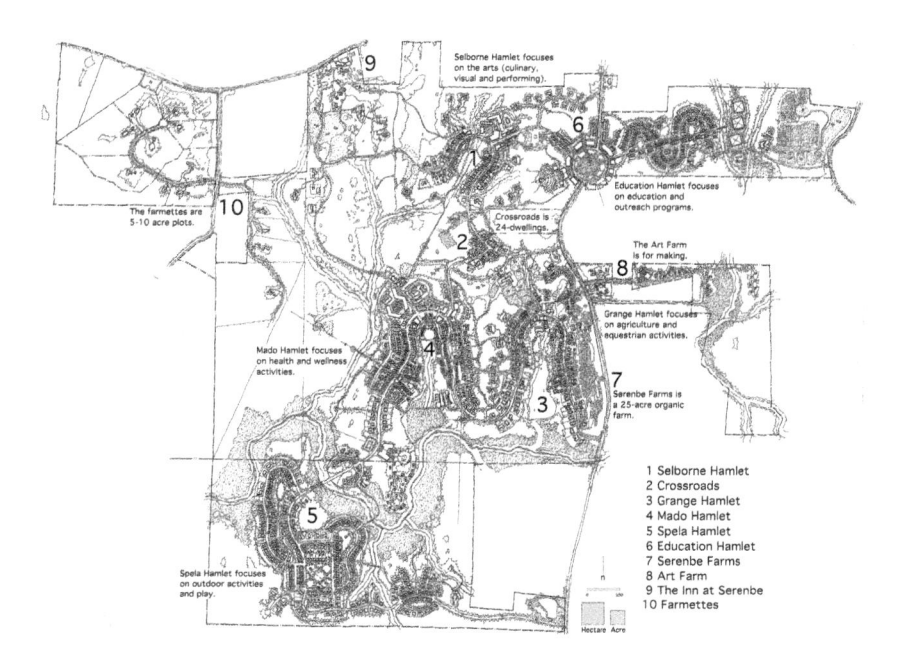

Selborne Hamlet focuses on the arts (culinary, visual and performing).

Education Hamlet focuses on education and outreach programs.

Crossroad is 24-dwellings.

The Art Farm is for making.

The farmettes are 5-10 acre plots.

Grange Hamlet focuses on agriculture and equestrian activities.

Mado Hamlet focuses on health and wellness activities.

Serenbe Farms is a 25-acre organic farm.

Spela Hamlet focuses on outdoor activities and play.

1 Selborne Hamlet
2 Crossroads
3 Grange Hamlet
4 Mado Hamlet
5 Spela Hamlet
6 Education Hamlet
7 Serenbe Farms
8 Art Farm
9 The Inn at Serenbe
10 Farmettes

1. The Plant Kingdom

The Serenbe location, southwest of Atlanta within the City of Chattahoochee Hills, is highly rural in character. 70 percent of the land area of Serenbe is undeveloped and will remain so after the final buildout. This allows for ample connections between the natural and developed portions of the site. This ratio of open space to developed land is even greater at the rural end of the transect. At higher densities, the amount of open space or natural areas is reduced. Nevertheless, it is important to include as much access to green space as possible. The inclusion of parks, trails, tree-lined streets, waterways, the 25-acre (10-hectare) Serenbe Farms, and other natural features is important. The trees and plants form important carbon sinks and produce of oxygen. As seen in Figures 9.7 and 9.8, the developed portion only takes up 30 percent of the land, leaving a generous amount of open space. Within a private garden, peaches are ripening, and a father and son look at raspberries on a trellis. The property encircling houses encourages private gardens. Herbs and flowers contribute color. Following is a list of primary examples of this attribute.

- Within Serenbe, 70 percent of the land is dedicated to open space.
- Most of the land is covered in conifer and deciduous trees, grass-filled pastures, paddocks, and wildflower meadows.
- Serenbe Farms is a dedicated 25-acre (10-hectare) organic farm.
- Streets are tree-lined and have seasonal edible plants.
- Open spaces tend to be either forestland, pastures, paddocks, wildflower meadows, or natural water features.

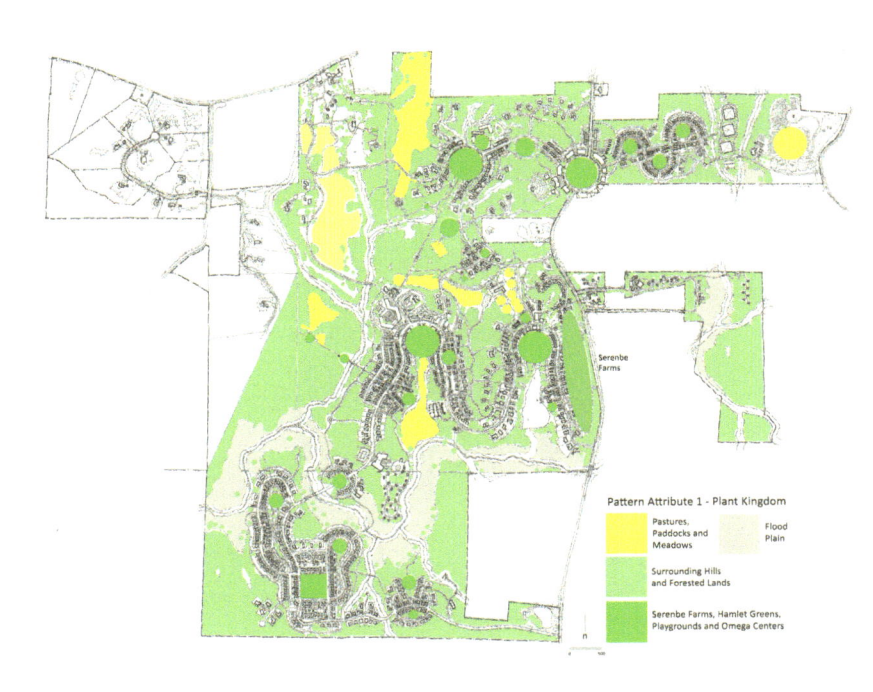

9.7
Pattern attribute 1:
the plant kingdom
(*Source: Phillip Tabb*)

- The abundance of plant life is carbon-sequestering and oxygen-producing.
- There is direct access to the open spaces for all dwellings.
- All dwellings are sited in a "first row" to the natural elements of the site.
- Traditional lawns are not allowed; instead there are smaller front greenspaces with native plantings.
- There is a local flower shop in Crossroads frequented by residents.
- Relative to the Coronavirus, the abundant greenspace allows easy access to nature and provides positive relief to sheltering-in-place.

9.8
Nature in Serenbe:
(a) Serenbe Farms,
(b) father and
son looking at
raspberries (*Source: Phillip Tabb*)

The Plant Kingdom pattern attribute at Serenbe can produce all five of the positive outcomes. For positive climate, it includes carbon sequestering, sustainable agriculture, and responses to the ecological flows of the region. For sustainability, it has dense pockets, clusters the built portions with increased accessibility and reduced automobile use. For placemaking, it surrounds the hamlets creating a sense of place. For health and wellness, it enhances sensory connections to nature and the elements, and contributes to nutrition, obesity reduction, improved productivity, reduction of stress and mental fatigue, accelerated healing processes, improved concentration and memory, increased energy, and improved performance. As for the numinous outcomes, it provides inspiration and lowers stress, and increases the potential for high-level wellness.

Approximately 25 acres (10 hectares) were initially allocated for Serenbe Farms, of which about 8 acres (3.2 hectares) are now being harvested. The farm participates in the CSA program, and serves the local restaurants and residents. Its workers offer many opportunities for farm education, from school farm tours to corporate tours to seasonal classes and Serenbe's apprenticeship program. They employ three organic methods that residents live by: composting, cover cropping, and crop rotation. Saturday mornings from May 8 to October 30 pay host to the Serenbe farmers' and artists' market, which takes place on Selborne Green. It is a wonderful venue for purchasing organic produce, fruit, culinary treats, and arts and crafts from local vendors. One of the purposes of the market is to improve the production and marketing of local agricultural and artisanal products and in turn stimulate community interest. Often there are music and games for children, while community members visit. The temporary tents and vendor stalls are pictured on the Selborne center green and people are congregating all along the omega road. Everything at the market is seasonal, which adds to authenticity and contextual response. The growing season averages 8 months from March to the end of October. During the Coronavirus pandemic, Serenbe residents have observed sheltering in place and social distancing of at least 6 feet (1.8 meters), and have often taken advantage of the abundant amount of natural open space within the community.

2. The Animal Kingdom

There are many ways residents can come into contact with both domesticated and wild animals in Serenbe. Many, if not most, households have domesticated dogs or cats. In the mornings and evenings dozens of residents walk their dogs throughout the community. There is a community dog-park where residents meet in the late afternoon for animal "socializing." Many board horses at the Serenbe stables and other nearby equestrian centers. A few households have chickens. Wild animals are plentiful as well, with deer, squirrels, opossums, turtles, frogs, toads, armadillos, and a wide variety to birds, reptiles, fish, and insects. Adjacent to the Inn at Serenbe is the animal village, which houses numerous animals, including goats, pigs, chickens, rabbits, and llamas. While venomous snakes, scorpions, ticks, chiggers, and mosquitos are unwelcome,

9.9
Pattern attribute 2:
the animal kingdom
(*Source: Phillip
Tabb*)

most other local animals are appreciated. Figures 9.9 and 9.10 show the site plan with the general location of animals found on the property, and a photograph of children riding horses while participating in the Serenbe Camp summer program.

- There are as many as 100 animals in the animal village.
- Horseback riding is a feature of Serenbe, both through the Inn at Serenbe and privately through Serenbe stables.

9.10
The animal
kingdom in
Serenbe:
(a) Serenbe Camp
horseback riding,
(b) local red-tailed
hawk (*Source:
Phillip Tabb*)

- It is not uncommon to see horses walking along the streets or along trails in the woods.
- On day trips, Serenbe Camp introduces children to farm animals, horseback riding, and wildlife in the forest.
- Due to the large amount of preserved land, there are many wild and free-roaming animals, especially white-tail deer, armadillo, opossums, squirrels, turtles, and many bird species.
- Nearly every household has domesticated pets.
- Walking dogs in the community and hanging out in the designated dog park encourages social interaction, increases opportunities for exercise, and provides interactions with animals.

The Animal kingdom pattern attributes contribute to an awareness of the climate and the seasons evidenced by the changes in absence and presence of birds and insects. For sustainability outcomes, this pattern can serve as an analogous form of sustainability and vitality. For placemaking outcomes, pet ownership garners social support. For health and wellness outcomes, they can provide opportunities for increased exercise, and contribute to visual and sensory connections to nature, heart health, lowered blood pressure, lower triglyceride levels, and reduced cardiovascular risk. For numinous outcomes, wild animals are a sign of vitality, and domesticated animals provide emotional support, as pet ownership can decrease depression, anxiety, and stress. And the wild animals reinforce a numinous connection to and regional sense of place.

The animal village lies between the Inn at Serenbe and Selborne hamlet, and is experienced by visitors staying at the Inn and by Serenbe residents. On one side of the animal village, a couple dozen goats roam on sloping topography filled with stands of pines, small rock outcrops, and fallen logs. On the other side of the village are smaller pens and holding areas for chickens, pigs, rabbits, goats, and, on occasion, llamas. The Inn at Serenbe offers feed-and-pet so guests can engage with the many animals, and they sponsor hayrides throughout the property. Adjacent to the animal village are large paddocks for donkeys, horses, and cows. The dog park has separate areas for larger and smaller dogs. It is located in Selborne Hamlet and is frequented by residents. After 5 pm, many locals bring their dogs for canine and human socializing. There is even an outdoor goat yoga class practiced by residents, where Nigerian dwarf goats provide emotional support. Wildlife is abundant and the deeper you go into the woods, the more likely you will come in contact with them. However, it is common for squirrels, chipmunks, white-tailed deer, opossums, and armadillos to roam the residential portions of the community. Published by a local resident is a book identifying 123 birds commonly found in Serenbe.[9] For residents, contact with the animal kingdom occurs as a part of everyday life. There are a few pests and dangerous animals, including fire ants, ticks, chiggers, and mosquitos – and, on occasion, kingsnake, cottonmouth, and copperhead snakes are spotted.

3. Views and Vistas

There are a variety of views and vistas available within Serenbe. One experiences an agrarian mood when entering the community, which is appropriate for the rural context. There are views of rural fences, paddocks, horses and cows, stables, barns, narrow rural roads, and the natural landscape of meadows and stands of trees. As one moves around the curvilinear omega-shaped roads, there are views of a changing landscape both natural and urban. Density increases and then decreases. Views into each hamlet center were also important, and as one walks along the omega street, view corridors exist between each of the cottage homes framing the natural interior of the hamlet, especially in Selborne, Grange, and Mado hamlets. For the Spela hamlet, it was important to have views to the large open park in its center and to the surrounding woods. Figures 9.11 and 9.12 show the masterplan and a view of Serenbe pond and the pavilion beyond it from another of the entry roads. The map shows long vistas and views into the omega centers.

- There are numerous views to the surrounding nature – hills, forests, lakes and ponds, meadows, greens, and Serenbe Farms.
- There are views to residential entries, creating wayfinding and spatial legibility.
- There is visual surveillance surrounding public spaces.
- There are changing views and vistas of the urban character while moving along the serpentine omega streets.
- Nearly every home has direct access to open space and views of nature.
- There are views to community activities along the omega streets.
- There are many open spaces for viewing the night skies.
- There are changing vistas upon entering the community, which feature its rural nature.

The Views and vistas pattern attribute can enhance visual connections to nature, the elements, changing weather patterns, and seasonal changes. Related to the placemaking outcomes, views and vistas encourage community interactions, can support surveillance, and provide a sense of protection. Internal spaces with views to streets, front porches, and the extensive network of sidewalks and paths throughout the community contribute to public safety. For the health and wellness outcomes, views and vistas to nature decrease stress, increase hospital recovery rates, encourage greater energy, direct attention, and reduce mental fatigue. Simply viewing nature can reduce anger, fear, and stress. It is particularly important to be able to experience nature daily, reinforced through the everyday functions of living.

Because of the large and dense portion of forested land, vistas only occur where there are expanses of open meadows and pastures, and where there is higher ground. Refer to Figure 9.12(a) for a view of the night sky at the top of a rise. Views, however, are everywhere in both the natural and urban areas. It was a design

9.11
Pattern attribute 3:
views and vistas
(*Source: Phillip
Tabb*)

intention to have changing views along the curvilinear omega roads, so that the community unfolded in changing vistas. Equally important was to have views between dwellings into the omega centers revealing the compelling natural space that exists there. There are more intimate views – to garden plantings and features such as wind chimes, fountains, rock gardens, and garden sculptures – in every hamlet, seen when walking about the community. For homes located along the eastern edge of Grange hamlet, there are views of Serenbe Farms, which change throughout the seasons. In Mado hamlet, every home

9.12
Views and vistas:
(a) dusk sky vista
over pasture,
(b) view of path
between two
buildings (*Source:
Phillip Tabb*)

aligned along the V-shape cluster faces into the healing garden. And from Anders Court, also in Mado, there is a long vista through a series of townhomes and gardens into the woods, and across a small stream to a circular yoga field. When built, there will be views from the assisted living complex across the street to the Montessori school and community swimming pool, where the elderly can observe the activities of children and families.

4. Sensory Connections

There are numerous opportunities to experience a variety of sensory interactions with the natural environment at Serenbe, in part due to the large percentage of natural open space. Visual connections occur because of the ever-present natural beauty of the place. However, the other senses can also be activated by emersion into these areas. Natural sounds are heard, from rustling leaves in the woods to running water in the streams and Cedar Creek, and in fountains in Selborne and Mado hamlets, as well as the sounds of animals at the stables, farm village, and pastures. The sounds of children are heard at the playgrounds and along the streets during the day, and theater performances in the woods can be heard at night. Walking in the woods, along the flower meadows, gardens, and through Serenbe Farms, or passing one of the five restaurants, triggers strong olfactory experiences. Most homeowners have domestic pets and regularly experience haptic interactions with them. Serenbe is filled with culinary opportunities through special programs, the integral restaurants, or in the homes of neighbors. Figures 9.13 and 9.14 show the base map and depict what are called the "larger waterfalls," found along one of Cedar Creek's tributaries. It is one of the favorite places to visit – looking at, listening to, and being mesmerized by the falling water.

- Primary natural features of the land are preserved and can be experienced directly using all the senses.
- There are views of nature in nearly every direction.
- The wildflower meadows provide an abundance of fragrances and living color.
- Water is an important element within the community. It is found in the lake, ponds, streams, rainfall, and built features, and the experience of the rhythmic ripples and sounds is serene.
- Edible seasonal plants occur along the omega streets and within individual resident gardens.
- With 123 bird species found in Serenbe, there is an abundance of singing, chirping and calling.
- Walking the streets, sidewalks, paths, and trails creates a sense of varying depths and touch to the feet.
- Walking by any of the five restaurants produces olfactory experiences.
- The many performing arts venues in the forest they create auditory and visual sensory experiences.
- Distracting sounds of air conditioners are eliminated in areas where use of geothermal heating and cooling systems are found.

9.13
Pattern attribute
4: sensory
connections
(*Source: Phillip
Tabb*)

9.14
Sensory
experiences:
(a) Serenbe
waterfalls,
(b) rose
(*Source: Phillip
Tabb)*

- Sensory engagements with the environment during the COVID-19 pandemic have been limited to sheltering at home, implementing social distancing and sanitation protocols throughout the community. Sidewalks on both sides of the streets allow for easy distancing.

The sensory connections pattern attributes contribute to enriched engagements within the community, nature, and the elements. The placemaking outcomes

include sensory experiences, along with the cultural and culinary functions within the community. The positive health and wellness outcomes include decreased stress, greater energy, improved direct attention, and reduced mental fatigue. Sensory integration is especially important for children of all ages, helping them refine the thresholds for differing sensory information. The numinous positive outcomes usually involve all the senses, creating enhanced perception, reduced temporal density, deeper noetic understandings, and an ineffable connection to nature.

Although the sense of smell is often taken for granted, it is critical for our wellbeing. We use olfaction to verify the cleanliness of our clothes and homes, and to fully enjoy foods, beverages, personal care products, flowers, and other aspects of our environment.[10] The sense of smell also alerts us to the danger of bad food or even pollutants in the environment, such as natural gas. There are olfactory experiences throughout Serenbe in both the natural and urban areas, and they vary with changes in weather and the seasons. There are five restaurants and when walking near them, olfaction occurs with the lingering scents in the air. In springtime and throughout the summer there is a cocktail of smells, including forest pine, the numerous flowering shrubs, bushes, vegetation, and damp earth. Becoming present within a place is linked to the quality of sensual perceptions experienced in that place, often triggering memories. In Serenbe, this occurs in both the natural and urban areas of the community, such as with the sounds of birds in the woods, the sound of rushing water at the two waterfalls, feeling the textured materials in the hamlets, rainwater striking a roof, the crackling of a night-time fireplace, seeing the streams of light in the forests, and with the sound of playing children and residents laughing at neighborhood gatherings.

5. Ecological and Biological Contexts

The primary ecoregion comprises a transitional area between the mostly mountainous ecoregions of the Appalachians to the northwest and the relatively flat coastal plain to the southeast. The geographical orientation of Serenbe is along the end of the Piedmont mountain range running northeast and southwest with irregular plains and many hills. Once largely cultivated, much of this region has reverted to pine and hardwood woodlands. The range determines the direction of the land contours and flow of water in Serenbe. Circling a large portion of the perimeter of Chattahoochee Hills is the Chattahoochee River. Most streams, creeks, and tributaries flow into it. And within Serenbe's rolling hills, water generally flows south through each of the hamlets, to Cedar Creek which in Serenbe moves east–west along the southern portion of the site. Figures 9.15 and 9.16 show a map of the primary waterways, landforms, water features, and Cedar Creek, and daylit stormwater drainage channels.

- The Piedmont range runs southwest so most of the landforms follow this pattern.
- The combination of landforms and waterways creates natural settlement sites.

9.15
Pattern attribute
5: ecological and
biological contexts
(*Source: Phillip
Tabb*)

Pattern Attribute 5 - Ecological
and Biological Connections

Wild Animal Habitats

Flood Plains

Natural Water Systems

Hills and Ridges

Prevailing Winds

9.16
Ecology: (a) swale
next to the
Montessori school,
(b) swale along Tabb
Way (*Source: Phillip
Tabb*)

- Stormwater is largely channeled through natural daylit swales and holding ponds.
- Development does not occur on the tops of landforms or within the basins and flood plains below, but along the interface between the two.
- The vegetated wetlands naturally process community wastewater, and have become a landscape feature of the community, with a tree-lined curvilinear boardwalk passing right through them.

- Exposed granite outcrops are not disturbed but rather are retained as natural features.
- The large forested areas, meadows, and farmland sequester carbon.
- The ecological context provides critical food and water resources for human consumption.

The ecological and biological connections pattern attributes seek to reverse adverse ecological effects and reduce disease ecology. They contribute to ecological thinking and connections to a diversity of natural processes subject to diurnal and seasonal climatic changes and hydrological cycles that are toxin free. This pattern expresses using biomorphic forms and infrastructures, such as the omega roads, which reinforce placemaking. From a sustainability point of view, local ecosystems provide vital food, water, and waste management. Variations of this pattern allow natural experiences in multiple venues. And the health and wellness outcomes produce positive abiotic factors, clean resources, healthy nutrients, and provide the possibility for deeper spiritual enrichment and cognitive development.

The Piedmont ecoregion is considered hilly because it is comprised of the foothills of the Appalachian Mountains. The ecology of Serenbe is connected to its geography, topography, climate, and changing weather patterns. One of the more dramatic weather events at Serenbe is rainfall, with on average about 50 inches (127 centimeters) per year. Often, when it rains, it pours. The daylit storm drainage systems adjacent to the roads offer a auditory and visual connection to and expression of the ecology of the place and its context. Certainly, walking through the woods presents the native first- and second-growth white pine, sugar maple, oak, and sweetgum trees, local flora and fauna, and the distinctive red color of the earth that are characteristic of the Piedmont ecoregion. Around the steep mesic slope forests close to the Chattahoochee river, the terrain shifts and reshapes because of the changing topography. In Serenbe paths along water habitats and the streambeds are particularly pleasant. The spatial structure and relationships, the energy, water, and flows, and the dynamic changes that occur over time are important for Serenbe.

6. Fire and Energy

Fire is energy, and it gives warmth and light. It is a source for social and ceremonial interactions. At the residential development scale at Serenbe, it is analogous to sources of thermal and electrical energy. Fire is expressed by passive solar and photovoltaic electric systems for heating and electricity production. To some extent ground-sourced heat pumps, used extensively in Serenbe, also serve as a source of heating and cooling. Most homes have fireplaces or wood-burning stoves. Outdoor uses include the ceremonial winter solstice site, the bonfire pavilion site, outdoor gas streetlights, and individual residential fire pits and fireplaces. Because Serenbe is a mixed automobile and pedestrian-oriented community, in-place transportation such as walking, bicycles, electric carts,

9.17
Pattern attribute
6: fire and energy
(*Source: Phillip
Tabb*)

Pattern Attribute 6 - Fire and Energy

Geothermal Heating and Cooling

Fire Pits Ceremonial Fires

Existing Stand-Alone Photovoltaic Electric Systems

9.18
Fire and energy:
(a) solstice bonfire,
(b) net-zero
dwelling (*Source:
Phillip Tabb*)

and electric and hybrid cars is commonly in use. There is low automobile use. Between-place transportation is reduced with the inclusion of mix uses, like the general store, bookstore, restaurants, retail shops, and schools.[11] In the Atlanta area, with 3,000 heating degree days annually, underheating in winter is a greater thermal problem than overheating in summer. Therefore, designing for on-site energy resources for heating is desired (passive solar heating and geothermal heating and cooling). Figures 9.17 and 9.18 show the base map and winter solstice bonfire and a home with a photovoltaic electric system on the roof.

- Currently all residential electricity is serviced by the public utility.
- Most residences in Serenbe have fireplaces and chimneys.
- Most residences in Serenbe have geothermal ground-sourced heat pumps.
- More than a dozen homes have photovoltaic electricity systems.
- Street and plot orientations are planned for rooftop solar access.
- Some homes employ passive solar heating.
- All homes have generous amounts of daylighting.
- There are seasonal ceremonial bonfires and fireworks.

The fire pattern attribute can utilize positive connections to nature and the elements. It supports the use of renewable resources of on-site thermal, electrical, and light energy that contribute to sustainability, and it reduces the need for fossil fuels which affect positive climate outcomes. The health and wellness outcomes of moderate sun exposure include thermal comfort, increased blood flow, reduced blood pressure, improved cardiovascular health, increased energy, a healthier immune system, enhanced vitamin D, better sleep, and improved mood. Solar energy has long been considered a numinous source of energy and inspiration.

Fire and energy are visually present at Serenbe in small doses. Buildings are presently powered by electricity and natural gas provided by the local utility and distribution companies, so the production, distribution, and end uses are not visible. Within the Atlanta area, most energy comes from coal and natural gas-fired power plants, while renewables provide approximately 8 percent of the energy (solar and biomass). In Serenbe, more and more residences are utilizing stand-alone photovoltaic electricity systems, and all new homes are required to use geothermal heating and cooling systems. In future, there are plans for a solar farm and electric utility. Nearly every home has a fireplace, and there are many outdoor barbecues, so the element fire is experienced directly. On certain occasions, bonfires celebrate special occasions, such as the autumn harvest organized by Serenbe Farms, and the winter solstice. Many residences have gas night lights on their porches. Solar radiation averages 5.2 kWh/m^2/day in Georgia, and about 4.5 kWh/m^2/day in the Atlanta area. Passive solar heating was not considered for most homes; however, sun tempering and roof access for photovoltaic systems were planned in. Most residential plots run east and west along both sides of the omega streets, allowing good solar access to south-facing roofs if desired.

7. Earth and Grounding

Earth is tangible and is associated with land, ground, soil, dirt, agriculture, minerals, mountains, hills, forests, deserts, caves, farms, and building materials. Its benefits are many: the provision of shelter and of nutrients and food grown in the earth; protection from severe climate and weather, and from insects and predators; the provision of strong materials for construction, enabling us to build larger, higher, and in more complex ways; the emergence and proliferation of

9.19
Pattern attribute
7: earth and
grounding (*Source:*
Phillip Tabb)

9.20
Earth and
grounding:
(a) Mado wetlands,
(b) newly planted
basil (*Source: Phillip*
Tabb)

technology in all its forms and uses, from wine-bottle openers to spacecraft; and finally, the sensual nature of materiality. Earth is expressed in many of these ways in Serenbe. Buildings are substantially constructed to EarthCraft green building standards.[12] Figures 9.19 and 9.20 show the site plan with major hills and valleys, along with photographs of the wetlands in the center of Mado Hamlet and freshly planted basil in a kitchen garden.

- 70 percent of the land is preserved land and was seen as a major lifestyle draw for residents.
- Acres of land are covered in first- and second-growth forests, meadows, paddocks, wetlands, and rock outcrops.
- Many of the rock outcrops and boulders are habitats with mosses, lichens, and aged eastern red cedars.
- There is a rock outcrop garden planned for the eastern side of Mado hamlet.
- Walking the miles of trails exposes the changing contours of the land.
- Buildings are well built to EarthCraft construction standards.
- All new buildings must employ ground-sourced heat pumps for heating and air conditioning.
- Waste is processed through sand filters and constructed wetlands.
- The landforms of hills and valleys contribute to the hamlets' natural site-fitted omega forms and placemaking.

The earth pattern attribute can form a grounding connection to nature and the elements, and can contribute to more energy-conserving building practices. The landforms help create a sense of place for the hamlets. The positive health and wellness outcomes occur through a process of "grounding" or "earthing," which reduces stress and promotes calmness, improving sleep, circulation, and the immune system.[13] The earth also provides nourishment and healthy food from Serenbe Farms. The numinous outcomes take the form of grounding, centeredness, and connectedness to the earth through haptic (tactile and kinesthetic) perception and the somatosensory (pressure, pain, or warmth) systems.

The red clay soils found throughout the development are the result of the effect of a warm, humid climate, and are primarily due to iron oxides, granite, gneiss, and marble. As an element earth is durable, withstanding decay, wear and tear, damage, and the effects of severe weather and time. Further, it suggests that material functions should endure without significant deterioration, over lengthy periods of time (years of life, hours of use, and operational cycles). Walking barefoot around the home, in the parks, or within the community is not commonplace, but when it happens, there can be a connection to the earth. Discovered by Clint Ober in 1998, "earthing" is the positive outcome of this process, especially when connected to natural surfaces such as sand, dirt, stone, concrete, water, or grass.[14] These kinds of surfaces are common in Serenbe in both the woods and urban areas. The greatest asset found at Serenbe is the large amount of open space – the land – offering exercise, healthy nutrition, sociability, children's independent play, and enchantment. Residents and schoolchildren are encouraged to visit and volunteer and get their hands dirty working at Serenbe Farms.

8. Air and Natural Ventilation
Given the rural location of Serenbe, air is fresh and accessible to all buildings. The prevailing wind direction is from the southwest to the northeast; Serenbe generally avoids polluted air from greater Atlanta. At Serenbe abundant forested

land replenishes the oxygen levels. Automobile usage is limited, and therefore carbon emissions are reduced. Most residents navigate Serenbe on foot, electric carts, skateboards, and bicycles, adding to the pedestrian nature of the community. All buildings employ operable windows for cross-ventilation, and most have ceiling-mounted fans. Because the community is largely pedestrian, the open omega forms are free of automobile emissions and allow fresh air to migrate to most homes. Because of the large forested areas, oxygen is produced, carbon dioxide is converted to oxygen through photosynthesis, and micro-particulates are absorbed. In Serenbe many meadows, greens, pastures, and other open spaces provide clear access to the open sky. Figures 9.21 and 9.22 show the attribute air map followed by images of the open sky with quarter moon, a wind sculpture, and a ceiling fan.

- Carbon sequestering with abundant landscape.
- Natural ventilation in buildings.
- Provision of ceiling fans in conditioned spaces.
- Provision of soffit fans in porches for insect control.
- Provision of adequate HVAC air changes per hour for replenishing oxygen.
- Encouragement of pedestrian movement with paths and sidewalks.
- Planned communities with pedestrian-accessible mix of uses.
- Eventually, Serenbe will limit gasoline-burning automobiles within the community.
- Encouragement of natural breezeways for air movement.

The air pattern attribute can enhance sensory connections to nature and the elements. Climate-positive outcomes include carbon sequestering and oxygen production with the abundant forested lands. Sustainability can be improved with the efficiency of fresh air, natural ventilation, and the use of internal filtering systems to reduce the need for outside make-up air. Use of non-toxic building materials reduces indoor air pollution. Positive health and wellness outcomes include fresh air that is good for the digestive system, improves blood pressure, strengthens the immune system, cleans the lungs, clears the mind, and improves mood, mental acuity, and energy. Numinous outcomes can occur through the experience of olfaction perception of fresh outdoor air.

Due to its location about 34 miles southwest of metropolitan Atlanta, Serenbe enjoys fairly fresh air. Atlanta is one of the largest ozone and nitrogen oxide emissions polluters from vehicles in the United States.[15] The prevailing and upper-level winds are mainly from the west and then move northward (67 percent of the time annually). This is good news for Serenbe as the polluted air moves away from the community. The average wind speed in the Atlanta area is 5.7 miles per hour. Every home in Serenbe is equipped with operable windows supporting cross-ventilation, and many homes have Christopher Alexander's pattern number 159, "light on two sides of every room,"[16] including natural ventilation. Outdoor rooms, porches, patios, and balconies also facilitate direct access

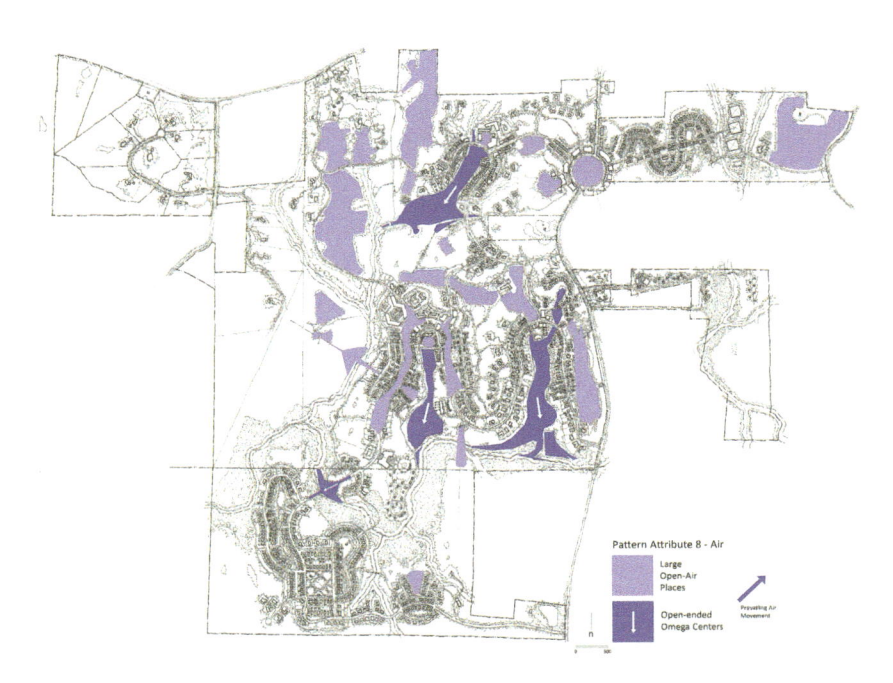

9.21
Pattern attribute
8: air and natural
ventilation (*Source:
Phillip Tabb*)

to fresh air. Many homes have wind chimes and bells, which can be heard on a day with breezes while walking throughout the community. Several of the Serenbe homes employ the "dog trot" building form where a natural breezeway through the dwelling helps cooling in summer.

9. Water and Waste

Water is necessary for life, and at Serenbe it is abundant. Fresh water is renewable and can be sourced naturally in several ways, including river diversion, collection from reservoirs, groundwater, wells, and rainwater harvesting. The

9.22
Air and natural
ventilation: (a) midday moon, (b) wind
sculpture, (c) ceiling
fan (*Source: Phillip Tabb*)

9.23
Pattern attribute 9:
water and waste
(*Source: Phillip Tabb*)

Pattern Attribute 9 - Water and Waste

Vegetated Wetlands
and Waste Collection

Water Ways
and Flood
Plains

Ponds, Lakes
and Water
Features

9.24
Water and waste:
(a) vegetated
wetlands, (b) Mado
fountain (*Source:
Phillip Tabb*)

City of Chattahoochee Hills presently supplies water. Rainwater harvesting is currently not allowed for domestic use in Chattahoochee Hills, but gray water can be used in gardens. Water can be found in other ways, including the streams, tributaries, ponds, lakes, and daylit storm-water drainage. Water is present with numerous fountains, pools, and water features. Figures 9.23 and 9.24 show the location of the waterways on the masterplan, with images of the Serenbe pond near the entrance to Selborne Hamlet and a fountain in Mado. Due to the

abundant rainfall, Serenbe receives water year-round. Water manifest as clouds, mist, fog, rain, high humidity, ice, and, infrequently, snow.

- The Atlanta region receives 50 inches of rain annually.
- Natural water sources are preserved and protected.
- There are accessible water features throughout the community (fountains, ponds, reflecting pools, and swimming pools).
- Wherever possible, there is daylit stormwater drainage.
- Gray water from the constructed wetlands is used to irrigate grazing fields.
- Serenbe employs a constructed wetlands water–waste system, which organically treats waste with water, plants, and microorganisms.
- Most houses have extended roof eaves, gutters and downspouts, and covered decks or porches for rain protection.
- There are extended water features, such as the small lakes and ponds.
- Water reservoirs are used for geothermal heating and cooling.
- Each hamlet has a major natural water feature: Selborne has a stream tributary, Grange a lake, Mado vegetated wetlands, and Spela Cedar Creek.

The water pattern attribute at Serenbe contributes to sensual, visual, and life-supporting connections to nature. Research shows that ponds and lakes absorb more carbon than woodlands.[17] With regard to sustainability outcomes, water can be used as an energy sink for geothermal systems, and can be stored for surface water runoff. Water is an integral part of the constructed wetlands water–waste system. The positive health and wellness outcomes include hydration and its effect on brain function, improved weight loss, better skin health, regulating body temperature, flushing out body waste, and maintaining blood pressure. The numinous outcomes of water reduce stress and produce calmness.

The constructed wetlands water–waste system was originally designed by John Todd, who is credited with inventing the "living machine," and then adapted by engineer Michael Ogden for Serenbe. Constructed wetlands are engineered systems that are described by other terms, such as vegetated wetlands, reed beds, soil infiltration beds, constructed treatment wetlands, and treatment wetlands. For Serenbe, grey and black wastewater are collected in individual cisterns located on each residential property where primary treatment is designed to separate the solids from the liquid effluent. Then gravity delivers waste to the one-acre (0.4-hectare) constructed wetlands, a biofilter system that uses natural functions of vegetation, soil, and organisms to treat anthropogenic discharge and remove sediments and pollutants. The associated filter bed, consisting usually of a combination of sand and gravel, has an equally important role to play in filtering the wastewater. The treated water is then piped to a nearby meadow where local cows graze. The meadow is located on low ground between Selborne hamlet and the Crossroads cluster. It was expanded in 2018 to land adjacent to the original wetlands.

10. Ether and Celestial Moments

The element ether is characterized in three ways. First is that ether is a combination of the other terrestrial elements. Second is that it is invisible, intangible, and immaterial. And third is that ether is related to celestial activity. Connecting to the cosmic order is important, from the flux of continuous occurrences to the dynamic movements around the sun. These connections help us understand our place in the universe. Due to the heavily forested nature of the land at Serenbe, celestial connections are difficult. However there are several sites, such as open land or on high south-facing ridgetops or the hamlet greens, which lend themselves to night-sky observations. Exterior lighting is designed to reduce night-sky pollution. Figures 9.25 and 9.26 show the base map and a view of the sunset and night sky.

- The calendrical function of the heavens helps mark the seasons, key occasions, and celebrations within them.
- Serenbe Playhouse produced quarterly productions associated with the changing seasons: *The Secret Garden* (spring), *A Midsummer Night's Dream* (summer), *Sleepy Hollow* (autumn), and *The Snow Queen* (winter).
- Provision of higher-elevation, open-space sites capable of night-sky observation.
- Exterior night lighting must be LED and/or no greater than 40 watts.
- Lighting standards direct light downward, reducing night-sky pollution.
- The masterplan indicates a special celestial observation site.
- Encountering flickering sunlight in the woods can generate awe.
- The hamlet omega forms are phototropic oriented to the south and sun, which is especially true for most residential sites.

The celestial connections pattern attribute provides visual and imaginative connections to nature, and the universe beyond. This is the source of light, warmth, and energy, and can contribute to positive health and wellness outcomes, including achieving inner stillness, stress reduction, and feeling a connection to the source. The outcomes include exposure to the sun and light, with their attendant benefits, including the enhancing vitamin D storage in the body, aiding dopamine production for healthy eye development, and possibly contributing to higher productivity. Stargazing can add a new perspective on everyday life, create a sense of stillness, give an expanded view of nature and the vastness of the universe, possessing to some extent the ancient function as a calendar, and facilitate a sense of wonder. Accessible to all, the celestial heavens are often overlooked and underappreciated. Therefore, it is important to plan for places in order to connect and be emplaced.

Ether has a magical way of entering Serenbe and is found in many natural places and during many cultural and ceremonial events. The more intimate numinous experiences occur in the woods and along the small streams, while the cultural moments are experienced during performing arts events, dining

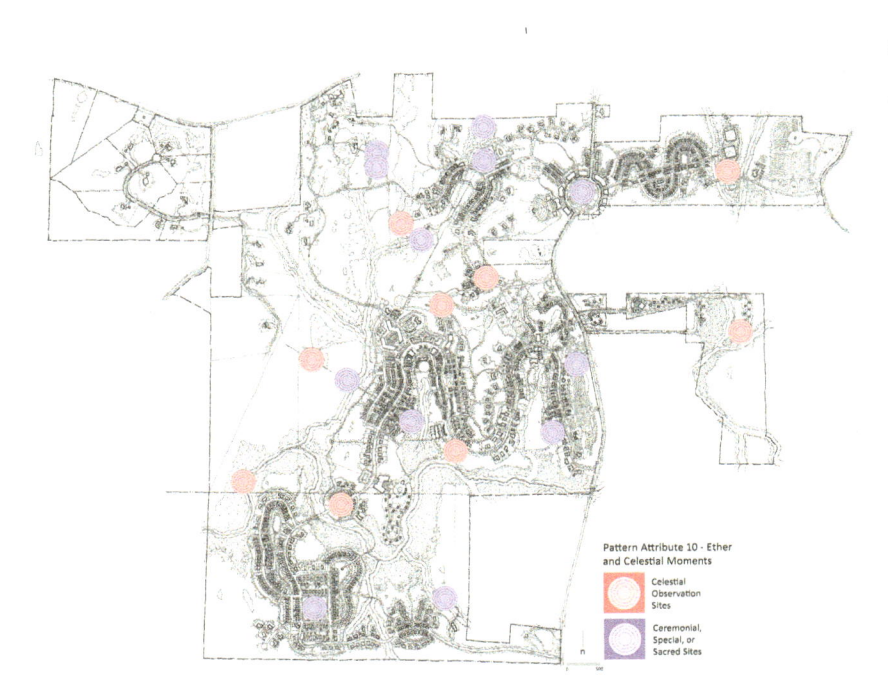

9.25
Pattern attribute 10:
ether and celestial
moments (*Source:
Phillip Tabb*)

experiences, and neighborhood gatherings. There are several stargazing places in Serenbe, located in the more open spaces, such as the greens at Crossroads, Selborne, and Grange hamlets. There is a designated celestial site in Mado hamlet as well. The labyrinth is another source of numinous experience. It is an outdoor 88-foot (27-meter) replica of the Chartres labyrinth in France. It is positioned along cardinal directions and is above and looking over the Inn pond. A slow walk around curving paths, it takes about 15 minutes to arrive at its center. In its center are five large granite stones, where one can sit and reflect on the journey. Often this process reduces temporal density and has a way of clearing

9.26
Ether and celestial
moments:
(a) evening sunset,
(b) night sky
(*Source: Phillip
Tabb*)

the mind, and becoming increasingly aware of the path, footsteps on the ground below, and the presence of mind.

11. Orientation and Direction

Orientation gives meaning and connections to the terrestrial world of a given place through connection to the natural features of the place, such as the cardinal directions, the natural contours of the site, or views of special features. To Christian Norberg-Schulz, orientation contributes to a sense of belonging or being-in-the-world.[18] At Serenbe the predominant orientation is toward the south and the southwest direction of the Piedmont range. Internally, orientation is to the land features, such as the omega interiors; tributaries, wetlands, ponds, and lakes. Planning for solar access was an important function of this pattern. A majority of residential plots were elongated along the east–west axis allowing for good rooftop orientation to the southern sun. In Figures 9.27 and 9.28, the map depicts orientations and the photograph shows axes to the yoga field and the healing garden in Mado hamlet.

- Hamlets are oriented to the south and southwest directions (with the exception of the Education hamlet).
- Residential lotting within hamlets is good for solar orientation for renewable energy systems as roofs generally face north–south, and plots are elongated along east-west direction.
- There is sympathetic orientation of the hamlets to the natural topography.
- Dwellings are oriented to the natural landscapes found within the omega interiors, and paths are directed into the hamlet centers.
- Most buildings are oriented to the streets for access to community engagement and surveillance, and to greens and parks for connections to nature.
- Higher density and a concentration of mix of a uses are located at to the hamlet omega apex for convenient access and theming identity.
- Each hamlet is oriented to a particular theme – the arts, agriculture, health and wellness, play, and education.

The orientation and direction pattern attribute can contribute to sensual, visual, and life- supporting connections to nature. The omega forms are phototropic as they orient to the sun and to the omega interiors. The sustainability outcomes include access to solar energy that can provide daylighting, passive and active heating, domestic hot-water heating, and electricity production. The theming of the hamlets allows for local placemaking and identity as hamlets are oriented to the natural contours of the land. The health and wellness outcomes and benefits can include stress reduction through orientation to the natural environment. Sunlight prevents vitamin D deficiency, boosts the immune system, can lower blood pressure, and reduces seasonal affective disorder.

The predominate orientations for Serenbe are determined by the topography of the land, access to sun, views to nature, and proximity to the omega road form.

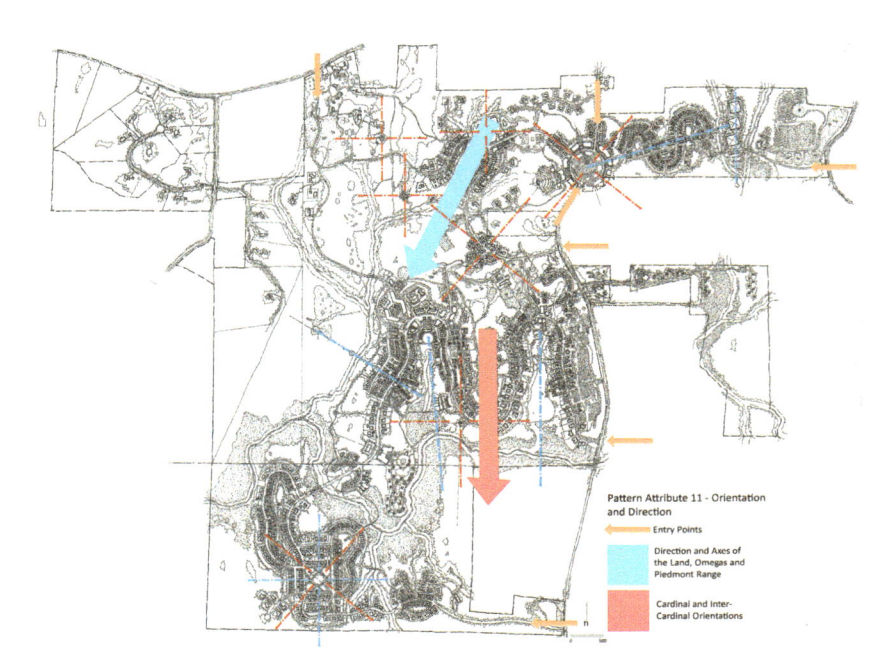

9.27
Pattern attribute
11: orientation and
direction (*Source:
Phillip Tabb*)

9.28
Orientation and
direction: (a) axial
view through
Anders Court to the
yoga field, (b) view
of the healing
garden in Mado
(*Source: Phillip
Tabb*)

Ridges and valleys tend to run south and southwest, creating bowl-like micro-places. It is in this context that the omega settlement forms were situated. For optimal performance both passive and active solar energy systems should be oriented within 30 degrees southeast or southwest of true south. The majority of residential land plots are aligned in the north–south direction of the omega legs, and each site's long axis runs east–west, which is good for placement of photovoltaic

panels on the south side of rooftops. Most dwellings have direct views to the natural hamlet centers or to the surrounding woods, and also to the tree-lined omega roads and the social activities they encourage. This orientation has a positive community-based surveillance function as well for identifying dangerous or criminal events. The orientation to the natural open spaces also provides relief during times of shelter-in-place.

12. Prospect and Refuge

Prospect and refuge are two very different pattern characteristics yet are inner connected. At the building scale, it means having a very protected space with a clear view outward. And at the urban design scale at Serenbe, the omega forms provide protection, outward views, and a sense of place. Nearly every dwelling in Serenbe backs onto an open space and faces the tree-lined streets. This sense of visual control contributes to reduced vulnerability. The houses have living spaces, kitchens, screened-in porches, and balconies facing the woods, and front entries facing the street that serve as observation lookouts. Figures 9.29 and 9.30 show the map of view corridors and refuge places. Figure 9.30(a) is an aerial view of Grange hamlet indicating the omega hamlet street shaped like a vessel and a dwelling, protected at the apex of the omega and open at the extremities. Figure 9.30(b) is of a dwelling showing the cave-like inner space beneath the barrel vault.

- Hamlets have an omega shape, providing a good prospect at urban design scale either along the streetscapes or into the omega centers.
- The omega hamlets also create refuge at the center, especially in the hamlets' public "outdoor rooms," where surveillance and communication readily occur.
- All homes face the street, most with front porches allowing surveillance of suspicious activities at the building and street scale.
- The friendly pedestrian scale and density encourages neighborly surveillance.
- Most homes have direct and discerning views outward to the open spaces and inward to the omega interiors.
- The restaurants have cozy and intimate dining settings.
- Refuge spaces can support passive survivability in natural disasters, severe weather, and power outages.
- Homes are constructed using substantial materials and are well insulated, adding a sense of safety and refuge.
- In sheltering-at-home, Serenbe dwellings have direct access to nature and safe distancing between neighboring homes, offering relief and safety during the pandemic.

The prospect and refuge pattern attribute can contribute to visual, safe, and supporting settings that connect to nature. Prospect allows for surveillance and the identification of danger. The sustainability outcomes occur in the form of passive survivability potentials coupled with refuge spaces. Together these pattern

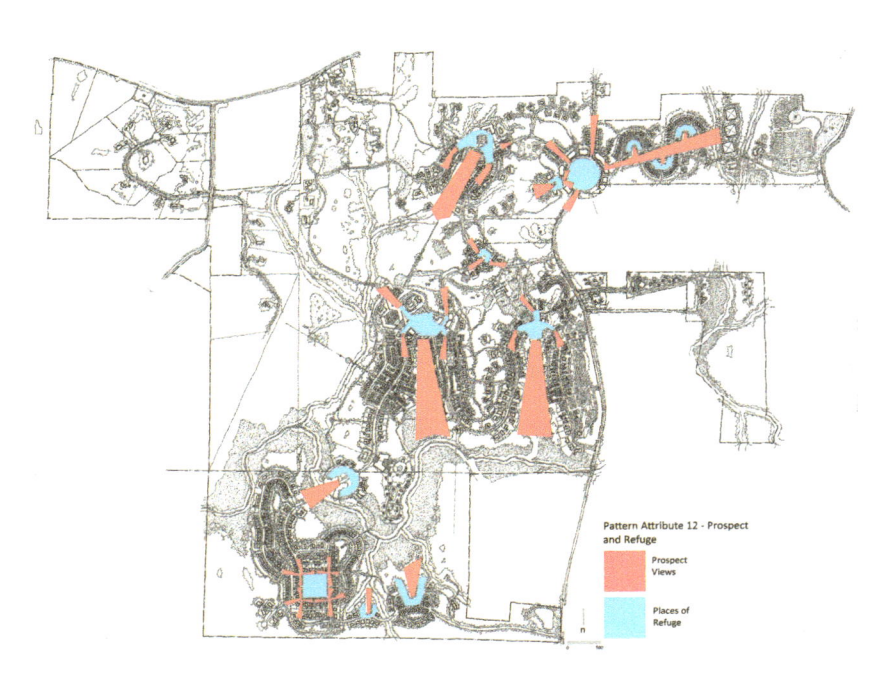

9.29
Pattern attribute 12: prospect and refuge (*Source: Phillip Tabb*)

attributes can produce positive health and wellness outcomes, including peace of mind, emotional security, stress reduction, and reduced boredom. Refuge also provides safety from potential intruders and suspicious activity, and from inclement weather without necessarily disengaging from it. According to Steven Kellert, they provide comforting and nurturing interior spaces.[19]

9.30
Prospect and refuge: (a) hamlet omega form as prospect and refuge, (b) refuge within a barrel vault dwelling (*Source: Phillip Tabb*)

Prospect occurs with dwellings facing the omega centers for observing children playing in the woods, or spotting the occasional wildlife passing by. Prospect along the streets also occurs from within the dwelling. Major interior rooms, porches, and balconies face the street for views, social connections to the community, and surveillance. There is a remarkable informal community network dedicated to supporting the health and wellbeing of fellow residents. Refuge occurs at the urban scale in the sense of place and the natural place boundedness that occurs in each omega hamlet. The omega apices offer a safe mix of uses and activities where residents can gather indoors or outdoors. For everyone, the home is a pleasant refuge. This is especially important when the home can function as refuge and passive survivability location simultaneously. During the Coronavirus pandemic, as throughout most of the world, residents have sheltered in place, and in the case of Serenbe they have been able to safely engage with the natural surroundings without direct contact with other residents. The attributes of prospect and refuge have been important during the COVID-19 pandemic, offering a safe haven from the spread of the disease.

13. Inside–Outside Relationships

The relationship between inside and outside could possibly be one of the most effective pattern attributes in achieving the biophilic effect at Serenbe. This is especially important in reversing the tendency of spending so much time indoors. This pattern not only suggests a visual connection to the natural features of the site and street activities, but also encourages a physical connection. Nearly every home in Serenbe directly faces some form of open space – the woods, meadows, Serenbe Farms, or natural water flows. There are porches on the street side and screened-in outdoor rooms on the forest side. Figures 9.31 and 9.32 show the built portions of Selborne hamlet and the relationship between building interiors and the adjacent outdoors. The dwelling photographs illustrate a fluid indoor–outdoor relationship with large windows and a diagonal inside wall form extending outside, creating visual and spatial continuity.

- The serpentine omega forms encourage screened-in porches and patios facing the woods on either side of the road.
- The indoor–outdoor spaces form a seamless transition, enable ease of access, and provide diversity and expansion to living functions in nature.
- Outdoor rooms expand and extend indoor living functions for recreation, work, relaxation, and entertainment.
- The extensive use of screened-in porches allows for closer contact with the outside without contact with menacing mosquitos.
- Most dwellings are positioned close to the street, set back between 8 and 10 feet (2.4–3 meters) from sidewalks, and have front porches and verandas directly facing the street.
- Each of the five restaurants has protected outdoor seating areas.

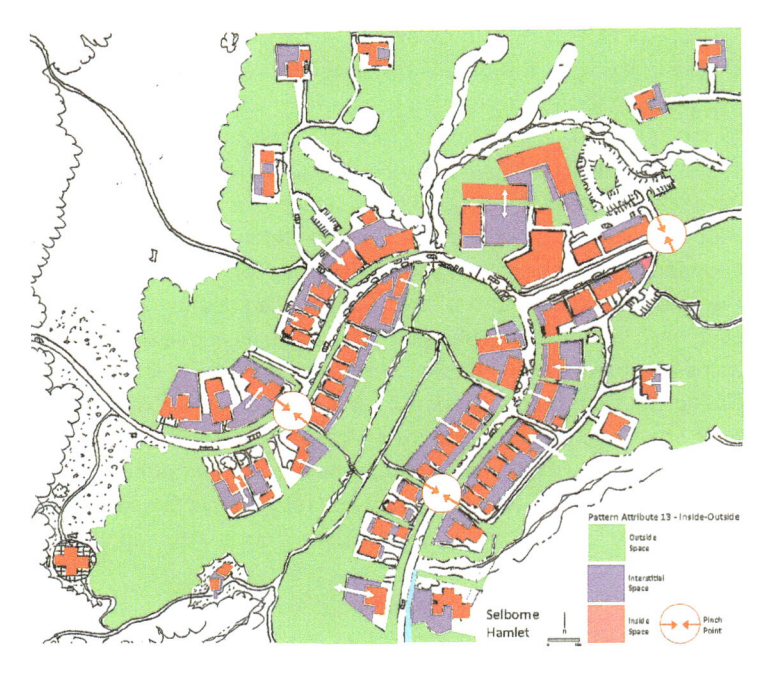

9.31
Pattern attribute
14: inside–outside
relationships
(*Source: Phillip
Tabb*)

9.32
Inside–outside:
(a) outside dwelling
space, (b) inside
dwelling space
(*Source: Phillip
Tabb*)

- Because Serenbe is a pedestrian-friendly community, people are constantly jogging, strolling, walking dogs, and attending events such as the farmers' and artists' market.
- All Serenbe Playhouse productions occur outdoors, with sets constructed within the Serenbe open spaces and woods.

The inside–outside pattern attribute can facilitate visual, sensual, physical, and social connections to nature, the elements, and place. Blurring the inside–outside relationship allows for a more direct experience with changing climatic and weather patterns. Many homes have outdoor rooms for entertaining family and friends. From a sustainability point of view, the preponderance of outdoor activities helps reduce indoor energy loads, as time spent in unconditioned spaces due to the buffering effect (transitional spaces) saves energy. The positive health and wellness outcomes include the greater experience of sunlight and exposure to fresh air, which positively affects physical health.

The inside–outside pattern attribute functions at two different scales. At the urban design scale, the omega forms create a bounded inside which is accessible nature, and the built forms create the container. Because the circulation systems are porous, visitors and residents can easily move into the hamlet centers. Building interiors open directly to the inner areas of the omegas or to surrounding forests. Most homes have porches, balconies, terraces, and outdoor rooms that directly connect to the natural areas of Serenbe. Weather conditions in spring, summer, and autumn are conducive to enjoying these outdoor transitional spaces. In summer, these spaces require screens to keep away the mosquitos. Due to the heavy presence of trees, natural breezes, and ceiling fans, most of these outdoor spaces do not overheat and are pleasant to use in summer. In good weather these spaces are used extensively and facilitate social interaction as neighbors walk by on their way to one of the restaurants, an event, or exercising their dog. Most homes enjoy fluid indoor–outdoor connections. All the restaurants within Serenbe have outdoor seating areas that overlook natural landscapes, which has allowed them to remain open during the pandemic.

14. Topography and Geography Patterns

The topographical patterns are landform characteristics of the site. At Serenbe the topography is quite varied with elevations ranging from approximately 795 to 915 feet above sea level, representing a change of 120 feet (36.6 meters). Traditional residential development tends to level the ground for ease of access for construction and to enable more cost-effective dwelling foundations. Building more densely allows for more land preservation and ease of site development. Within Serenbe, however, development is sensitive to the terrain, following land found between the higher hills and lower flood plains. The orography (hilly geography) through Serenbe contributes certain microclimates. In Figures 9.33 and 9.34, the map shows the highs and lows of the topography, and photographs

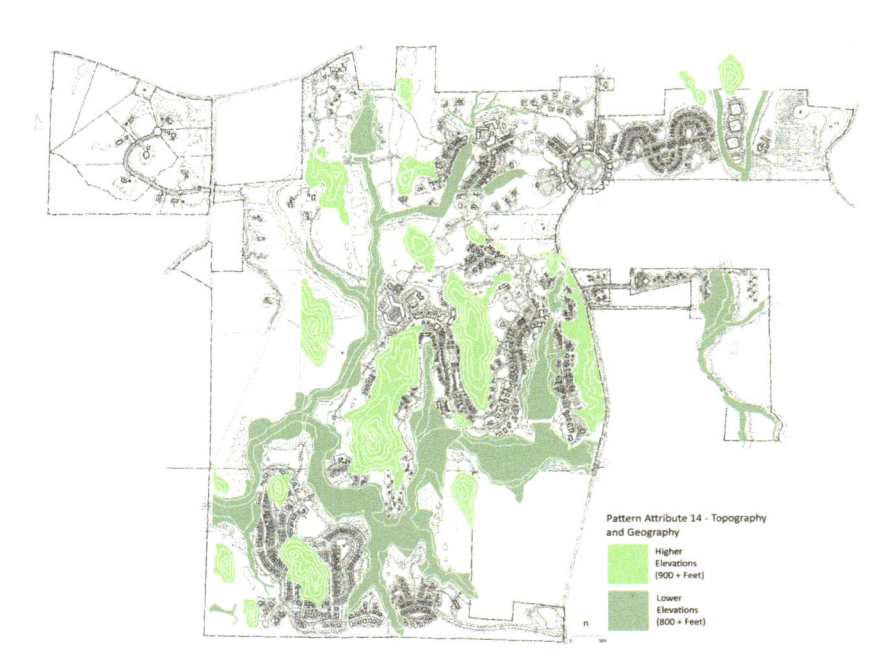

9.33
Pattern attribute
14: topography and
geography (*Source:
Phillip Tabb*)

illustrate the topographical changes in the hills separating Mado and Grange
hamlets.

- Built portions of the development follow the natural contours of the land
  typically located between the hilltops above and flood plains below.
- Rather than leveling out roads with cut-and-fill, the roads follow the natural
  contours within development code limits.
- Development avoids building on the extreme tops and bottoms of the
  changing contours.

9.34
Topography
and geography:
(a) hillside toward
Mado hamlet, (b)
hillside toward
Grange hamlet
(*Source: Phillip
Tabb*)

- Sloping land allows for a natural means of channeling stormwater and creating natural water-retention swales and daylit storm drains.
- Changing topography creates more visual interest.
- Changing topography allows for views and vistas.
- Paved, gently sloping paths occur between hamlets for ADA compliance.
- The developed portions simulate and complement rather than replicate the natural features of the site.
- The miles of trails and varying topography contribute to physical health.

The topography and geographic pattern attributes contribute the sensitivity, preservation, and visual interest of the natural features of the site. Development occurs with minimal negative impact upon the land. The climatic benefits are a result of concentrating development and thereby preserving greater forested areas for carbon sequestering. The sustainability outcomes of topography include the natural effects of gravity for ease of groundwater movement, and induced air circulation. Changing topography creates place-location and contributes to place-identity. The positive health and wellness outcomes include increased cardiovascular exercise, weight loss, and toning of multiple lower-body muscles, especially hamstrings (knee flexion) and hip extension.

Topography played an important role in the placement of the hamlets and the designs for the individual buildings within them. The omega roads and utilities follow the shape of the land, slightly rising and falling according to the natural variations in height along a similar contour. The combination of this slight elevation change and the curvilinear nature of the omega shape creates an interesting changing perspective of the urbanized portions of the design. The street curvature causes closed or contained views and exposure to the changing perspectives of building facades, and helps to help facilitate traffic calming. Dwellings typically are sited either on relatively flat parcels of land or on sloping ones with as much as 10 to 20 feet (3 to 6 meters) variation in height. From a biophilic point of view, this changing topography is an experiential and perceptual connection to the land and usually affords good views, allowing for other biophilic pattern attributes. As described by Orlians and Heerwagen, preferable landscapes contain changes of elevation, tall trees, and semi-open space.[20] The landforms, landscape features, and topological changes of the Serenbe site are reminiscent of landscapes described in the Savanna Hypothesis.

15. Spatial Order and Connectiveness

There are contrasting spatial ordering systems present at Serenbe in both the natural and built environments. The natural environment contains a more random pattern created by the geological, topographical, and ecological systems. The constructed environment is organized by an intentional hierarchal pattern of single-loaded omega spatial organizing forms, and their replication within favorable site locations. The serpentine omega road system gives structure to the plots, density gradient, and composition of the mix of uses. The primary order

9.35
Pattern attribute 15:
spatial order and
connectiveness
(*Source: Phillip Tabb*)

9.36
Spatial order and
connectiveness:
(a) Thorburn
transect diagram,
(b) Thorburn
transect along
Selborne Lane,
(c) Selborne Hamlet
(*Source: Phillip Tabb*)

of the hamlets follows sympathetic land contours, and the Thorburn transect allows for varying building plotting and landscape themes along changing densities. At the architectural scale, building types vary from detached to attached dwellings with differing architectural languages. The simple omega road form is powerful enough to be able to accommodate these widely varying architectural forms. The omega road has spatial continuity, and the dwellings have spatial diversity, complexity, and varying detail and materials. Figures 9.35 and 9.36 show the map detailing urban and landscape forms along with methods of

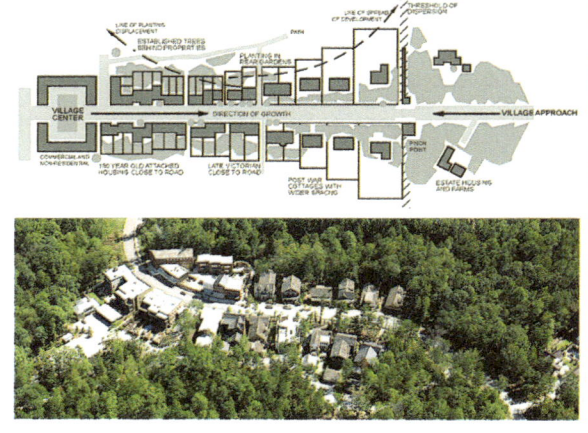

circulation, and a Thorburn transect diagram along Selborne Lane with accompanying photographs.

- All ordering systems are present at Serenbe: simple, ambiguous, and complex.
- The omega hamlet planning form allows for interesting and structured order that is easily comprehended yet filled with dynamic changes of viewpoint.
- The omega hamlets increase in density, scale, and mix of uses along the Thorburn transect, and they increase spatial cognition.
- Complexity at the human scale is information rich.
- The serpentine omega order naturally follows the contours of the land.
- The omega forms are easily identified and contribute to coherent wayfinding.
- Buildable sites within each plot are designated to conform to the Thorburn transect.
- Dwelling types vary and include apartments, condominiums, townhomes, cottage homes, live–work units, and estate homes; plot size for dwellings varies from 900 square feet (84 square meters) to more than 4,000 square feet (372 square meters).
- Within the strong omega form, dwellings can have individualized architectural languages adding to the diversity, identity and need for self-expression, and complexity of human scale.
- Each of the hamlets are connected by the serpentine roads and pedestrian paths.

The spatial order and variability pattern attribute contributes to multiple connections to nature and urban activities. It provides efficient access to the diverse land uses and adaptations to changing conditions, and the expression of extreme and combinatory ordering systems from simplicity to complexity. With regard to placemaking outcomes at Serenbe, the omega ordering geometry contributes to wayfinding, spatial legibility, and to creating a sense of place and identity. The health and wellness benefits derive from spatial diversity and pattern complexity, yet obvert boredom and overstimulation. Varying spaces contribute not only to functional demands, but also to psychological and emotional needs.

The most powerful spatial structure for Serenbe is the omega form. The omega is a symbol for the last or 24th letter of the Greek alphabet and means the completion of a sequence.[21] It also suggests the volume of an object and the containment of an open-loop system. The geometry related to this form has two qualities. The first is the creation of a sense of place through its embracing nature where center, boundary, and domain are clearly given form. The shape is not a 'U', but it is an 'Ω,' which supports greater containment. The second occurs with the open end of the omega, which allows for natural ecological flows – solar energy, water, resident animals, and people. The unique qualities and interesting properties or shape grammars include the linear, nucleated, and transected characteristics, along with the power of circularity. As a double-loaded organization of building sites along the omega road, it allows access to the center and perimeter for direct contact with nature. The road widths are narrow, creating an increase in what is called "side-friction." This term describes the degree of activity complexity and spatial constriction of the activities along a residential street, which contributes to slower automobile speeds. Growth at Serenbe occurs by multiplication as hamlet size is determined by the topographical features of the land. The pedestrian network is vast and seamless with more than 15 miles (24 kilometers) of walkways, paths, and trails throughout Serenbe.

16. Centering and Nucleation

Centering is a point of attraction and a seed encoding growth of a place. The place can be a special one such as a square, green, temple, market, street, building, landmark, natural feature, or fountain. Centering can be real or perceived. It is a physical focal point and usually contains an intense activity and meaning. According to Yi-Fu Tuan, the center is what he calls the "middle place," or the center of the world.[22] Centering happens on several levels at Serenbe. It happens within each of the homes, the center of the hamlets, the apex of the omega forms, and the center of the entire community. The center can be a physical place or network and constellation, as in the case of Serenbe, or an emotional sense of place. Centering also occurs within the individual while experiencing the abundant natural beauty of Serenbe. Living in Serenbe promotes a sense of serenity and isolation from outside development, yet it is connected to the larger world around it. The world's busiest airport is 25 minutes away, and the city center of Atlanta is 45 minutes to an hour away depending upon traffic. Figures 9.37 and 9.38 show a site plan indicating center points within Serenbe and a photograph of the Serenbe labyrinth and path in the center of Selborne hamlet.

- There is no marked center for the entire community, but there is a strong sense of place.
- The community is a constellation of interrelated hamlets, each with a perceived center.
- The cultural centers of each of the hamlets occur at the omega apex. Each hamlet has its own theme, function, outdoor gathering place, and gathering point.
- The natural centers of the hamlets occur near the interior of the omega and each frames a different natural feature – stream, lake, wetland, park, and rock garden.
- Each hamlet center is a place-maker, giving identity to the place.
- Centering encourages the presence of pedestrians and social interaction.
- When inside your own dwelling, there is a connection to the whole.
- Centering can increase a sense of presence with enhanced perception, grounding, and a sense of nearness.

9.37
Pattern attribute
16: centering and
nucleation (*Source:
Phillip Tabb*)

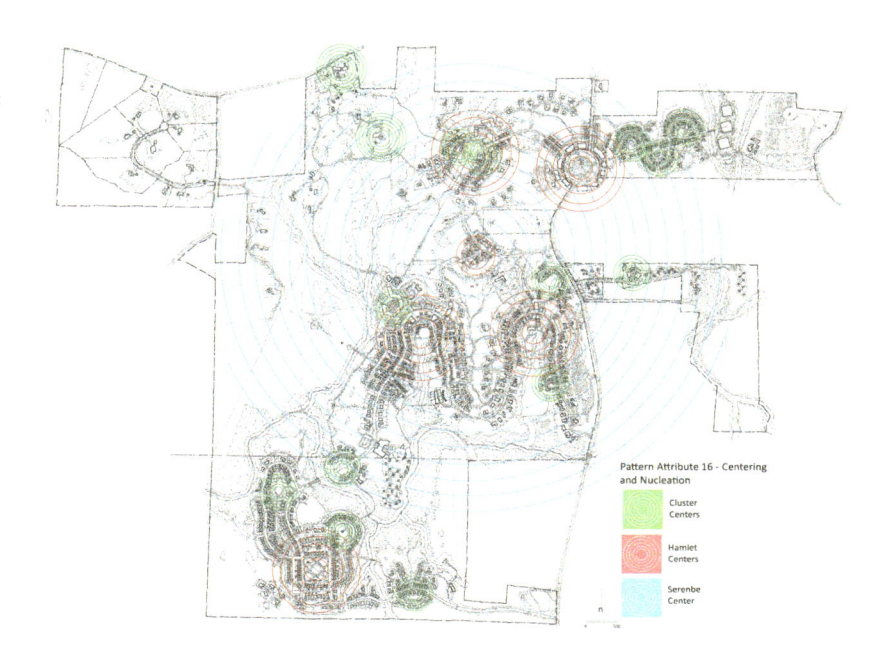

9.38
Centering:
(a) omega center
walking path and
bridge, (b) Serenbe
labyrinth (*Source:
Phillip Tabb
and Serenbe
Development*)

The centering pattern attribute contributes to a more intense and vital connection to nature, the elements, and numinous dimensions. The sustainable outcomes focus on concentration, density, and agglomeration of activities. The positive health and even high-level wellness outcomes include increasing focus and mental acuity, enhancing presence, grounding or centering, and the reduction of temporal density, anxiety, and stress. The numinous outcomes derive from the strong sense of community (e.g. at community events), special places

like the labyrinth, the natural water features, and experiences within the omega centers.

The labyrinth has become a favorite destination for both residents and visitors. It was built over a weekend in July of 2003 by family and friends of the developer. The Serenbe labyrinth is an 88-foot-diameter replica of the one in the west nave or Royal Portal of the 12th-century Chartres Cathedral in France. However, it is twice the size and is sited outdoors overlooking the Inn pond. Walking at a deliberate pace, it takes 15 minutes to navigate to the center of the labyrinth. For most, it is a calming and contemplative experience. There is no designated center in Serenbe, as it is not a single place but rather an agglomeration of smaller places. When you are there, however, you do feel that you are in a special place. There is an organic network or constellation of hamlets. When considering the northern parts of Serenbe that include Selborne, Grange, Mado, and the Education Hamlets, the intersection in Crossroads is at the geographic center of the site. The feeling of center does occur within the natural areas of the omegas, and a sense of nucleation occurs at the apex where there are more compact forms and mix of uses. During the Coronavirus, having direct access to fresh produce, goods from the general store, and take-away food from four of the on-site restaurants has been a benefit from nucleation.

17. Bounding and Containment

Serenbe is not a gated community, but rather is a porous open-access one. Automobile access to the developed portions of the community occurs through four road entrances. There is a large amount of containment as bounding exists by both natural and architectural means. However, Serenbe's boundedness is porous, allowing for vital natural elements and wildlife to flow in and out. Bounding and the constellation of hamlets give a clear sense of place and contribute to each hamlet's identity. The built portions of the development are surrounded by woods, and the omega forms are a bounding urban spatial organization containing the natural centers. Greenspaces, recreational areas, and courtyards are bounded. Figures 9.39 and 9.40 provide a map with these two bounding patterns of the natural and built portions of the site, an aerial view of Grange hamlet, and a Selborne hamlet omega street view with architectural bounding.

- Each of the hamlet omega forms is bounded by forests, or in the case of the east side of Grange, with the Serenbe Farms.
- Each built portion of the omega forms a boundary around its natural center.
- The bounded and contained omega forms give a clear sense of protection and individual identity.
- There are bounded greens, recreation areas, or open spaces within each hamlet.
- With the boundaries is an increased sense of containment, protection, and peace.
- The boundaries create a safe territory for free-ranging children to play.

9.39
Pattern attribute
17: bounding
and containment
(*Source: Phillip
Tabb*)

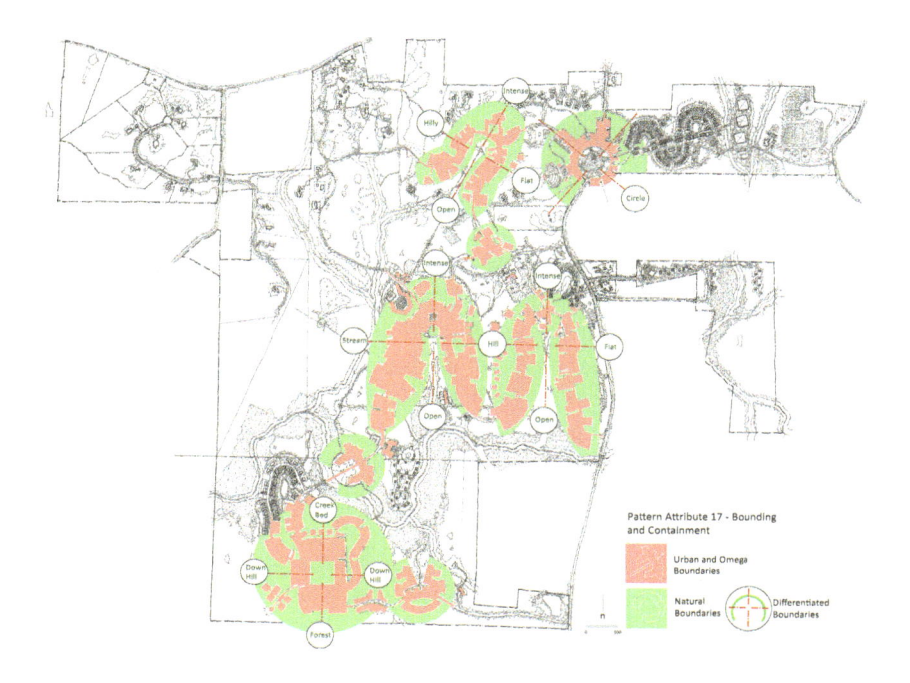

9.40
Bounding:
(a) Grange hamlet
omega bounding,
(b) Selborne hamlet
and fresco dining
with architectural
bounding
(*Source: Serenbe
Development and
Phillip Tabb*)

- The bounded areas are always porous, allowing for vital elements and wild-life to flow through and between the built portions.
- Serenbe is accessed by county roads on two sides, the north and east, leaving the other two sides forested and protected.
- Animal enclosures and paddocks are bounded by fences.

The bounding pattern attribute contributes to a strong sense of place with protected connections to nature and the elements. It provides a context for recreational, cultural, and social activities. The sustainability benefits from

boundaries include setting a clearly defined territory for on-site renewable resource management, the reduction of automobile use, and the protection of non-urbanized land. From a placemaking perspective, it provides a safe territory for slow automobile traffic and electric carts, and also for pedestrian movement. The positive health outcomes include feelings of peace, safety, and privacy, the protection of home and community, and the reduction of stress and anxiety. The numinous benefits occur through the isolation and protection of sacred spaces.

Serenbe is surrounded by woods and is contained within this natural barrier. Within this fabric of forest land, the built portions of the omegas define and bound the natural omega centers. The bounded hamlets are a simultaneous process of place-making and a growth strategy by multiplication. They too are porous, allowing access from the road and sidewalks into the center. The omegas are open-ended, allowing for natural flows in and out of the center. Because of the generally cardinal orientation of the omega hamlets, the four directions are articulated differently – open to the south, apex in the north, east and west legs usually different in topography or architectural language. The containment, like a caldron, contributes to a sense of place. In ancient China, the *ting* was a cooking vessel suggesting nourishment, and at Serenbe the omega centers function similarly.[23] Home properties typically do not have exterior enclosing walls and fenced-in lawns (though there are some small fenced-in areas for dogs). So there is not really a sense of bounding other than the exterior walls of the dwelling. Dwellings' exterior walls contribute to resident bounding and a sense of refuge. During the Coronavirus pandemic, Serenbe residents have observed sheltering-in-place, for the most part sheltering within their homes and hamlets.

18. Natural Materiality

Materials define form. Natural materials are found everywhere in Serenbe. In the built environment wood, plant-based fibers, stone, slate, brick, stucco, and iron are often used in construction. Typical in this part of Georgia are the black-stained four-board and post-and-rail wood fences enclosing pastures and defining entrances within the community. There is an interesting contrast between the natural materials associated with the buildings and high-tech materials used in automobiles, bicycles, and smartphones. Natural materiality expresses non-objective, nonlinear, and random patterning. Experiences of natural materials, according to Bill Browning, create a semiotic narrative back to its living source.[24] Figures 9.41 and 9.42 show a map with prominent built natural materials used in the community, and the Swan Ridge bridge and a folly next to the labyrinth which illustrate a contemporary living vernacular architectural language of natural materials.

- Building foundations are made of concrete, stone, and brick.
- Exterior walls are constructed with board and baton, baton and board, lapped siding, wood trim, stone, brick, stucco, and concrete.
- Roofs are typically wood shingles or metal.
- Decks and balconies are stained or painted wood.

9.41
Pattern attribute 18:
natural materiality
(*Source: Phillip
Tabb*)

9.42
Natural materiality:
(a) Swan Ridge
bridge, (b) the Inn
pond folly (*Source:
Phillip Tabb*)

- Stair and balcony rails are wood and wrought iron.
- Dwelling interiors have indoor plants, natural materials (wood, straw, hemp, cork, bamboo, and recycled fibers), exposed wood structure, wood floors, marble countertops, and wood furniture.
- Hamlet street curbs are made of granite.
- Rural elements, like fences, benches, and follies are wood.
- Many materials are recycled and repurposed.

The natural materiality pattern attribute can enhance visual and sensory connections to nature and the elements. Climate-positive outcomes occur with carbon sequestering and storage through the use of building materials, and the high percentage of woodlands. Sustainability outcomes include on-site renewable resources. The use and continuity of natural materials can contribute to place identity. The positive health and wellness outcomes include improved attention and creativity, reduction of stress, and reduction of passive inhalation of toxic chemical off-gassing from construction and synthetic products. The numinous outcomes suggest that natural materials offer a sensory benefit because of their different sizes, textures, colors, and tactile sensations.

Generally, exterior building envelope materials are selected in response to underheating and overheating conditions, and at times excessive rain. At Serenbe, the two- and three-story Southern contemporary vernacular designs are usually sheathed in lapped wood-painted siding, board and batten, batten and board, and stucco. They usually have stone or brick chimneys. Commercial and townhome building types are typically finished with brick veneer or stucco. Most roofs are covered with either standing-seam metal or asphalt shingles, and some have wood shingles (usually increasing fire insurance costs). Foundations are typically concrete or concrete block, faced with either stone or stucco. Most dwellings have wood porches and/or balconies. Landscapes are a natural extension of the materiality of most buildings in Serenbe. Since there are no lawns, dwellings are accompanied by the existing trees and extensive vegetation and native species. Split-rail fences are placed around pastures and paddocks, and there are wood and cast iron benches in both the natural and urban areas. It is the combination of the materials of the natural environment, and the preponderance of natural building materials, that contributes to the unity and rural character of Serenbe. The preponderance of wood and stone are intended to reflect back to the living forests and land from which they derived.

19. Form Language and Natural Analogs

There are several form languages at play in Serenbe. First and foremost is the response to the natural, rural character of the place, and as such there has been a concerted effort to protect and preserve the natural areas while minimizing the urban impact on them. In some places there remain gravel roads lined with dark four-rail fences defining pastures, creating vistas, and retaining an agrarian landscape. Second is the progressive nature of the omega spatial structure that organizes the street system and built portions of the community. The curvilinear form provides strong organizing geometric properties, the rural-to-urban transect, and a changing perspective while moving throughout the community. And third is the development's varied building types and architectural languages. Unlike the more prescribed architecture of many new urban projects and single use developments, at Serenbe building size, form, complexity, material choices, colors, and image can vary. Often though, the overall building forms are encouraged to correspond to the massing and density gradient ascribed by the Thorburn transect. Hamlet centers and commercial buildings also have

9.43
Pattern attribute 19:
form language and
natural analogues
(*Source: Phillip
Tabb*)

Pattern Attribute 19 - Form Language
and Natural Analogues (as of 2020)

Existing
Urban
Architecture

Hamlet
Omega
Forms

Existing
Southern
Vernaculars

European
Contemporary
Vernaculars

Existing
Contemporary
Forms

9.44
Form language and
natural analogues:
(a) Serenbe
stables (rural),
(b) Blue Eyed Daisy
Bakeshop with
outdoor social
distancing (urban)
(*Source: Phillip
Tabb*)

certain thematic languages: Southern revival in Selborne, Southern vernacular in Crossroads, Western agrarian in Grange, English vernacular in Swan Ridge, and Nordic vernacular in Mado. And sprinkled throughout each of the hamlets are contemporary works. Refer to Figures 9.43 for the masterplan map, and 9.44 showing locations of existing buildings and differing form languages for the Serenbe Stables and Blue Eyed Daisy Bakeshop.

- 70 percent of the land is preserved and therefore retains a rural character.
- The natural areas of Serenbe include large stands of trees, pastures, meadows, wetlands, and other water features.

- The urban structures utilize the form grammar of the omega geometry, supporting containment, bounding, a sense of entry/exit, and open-endedness.
- Buildings within the urban areas of the hamlets generally conform to the rural-to-urban transect in their positioning on the land plots, massing of building envelopes, and material choices.
- Architectural building types vary throughout the community, including five different kinds of residential types, and commercial and rural uses.
- The varying form languages contribute to building identity among the different hamlets.
- Dwellings in particular are required to have front porches facing the street, to help residents engage with the community and also to encourage indoor–outdoor experiences.
- The wide variety of building images and languages vary allowing residents to select housing aesthetics that express their personal concept of home.

In general, form refers to the shape and structure of something; and it can also mean the organization and placement of, and relationship between, things. As a language, it influences the entire built portions of the community. In Serenbe there is a serene quality, a pastoral quality, and a strong sense of community, all of which serve to inform its biophilic character. It is the integration of the natural qualities of the site with the built form that gives it its character. The analogue for the omega forms is a vessel or mouth that opens for fresh air and nutrients provided by the forest in which it is contained.

In the Mado hamlet, the architectural language is an anthroposophically based philosophy and was inspired by the architecture of Erik Asmussen and his work at the educational center at Järna, Sweden.[25] His architecture is human-scaled, with both abstract geometric and biological references. In Malmo, Sweden there is a mix of modern architecture and ecologically sustainable neighborhood designs. Buildings are colorful, eccentric, and playfully iconic.

In Serenbe, the One Mado building is a three-story blue wellness center housing the Halsa restaurant. The community swimming pool is pink, and dwellings vary in color from red, green, blue, yellow, and aubergine to cream, gray, charcoal, and white. In the Crossroads, all dwellings reflect the character of rural clustered intersection development of the 19th century in the South. They are white and mostly contain porches and white-painted picket fences. In Selborne hamlet, houses utilize more natural materials because it was the first hamlet constructed, the dwellings blending with a healthy mix of mature landscaping and trees. Each of the hamlets has its own unique character, which emphasizes their thematic differences.

20. Cultural, Social, Historic Connections

Cultural, social, and historic connections are very much present within Serenbe. There are two historic sites within Serenbe. One is a Native American archeological site and the other is a 19th century homestead and cemetery site. With five restaurants and numerous other culinary events, social connections occur often. Not only do residents socialize with one another, they also meet visitors, especially on weekends. Food is central to Serenbe, and its farm-to-table dining and the produce purchased from Serenbe Farms lead to healthy eating. The performing arts offer many opportunities for community engagement. Serenbe Playhouse, Terminus Ballet, and the artist-in-residence program provide multiple venues for cultural development and social interaction. Figures 9.45 and 9.46 show Serenbe's many historic, agricultural, community, culinary, and performing arts locations, with photographs of the Jungle Book poster, and the Farmer's and Artist's Market.

- Within Serenbe, there are two historic sites: Native American and Colonial Georgia.
- There are numerous cultural events, activities, and programs organized throughout the year, and there are many spontaneous community gatherings and chance encounters.
- The urban form and abundant cultural and social activities contribute to the strong sense of community-building within Serenbe that fosters collective identity.
- Serenbe Playhouse draws spectators from throughout the regions and community, who meet and patronize the local shops and restaurants.
- The mandated front porches and balconies and pedestrian nature of the hamlets contribute to opportunities for community interactions.
- Greater community interactions can contribute to the "upgrade effect" for individual residences and neighborhoods, including creating aesthetic, landscaping, and sustainable technology improvements.
- Seasonal events are celebrated community-wide: Mayday, the 4th of July, Halloween, and Christmas (corresponding with spring, summer, autumn, and winter).

The cultural, social, and historic pattern attribute can facilitate communal connections to nature, the elements, and place. The preponderance of social activities helps provide opportunities for interaction and the development of a shared environmental awareness. The opportunities for enhanced experiences with family and friends can produce positive health and wellness outcomes, including lowering the risk of dementia, improving mental health, improving memory, improving longevity, and reinforcing healthy habits. Social interactions contribute to physical wellbeing, and help provide a more positive outlook on life. The natural, cultural, and social interactions can produce numinous experiences.

The creation of community in Serenbe was one of the original goals of the town founders. To new property owners, Serenbe is a friendly place with many social activities and opportunities to interact with fellow neighbors. As time goes on, the full range of events unfolds throughout the year. Several times a year there is a special dinner at the town founder's home, where potential homebuyers dine

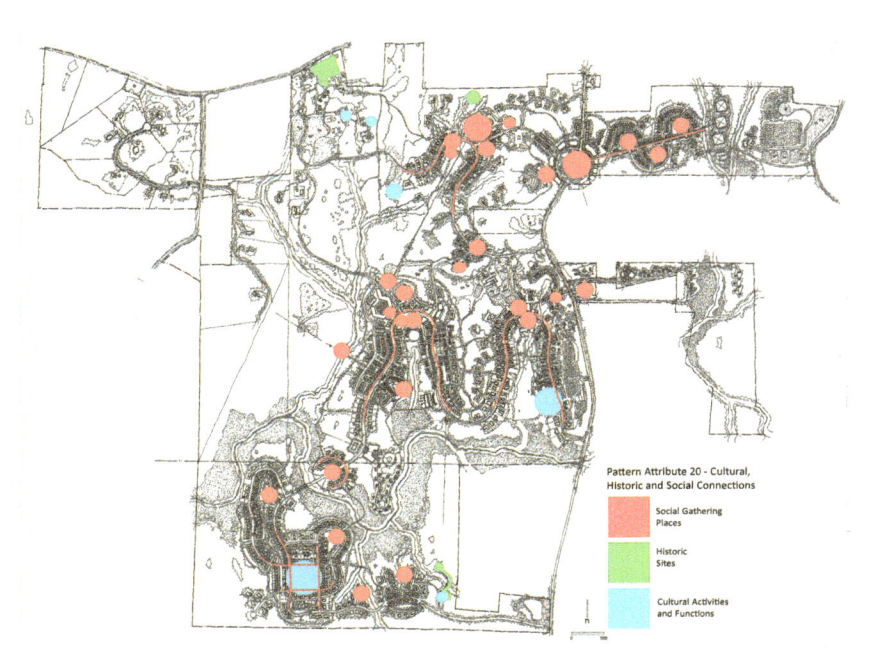

9.45
Pattern attribute 20: cultural, historic, social connections (*Source: Phillip Tabb*)

9.46
Cultural and social activities: (a) Serenbe Playhouse poster, (b) farmers' and artists' market (*Source: Phillip Tabb*)

and mix with established community members. This is a wonderful opportunity for existing and potentially new members to meet and interact. Les Dames d'Escoffier is an afternoon culinary event where many of the favorite chefs from Atlanta's restaurants come with scrumptious gourmet creations. In addition, Georgia's organic farmers share their wine and organic produce. In the spring there is a Holiday Bazaar where one-of-a-kind arts and crafts pieces are displayed for sale. There are special vendors, live music, and marshmallow roasting, and raffle prizes are given out by local Serenbe shop owners. The event is held in the Selborne courtyard spilling into some of the live–work units, and it occurs in the Pavilion. The 4th of July is important at Serenbe, and community residents participate in the annual parade that features fire trucks, horses, and a tractor or two from local farmers. The holiday is celebrated in the evening with fireworks over the Grange lake. During the Coronavirus pandemic, Serenbe residents have observed sheltering-in-place, limited social interactions, and social distancing. Socializing has occurred with safe distancing between sidewalks and porches and as people pass one another along sidewalks.

21. The Arts and Mythopoeia

One of the original goals for Serenbe was to include the arts and crafts into the development process. The first hamlet, Selborne's, theme focused on the arts, which contributed to the initial success of the development. This included the visual, performing, and culinary arts as well as building crafts. Initially the visual arts were expressed with follies, exterior wall graphics, street furniture, lighting standards, and signage. The performing arts supply many opportunities for community engagement. Serenbe Playhouse, Terminus Ballet, and the artist-in-residence program are divisions of the Serenbe Institute for Arts, Culture, and the Environment. They provide multiple opportunities for cultural development and social interaction. The artists involved with these groups are professionals in their fields. Serenbe residents can also participate in its community theater program. As mentioned above, food and the culinary arts are central to Serenbe through its farm-to-table dining and the ability to buy the farm's produce. The Art Farm, a program funded by Serenbe Development, provides a forum for cultural dialogue by creating vibrant creative facilities and artist workspaces, and dinners where residents can meet and converse with artists in all fields. There are two residential cottages with long-term land leases for the artist-in-residence program. The Art Farm is located on 4 acres (1.6 hectares) directly next to the Serenbe community. Figures 9.47 and 9.48 show the map with the many locations of arts activities within Serenbe including the culinary, visual, and performing arts, and the Art Farm; and appropriate photographs.

- Inclusion of the arts contributes to civic pride.
- There are numerous cultural events, activities, and programs organized throughout the year, and there are many spontaneous community gatherings.

9.47
Pattern attribute
21: the arts and
mythopoeia
(*Source: Phillip
Tabb*)

Pattern Attribute 21 - The Arts
and Mythopoela

Performing Arts

Writing and Story Telling

Culinary Arts

Visual Arts

- There can be economic benefit through jobs, tourism, and property sales.
- Serenbe Playhouse and Terminus draw spectators from the regions, who patronize the local shops and restaurants and interact with residents.
- The culinary focus not only provides convenient, sustainable, and healthy access to food, but also encourages community-building and social interactions.
- With an arts orientation, the community provides incubation for local and resident artists.
- The arts can become a conduit for numinous and noetic experiences.

The arts pattern attributes can facilitate communal connections to nature, the elements, and place. The preponderance of activities helps provide opportunities

9.48
The arts and
mythopoeia:
(a) artists in
residence, (b) wall
mural (*Source:
Phillip Tabb*)

for interaction, civic pride, development of a shared environmental awareness, and enhanced experiences with family. From a placemaking viewpoint, the arts can have a positive economic and social impact. Educational impacts include increased attendance and academic achievement. The positive health and wellness outcomes include lowering the risk of dementia, improving mental health, improving memory, improving longevity, and reinforcing healthy habits. Viewing art increases empathy, tolerance, and feelings of love.

The Serenbe Institute is a non-profit, tax-exempt community organization that supports three divisions: an artist-in-residence (AIR) program, Terminus Modern Ballet Theater, and the Serenbe Playhouse. These programs are supported and partially funded by a property transfer fee. All programs also participate in their own fundraising. The artists in the AIR program are selected to reside in the community and produce work to be shared by everyone. Two Auburn University Rural Studio 20-K dwellings were constructed on the Art Farm site for AIR residencies. The purpose of the program is to provide uninterrupted space and time for artists to create their work. The Serenbe Playhouse is a professional theatre company committed to producing bold new works connected to nature and the community.[26] All of the Serenbe Playhouse performances use the outdoor environment as a theater and stage, and often they perform in the woods or meadows. On production, *The Ugly Duckling*, was even performed on a stage constructed a foot below the top of one of the Serenbe ponds. Terminus Modern Ballet Theater is a professional dance company that performs in their Atlanta venue and outdoors in Serenbe. They create new dance works and offer classes for all ages. A podcast called "Serenbe Stories" that started in 2019 is a series of interviews, both with professionals who helped plan and construct Serenbe, and with residents regarding their stories about coming to live and work in the community.

22. Living Color

Natural living color is plentiful in Serenbe. It can be found in the plants, wildflower meadows, trees, insects, birds, the red clay earth, and the skies. In spring there is the emergence of new life and spring flowers. In summer there is an abundance of flowering plants. In autumn there is the deciduous tree change. And in winter there is an abundance of green in the Southern pine trees. Most homes provide views to the outdoor natural colors and seasonal plantings. Yet, the more meaningful experiences happen in the surrounding environment. Like the buildings in Järna Community in Sweden or the island city of Burano, Italy, dwellings are painted a variety of colors, with the especially vivid found in Mado hamlet. In Crossroads, however, all buildings have white exteriors. Refer to Figures 9.49 and 9.50 showing the color-laden map of the community, along with a local wildflower, the community swimming pool building, and a butterfly.

- Nature's color is abundant year-round in Serenbe.
- In spring the colors are green and vibrant, and are found everywhere.
- In autumn the colors are warm and everywhere throughout the forest.

9.49
Pattern attribute 22:
living color (*Source:
Phillip Tabb*)

Pattern Attribute 22 - Living Color

Grassland and Wetland Colors		Natural and Colorful Architecture	
Predominantly Deciduos Trees Color		Water Color	
Predominantly Conifer Tree Colors			

- Omnipresent is Georgia's red clay earth, or ultisol, its color due to the presence of iron oxide.
- The wildflower meadows are a visual composition in living color.
- Dwelling dark values absorb and light values reflect energy.
- While many buildings have fairly neutral colors, many are very colorful; while most are natural wood or brick colors, some are blue, red, yellow, green, cream, white, light and dark gray, and there is even a pink pool building.

9.50
Living color:
(a) local fuchsia
thistle, (b) Serenbe
swim club building,
(c) butterfly (*Source:
Phillip Tabb*)

From a sustainability point of view darker values absorb solar energy and lighter values reflect it. The living color pattern attribute can accentuate visual connections to nature and the elements, engender an appreciation of the sun and solar energy, and contribute to positive health and wellness outcomes, including enhanced perception, mental stimulation, and eating colorful foods. According to Lin Yun, living color refers to the physical and visible elements of life, and it is often accepted as having substance and being an integral part of knowledge.[27] The healing qualities in chromotherapy vary, from increases of energy and stimulation with warmer colors (red, orange, and yellow) to an increase of calmness with cooler colors (green, blue, and purple). The numinous effects of color include stimulating sensory perception resulting in symbolic, associative, synesthetic, and emotional associations; it influences us psychologically and physiologically.

Color in the architecture is generally representative of the natural environment or often white reflecting traditional Southern vernaculars. In some instances brighter and more vibrant primary colors are introduced into the streetscape. This was inspired by the anthroposophical architecture of Erik Asmussen found at Järna, Sweden. The color explosion occurs mainly in Mado hamlet. The Design Review Board reviews more conventional dwellings recommending materials and colors for the roofs, primary exterior walls, front doors, windows, and trim. Serenbe's natural environment also provides a rich pallet of colors year-round. In spring, the many wildflower gardens sparkle with color, and in autumn the numerous deciduous trees turn to gold. Living color derives from the practice of Feng Shui. Color normally refers to the concrete and visible elements of life and in light it is differentiated according to electromagnetic wavelength. Color, too, has a biophilic function and transcendent dimensions that effect health and emotions, and influence behavior. Serenbe is full of the color green, which according to Stephanie Lichtenfeld et al. enhances creative performance.[28]

23. Temporal and Transformative Processes

Time affects Serenbe in several ways, from development construction and growth to the changing composition of the resident population. In Serenbe one can observe that the earlier hamlets are nearly completely built out, and have become more mature and settled and more placebound over time. The newer developments tend to be denser with more residents, the public and private landscapes are less mature, and the new commercial functions have added expanded opportunities for engagement. The aging process is what Stephen Kellert calls the "patina over time."[29] The diurnal and seasonal variations affect the character of the environment. Time also affects the weathering of building materials, which is especially true in northern Georgia, where the climate is quite humid and receives a great deal of rain annually. Figures 9.51 and 9.52 illustrate the development construction sequence by phases over time, with seasonal

Pattern Attribute 23 - Temporal and Transformative Processes

Grange West Leg (2013-2020)
Grange East Leg (2010-2019)
Selborne East Leg (2007-2009)
Selborne West Leg (2005-2007)
Mado West Leg (2018-2020)
Mado East Leg (2020-)
Spela Hamlet (Future)
Education Hamlet (Future)

9.51
Pattern attribute 23: temporal connections (*Source: Phillip Tabb*)

images of the Crossroads neighborhood in spring and autumn, and an aerial view of Mado hamlet under construction.

- Plan development sequence follows a natural morphology with minimal disturbance to the land over time.
- The climate of north Georgia is subject to dynamic seasonal changes (with approximately 3,000 heating degree-days and 1,800 cooling degree-days annually).

9.52
Temporal connections: (a) crossroads in spring, (b) autumn deciduous trees (*Source: Phillip Tabb*), (c) Mado hamlet under construction (*Source: Serenbe Development*)

- With a latitude of 33.75° north, daily sunlight hours vary from approximately 10 hours in winter to 15 hours in summer.
- Buildings are designed for diurnal and seasonal changes, reflecting Southern vernacular architectural forms.
- Geothermal systems are designed for both heating and cooling.
- Sustainable approaches to Serenbe occur over time with increasing standards, technologies, effectiveness, and sustainable lifestyle practices.
- Community-building is a dynamic social process and deepens over time.

The temporal variations pattern attribute reflects the naturally changing connections to nature, the dynamic flux of community numbers and members, and the evolving character of the built environment. The changing seasons create varied outdoor choices and activities. They contribute to positive health and wellness outcomes in terms of spatial variability, availability of local foods, types of physical activities, improved metabolism, and frequency of social interactions can result in increased focus, improved memory, and creative brain activity; to Mikey Rox, changing your lifestyle and breaking repetitious routines with new input can increase creativity and contribute to feelings of happiness.[30] Biophilic experience may contribute to slowing down the effect of senescence or biological aging. The construction sequence shown in Figure 9.51 begins with the color yellow and follows with orange, pink, red, violet, blue, green, and finally brown.

Temporal connections occur on several levels, from the changes caused by the evolving development process itself, to changes of the seasons and from day into night. The developmental process of Serenbe has transformed from completely forested land to incrementally growing developed land. Typically, one leg of an omega hamlet is constructed with a half-dozen dwellings at a time, until it is substantially built out. The building elements within the apex are next in the process and provide mix of uses and community gathering spaces, and finally the second leg of the omega form is constructed. Also, as hamlets are created, sustainable technologies are implemented or encouraged. For example, geothermal heating and cooling technologies were encouraged for Grange, but mandated for Mado, Spela, and the Education hamlets. At Serenbe, the transformation from a naked forest to a community of 850 residents marks a great deal of change. This will intensify when the community reaches its final buildout. The growth at Serenbe does not occur by addition, but rather by incremental multiplication. Serenbe experiences the four seasons distinctly with temperature changes, the changing quality of light, and especially changes in the deciduous forests. In addition, there is an increase in activity in the warmer seasons. Certainly there was a dramatic change from abundant outdoor and social activities to sheltering in place caused by the COVID-19 pandemic.

24. Light in All Forms

Light impacts health and performance, and is expressed in many forms related to luminosity, inspiration, the ethereal, and the numinous. Fluid luminosity refers to the changing qualities of light, whether due to fluctuating conditions, differing sources, color, or architectural design. Light has a coexisting dance with shadow to give expression to form. In Serenbe, light comes in many forms. It filters through the forest creating dynamic patterns and pools of light. Within Serenbe artificial night-light is designed to reduce night light pollution, and the yellow color LED lights are less attractive to insects. Light filters through the trees along walks in the woods and casts shadows on through-screens, trellises, fences, and other porous architectural elements. Natural daylight is everywhere and is accessed by all buildings within the community. Figures 9.53 and 9.54 show the base map with differing colors according to varying orientations, interesting light and shadows formed along the forested paths, and moonlight and domestic lighting.

- Light in Serenbe includes natural light, pools of light, diffused light, filtered light, insect-repelling light, and shade patterns.
- LED, low-wattage, and downward-facing exterior night-lights reduce light pollution.
- Natural daylighting reduces AC and electricity demands and is used extensively in every residence.
- Daylighting provides the full spectrum of natural light.
- Light and shadow accentuate architectural forms and create discernment.
- Pools of light can be observed during walks through the woods.
- Sunshades and sunscreens modulate the changing qualities of natural light.
- Each hamlet has its own unique exterior lighting standard design.
- Light gradients are formed with landscaping, porches, and other buffering spaces.
- Natural light creates ambiance and aesthetic pleasure and can enhance perception.

The light pattern attribute can enhance visual connections to nature and the urban environment. Natural light and efficient LED lights can contribute to sustainability through reduced electricity demands. Natural light can reduce mildew and mold build-up. It is also linked to an increase in work satisfaction. The positive health outcomes include boosting vitamin D, warding off seasonal depression, improving sleep, producing serotonin, and expediting healing. Natural light is easier on the eyes and can increase visual appeal. It regulates the sleep–wake cycles and informs the body's metabolic processes. The numinous outcomes include luminosity and the potential for high-level wellness.

Within the natural areas of Serenbe, light is found in varying forms. Walking through the woods, pools of light can be seen shining down through the trees and producing dramatic patterns of light and dark caused by the shadows. In the denser areas of the woods, the light tends to flicker. At the two waterfalls, light reflects off the moving water. At night the outdoor lighting standards vary from

9.53
Pattern attribute 24:
light in all its forms
(*Source: Phillip
Tabb*)

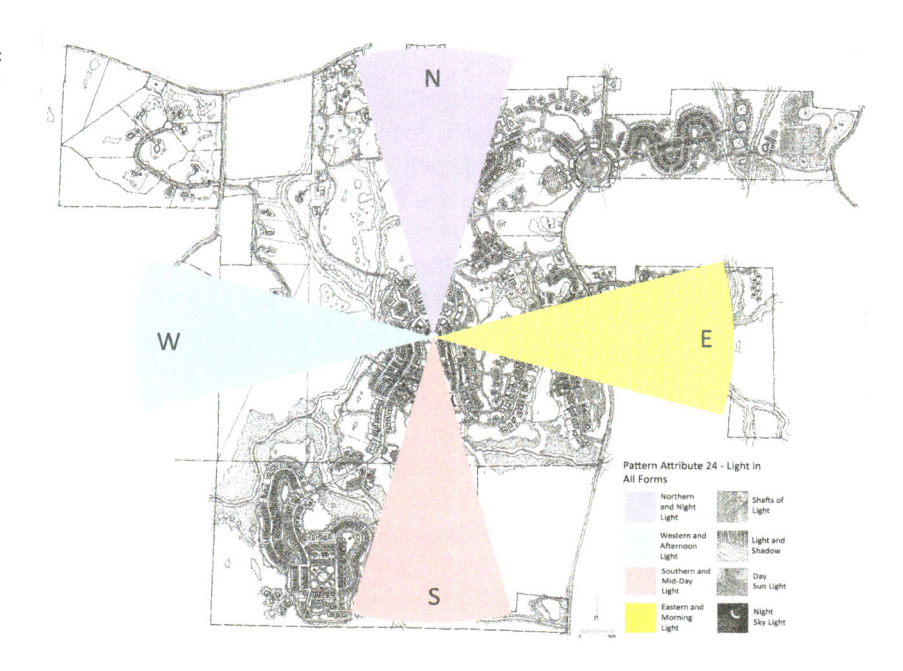

9.54
Light in all its forms:
(a) tree shadows
along footpath,
(b) moonlight in
Crossroads (*Source:
Phillip Tabb*)

hamlet to hamlet. The one in the Mado hamlet is particularly interesting because it is made with perforated metal with geometric patterns. Also in Mado, there are several places where similar lights are placed under dome-like spaces and the patterns they cast on surrounding surfaces are magical. Each hamlet requires porch lights to be pointed downward, with low-wattage bulbs to reduce night light pollution. Walking between hamlets at night is done in complete darkness except for the stars on a clear night.

25. Numinous and Noetic Moments

There are numerous opportunities for numinous experiences in Serenbe. Some occur in special places like the small and large waterfalls, the labyrinth, the wedding green, the Mado celestial observation site, and the cemetery site. Other numinous experiences happen spontaneously anywhere within the community. The interfaith meeting each Sunday in Gainey Hall is a noetic opportunity. Numinous experiences can occur at the numerous performing arts events (music, ballet, and theater); many of these events can be elevating and transformative. And certainly, an incredibly prepared meal with fresh organic ingredients can be very satisfying. These numinous experiences also occur in the sanctity of one's own home. The noetic experiences, meaning an intellectual or mental understanding, contribute to a profound sense of knowing and revelation. They can be the reflective trace of a numinous experience. Intimate connections occur at the two waterfall sites within the woodlands of Serenbe. Figures 9.55 and 9.56 show on the masterplan special sites where numinous experiences have been reported either in nature or within the built portions of the community, and an exterior night light in Mado casting its geometric pattern on adjacent walls and a poetic message inserted in a concrete pad on the ground.

- There are celestial observation sites found in Serenbe where clearings open to the night sky.
- There are ceremonial sites that contribute to numinous experiences.
- The Sunday morning interfaith gathering is a positive connection to community and a source of numinous experiences.
- Culinary, visual, and performing arts activities are in constant transformation and numinous experiences.
- Profound experiences can occur with chance encounters with wildlife in the woods as deer often pass by residents' homes.
- Intimate sites within the woodlands are mysterious and fascinating.
- There is something compelling about an overall ethereal feeling to Serenbe that most residents and visitors seem to experience when entering the community.

The numinous and noetic pattern attributes can form deeper connections to nature, the elements, and place. There exists the opportunity for an enlightened sense of sustainability and climate neutrality. The positive health outcomes include the potential for high-level wellness, with temporary stress reduction, and a feeling euphoria. There are numerous thin-place experience opportunities.[31] This can lead to a profound respect for and reverence toward nature and the community, and a greater understanding of the connection between our styles of living and our relationships with nature.

The numinous experiences at Serenbe are identified by various conditions, usually considered sanctified, transcendent, and extraordinary. These

9.55
Pattern attribute
25: numinous and
noetic experiences
(*Source: Phillip
Tabb*)

Pattern Attribute 25 - The Numinous
and Noetic

Potential Numinous
Moments Found in
Nature

Potential Numinous
Moments Found in
Social Engagements

9.56
Numinous and
noetic experiences:
(a) exterior light
from Mado lantern,
(b) message
embedded in a
concrete pad next
to small waterfalls
(*Source: Phillip
Tabb*)

numinous encounters are venerated in various places and at differing times, and it is not necessarily important that they be overtly stated or obviously expressed. Rather, the numinous design moments are integrated into the fabric of the secular place, contributing to a process of revelation. They are to be discovered and experienced through the ensouling qualities of the place. They most often occur in nature that surrounds Serenbe and sometimes within the built portions through social interactions and cultural events. Understanding of these encounters occurs with a self-reflective consciousness and noetic

experience. There is, in Edward Casey's terms, "a refractory survival of the hidden presence of the sacred in certain spatial oppositions" – ordinary versus special places or urban versus rural.[32] At night in Mado hamlet, the streetlights are thin conical perforated shapes that create geometric patterns reflecting off nearby objects and surfaces. The visual effect is mesmerizing. These moments create a core effect, a sense of natural knowing and connections to source. Unfortunately, the Coronavirus has curtailed many of the opportunities for social numinous experiences.

9.57
Serenbe biophilic experiences:
(a) Serenbe Farms,
(b) farm-to-table,
(c) children at fountain,
(d) Serenbe Playhouse (*Source: Phillip Tabb*)

The biophilic urbanism orientation of communities, like Serenbe, typically seeks to preserve land for future generations and provides diverse kinds of spatial experiences, both urban and rural, that reflect evolving contemporary needs and opportunities for varying natural experiences. The geometry of Serenbe provides an explicit structure, spatial order, and context for a nature–urban lifestyle. Socially, community is expressed by resident gatherings; it can also be experienced in immaterial ways as a felt sense of belonging and a true sense of community. In this regard, residents are sharing a similar place-centered style of living and are part of the larger collective of residents. The social environment also creates the place through which a living Serenbe thrives in a biotic community of inclusiveness, interdependence, and participatory interaction. And positive outcomes can be found throughout Serenbe.

According to cofounder Marie Nygren, the Serenbe Playhouse 2015 production hidden deep in the woods of *The Secret Garden* was a metaphor for the spirit of Serenbe – a place contained in magic and healing powers.[33] A positive unintended consequence of the biophilic principles and patterns operating in Serenbe during the pandemic has been the relative ease of sheltering place. This has been due to its isolation away from dense urban centers, direct access to nature, sidewalks on both sides of the streets, and the function of front porches, which have built-in physical spacing. A large percentage of residents work in the community or have been easily able to telework at home.

NOTES

1. The name was created by co-founder Marie Nygren; the name Serenbe derives from a portmanteau or the blend of two root terms: *serene* or *serenity*, and *be* or *being*.
2. Atlanta metropolitan area, https://en.wikipedia.org/wiki/Atlanta_metropolitan_area (accessed February 12, 2020).

3. Steven Corver, Director of Environment and Community Development, Fulton County, Georgia email quote, June 1, 2020.

4. Phillip James Tabb, *Serene Urbanism: A Biophilic Theory and Practice of Sustainable Placemaking* (London, UK: Routledge, 2017).

5. Mado was the name proposed by Serenbe resident, Karen Reed.

6. R. Alfred Vick, from a personal email, (accessed March 17, 2020).

7. Phillip James Tabb, *Serene Urbanism: A Biophilic Theory and Practice of Sustainable Placemaking* (London, UK: Routledge, 2017). pp 144–147.

8. Serenbe's first thought leaders meeting occurred in September of 2000, led by the Rocky Mountain Institute and documented by Georgia Tech, and they generated the goals in forming an environmentally oriented community.

9. Sam Murray, *123 Birds of Serenbe*, (Chattahoochee Hills, GA: Self-published, 2020).

10. Dana Foundation, *Olfaction: Smell of Change in the Air* https://www.dana.org/article/olfaction-smell-of-change-in-the-air/ (accessed January 29, 2020).

11. Haleh Moghaddasi and Phillip James Tabb, material discussed together while I was Chair of her PhD committee at Texas A&M University, 2018–2019, for research in the area of net-zero developments.

12. EarthCraft was established in 1999 by the Greater Atlanta Home Builders Association and Southface, and EarthCraft is a green building certification program that serves the Southeastern United States.

13. Earthing: Health Implications of Reconnecting the Human Body to the Earth's Surface Electrons https://www.ncbi.nlm.nih.gov/pmc/articles/PMC3265077/ (accessed January 29, 2020).

14. Clinton Ober, Dr. Stephen Sinatra, Martin Zucker, and Gaetan Chevalier, *Earthing: The Most Important Health Discovery Ever!* (Laguna Beach, CA: Basic Health Publications, Inc., 2014).

15. Facing the Facts about Atlanta's Air Quality https://www.southernenvironment.org/cases-and-projects/fact-sheets/facing-the-facts-about-atlantas-air-quality (accessed January 30, 2020).

16. Christopher Alexander, Sara Ishikacca, and Murry Silverstein, *A Pattern Language: Towns, Buildings, Construction* (New York, NY: Oxford University Press, 1977). p 177.

17. The Conversation, *Ponds can absorb more carbon than woodland – here's how they can fight climate change in your garden*, https://theconversation.com/ponds-can-absorb-more-carbon-than-woodland-heres-how-they-can-fight-climate-change-in-your-garden-110652 (accessed March 17, 2020).

18. Christian Norberg-Schulz, *Genius Loci: Towards a Phenomenology of Architecture* (New York, NY: Rizzoli, 1980).

19. Stephen R. Kellert, Judith H. Heerwagen, and Martin Mador, *Biophilic Design: The Theory, Science, and Practice of Bringing Building to Life* (New York, NY: John Wiley & Sons, Inc., 2008). p 13.

20. Gordon H. Orians and Judith H. Heerwagen, "Evolved Responses to Landscapes," in Jerome H. Barlow, Leda Cosmides, and John Tooby (eds.) *The Adapted Mind: Evolutionary Psychology and the Generation of Culture* (New York, NY: Oxford University Press, 1992). p 560.

21. Phillip James Tabb, *Serene Urbanism: A Biophilic Theory and Practice of Sustainable Placemaking* (London, UK: Routledge, 2017). pp 141–42.

22. Yi-Fu Tuan, *Space and Place: The Perspective of Experience* (Minnesota, MN: the University of Minnesota Press, 1977).

23. *I-Ching: The Chinese Book of Changes*, Welhelm Translation, (Princeton, NJ: Princeton University Press, 3rd Edition, 1967). pp 193–197.

24. Terrapin Bright Green, *14 Patterns of Biophilic Design: Improving Health and Wellbeing in the Environment* https://www.terrapinbrightgreen.com/reports/14-patterns/ (accessed January 2020).

25. Gary Coates, *Erik Asmussen, architect* (Stockholm: Byggforlaget, 1997).

26. Serenbe Playhouse http://www.serenbeplayhouse.com/serenbe-playhouse-about/missionvision (accessed January 18, 2020).

27. Sarah Rossbach and Lin Yun, *Living Color* (New York, NY: Kodansha America, Inc., 1994). pp 9–11.

28. Stephanie Lichtenfeld, Andrew Elliot, and Markus Maier, "Fertile Green: Green Facilitates Creative Performance" https://journals.sagepub.com/doi/abs/10.1177/0146167212436611 (accessed January 29, 2020).

29. Stephen R. Kellert, Judith H. Heerwagen, and Martin Mador, *Biophilic Design: The Theory, Science, and Practice of Bringing Building to Life* (New York, NY: John Wiley & Sons, Inc., 2008).

30. Mikey Rox, *The Benefits of Changing Your Routine*, https://www.wisebread.com/the-benefits-of-changing-your-routine (accessed June 15, 2020).

31. Phillip James Tabb, *Elemental Architecture: Temperaments of Sustainability* (London, UK: Routledge, 2019). pp 116–122.

32. Edward Casey, *The Fate of Place: A Philosophical History*, (Berkeley, CA: The University of California Press, 1998).

33. The play was an adaptation of Frances Hodgson Burnett's *The Secret Garden* written in 1911.

10 CONCLUSIONS

The six precedents showed a range of biophilic urban characteristics, from the tightly knit medieval hamlet of Castello di Gargonza, the innovative biome and progressive contemporary work environments found at the Googleplex and new Google Headquarters, and the 25 clustered hamlets of Helsinge Haveby to the efficient sustainable community infrastructure and super-block designs that simultaneously house residents and protect greenspace at Kronsberg District, the incredible automobile-free zone in the Pontevedra city center that promotes a vibrant and safe work–family relationship, and the magical garden loop connector landscapes in Singapore's park network. Thereafter, the case study of Serenbe demonstrated the full complement of biophilic pattern attributes integrated throughout the community. Taken together, these preceding examples combine to present a wide menu of actionable biophilic strategies at varying urban scales.

SUMMARY OF PATTERN ATTRIBUTES AND POSITIVE OUTCOMES

The following tables illustrate the biophilic functions of the pattern attributes of the six precedents and the Serenbe case study, and identify the positive outcomes for climate neutrality, sustainability, placemaking, health and wellness, and the numinous. They were created through a process of extrapolations in the Internet literature search space, through professional books on related topics, through analysis and coalescence of the precedent studies, and through a process of actualistic immersion and direct experience while visiting Gargonza, Google and Kronsberg and living in Serenbe. The tables are intended to show the relationships between the major pattern attributes and the positive outcomes for each of the precedents and case study. For climate neutrality, the outcomes are divided into: (a) carbon sequestering, (b) greenhouse gas reduction, and (c) afforestation/reforestation.[1] The sustainability outcomes are (a) energy demand reductions, (b) on-site resource use, and (c) pedestrianization.[2] The placemaking outcomes are (a) social interaction, (b) place identity, and (c) community building.[3] The health and wellness outcomes are (a) stress and anxiety reduction, (b) cognitive activity, and (c) emotional effects.[4] The numinous outcomes are (a) heightened awareness and alertness, (b) insights and understanding, and (c) the experience of awe.[5]

■ CONCLUSIONS

The first six tables for the precedents show ten pattern attributes that appear to be the most important attribute for each precedent. They are related to each of the sets of positive outcomes. The outcomes are rated as "highly present" (X), or "not applicable" (blank). These rates are derived from published scientific research papers, literature searches, and observations of the pattern analysis for each of the precedents. The author visited Gargonza, the Googleplex, and Kronsberg, and lives in Serenbe. The case study of the Serenbe Community shows all 25 pattern attributes compared to each of the five outcome sets. Each cell is given a value of 0–4, with 0 as "not applicable" and 4 as "highly present." This analysis is intended to give a rough indication and account regarding the outcome impacts of each pattern attribute for each of these projects. For the precedent tables, numbers occurring along the far right column represent the frequency of positive outcomes down the ten selected pattern attributes. The numbers that occur at the bottom represent the frequency of pattern attributes across the 15 positive outcomes. The following summaries of key biophilic pattern attributes and outcomes of the six precedents and case study are not intended to be an exhaustive analysis, but rather an indication and guide that highlights the most prominent patterns and their probable positive outcomes appearing within each of the projects.

Table 10.1 indicates in Castello di Gargonza a strong relationship between the integrated and surrounding nature, largely due to the forested site within which it is sited, views and vistas to the east to the Val di Chiana below the site, the grounding and bounding due to the massive stone tapered foundation and retaining walls, and natural materiality of the buildings themselves. Due to its function as a destination resort, there is the potential for social interactions, especially through corporate retreats, and the restaurant La Torre di Gargonza. The parish church of St Tiburzio and Susanna draws from the surrounding community and serves destination weddings as well. While Castello di Gargonza no longer functions as a residential community, it does have a strong sense of place, and the tower serves as a place marker. As a result, the outcome categories of placemaking, health and wellness, and the numinous are most present. The pattern attributes that are most present include plant kingdom and earth and grounding, and the highest scores for outcomes are pedestrianization, social interaction, place identity, stress reduction, emotional effects, and the experience of awe.

Table 10.2 identifies the combination of key pattern attributes and positive outcomes at the Googleplex and speculates about the outcomes at Google's Charleston Street Headquarters. Interactions with and views to nature were important in the Googleplex and the new design for Charleston East. Replanting trees and the provision of natural outdoor spaces were also important. The use of renewable energy for heating, cooling, and electricity production is highly visible at the Googleplex and will be a major feature of the new biome. Employee interactions, group spaces, outdoor teleworking spaces were integral to the design. The surrounding community is encouraged to interact with the place. The major outcome categories include sustainability, placemaking, and health and wellness. The pattern attributes that are most present include plant kingdom and spatial order and connectivity, and the highest scores for outcomes are social interaction, place identity, community building, stress reduction, emotional effects, and the experience of awe.

Table 10.1

PATTERN ATTRIBUTES	CLIMATE NEUTRAL OUTCOMES			SUSTAINABILITY OUTCOMES			PLACEMAKING OUTCOMES			HEALTH/WELLNESS OUTCOMES			NUMINOUS OUTCOMES			
	A	B	C	A	B	C	A	B	C	A	B	C	A	B	C	
1 Plant Kingdom	X	X	X	X	X	X	X	X	X	X	X	X	X	X	X	15
2 Views and Vistas			X			X	X	X	X	X	X	X	X	X	X	11
3 Earth and Grounding	X	X	X	X	X	X	X	X	X	X	X	X	X	X	X	15
4 Orientation and Direction				X	X	X	X	X	X	X	X	X	X	X	X	12
5 Prospect and Refuge						X	X	X	X	X	X	X	X	X	X	10
6 Spatial Order and Connectivity		X		X	X	X	X	X	X	X		X			X	10
7 Centering and Nucleation					X	X	X	X	X	X	X	X	X	X	X	11
8 Bounding and Containment	X	X	X		X	X	X	X	X	X		X		X	X	12
9 Natural Materiality	X	X			X	X	X	X		X	X	X	X	X	X	12
10 Cultural, Social, Historic			X		X	X	X	X	X	X	X	X	X	X	X	12
	4	5	5	4	8	10	10	10	9	10	8	10	8	9	10	

☒ Presence of Outcome
☐ Not Applicable

A Carbon sequestering	A Demand reductions	A Social interaction	A Stress reduction	A Heightened awareness
B CO$_2$ reduction	B On-site resources	B Place identity	B Cognitive activity	B Insights/understanding
C Reforestation	C Pedestrianization	C Community building	C Emotional effects	C Experience of awe

Castello di Gargonza – Key Biophilic Pattern Attributes and Outcomes (*Source: Phillip Tabb*)

PATTERN ATTRIBUTES	CLIMATE NEUTRAL OUTCOMES			SUSTAINABILITY OUTCOMES			PLACEMAKING OUTCOMES			HEALTH/WELLNESS OUTCOMES			NUMINOUS OUTCOMES			
	A	B	C	A	B	C	A	B	C	A	B	C	A	B	C	
1 Plant Kingdom	X	X	X	X	X	X	X	X	X	X	X	X	X	X	X	15
2 Views and Vistas		X	X		X		X	X	X	X		X	X	X	X	11
3 Fire and Energy	X	X		X	X	X	X	X	X	X	X	X			X	12
4 Orientation and Direction				X	X		X	X	X	X	X	X			X	9
5 Inside-Outside				X	X	X	X	X	X	X	X	X	X	X	X	12
6 Spatial Order and Connectivity	X		X	X	X	X	X	X	X	X	X	X	X	X	X	15
7 Form Language			X	X	X	X	X	X	X	X	X	X	X	X	X	13
8 Cultural, Social, Historic	X	X	X	X	X		X	X	X	X	X	X	X	X	X	14
9 Light in all Forms				X	X	X	X	X	X	X	X	X	X	X	X	12
10 Temporal Transformations	X	X	X			X	X	X	X	X	X	X			X	11
	5	6	6	8	9	7	10	10	10	10	9	10	7	7	10	
	A Carbon sequestering	B CO$_2$ reduction	C Reforestation	A Demand reductions	B On-site resources	C Pedestrianization	A Social interaction	B Place identity	C Community building	A Stress reduction	B Cognitive activity	C Emotional effects	A Heightened awareness	B Insights/understanding	C Experience of awe	

⊠ Presence of Outcome
☐ Not Applicable

Table 10.2

Google Headquarters – Key Biophilic Pattern Attributes and Outcomes (*Source: Phillip Tabb*)

Table 10.3 speculates the presence of the pattern attributes and positive outcomes for Helsinge Haveby. The design and development objectives seem to suggest strong relationships among nature, animals, and the earth, due to its integrated agriculture and animal husbandry. They also include energy efficiency and use of renewable sources. While residents are not necessarily required to work in the agricultural production within the village, they do live in close proximity to it and can observe it. The spatial structure of informal roads and pathways, and of clustered neighborhood loops, contributes to social interactions, community building, sense of place, and surveillance. The food hub is a catalyst for social and cultural interactions. The outcome categories of sustainability, placemaking, health and wellness, and the numinous are most present. The pattern attributes that are most present include plant kingdom and spatial order, and the highest scores for outcomes are on-site resources, place identity, and emotional effects.

Table 10.4 for the Kronsberg District integrates nature with a compact urban design. Its super-blocks, swales, parks, and agriculture stand out as biophilic measures. The plan indicates a strong commitment to power, transportation, and to building renewable energy systems. Reduction of automobile use and the impact of parking is also addressed. The views and vistas, indoor–outdoor spaces, and prospect and refuge are also present. The spatial structure supports density, mix of uses, pedestrianization, and the super-blocks. The major outcome categories include sustainability, placemaking, health and wellness, and the numinous. The pattern attributers that are most present include plant kingdom, and spatial order, and the highest scores for outcomes are on-site resources, place identity, community building, stress reduction, and insights/understanding.

Table 10.5 indicates Pontevedra city center's patterns of connections to nature, banning automobiles, pedestrianization, mix of uses, connections to water, public space design, and social and cultural interactions. The vast matrix of naturally occurring pedestrian streets connect parks, plazas, culturally significant buildings and social functions. The pattern attributes that are most present include plant kingdom and water and waste, and the highest scores for outcomes are pedestrianization, social interaction, place identity, community building, stress reduction, and emotional effects.

Table 10.6 indicates the Singapore Park Connector Neighborhood connections to nature, biodiversity, nature preservation, access to dense urban areas, views and vistas, connections to the elements, and the promotion of outdoor physical activities. The outcomes of climate neutrality, placemaking, health and wellness, and the numinous are most present. The loops with nature contribute to a strong sense of place – the city within a garden. It is clear with this precedent that the extensive natural network of parks allows connections to nature citywide. The pattern attributes that are most present include plant kingdom, water and waste, centering and nucleation, spatial order and connectivity, and pedestrianization, and the highest scores for outcomes are pedestrianization, place identity, community building, stress reduction, emotional effects, and the experience of awe.

Table 10.7 indicates the 25 biophilic patterns and outcomes for the Serenbe Community, with connections to nature, agriculture and farm animals, 70 percent

PATTERN ATTRIBUTES	CLIMATE NEUTRAL OUTCOMES			SUSTAINABILITY OUTCOMES			PLACEMAKING OUTCOMES			HEALTH/WELLNESS OUTCOMES			NUMINOUS OUTCOMES			
	A	B	C	A	B	C	A	B	C	A	B	C	A	B	C	
1 Plant Kingdom	X	X	X	X	X	X	X	X	X	X	X	X	X	X	X	15
2 Animal Kingdom					X	X	X	X	X	X	X	X	X	X	X	11
3 Views and Vistas			X	X	X	X	X	X	X	X	X	X	X	X	X	13
4 Fire and Energy	X	X	X	X	X			X	X	X	X	X	X	X	X	13
5 Inside-Outside					X	X	X	X	X	X	X	X	X	X	X	11
6 Spatial Order and Connectivity	X	X	X	X	X	X	X	X	X	X	X	X	X	X	X	15
7 Bounding and Containment			X	X	X	X	X	X	X	X	X	X	X	X	X	13
8 Natural Materiality		X			X		X	X	X	X	X	X	X	X	X	11
9 Cultural, Social, Historic			X		X	X	X	X	X	X	X	X	X	X	X	12
10 Temporal Transformations	X	X	X	X	X		X	X				X				8
	4	5	7	6	10	7	9	10	9	9	9	10	9	9	9	

Legend:

☒ Presence of Outcome
☐ Not Applicable

CLIMATE NEUTRAL OUTCOMES
A Carbon sequestering
B CO$_2$ reduction
C Reforestation

SUSTAINABILITY OUTCOMES
A Demand reductions
B On-site resources
C Pedestrianization

PLACEMAKING OUTCOMES
A Social interaction
B Place identity
C Community building

HEALTH/WELLNESS OUTCOMES
A Stress reduction
B Cognitive activity
C Emotional effects

NUMINOUS OUTCOMES
A Heightened awareness
B Insights/understanding
C Experience of awe

Table 10.3
Helsinge Haveby – Key Biophilic Pattern Attributes and Outcomes (*Source: Phillip Tabb*)

Table 10.4
Kronsberg District – Key Biophilic Pattern Attributes and Outcomes (*Source: Phillip Tabb*)

PATTERN ATTRIBUTES	CLIMATE NEUTRAL OUTCOMES			SUSTAINABILITY OUTCOMES			PLACEMAKING OUTCOMES			HEALTH/WELLNESS OUTCOMES			NUMINOUS OUTCOMES		
	A	B	C	A	B	C	A	B	C	A	B	C	A	B	C
	4	5	5	7	10	8	8	10	10	6	9	9	6	10	6
1 Plant Kingdom	X	X	X	X	X	X	X	X	X	X	X	X	X	X	X	15
2 Views and Vistas				X	X	X	X	X	X	X	X	X	X	X	X	11
3 Fire and Energy	X	X	X	X	X	X	X	X		X	X	X	X	X	X	13
4 Water and Waste	X			X	X	X	X	X	X	X	X	X	X	X	X	13
5 Orientation and Direction	X			X	X	X	X	X		X		X		X		8
6 Inside-Outside		X	X	X	X		X	X	X	X	X	X	X	X	X	13
7 Prospect and Refuge				X			X	X	X	X	X	X	X	X	X	10
8 Spatial Order and Connectivity	X	X	X	X	X	X	X	X	X	X	X	X	X	X	X	15
9 Centering and Nucleation		X		X	X	X	X	X	X	X	X	X	X	X	X	13
10 Cultural, Social, Historic				X	X		X	X	X	X	X	X	X	X	X	11

Presence of Outcome [X]
Not Applicable [ ]

A Carbon sequestering
B CO_2 reduction
C Reforestation

A Demand reductions
B On-site resources
C Pedestrianization

A Social interaction
B Place identity
C Community building

A Stress reduction
B Cognitive activity
C Emotional effects

A Heightened awareness
B Insights/understanding
C Experience of awe

PATTERN ATTRIBUTES	CLIMATE NEUTRAL OUTCOMES			SUSTAINABILITY OUTCOMES			PLACEMAKING OUTCOMES			HEALTH/WELLNESS OUTCOMES			NUMINOUS OUTCOMES			
	A	B	C	A	B	C	A	B	C	A	B	C	A	B	C	
1 Plant Kingdom	X	X	X	X	X	X	X	X	X	X	X	X	X	X	X	15
2 Views and Vistas					X	X	X	X	X	X	X	X	X	X	X	11
3 Water and Waste	X	X	X	X	X	X	X	X	X	X	X	X	X	X	X	15
4 Orientation and Direction	X	X	X	X	X	X	X	X	X	X	X	X		X		13
5 Inside-Outside				X	X	X	X	X	X	X	X	X	X		X	11
6 Prospect and Refuge				X	X	X	X	X	X	X	X	X	X	X		11
7 Spatial Order and Connectivity	X	X	X		X	X	X	X	X	X	X	X	X	X	X	14
8 Centering and Nucleation	X	X		X		X	X	X	X	X	X	X	X	X	X	13
9 Bounding and Containment	X	X		X	X	X	X	X	X	X		X	X	X	X	13
10 Cultural, Social, Historic						X	X	X	X	X	X	X	X	X	X	10
	6	6	4	7	8	10	10	10	10	10	9	10	9	9	8	

☒ Presence of Outcome
☐ Not Applicable

CLIMATE NEUTRAL: A Carbon sequestering B CO_2 reduction C Reforestation

SUSTAINABILITY: A Demand reductions B On-site resources C Pedestrianization

PLACEMAKING: A Social interaction B Place identity C Community building

HEALTH/WELLNESS: A Stress reduction B Cognitive activity C Emotional effects

NUMINOUS: A Heightened awareness B Insights/understanding C Experience of awe

Table 10.5
Pontevedra city center – Key Biophilic Pattern Attributes and Outcomes (*Source: Phillip Tabb*)

PATTERN ATTRIBUTES	CLIMATE NEUTRAL OUTCOMES			SUSTAINABILITY OUTCOMES			PLACEMAKING OUTCOMES			HEALTH/WELLNESS OUTCOMES			NUMINOUS OUTCOMES			
	A	B	C	A	B	C	A	B	C	A	B	C	A	B	C	
1 Plant Kingdom	X	X	X	X	X	X	X	X	X	X	X	X	X	X	X	15
2 Animal Kingdom					X	X	X	X	X	X	X	X	X	X	X	11
3 Views and Vistas			X	X	X	X	X	X	X	X	X	X	X	X	X	13
4 Water and Waste	X	X	X	X	X	X	X	X	X	X	X	X	X	X	X	15
5 Inside–Outside				X		X		X	X	X	X	X			X	8
6 Toppography and Geography	X	X	X		X	X	X	X	X	X	X	X	X	X	X	14
7 Spatial Order and Connectivity	X	X	X		X	X	X	X	X	X	X	X	X	X	X	14
8 Centering and Nucleation	X	X	X	X	X	X	X	X	X	X	X	X	X	X	X	15
9 Bounding and Containment	X	X		X	X	X	X	X	X	X	X	X	X	X	X	14
10 Cultural, Social, Historic				X	X	X	X	X	X	X		X	X	X	X	11
	6	6	6	7	9	10	9	10	10	10	9	10	9	9	10	

⊠ Presence of Outcome
☐ Not Applicable

CLIMATE NEUTRAL	SUSTAINABILITY	PLACEMAKING	HEALTH/WELLNESS	NUMINOUS
A Carbon sequestering	A Demand reductions	A Social interaction	A Stress reduction	A Heightened awareness
B CO$_2$ reduction	B On-site resources	B Place identity	B Cognitive activity	B Insights/understanding
C Reforestation	C Pedestrianization	C Community building	C Emotional effects	C Experience of awe

Table 10.6
Singapore Park Connector Network – Key Biophilic Pattern Attributes and Outcomes (*Source: Phillip Tabb*)

PATTERN ATTRIBUTES	CLIMATE NEUTRAL OUTCOMES			SUSTAINABILITY OUTCOMES			PLACEMAKING OUTCOMES			HEALTH/WELLNESS OUTCOMES			NUMINOUS OUTCOMES			
	A	B	C	A	B	C	A	B	C	A	B	C	A	B	C	
1 Plant Kingdom	4	4	3	3	3	3	4	4	4	4	3	4	4	4	4	55
2 Animal Kingdom	1	1	0	0	2	4	4	3	3	4	3	4	3	3	4	39
3 Views and Vistas	0	0	3	0	0	4	3	4	3	4	3	4	4	4	4	40
4 Sensory Connections	0	0	4	3	4	4	3	4	3	4	3	4	4	4	4	48
5 Ecological & Biological	4	4	3	3	3	0	2	3	2	2	2	2	3	2	3	38
6 Fire and energy	2	4	0	4	3	3	3	2	2	3	2	3	2	2	3	38
7 Earth and Grounding	4	3	3	4	3	3	4	4	3	4	3	4	3	3	4	52
8 Air and Natural Ventilation	3	4	0	3	3	0	3	2	3	4	2	3	3	2	4	39
9 Water and Waste	4	4	3	3	1	3	3	3	3	4	3	4	4	3	4	49
10 Ether and Celestial Moments	0	0	0	0	4	3	3	3	3	4	3	4	4	3	4	38
11 Orientation and Direction	0	0	2	2	3	3	3	3	2	2	2	3	3	3	3	34
12 Prospect and Refuge	0	0	0	0	3	3	4	3	4	4	3	4	4	4	3	39
13 Inside-Outside Relationships	0	0	0	3	3	4	4	3	4	4	3	4	3	3	3	41
14 Topography and Geography	0	0	3	1	3	2	2	4	2	3	3	3	4	3	3	36
15 Spatial Order and Connectivity	3	4	3	3	3	4	4	4	4	3	3	4	3	3	3	51
16 Centering and Nucleation	0	3	4	3	3	4	4	4	4	4	3	4	3	3	3	49
17 Bounding and Containment	3	3	3	0	0	3	4	4	4	3	2	3	3	3	3	41

Table 10.7

Serenbe Community – Biophilic Pattern Attributes and Outcomes (*Source: Phillip Tabb*)

(*Continued*)

PATTERN ATTRIBUTES	CLIMATE NEUTRAL OUTCOMES			SUSTAINABILITY OUTCOMES			PLACEMAKING OUTCOMES			HEALTH/WELLNESS OUTCOMES			NUMINOUS OUTCOMES			
	A	B	C	A	B	C	A	B	C	A	B	C	A	B	C	
18 Natural Materiality	4	3	0	3	3	0	3	4	3	4	3	4	3	3	3	43
19 Form Language and Analogues	2	4	2	3	3	3	3	4	4	3	3	3	3	3	3	46
20 Cultural, Social, Historic	0	0	4	0	3	3	4	3	4	3	3	4	3	3	4	41
21 Arts and Mythopoeia	0	0	0	0	3	3	4	3	4	4	3	4	3	3	4	38
22 Living Color	0	0	0	0	4	3	3	4	3	3	3	4	3	3	4	37
23 Temporal and Transformation	3	0	0	3	3	0	3	3	3	2	2	2	3	2	3	32
24 Light in All Forms	0	0	0	3	3	3	3	3	3	3	3	4	4	3	4	39
25 The Numinous	0	0	4	0	4	0	4	4	4	4	4	4	4	4	4	44
	37	41	44	47	70	65	84	85	81	86	70	90	81	74	88	

4 - Highly present
3 - Very present
2 - Moderately present
1 - Rarely present
0 - Not applicable

A Carbon sequestering
B CO_2 reduction
C Reforestation

A Demand reductions
B On-site resources
C Pedestrianization

A Social interaction
B Place identity
C Community building

A Stress reduction
B Cognitive activity
C Emotional effects

A Heightened awareness
B Insights/understanding
C Experience of awe

Table 10.7
Serenbe Community – Biophilic Pattern Attributes and Outcomes (*Source: Phillip Tabb*) (*Continued*)

preserved land, views and vistas, connections to the elements, abundant water features, indoor–outdoor connections, constellating urbanism and omega spatial order, Thorburn transect, themed hamlets, social programs and activities, and opportunities for the numinous. The outcomes of placemaking, health and wellness, and the numinous are most present. The Likert scale numbers for Serenbe indicate that the most effective patterns are connections to the plant kingdom, sensory connections, access to water and waste ameliorations, effectiveness of the spatial order, and encouragement of social interaction. The pattern attributes that are most present include plant kingdom, sensory connections, earth and grounding, water and waste, inside-outside relationships, spatial order and connectivity, centering and nucleation, natural materiality, cultural, social, historic, and the numinous; and the highest scores for outcomes are social interaction, place identity, community building, community building, stress reduction, emotional effects, heightened awareness, and the experience of awe. The outcome category of climate neutrality did not score high with any of the studies probably due to the fact that most of the pattern attributes are more detailed and not directly related to the larger considerations of carbon sequestering and reforestation.

CONCLUSIONS ABOUT BIOPHILIC URBANISM

It is ironic that our ancestors, during the Pleistocene era within the savanna plains of the Rift Valley, preferred horizontal territories with undulating topography and sparsely placed trees, and occasional water features where life congregated. Fast-forward to today and migration is generally to dense cities full of high-rise towers, such as Manila, Hong Kong, Sao Paulo, Singapore, Seoul, Tokyo, and New York City. Will modern humans elect to descend from their urban "trees," returning to the ground to find alternative ways of living? What are the characteristics of the contemporary savanna of today? It is certainly not the monoculture of suburban development found worldwide, because this lack biodiversity and essential mix of uses. Fundamental to Wilson's Biophilic Hypothesis is the idea that the crucial first step to survival for all organisms is habitat selection.[6] This brings up a further question: what are the characteristics of the contemporary savanna of today that are crucial for our survival? This includes our need to respond to the spread of infectious diseases, like COVID-19.

Because migration patterns show more and more people are moving to urban areas, it will be a challenge to implement effective biophilic patterns to existing urban forms. The effects of climate change in general, but more specifically in coastal cities, should lead top government officials to gently look toward rural and suburban areas for opportunities to mitigate risks associated with climate change and overcrowded cities. The development of more sustainable models is essential. Furthermore, these territories could be reinvigorated with a greater connection to nature, healthier food production and delivery systems, renewable energy sources, and accessible cultural amenities. Another challenge is to transcend piecemeal, remedial architectural applications to the full range of biophilic urban patterns, and generate ones that are more comprehensive, inclusive, and regenerative at all scales.

Many years ago, Wayne Nichols, who developed a number of passive solar projects in Santa Fe, New Mexico in the 1970s, said that if you think a passive solar home costs less than a conventional home, then you have never built one.[7] More recently, Julia Africa et al. suggested that the biophilic design approach "is most accessible among clients of means."[8] Because biophilic design functions as a facilitator of pre-existing natural conditions, the costs should normalize over time. This includes the introduction of renewable energy technologies. At the residential development scale, issues of land cost, utility costs, density, number of dwelling units, and percentage of open space have a large impact on the economics of biophilic planning. As Timothy Beatley suggested in the Foreword to this book, we must put equity and social justice front and center.

The six precedents and the case study show the ways in which the biophilic principles, pattern attributes, and positive outcomes are integral to each of these projects. While the projects demonstrate similar design patterns, they do so in differing ways, which is intended to illustrate the universality as well as the local individuation of the patterns. For example, the first pattern attribute of the plant kingdom is utilized in so many different ways, from the cypress trees surrounding Castello di Gargonza and trees in Google's biome to farming in Helsinge Haveby, and from the varying tree species along the streets in Kronsberg to parks and gardens sprinkled throughout the Pontevedra city center. Nature abounds in the impressive infrastructure landscape architecture of Singapore's Park Connector Neighborhood. And finally, the plant kingdom is found in Serenbe's organic farm, farm-to-table, and large percentage of open space. Biophilic Urbanism is a regional, natural, and cultural response to place. It is uncanny how Serenbe's natural landscape is similar to the ancient savannas with its changing elevations, tall trees, open pastures with views of the horizon, the presence of water, and wild animals.

The recent pandemic caused by the Coronavirus has brought to light the critical need for social distancing, sheltering-in-place, and wearing face masks. The spatial consequence of these measures has counteracted our natural tendency to thrive at social gatherings, populated events, and entertainment and sports venues, and with human interaction and closeness. The supply chain of essential goods and services has also been interrupted with high demands for food, household goods, and contagion-protective products. From a biophilic point of view, this pandemic health crisis has revealed the need for periodic escape from the prolonged isolation of home-boundedness to the relief of direct contact with nature. While Americans normally spend as much as 93 percent of their time indoors, during the pandemic it was being confined to one space without social interaction outside the family unit that was the primary cause of stress and consternation. Spending time outdoors, with adjustments for social distancing, has been a sustainable, proven approach to preserving mental health.[9] As previous scientific research has revealed, this interaction reduces stress and strengthens the immune system.[10] Also, it has been shown that people who have congregated without these protective protocols have spread the disease.

As terrible as this health and economic event has been, staying-in-place could be seen as a harbinger of future pedestrianization, resulting in improved air quality because of the removal of millions of vehicles from our roads and airplanes from the skies. According to Skip Descant, the Coronavirus-related traffic reduction "creates an unprecedented natural experiment and helps us understand how pollution levels are impacted by large-scale behavioral change."[11] It also underscores the need for possible changes in dwelling design as places of prospect–refuge provide buffer spaces, home offices, remote learning spaces, outdoor rooms, greater stockpiles of food, and other essentials for prolonged stays at home. We must also plan for surge capacities at hospitals. The presence of COVID-19 has highlighted the urgent need for greater levels of biophilic planning and design in the hope of reducing the possible effects of a second wave of the virus.

A more advanced form of biophilic refuge occurs when passive survivability focuses planning and design adaptations on devastating weather events and natural disasters, including power outages, extreme temperatures, wildfires, drought, viral transmissions, and terrorism threats. Critical life-support systems are kept intact and maintained throughout the debilitating event. This means providing decentralized essential resources, including energy, food and water, telecommunications, and safe shelter for individual buildings, neighborhoods, communities, and even regions. This resilient strategy includes on-site power production, water harvesting, daylighting, passive solar heating or heat avoidance, natural ventilation, and even some on-site food production. Designs for sheltering-in-place and passive survivability provide new biophilic opportunities, especially in the face of transformations of public health-oriented cities. According to Prem Chandavarkar, while climate change and pollution are concerning products of human activity, the Coronavirus is a consequence of our problematic relationship with nature.[12] In a little more than 100 years, we have experienced numerous plagues, including the 1918–1919 pandemic, the 1957 flu pandemic, the 1968 flu pandemic, the HIV/AIDS pandemic, the 2002–2003 SARS and 2012 MERS outbreaks, the 2014 Ebola epidemic, and now the 2020 COVID-19 pandemic. While it still remains unknown as to how long this wave of COVID-19 will last or whether or not it will become a reoccurring disease, what is clear is our need to become more resilient and to better plan for infectious diseases like it in the future. It is here that responses to airborne diseases and Biophilic Urbanism intersect. Refer to Figure 10.1(a) showing social distance markers in Washington Square Park in San Francisco, California; and to Figure 10.1(b), which is a cascading outdoor fresco dining area in Siena, Italy.

10.1
Social distancing:
(a) Washington
Square Park,
San Francisco,
California (*Source:
Shutterstock*),
(b) fresco dining in
Siena, Italy (*Source:
Phillip Tabb*)

Our ability to transition from an indoor generation and a fossil-fuel economy to one that is more connected to nature and renewable resources will not be easy and will take time to evolve, perhaps a lot of time. In the last chapter of his book *Biophilic Cities*, Tim Beatley suggests there is a remarkable amount of nature around and within cities that includes designed nature and green building elements.[13] The challenge is to preserve this nature and create meaningful access to it through planning and design methods including reforms in land use allocations, zoning, essential mix of uses, urban agriculture, transportation networks, infrastructure planning, urban and suburban growth strategies, and building designs. This must be a multi-scalar approach. Within existing communities, this process will most likely be successful utilizing incremental changes, especially at the building and street scales. In new development, the transformations can be more aggressive and inclusive of the full range of biophilic patterns at each of the scales of development. Where tuberculosis shaped modern architcture and planning a century ago, COVID-19 is now shaping biophilic urbanism.

The study of biophilia and its application to urbanism brings many questions. How will the Biophilic Hypothesis change or evolve if we do not view nature and humans separately, but rather see them as a necessary unity? What becomes of the innate affiliation then? Is there a migration tendency to move away from dense urban cities to surrounding communities, peri-urban areas, and hinterlands of lesser density and greater access to nature? In a concrete sense, how can biophilia inform reforms to our existence, our current ways of surviving, and our urban tendencies within the global ecosystem? How can biophilic urbanism equitably help communities of minorities who bear the impacts of unhealthy, energy-inefficient, and disaster-vulnerable environments? What lessons can we learn from a view of our ancient ancestors who migrated to the Rift Valley in the savanna of East Africa Contemporary examples of advantage-settings might include access to clean air and water, on-site energy, local agriculture, grocery stores, medical facilities, and parks and recreation, with community surveillance and protective community spatial structure. Biophilic urbanism is an intermediate focus ranging from individual biophilic buildings to biophilic cities. Ultimately, it will be the seamlessness of the applications and survival advantages on all the scales that should be most effective. Figure 10.2 is an image of East Africa's Great Rift Valley.

10.2
The Great Rift
Valley, East Africa
(*Source: Getty Images*)

NOTES

1. Julia Africa, Judith Heerwagen, Vivian Loftness, and Catherine Ryan Balagtas, *Biophilic Design and Climate Change: Performance Parameters for Health* https://www.frontiersin.org/articles/10.3389/fbuil.2019.00028/full (accessed February 14, 2020).

2. Terrapin Bright Green, *14 Patterns of Biophilic Design: Improving Health and Wellbeing in the Environment* https://www.terrapinbrightgreen.com/reports/14-patterns/, published on-line in 2014. (accessed December 15, 2020).

3. Phillip James Tabb, *Serene Urbanism: Biophilic Theory and Practice of Sustainable Placemaking* (London, UK: Routledge, 2017).

4. Stephen R. Kellert, Judith H. Heerwagen, and Martin Mador, *Biophilic Design: The Theory, Science, and Practice of Bringing Building to Life* (New York, NY: John Wiley & Sons, Inc., 2008).

5. Phillip James Tabb, *Elemental Architecture: Temperaments of Sustainability* (London, UK: Routledge, 2019).

6. Edward O. Wilson, *Biophilia: The Human Bond with Other Species* (Cambridge, MA: Harvard University Press, 1984). p 106.

7. Wayne Nichols developed small passive solar communities in Santa Fe, New Mexico. In the mid 1970s, Wayne and Susan Nichols, along with Doug Balcombe, at Los Alamos National Laboratory, and architect Ed Mazria, conducted nationwide workshops "teaching thousands of people all over America how to do passive solar design, construction, architecture and development."

8. Julia Africa, Judith Heerwagen, Vivian Loftness, and Catherine Ryan Balagtas, *Biophilic Design and Climate Change: Performance Parameters for Health* https://www.frontiersin.org/articles/10.3389/fbuil.2019.00028/full (accessed February 14, 2020).

9. Eugenia C. South and Raina M. Merchant, "How Can you Responsibly Enjoy Nature During Coronavirus? – Opinion" https://www.inquirer.com/opinion/commentary/coronavirus-outside-nature-safety-philadelphia-20200320.html (accessed April 7, 2020).

10. Barton, R. Hine and Jules Pretty, *The health benefits of walking in greenspaces of high natural heritage* value https://www.tandfonline.com/doi/full/10.1080/19438150903378425 (accessed January 12, 2020).

11. Skip Descant, *Sensor Data Shows Environmental Benefits of Home Isolation* https://www.govtech.com/fs/data/Sensor-Data-Shows-Environmental-Benefits-of-Home-Isolation.html (accessed April 7, 2020).

12. Prem Chandavarkar, *The Covid Pandemic: Seven Lessons to be Learned for a Future* https://medium.com/@premckar/the-covid-pandemic-seven-lessons-to-be-learned-for-a-future-81792f7f175 (accessed May 4, 2020).

13. Timothy Beatley, *Biophilic Cities: Integrating nature Into Urban Design and Planning* (Washington, DC: Island Press, 2011). pp 151–152.

Suggested Reading

Alexander, Christopher, Sara Ishikacca, and Murry Silverstein *A Pattern Language: Towns, Buildings, Construction* (New York, NY: Oxford University Press, 1977).

Barker, Graeme *The Agricultural Revolution in Prehistory: Why Did Foragers Become Farmers?* (Oxford, UK: Oxford University Press, 2009).

Beatley, Tim *Biophilic Cities* (Washington, DC: Island Press, 2011).

Brill, Michael *Using the Place-Creation Myth to Develop Design Guidelines of Sacred Space* (Champagne-Urbana, IL: Council of Educators in Landscape Architecture, 1985).

Browning, William D. and Catherine O. Ryan *Nature Inside: A Biophilic Design Guide* (London, UK: Royal Institute of British Architects, 2020).

Buettner, Dan *The Blue Zones: 9 Lessons Learned from the People Who've Lived the Longest*, 2nd edition (Washington, DC: National Geographic, 2012).

Carrol, John E. *Sustainability and Spirituality* (Albany, NY: State University of New York Press, 2004).

Carson, Rachel *Silent Spring* (anniversary edition) (New York, NY: Haughton Miffin Company, 2002).

Chandavarkar, Prem *The Covid Pandemic: Seven Lessons to be Learned for a Future* https://medium.com/@premckar/the-covid-pandemic-seven-lessons-to-be-learned-for-a-future-81792f7f175 (accessed May 4, 2020).

Chermayeff, Serge *Community and Privacy: Toward a New Architecture of Humanism* (New York City, NY: Doubleday, 1963).

City of Hanover, *Hannover Kronsberg Handbook: Planning and Realisation* (Hanover: City of Hanover, 2002).

Coates, Gary The City as Garden: A Study of the Sustainable Urban District of Kronsberg (Hannover), Germany (accessed January 6, 2020). https://www.academia.edu/8041051/The_City_as_Garden_A_Study_of_the_Sustainable_Urban_District_of_Kronsberg_Hannover_Germany

Corbett, Lionel "Varieties of Numinous Experiences: the Experience of the Sacred in the Therapeutic Process," in Ann Casement and David Tacey (eds.) *The Idea of the Numinous: Contemporary Jungian and Psychoanalytic Perspectives* (London: Routledge, 2006).

Cotton, William and Riley Dunlap "A comparison of major assumptions in the dominant western worldview" https://www.researchgate.net/figure/A-comparison-of-major-assumptions-in-the-dominant-western-worldview-sociologys-human_tbl1_267802272 (accessed June 1, 2020).

Day, Christopher *Places of the Soul: Architecture and Environmental Design as a Healing Art* (Wellingborough, UK: Aquarian Press, 1990).

Densworth, Lydia "How the COVID-19 Pandemic Could End," *Scientific American* https://www.scientificamerican.com/article/how-the-covid-19-pandemic-could-end1/ (accessed May 28, 2020).

Doxiadis, Constantinos *Ekistics: An Introduction to the Science of Human Settlement* (London: Hutchinson & Company, 1968).

Dunn, Halbert L. *High Level Wellness* (Arlington, VA: Beatty, 1971).

Ehrenfeld, John R. *Sustainability by Design* (New Haven, CT: Yale University Press, 2008).

Eliade, Mircea *The Sacred and The Profane: The Nature of Religion* (Orlando, FL: Harcourt Brace, 1959).

Fraker, Harrison *The Hidden Potential of Sustainable Neighborhoods: Lessons from Low-Carbon Communities* (Washington, DC: Island Press, 2013).

Fromm, Dorit *Collaborative Communities: Cohousing, Central Living, and Other New Forms of Housing With Shared Facilities* (New York, NY: Van Nostrand Reinhold, 1991).

Fromm, Erich *The Heart of Man: Its Genius for Good and Evil* (Herndon, VA: Lantern Books, 2010).

Gunderson, Lance, Craig Allen, and C.S. Holling *Foundations of Ecological Resilience* (Washington, DC: Island Press, 2009).

Holland, Mark and Janine de la Salle *Agricultural Urbanism: Handbook for Building Sustainable Food & Agriculture Systems in 21st Century* (Winnipeg, Manitoba: Green Frigate Books, 2010).

Hoskins, William *The Making of the English Landscape* (Middlesex, UK: Penguin Books, 1970).

Jacobs, Jane *The Life and Death of Great American Cities* (New York, NY: Vintage, 1992).

Jiacheng Jiao, Sheng He, and Xiaochen Zeng "An Investigation into European car-free development models as an opportunity to improve the environmental sustainability in cities: The case of Pontevedra," https://uniqueca.com/archives/proceedings/HUSO2019.pdf#page=84 (accessed March 28, 2020).

Kaplan, R. and S. Kaplan. *The Experience of Nature: A Psychological Perspective* (Cambridge, MA: Cambridge University Press, 1989).

Kellert, Stephen R., Judith H. Heerwagen, and Martin Mador *Biophilic Design: The Theory, Science, and Practice of Bringing Building to Life* (New York, NY: John Wiley & Sons, Inc, 2008).

Knowles, Ralph *Sun Rhythm Form* (Cambridge, MA: MIT Press, 1981).

Krier, Leon *Leon Krier: Houses, Palaces, Cities* (London: Architectural Design, 1984).

Kunstler, James Howard *The Geography of Nowhere: The Rise and Decline of America's Man-Made Landscape* (New York, NY: Free Press, 1994).

Lamark, J.B., C.R. Darwin, and A.R. Wallace *Savanna hypothesis* https://en.wikipedia.org/wiki/Savannah_hypothesis (accessed January 30, 2020)

Levy, Steven *In The Plex: How Google Thinks, Works, and Shapes Our Lives* (New York, NY: Simon & Schuster, 2011).

McDonough + Partners *The Hannover Principles: Design for Sustainability* (Hanover: City of Hannover, 1992).

Newman, Peter et. al. "Can Biophilic Urbanism Deliver Strong Economic and Social Benefits in Cities?" https://sbenrc.com.au/app/uploads/2013/11/sbenrc_1.5biophilicurbanism-industryreport.pdf (accessed June 4, 2020).

Ng, Peter K.L., Richard T. Corlett, and Hugh T.W. Tan *Singapore Biodiversity: An Encyclopedia of the Natural Environment and Sustainable Development* (Singapore: Raffles Museum of Biodiversity Research, 2011).

Norberg-Schulz, Christian *Genius Loci: Towards a Phenomenology of Architecture* (New York, NY: Rizzoli, 1980).

Olgyay, Victor *Design With Climate: Bioclimatic Approach to Architectural Regionalism* (Princeton, NJ: Princeton University Press, 1963).

Orians, Gordon H. and Judith H. Heerwagen "Evolved Responses to Landscapes," in Jerome H. Barlow, Leda Cosmides, and John Tooby (eds.) *The Adapted Mind: Evolutionary Psychology and the Generation of Culture* (New York, NY: Oxford University Press, 1992).

Otto, Rudolf *The Idea of the Holy* (Oxford: Oxford University Press, 1950).

Owens, Susan *Energy Planning and Urban Form* (London: Pion, 1986).

Postman, Neil *Technopoly: The Surrender of Culture to Technology* (New York, NY: Vintage Books, 1993).

Relph, Edward *Place and Placelessness* (London, UK: Pion, 1984).

Rowley, T. *Villages in the Landscape* (London, UK: Dent & Sons Ltd, 1971).

Rossbach, Sarah and Lin Yun *Living Color* (New York, NY: Kodansha America, Inc, 1994).

Soja, Edward W. *Thirdspace* (Malden, MA: Blackwell, 1996).

Tabb, Phillip James *The Solar Village Archetype: A Study of English Village Form Applicable to Energy-Integrated Planning Principles for Satellite Settlement in Temperate Climates* (London: PhD Dissertation, 1990).

Tabb, Phillip James *Serene Urbanism: A Biophilic Theory and Practice of Sustainable Placemaking* (London: Routledge, 2017).

Terrapin Bright Green "14 Patterns of Biophilic Design: Improving Health and Wellbeing in the Environment" https://www.terrapinbrightgreen.com/reports/14-patterns/ (accessed January 2020).

Tuan, Yi-Fu *Space and Place: The Perspective of Experience* (Minnesota, MN: University of Minnesota Press, 1977).

van Effelen, Chris *Pedestrianization Zone: Car-Free Urban Spaces* (Salenstein: Braun Publishing AG, 2015).

Velazquez, Jaime "What happens to Kid Culture When You Close the Streets to Cars" https://www.citylab.com/design/2018/11/car-free-pedestrianization-made-pontevedra-spain-kid-friendly/576268/ (accessed January 7, 2020).

Wilson, Alex "Passive Survivability: A New Design Criterion for Buildings" https://www.buildinggreen.com/feature/passive-survivability-new-design-criterion-buildings (accessed January 12, 2020).

Wilson, Edward O. *Biophilia: The Human Bond With Other Species* (Cambridge, MA: Harvard University Press, 1984).

Wilson, Edward O. *Half-Earth: Our Planet's Fight for Life* (New York, NY: Liveright Publishers, 2017).

World Commission on Environment and Development (WCED) *Our Common Future* (Oxford, UK: Oxford University Press, 1987).

World Health Organization, *Bulletin of the World Health Organization: Urbanization and health* http://www.who.int/bulletin/volumes/88/4/10-010410/en/ (accessed March 28, 2020).

Yamin, Farhana "What is 'Carbon Neutrality' – and How Can We Achieve It by 2050?" https://theelders.org/news/what-carbon-neutrality---and-how-can-we-achieve-it-2050 (accessed February 16, 2020).

Index

Note: Locators in *italics* represent figures and **bold** indicate tables in the text.

actualistic 75, 144, 204
advantage-settings 5, 217
affiliation 3–5, 27–28, 36, 41, 46, 217
afforestation 68, 203
Africa, Julia 72, 218
agglomeration 33, 179–180
aggregate 18, 54, 58, 85, 143
aging 54–55, 61–62, 193, 195
    in place 54, 61–62
agricultural urbanism xxxvii, 46, 54, 62, 143
Agricultural Urbanism 70, 96
agriculture 6, 30–31, 59, 66, 95, 98, 111–113,
    136–137, 139, 141, 143, 147, 158, 212, 217
agrihoods 96, 100
air 7–8, 14, 16–18, 20, 22, 26, 34, 42–43, 49,
    101, 113, 116, 130, 160–162, *162*, 186, **213**
    air-borne 18, 20, 49, 54, 57, 216
amenity xxxi, 80
amnesia 13
Anglo-Saxon villages xxvi–xxvii, *xxix*
animals 4–5, 47–48, 53, 56, 63, 67–68, 80, 120,
    125, 147–149, *148*, 177, 181, **208**, **211**, **213**
    domesticated 47, 149
    husbandry 5, 89, 99, 101, *112*, 207
    wild 16, 47, 56, 63, 101, 147, 149, 215
Anthroposophic 44, 186, 193, 196
apex 137–139, 142, 167, 178, 180, 195
Appleton, Jay 50, 71
Aquatic Ape Hypothesis 4
archetype xvii, xxxviii, 55
architecture 3, 9, 25, 29, 63–64, 98, 102, 117,
    121, 127, 135, 186, 193
art 43–44, 54–55, 63, 67, 83, 87–88, 91–92, 107,
    114, 117, 121, 135, 141, *188*, 189–191,
    190
Art Farm xxxvii, 189, *190*, 191

A-S-I (Avoid-Shift-Improve) 121
Asmussen, Erik 186, 193, 202
attributes 6, 34, 40–43, 45–46, 75, 82, 90, 100,
    111, 119, 129, **205**, **206**, **208–211**, **213**,
    214
auditory sense 47, 130, 152, *153*, 156
Aurora Borealis 50, 56, 62
authentic 13–14, 24–25, 40, 48, 61, 77, 79, 147
automobile 7, 17, 29, 53, 109, 114–116, 119, 161,
    182, 207
    fatalities 26, 122, 132
awe 3, 6, 12, 43, 58, 62–63, 204, **205**, **208**,
    210–211, **213**
axis 11, 79, 139, 167, *168*

Bailey, Robert 39
balance 5, 22, 35, 41, 47, 62, 85, 93, 107–108,
    136, 140
Beatley, Timothy 6, 33, 43–45, 70, 110, 113,
    216
Beery, Thomas 4, 36
BIG 7
biochar 59
bioclimatic 73, 220
biodiversity 8, 14, 15–16, 26, 58, 96, 98,
    124–125, 127, 131–132, 207, 212, 220
bio-indifference 13
biology xxv, 3, 28–29, 95
biomarker 54
biomass 101, 111, 158
biome *9*, 75, 88, *89*, 91–92, 203–204, 215
biomimicry xxxvii, 54, 71
biophilia 3–6, 13, 27–28, 40, 44–46, 135, 217,
    221
    patterns 5–6, 8, 31, 43, *81*, *90*, 100, *101*, *110*,
    118, 120, *129*, 212, 217
biophilic cities xx, xxiii, 6, 36, 45, 131, 217
biophobia 5, 13
bioregions 30

bioswale 138, *155*

biourbanism 6, 23, 28–29, 36

block xx, 11, 28, 30, 32, 45, 105–107, 109

Blue Eyed Daisy 139, *185*

Blue Marble 22

Blue Zones 62, 72

Browning, Bill xxxix, 182

boundary 10, 30, 44, 78, 81–84, 100, 121, 177, 180

bounding 52–53, 67, 82, 102, 180, *181*, **205**, **208**, **210–211**, **213**

Brill, Michael 43–44, 53, 219

Brin, Sergey 85

Brundtland Commission Report 12

Buettner, Dan 62, 72

Buildings 12, 17, 26, 30–32, 34, 58, 81, 86, 106–107, *151*, 159, 161, 186, 191, 219

Bullitt Center xxii

Caperna, Antonio 6, 26, 30, 36

car-free 30–32, 70, 75, 78, 82, 114–116, 121, 220

carbon 14, 17–18, 26, 28, 46, 48–49, 51, 58–59, 116, 161, 164

emissions xxxvii, 95, 161

farming 58, 68

footprint xxi, 8, 16

neutrality 12, 80, 119, 221

sequestering 8, 53, 57–59, 68, 80, 83, 92, 102, 121, 130, 146, 161, 175, **205–206**, **208–211**, **214**

Cardinal directions xxxviii, xxx, 50, 53, 166–167, 182, **168**

Carrol, John E. 64, 72

carrying capacity 22

Carson, Rachel 16–17, 26, 219

Castello di Gargonza 35, 70, 75, 77, *78*, 80, 82, 84, 203–204, **205**, 215

Castiglion Fiorentino, Italy xvii, *xxxi*

cave paintings 5, *6*

celestial 11, 44, 50, 71, 165, *166*, 167, **213**

Celtic farmsteads xxvi, *xxix*, 56

center xxx, 50, *79*, 82, *99*, 114–115, *115*, 117–119, *120*, 178–180, *179*, **209–211**, **213**

centering 44, 52, 82, 91, 112, 121, 130, 178, *179*, **205**, **209–211**, **213**

Chandavarkar, Prem 47, 69–70, 216

charged places 43, 69

Chermayeff, Serge 71

Chesterton, Andrew 38

city 9, *10*, 19, 28, 64, 95, 105, 114, *115*, *117*, 124, 126–127, 130

center 12, 70, 97, *117*, 119, *120*

cityscape 90–92

Clay, Elonda 5, 36

climate 9, 15, 28, 33, 87, 97, 114, 160, 194

change 4–5, 14–16, 22–23, 35, 46, 48, 58, 68, 89, 105, 112, 131, 212, 216

neutrality 12, 27, 29, 83, 92, 97, 102, 207, 112, 121, 198, 203, **205**, **208–211**, **213–214**

positive 57–58, 68, 130, 136–137, 158, 161, 193

zones 9, 98, 102

CO_2 14, 18, 73

cogeneration **110**

cognitive 56–57, 62, 84, 156, 203

activity 92, **205–206**, **208–211**, **214**

content 42, 56, 63

coherence 52–53

community 31, 33, 55, 57, 69, 77, 95, 105, 125, 135, 143

building 43, 53–54, 57–58, 69, 95, 135, 187, 190, 195, **205–206**, **208–211**, **214**

climax 55

ecological 15, 28

pioneering 55

scale 31, 33, 58–59, 65–66, 108, 144

size 23, 33, 58, 75

sustainable xvii, 203

composting 101, 147

conduit moment 43, 56, 190

congregate housing 18–20, 51, 53–54, 66–67

connections 6, 34, 90–91, 95, 100–101, 111–112, 120, 130, 135, 142, 167, 186, *188*

celestial 165–*166*, **213**

sensory 8–9, 43, 47, 147, 149, 152–*153*, 161, 184, **213**

social 171, 173, 187, *188*

temporal *194*, 195

visual 51, 90, 150, 152, 193, 196, 207

conservation xxi, 6, 16, 34, 57–59, 69, 124–125, 127, 143

constellating urbanism 24, 33, 67, 141, 212

constellation xxxi, 33, 50, 95–96, 136, 141–142, 178, 180

constructed wetlands 33, 160, 164

contact tracing 19, 67, 132

contaminants 16–18, 26, 48, 58

cooling 15, 30, 48, 101, 156–157, 162, 194–195, 204

Corbett, Lionel 63, 69–70

core effect 63, 200

Coronavirus xix, xx, 18–20, *19*, 32–33, 49, 51–53, 60, 64–67, 92, 130, 144, 146–147, 171, 180, 182, 189, 215–216

corridors 34, 39
   systems xxxii, 59, 152, 158
COVID-19 xxii, 14, 18, 25, 31, 64–65, 67–69, 72,
   103, 153, 171, 195, 212, 216, 218–219
cross pollination 86
Crossroads xxxi–xxxii, 138, 141, 146, 164, 166,
   180, 185–186, 191, *194*, *197*
culinary arts 54–55, 80, 92, 136, 139, 141, 147,
   152, 154, 187, 189–190, 198
culture xxxvi, 5, 13–14, 21, 23, 25, 35, 42, 45,
   56, 63–64, 85–87, 91, 131, 189

damp 7, 20, 154
dawn and dusk 56
Day, Christopher 56, 71
deep ecology 28, 39
density 12, 15, 19, 29, 31–33, 38, 48, 52, 54, 58,
   166–167, 169, 177, 179, 207, 215, 217
density gradient 106, 138, 111, 175, 184
Devall, Bill and George Sessions 39
development 30–31, 45, 64, 95–96, 105, 108,
   143, 173–174, 189
   car-free 123, 220
   residential xxxi, 34–35, 58, 68, 75, 97, 103,
    110, 135–136, 143–144, 156, 173, 215
   single use xxxvii, 184
   sustainable 12, 42, 132, 143
   urban 13, 15, 69, 129, 135, 212
differentiated boundary 44, 82
direction xxx, 43, 50, 53, 62, 105, 152, 154,
   166–167, *168*, 182, **205–206**, **209–210**,
   213
disasters 14, 23, 29, 59–60, 169, 216–217
diurnal 57, 156, 193, 195
dog park 140
dog trot 162
Doxiadis, Constantinos 43, 70
Dunbar Number 33, 39
Dunn, Halbert 12, 62, 69, 72
dwelling 66, 97, 139–141, *157*, 167, *172*, 176–177,
   183

E-learning 65
earth 26, 48–49, 82, 158–160, *159*, 191–192,
   205, **213**
earthing 160, 201
ecology 24–25, 28, 33–34, 36, 41–43, 48, 45,
   111, 154–156, *155*, 175, 177, **213**
ecoregion 30–31, 33–34, 39–40, 154, 156
ecosystem xx–xxi, 4, 15–16, 26, 37, 47–49, 140,
   156, 217
ectype 40

Eden Project 9, *10*
Ehrenfeld, John 12, 14, 21, 37, 59, 69
Ekistics 43–44, 70, 219
electricity 8, 17, 27, 32, 58–60, 87, 105, 110–111,
   124, 158, 196, 204
elements 99, 146, 153, 187, 190, 193
emissions 58–60, 95, 102–103, 115–116, 121
empower xxvi, 118
English villages 136–137, 143
ether 42–43, 50, 165, *166*, **213**
etherial 56, 195, 198
everyday xxx, 5, 25, 32, 62, 149–150, 165
exercise 17, 47, 61, 68, 85, 87, 113, 149, 160, 175
experience 4, 40, 46–47, 49, 57, 68–69, 83, 99,
   102, 130, 152, *153*, 182, 190, 198, *199*, *200*
EXPO 2000 xxx, 7, 70, 76, 105
exurbs 23
eyes on the street 47

Facebook xxxv
farm-to-table 47, 187, 189, *200*, 215
farmer's market *xxxiv*, 116, 147, 173, *188*
farming 5, 16, 47, 58, 68, 96, 101, 215
farmstead xxvi, xxviii
Feng Shui 55, 193
fire 18, 32, 48, 90–91, 111, 156–158, *157*, **206**,
   208–209, **213**
first row 96, 146
fixation capacity 51
flatscape 25
flood plains 31, 140, 155, 173–174, **159**
fluid luminosity 56, 195
food xxii, 3–5, 13, 46–47, 97–98, 131, 158, 187,
   189–190, 193, 195, 215–216
   forest 140
   hub *97*, 97–100, 102, 207
   production 96–97, 99–100, 102
forest free approach xxiv
form language 9, 53, 82, 91, 102, 112, 121, 184,
   185, **206**, **214**
fractals 34, 39, 54
fractured 119
fresco dining xxi, 117, 181, 217
Fromm, Erich 4, 6, 220
functional zoning xxxvii, 24

garbage 27
gardens 5, 81–82, *83*, 91, 98, 117, 124–127, 130,
   131, 151–152, *153*, 165, *168*
   city 95, 100, 113, 125, 127, 131, 207, 219
   community 32
   healing *140*, 152, 167

kitchen 30, 66, 96, 159

roof 44

secret 165, 200, 202

walled-in *xxxiii*, 137

geographic 15, 25, 32, 48, 51, 53–54, 61, 130, 144, 154, 175, 180, **213**

geological 42, 46, 51, 91, 175

geology 48, 50, 139

geometry xxv, 34, 81, 89, 135, 140, 177, 186, 200

sacred 34, 135, 143

geothermal xxv, 30, 59, 98, 101, 152, *157*, 158, 164, 195

Global Seed Vault 46

global warming 15, 26–27

Google Headquarters 35, 70, 75, 85–94, *87*, 203, **206**

grammar 53, 177, 186

Grange Hamlet *139*, 139–141, 151, 166, 169, *174*, 180, *181*

gray water 163–164

Great Pacific Garbage Patch 27

green 7–8, 70, 78, 91, 111–112, 186, 192, 195

roofs 49, 53–54, 101, 127

verges 49

walls 49, 54, 93, 127

greenhouse 9, 14, 29, 58, 62, 68, 86, 98–100, 102, 106–107, 121, 121

gas emissions 29, 53, 60, 121

greenspace 15, 32, 48, 112, 121, 124, 140, 145–146, 180, 203, 217

greenways 58

grounding 48–49, 158–160, *159*, 179, 204, **205**, 212, **213**

growing seasons 5, 98, 147

growth 5–6, 22–23, 42, 38, 48–49, 52, 54, 65, 95, 105, 156, 160, 178, 182, 193, 217

by addition 23–24, 141, 195

by multiplication 23–24, 52, 96, 98, 103, 141–142, 178, 182, 195

population 22, 26, 48, 55

habitat 15–16, 27, 29, 31, 34, 63, 105, 108, 156, 160

habitat selection 212

half earth xxi, xxiv

hamlet 77–78, 81–82, 136–137, *138–140*, 141, 169, *170*, 180, *181*, *194*, 195, 197, 203

haptic sense 47, 152, 160

Hancocks, David 16, 38

health 17–20, 25–28, 49, 57, *63*, 69, 139–140, 165, **206**, **208**, **210–211**, **213–214**

emotional 13, 43, 193

mental 52, 62, 187, 216

physical 7, 69, 160, 173, 175

public 64

healthscapes 84

Heerwagen, Judith 13, 218

Helsinge Haveby 75, 95, *96*, 97, *99*, 100, *101*, *103*, 207, **208**

high-level wellness 12, 37, 41, 58, 62, 68–69, 147, 179, 196, 198, 219

High Line Park 9, *10*

hill 77–78, 105, 109, 111, *112*, 126, *128*, 141, 174

Hill, Christina 14, 37

Hillfort *xxix*

Holland and de la Salle 96, 220

homebound living 65

homestead xxvi, *xxix*, 186

Hooke, Della xxvii, xxxviii

horticulture 124, 127

Hoskins, William xxvii, 220

human 4–5, 8, 12–14, 21, 25, 29, 35, 41, 56–57, 129, 212, 215–217

activity 7, 14, 16, 22, 31, 215

scale 12, 23–24, 30, 80, 83, 98, 121, 177, 186

spirit 42

hydrological cycle 27, 33, 47–49, 111, 156

immune system 18, 20, 49, 56, 69, 74, 158, 160–161, 167, 216

immaterial 165, 200

inborn tendencies 3

inclusive xxiii, 28, 41, 87, 121, 143, 200, 215, 217

indoor 7, 14, 20, 36, 51, 66, 92, 171, 215

air pollution 17–18, 20, 49, 161

Industrial villages xxvii, *xxix*

Ineffable 56, 58, 63, 154

Infiltration gardens 49

influenza xxi

epidemic of 1918 216

innate xxi, 3, 6, 41, 50, 217

insulation 9, 17

interiors 29–31, 34, 49, 80, 85, 105–107, 136, 167, 169, 171, 173, 183

interstitial spaces xxi, 24, 51

invasive species 15

Island of Sculptures 117

James, William 42, 63

Jarna, Sweden 186, 191, 193

Jonssen, Ingemar K. 4, 36

Kaplan, Steven and Rachel 4, 6, 35, 36

Kellert, Stephen xxiii, 6–7, 36, 43–44, 170, 193

Kendeda Center xxii
Knowles, Ralph 58, 72, 220
Krakow, Poland 7
Krier, Leon 23–24, 38, 220
Kronsberg District xxii, xxx, 70, 76, 105, *106–108*, 109, *110*, *112*, **209**
Kunstler, James Howard 25, 38, 220

Labyrinth 117, 166, 168, *179*, 180, 182, 198
Lamark, J. B. 220
land 14–15, 24, 97, 103, 109, 135–136, 139, 143, 149, 175–177
    land plots 31–32, 168, 186
    land use xxviii, 12, 14, 52, 58, 67, 73, 116, 177, 217
    landform xxxvii, 34, 48, 51, 137, 154–155, 160, 173, 175
landscapes 24, 32, 52, 91, 96, 100, 106, 111, 121, 124–127, 137, 155, 167, 173, 175
Lane, Belden 69, 74
lawns 31, 146, 182, 184
Lerez river 114, 117, 119–121
life expectancy 17, 22–23, 38
light 158, 161, 165, 192–193, 195–196, *197*, **206**, **214**, 216
    day 7, 20, 56, 60, 88, 158, 167, 196, 216
    natural 8–9, 30–31, 44, 56, 59, 68, 86, 90–93, 196
    night 33, 50, 56, 158, 165, 196–198
    numinous 56
    sun 44, 56, 66, 136, 167, 173, 195
Limits to Growth 22, 38
living color xxxiv, 8–9, 43, 55, 191–193, *192*, **214**
living machine 73, 102, 104, 164
lotting 34, 56, 167
Lovejoy, C. Owen 36
Lovejoy Hypothesis 4, 36

Mado Hamlet 126–127, *139–140*, 141, *163*, *168*, *174*, 186, *194*, *199*
Malin, David 71
Malmo, Sweden 186
Marchett constant 119, 123
Marina Bay Sands 127
material 31, 48–49, 53, 80, 82, 90, 138–139, 158, *161*, 176, *183*, 184
    natural 53, *80*, 82, 91–92, 96, 102, 112, 121, 130
    sustainable 69
materiality 8, 30, 53, 159, 182, *183*, 184, 204, **205**, **208**, **214**

medieval xxvi, *xxix*, 7, 70, 82, 84, 115, 119, 203
memory xxviii, 3, 47–48, 84, 91, 147, 187, 191, 195
mental health 52, 62, 72, 187, 191, 216
Mexcaltitan, Mexico 10–*11*
migration 4, 6, 22–24, 27, 55, 61, 212, 217
mix of uses 12, 29, 31–32, 52, 60–61, 116, 135, 142, 161, 171, 175, 177, 207
modal 109
modern *xxix*, 6, 13, 16, 20, 25, 50, 54, 186, 191, 212
modernity 12, 21, 23, 27, 59
morphology xxvii, *xxix*, 194
multiplication 23, 34, 52, 96, 98, 103, 141–142, 178, 182, 195
multi-sensory 91
mythopoeia 50, 54–55, 189, *190*, **214**

National Oceanic and Atmospheric Administration 14, 37
nature 3–7, 13, 29, 41–42, 50–51, 53–54, 56–58, 62, 102, 105, 125, *128*, 130, 142, *146*, 150, 207
nature deficit disorder 69, 73
neighborhood xx, 24, 32, 61, 75–76, 95–96, 106–107, 124, *129*, 130
    sub xxxv, 100, 102–103
net-zero xxxi, 70–71, *157*
New Urbanism xxx, 143
Newman, Peter and Isabella Jennings 15, 29, 37, 126, 132
night light 33, *42*, 50, 55–56, 138, 152, 154, 165, 195, 197, 200
    sky 31, 47, 84, 150, 165, *166*, 198
    night light pollution 33, 50, 56, 196–197
noetic 42, 56, 63, 154, 190, 198–*199*,
Norberg-Schultz, Christian 25, 38, 69, 73, 167
nucleation xxvii, 23, 29, 31, 43, 52, 61, 67, 178, 180, **205**, **209–211**, **213**
numinous 43, 54, 58, 62–63, *64*, 69, 179, 198, *199*, **205–206**, **208–211**, **213–214**
nutrition 13, 46, 55, 57, 147, 160

obesity 17, 61–62, 147
off-grid xxxi
Oglethorpe, James 11
olfactory sense 47, 91, 130, 152, 154
omega 136–140, 165, 167, 169, *170*, 175–177, *179*, 180, *181*, 186
on-site 8, 31, 57, 59–60, 98, 105–106, 112, 144, 157, 182, 184, 203, **205–206**, **208–211**, **214**
orchards 46, 79, 95–96, 98, 101
Orians, Gordon H. 52, 71, 201

orientation 3–4, 43, 50, 58, 106, 167, *168*, **205–206**, **209–210**, **213**

Ott, Wayne 7, 36

Otto, Rudolf 12–13, 37, 56, 63, 69

outcomes 40–41, 57–58, *59–61*, *63–64*, 68–69, 83, 92, 102, 112, 121, 130, 203–204, **205–206**, **208–211**, **213–214**

outdoors 20, 51, 61, 66, 92, 118, 120, 122, 171, 173, 191

oxygen 49, 130, 145–146, 161

Page, Larry 85

Park Connectors 35, 70, 76, 124–125, 127, *129*, 131–132, 207, **211**, 215

parking 29–31, 53, 80, 88, 92, 109, 119, 138, 140, 143, 175–176, 207

passive xxx, 54, 108, 184
   solar heating 58, 60, 66, 82, 98, 100, 102, 156, 158, 167, 215–216, 218
   survivalism 8, 31, 48, 51, 57, 59–60, 69, 169, 171, 216, 221

pathways 111, 125, 207

pattern attributes 40, 42–46, 75, 82, 90, 100, 111, 119, 129, 144, 203–204, **205–206**, **208–211**, **213–214**

Pawlyn, Michael 54, 71

peak experience 63

pedestrianization 57, 69, 83, 102, *117*, 121–122, **206**, **208–211**, **213–214**

performing arts 55, 67, 152, 165, 187, 189, 198

peri-urban xxviii, 12, 23, 34, 65, 67, 135, 143, 212

permaculture 96

Phon, Abby 49, 71

phototropic 165, 167

photovoltaic xxxii, 8, 58, 86, 88, 91–92, 98, 105, 107–108, 111, 156–158, 168

physical distancing 32, 54, 66–67

place 4, 7, 20, 24–25, 32, 52, *61*, 66–70, 79, 102, 119–121, 178, 180, 184, 198–200, 204
   creation 45, 53, 70, 84
   identity 30, 43, 51, 61, 69, 175, 184, 203–204, **205–206**, **208–211**, 212, **214**

placelessness 12, 24–25, 37, 61–62, 69, 221

placemaking 13, 54, 57, *61*, 69, 98, 102, 127, 203, **205–206**, **208–211**, **213–214**

placemarker 82

plaza 11, 51, 53, 78–80, 111–112, *116–117*, 118–119, 121

pollution 15–16, 26, 30–31, 59, 165, 196–197, 216

Pontevedra, Spain 35, 70, 76, 114, *115–118*, 119, *120*, 121, *122*, 123, 207, **210**

porosity 30, 51–52

Postman, Neil 20, 38

preservation 6, 15, 23, 34, 58–59, 97, 135–136, 143, 173, 175, 207

productivity xxiii, 15, 83, 86, 91–92, 147, 165

profane 25, 56, 64, 220

proliferation xxvii, 13, 20, 48–49, 158

psychology 3, 71

public 75, 88–89, 91–92, 99, 121, *128*, 137, 140, 150

Putnam, Robert 69, 71

qualitative 41, 54

quarantine xix, xxxvi, 20

Rafferty, John P. 15, 37

rainwater 26, 49, 106–108, 154
   harvesting 8, 31, 60, 62, 92, 162–163, 107, 111

reforestation xxviii, 34, 38, 100, 203, **205–206**, **208–211**, **214**

regenerative 28, 45, 55, 60, 64, 70, 75, 95, 98, 215

region 6, 28, 31, 33–34, 40–43, 45, 67, 69, 105–106, 130, 154, 156

Relph, Edward 12, 24–25, 37, 61, 69

renewable 30–31, 57, 59–60, 107–109, 113, 131, 158, 204

Reno, Josh 27, 39

resilience 28, 30, 39, 55, 69, 127

restoration 29, 48, 58, 88, 95, 107

Rift Valley 4, 212, 217, *218*

riparian 31, 88, 101, 117

Romano-Christian xxvi, *xxix*

Rose, Michael 39

Rowley, T. xxxviii, 271

sanctuary spaces 51, 65

sanitation protocol 19, 54, 65–67, 113, 153

Savanna Hypothesis 4, 35, 220

scalar 28, 68, 217
   conflicts 34
   integration xxxvii, 58

scale 6, 10, 12–13, 29–34, 54, 59, 65–66, 143–144, 169, 177

seasons xxxiii, 5, 58, 149, 151, 154, 165, 195

Selborne Hamlet 136, *138*, 141, 163–164, *176*, *181*, 189

self-sufficient 6, 12, 95

sense of place 13, 31–32, 53, 119, 127, 177–178, 204, 207

sensory 47, 82, 91, 101, 111, 130, 152, *153*, 184, 193, **213**

Serenbe Community xxx, 35, 135, 141, 189, 204, 212, **213–214**

shading 32, 66, 87–88

sheltering-in-place 19, 30–32, 60, 64, 66, 68, 99, 146–147, 189, 195, 215–216

Shepard, Roger 71

side friction 178

silence 56, 71

Singapore 124–132, *125*, *128*, *129*, *131*, 207, **211**

sky xxxii, 30–31, 47, 50, 56, 84, 127, 132, 150, *151*, 161, 165, *166*, 198

skyglow 56

Skypark 127

soakaway 108, 111

social distancing 18–19, *65*, 66–67, 153, 215–216, *217*

social media xxxvii, 20

socialization 100, 102

Soja, Edward W. 69, 72, 221

solar energy 58–59, 101, 111, 130, 137, 158, 167–168, 177, 193

   access 11, 30, 34, 48, 50, 57–58, 60, 69, 73

   envelope 58

space 24, 47, 50–52, 78–79, 98–100, 119, 150, 169, 173, 203, 215–216

spatial structure xxvii, 28, 30, 82, 91, 102, 111, 121, 130, *176*, 177

specialization xxvi–xxvii

species xx, 4, 6–9, 15–16, 23, 30, 47, 49, 88, 125, 130, 149, 152, 184, 215

Spela Hamlet 126, 137, 140–141, 150, 164, 195

stay-at-home 92, 144

Steele, John 47, 69, 71

stewardship 6, 13, 29, 41, 61, 125

store xxi, 8, 33–34, 41, 47, 58, 67, 77, 110, 139, 141, 157, 164, 180

streets 30, 32, 64, 105–106, 109, 115, 119, 145, 150, 152

stress reduction 52, 62–63, 68–69, **206, 208–211, 214**

sublime 62–63, 72

suburbs 12, 19, 25

super-block 105–109, *107*, *108*, 111–113, 203

super cluster 96

supertrees 127, 130, 132

surge capacity 18, 33, 52, 67, 216

surveillance 4, 30, 41, 47, 50–51, 61, 150, 167, 169, 171, 207

sustainable development 12, 15, 42, 132, 220

swale 30, 49, *108*, 111, 138, *155*, 175, 203, 207

technology xxv, 8, 21, 23, 28, 49–50, 65, 88, 106, 159, 187, 221

telework 19, 65–66, 92, 200, 204

temporal density 63–64, 69, 154, 166, 179

Terrapin Bright Green 6, 36, 43, 45, 71

territory 25, 61, 79, 88, 180, 182

Texas A&M University xxxi

thin places 44, 56, 69

Thirdspace 56, 72

Thorburn transect 137–138, *176*, 177, 184, 212

Titchfield Village, UK xxviii, *xxx*

topography 82, 111, 126, 140, 149, 156, 167, 173–175, *174*, **213**

Topophilia Hypothesis 4, 36

Tracada, Eleni 6, 30, 36

traffic 26, 29–30, 40, 53, 88, 109, 114

tram xxxv, 66–67, 105–107, 111–112

transect 15, 30, 40, 42–43, 48, 51, 137–138, 144–145, *176*, 177

transfer of density rights xxxi, 136

transportation 14, 17, 29–30, 48, 67, 69, 109, 113–114, 121

trees 4, 8, 12, 46, 77–79, 83, 106, 145, 175, 184, *194*

triad 29, 40–41

true sustainability 12, 14, 27, 41, 57–59, 68–69, 136

Tuan, Yi-Fu 178, 201

tuberculosis 64

uncertainty xix

unity 5, 44–45, 217

unsustainability 12, 21, 59

upgrade effect 187

urban 6–7, 9–12, 15, 23–25, 28–30, 114, 118, 121, 125, 135–136, 186, 217

   core 19, 23

   density 124, 150

   design 44, 50, 52–53, 59–60, 169, 173, 207

urbanism 21, 23–24, *27*–29, 44–48, 50–52, 141, 143, 212, 215

utility 28, 59–60, 67, 103, 158, 215

veil 4, 30, 44, 56

ventilation 30–31, 49, 60, 66, 87, 108, 160–161, *162*, **212**, 216

views 42, 44, 47, 78–79, 82, 91, 111, *140*, 150–*151*, **205–206**, **211**, **212**

viral load 20

vistas 9, 47, 111, 120, 130, 150–*151*, **205–206**, **211**, **213**

visual 8, 47, 51, 54, 91, 130, 136, 150, 152, 171, 196

visual arts 55, 64, 189–*190*, 198

vitality 13, 55, 149

vulnerability 18, 169

walking 4, 24, 32–33, 47, 62, 78, 83, 112, *117*, 118, 122, 152

walking distances 24

wall 49, 51, 54, 77–78, 80, 82, 86, 90, 126–127, 171, 182, 204

walled-in garden xxx, xxvii, *xxxiii*, 137

waste 7–8, 17, 26–27, 43, 49, 54, 69, 101–102, 121, 124, *163*, 164, **209–211**, **213**

water 26, 31, 49, 111, 152, 162, *163*, 164, **209–211**, **213**

   feature 32, 46, 82, 91, 111, 120–121, 130, 145–146, 154, *162*, 163

   fresh 127, 162

   potable 22

   rain 8, 26, 31, 49, 60, 92, 106–108, *108*, 111, 163, 215

   storm 32, 92, 111, 154–155, 162, 164

weather 14–15, 57, 79, 87, 156, 158, 160, 163–164

wellbeing 47

wellness 13, 62, *63*, 68–69, 72, 136, 139–141, **205–206**, **208–211**, **213–214**

wetlands 23, 48–49, 95–96, 128, 140–141, 155, *158*, 159, *163*, 164, 185

wholeness 21–22, 64

wholly other 56

wildlife xx, 14, 125–126, 130, 149, 171, 180–181

Wilson, Alex 60, 69, 72

Wilson, Edward O. xxi, 3–4, 6, 36, 212

wind xxi, 58, 80, 97, 105, 108, 111, 113, 151, 160–162

wind power 110, 112

windows xxi, 44, 51, 56, 78, 161, 171, 192

wood 4, 7, 69, 78, 82–83, 88, 102, 117, 126, 182–183

work-family 118, 202

World Health Organization 7, 36, 39

worldview 13–14, 41, 102

Wrangham, Richard 4, 36

Wuhan, China xxxvi, 18

zoning 24, 31, 60–61, 109, 135–136, 217

   functional xxxvii, 24

   integrated 24, 60

   land use 24

zoonotic 18

zoos 14, 16, 37